HUMANITY'S RUINS

HUMANITY'S RUINS

ETHICS,
FEMINISM, AND
GENOCIDAL
HUMANITARIANISM

Danielle Bouchard

DUKE UNIVERSITY PRESS
Durham and London
2025

© 2025 DUKE UNIVERSITY PRESS
All rights reserved
Printed in the United States of America on acid-free paper ∞
Project Editor: Bird Williams
Designed by David A. Rainey
Typeset in Minion Pro and Real Head Pro
by Westchester Publishing Services

Library of Congress Cataloging-in-Publication Data

Names: Bouchard, Danielle, [date]– author
Title: Humanity's ruins : ethics, feminism, and genocidal humanitarianism / Danielle Bouchard.
Description: Durham : Duke University Press, 2025. | Includes bibliographical references and index.
Identifiers: LCCN 2024050768 (print)
LCCN 2024050769 (ebook)
ISBN 9781478032069 paperback
ISBN 9781478028796 hardcover
ISBN 9781478060994 ebook
Subjects: : LCSH: Humanitarianism—Political aspects | Imperialism—Moral and ethical aspects | Feminist ethics | War and society | Human rights and globalization | International relations | Genocide
Classification: LCC BJ1475.3 .B683 2025 (print)
LCC BJ1475.3 (ebook)
DDC 361.7/4082—dc23/eng/20250519
LC record available at https://lccn.loc.gov/2024050768
LC ebook record available at https://lccn.loc.gov/2024050769

Contents

Acknowledgments — *vii*

Introduction — **Cynicism, Death, and Humanitarianism**
THE AESTHETICS OF RUINATION — *1*

1 — **Bomb Ethics**
VULNERABLE HUMANITY IN THE ANTHROPOCENE — *41*

2 — **Postcolonial Histories of the Bomb**
DIFFERENTIAL TEMPORALITIES OF DESTRUCTION IN KIDLAT TAHIMIK'S *MABABANGONG BANGUNGOT* AND SOULEYMANE CISSÉ'S *YEELEN* — *77*

3 — **Converting Absences into Signs**
THE WAR ON TERROR AND THE HUMANITARIAN NECESSITY OF VIOLENCE — *111*

4 — **Documentation as Eradication**
THE AMAZON'S "UNCONTACTED TRIBES" AND THE SECURITIZING OF HUMANITY — *149*

5 — **A Differential Humanity**
BEYOND THE NEW FEMINIST ETHICS OF VULNERABILITY — *183*

Coda — **Zero Logics, Atomic Semiotics;**
OR, AN AESTHETICS OF DEBRIS — *218*

Notes — *227*
Bibliography — *263*
Index — *283*

Acknowledgments

It has felt very meaningful to get to work on this project for the last decade, and I have many people to thank for the fact that it now exists in this form. It's a commonplace of Buddhism that everyone—really, every being—is a teacher. The communities of teachers I am a part of make everything possible.

I feel incredibly fortunate to have gotten to work with Courtney Berger and Laura Jaramillo. I had never dared to imagine that I might have a chance at publishing with Duke, but Courtney's support right from the beginning helped me to accept that yes, it was really happening. Courtney is a brilliant and dedicated editor; her feedback on my work was both incisive and supportive, and she knew exactly what I needed to hear in order to do the work that would most benefit the manuscript. This book is immeasurably better because of it. As a team, Courtney and Laura struck a perfect balance between very clear and specific guidance, and trusting me to use my own good judgment. And their patience and enthusiasm for the project carried me through when my inner voice of doubt spoke up; I can't thank them enough. Many thanks, too, to Bird Williams, project editor extraordinaire.

This book would quite simply not be what it is without the generous, incisive, and deeply thoughtful work of two anonymous readers. They could see clearly what I could not, and it was only after receiving their comments that the project fully crystallized for me. And they read it not just once, but twice, in an eminently committed and thorough way both times. They offered me the best kind of intellectual engagement one could hope for.

Getting to think with Jigna Desai over the years has helped to remind me of why I am here in the first place. When I think of how I want to move in the world and in my work, and what kind of a place the university can be at its most ethical, intellectually curious and rigorous, creative, and revolutionarily just, I think of Jigna.

Qadri Ismail, who passed away suddenly in 2021, asked me during my dissertation defense what books should be arranged next to my dissertation on a hypothetical bookshelf. I take that question, along with many others that he posed, as one to practice and learn with, rather than one to be definitively answered. It shaped how I thought about what it meant to write this book, as it did my first one. I continue to learn from the questions he asked, and by what I have come to see as his hope for the possibilities opened up by a committed critique.

This book has benefited greatly from audiences at the many conferences where I have workshopped my ideas. Ann Braithwaite and Catherine Orr generously offered me the opportunity to write a chapter for their most recent edited collection; writing that piece allowed me to develop my thinking about the concept of humanity in a way that would become foundational for the book. A UNCG College of Arts and Sciences research assignment in the spring of 2017 afforded me crucial time for new research and a lot of reading. Participating in a National Center for Faculty Development and Diversity coaching program in the spring of 2021 gave me new tools and a lot of confidence at a time when I sorely needed both. And it has been so lovely to get to know Katie Kent as we have helped each other hold on to the skills we developed in the program.

At UNCG, I continue to have the great fortune of getting to work with many dedicated, compassionate people. In the WGSS Program, I am proud to be one member of a core faculty power trio that includes Tiffany Holland and Sarah Cervenak. Lisa Levenstein, our incredible program director, is both brilliant and kind. She is an expert at making people feel seen, appreciated, and trusted, just as she is at seeing exactly what the moment calls for and how to get it done. Kelly Taylor has been the driving force in helping WGSS fulfill its full potential as a vibrant presence at UNCG and in the wider community, and she has helped me in innumerable ways over the last several years. Faye Stewart, Gwen Hunnicutt, Silvia Bettez, Risa Applegarth, Heather Adams, Leila Villaverde, and Mark Rifkin have helped me to better understand who I am and what I am capable of, and they, along with the broader group of WGSS faculty, generously and enthusiastically make WGSS a strong and thriving center of engaged research and pedagogy on campus. I am grateful for Janine Jones's intellectual engagement and our conversations over the years. I feel honored to have gotten to work with Teresa Walch, Mark Elliott, John Stehlin, Anne Parsons, Denisa Jashari, Claudia Cabello, and many others—some of them still at UNCG, some now elsewhere—who show me how to engage in skillful livelihood and stand up for each other. I still have a lot to learn, and I am grateful to get to do so with them. I have been happy to keep up with my colleague Kathy Jamieson from afar—if there is a more thoughtful, generous, principled, and committed person and academic out there, I haven't met them.

The best part of this job is getting to meet, spend time with, and work with students. Every semester, I feel overcome by how special it is to have a room full of strangers trust me and each other enough to try out new ideas, ask the most important questions, and share their joys and fears alike. I have learned much of what I know from them, and I regret that I cannot remember or name all of them. When luck is really with me, I get to keep working with a former student and maybe even over time be called their friend. I'm so happy to get to be on Danielle LaPlace's dissertation committee even though she's no longer at UNCG. Zac Johnson inspired me with his astonishing intellect as an undergraduate student, and continues to do so. I love being able to call both Caitlin Spencer and Eric Toler my colleagues. Kelton Hollister is a fantastic pedagogue and I'm grateful for our many conversations about teaching and everything else. And getting to write an article with Aalih Hussein has been a true joy.

In the Chapel Hill Zen Center sangha, I have discovered that there is space for quiet in this world. My feeling of gratitude for getting to practice with this group is just not expressible in words. When I first started practicing there, I needed a lifeline; now it has become something more, as I am inspired by these friends and their dedication to finding the capacity for a nonviolent way of being together.

Dad, Josh, and Minori have shown up for me more times than I can count. I'm so lucky to have their friendship in addition to being able to call them my family. It means everything that I spent so many hours working on this book at Dad's house. Our relationship has been a safe place for me; he has kept me grounded and oriented over the years. His and Mom's presences show up in this book in so many ways. Sheryl Ketner has become a true and trusted friend. In the times when I have been in the most pain and my hope has been at its lowest, she has compassionately shown me how to reconnect with the part of me that knows that I can make it.

Diane Detournay, with her cloak of stars, has been at my side for over twenty years. She is the very definition of kindness, joy, commitment, and dazzling intellect. I just wouldn't be the person I am or be doing the work that I do without her. The many hours and days we spent together on video calls during the pandemic, when we couldn't visit each other, were the most special time. She and Brian Johnson have shown me that I always have a place to go. And Daniel Rhodes makes life sweeter than I knew was possible. Getting to live life with him has made the world open up into something newly beautiful. He is lovely beyond words. His very presence, his seemingly infinite patience, and our many conversations kept me going in the final stretch.

All faults, oversights, and omissions are my own.

Introduction

CYNICISM, DEATH, AND HUMANITARIANISM:
THE AESTHETICS OF RUINATION

Ruin, n.
- I. The state or condition of collapse or downfall. . . .
    - I.1.a. The state or condition of a fabric or structure, esp. a building, which has given way and collapsed.
    - I.1.b. The state or condition of a person who or society which has suffered decay or downfall. . . .
- II. The action of falling down; collapse, destruction, downfall. . . .
    - II.4.a. The downfall or decay of a person or society; complete loss of resources, wealth, moral or social standing, well-being, etc. . . .
    - II.5.a. Destruction; complete overthrow or devastation of a thing. . . .
- III. That which remains after collapse or downfall.
    - III.8. Material which remains after the decay and collapse of a structure; ruined buildings (cf. sense III.9b); debris, wreckage, remains. Also in extended use. Now *rare*.

III.9. In *plural*. The remains of a person who or thing which has suffered collapse, destruction, or downfall. Frequently in **in ruins**.

—"Ruin (n.)," *Oxford English Dictionary Online*

"We Have Reached the Last Threshold of the Human Heartbeat"

Abderrahmane Sissako's 2006 film *Bamako* stages a trial in which the plaintiff, African Society, accuses International Financial Institutions of certain crimes. The trial unfolds over the course of the film before it is revealed, in the closing argument made by a lawyer for the plaintiff, that the specific charge is "crimes of inhumanity and cynicism." The charge of inhumanity is perhaps expected, even as that expectedness is the proof of its abiding truth. The additional charge, of cynicism, catches the attention. In everyday use, "inhumanity" suggests a deep and enduring deficit, and "cynicism" something more like an attitude that might be ephemeral or contextually bound. But cynicism is also about an inability and/or unwillingness to imagine, to hope, or to admit that something else is possible. To be cynical is to claim that humanity writ large is incapable of kindness and compassion; for the cynic, humanity is, by definition, selfish and violent.[1]

This cynicism about humanity is anchored in the killing logics of colonialism and conquest, according to which theft and destruction are just what humans do to each other. In charging the global economic infrastructure not just with inhumanity but also with cynicism, *Bamako*'s representatives of African Society—who are not simply actors, but a professor, a lawyer, a refugee, a teacher, and a griot, among others, playing versions of themselves—call for its very concept of humanity to be put on trial, given that it requires that Africa, and Africans, die. The witnesses for the plaintiff all speak to the many and various forms of death they have been made to endure, witness, and at times themselves embody. Mr. Keita, a professor, is asked by a lawyer for the defense whether he can imagine a world without "funds or banks"—a question posed with an answer in mind, one that reveals the asker's own failure of imagination. When Mr. Keita responds that "absolutely" yes, he can, the lawyer suggests that Africa should accept death rather than be released from the debt it cannot pay back. Mr. Keita's own ability to hold both in mind—the death he has witnessed, as well as the possibility for a different world—and the necessity of not seeing these as mutually exclusive, becomes apparent in the rest of his testimony. He notes that colonization "took everything," that "they don't just take our resources, our work, and our money, they take our minds too. We have reached the last threshold of the human heartbeat," implying that "they" will try to take this too, the final human thing remaining, the very thing that keeps the body and the spirit alive and also where, perhaps, a non-cynical experience of humanity could be located. Mr. Keita concludes that the World Bank's policies are predicated on the teleological assertion that "some countries are destined to disappear," that is, to be eliminated as the ultimate fulfillment of humanity's quintessence.

Bamako exposes the aestheticizing—the artistic and sensorial rendering, and the onto-political categorizing—of Africa as destined to disappear precisely by those discourses and projects that declare the intention of saving it, as the testimony given by the witnesses for African Society focuses on the necropolitical depredations wrought by development's extractivism and the humanitarian legal apparatus that supports it. The trial's staging in a neighborhood courtyard is itself a sustained visual reminder of the law's positioning of human bodies in relation to each other in a highly prescribed and hierarchical way. The witnesses for the plaintiff stand in this makeshift court, speaking of their humanity, while signs of the deep presence of "International Financial Institutions" in their lives abound. It becomes clear that many forms of suffering create the conditions for the very law that the trial's proceedings are meant to embody and express. These forms would be exceedingly familiar to anyone who has imbibed popular Western media about Africa—the economic refugee who perishes on her way to Europe, the silent and sickly young child, the man slowly succumbing to an unnamed illness at home—and indeed the film implicitly poses multiple questions about the stakes of filmmaking, especially for those whose appearance within this juridical/political/media scenography is structured in relation to violence and ruin. In doing so, it allows us to see the aesthetic conjunction of artistic and political practice: The distribution of bodies in space, the type and tenor of sensorial experience, and the enforcement of "proper" social roles for different subjects that both imperial legal logics and "coherently" structured films rely upon and reproduce are very much the same.

Perhaps one of the most striking features of *Bamako* is the emphasis on the practices of looking of so many of the people in the film itself, and how those practices describe the ordering of social and political space—sometimes reifying the given places of individuals in that order, sometimes disrupting that order, and sometimes doing something more ambiguous. Looking is thematized as contextual and deeply complicated, guided and oriented by the literal and symbolic architectural features of various social milieux. The character Falaï, frequently seen with a video camera recording various goings-on, describes himself as a criminologist who takes photographs for the police and also for family events, noting that "There's another market now—funerals. There's money in that," and that "The faces of people who talk don't interest me. There's no truth in them. . . . I prefer the dead. They're truer." This conversation occurs outside the walls of the courtyard, during the testimony given by a witness for the plaintiff, who notes that development is a system based in deception that makes those subject to it into unwitting accomplices in their own "pauperization": "pay or die. That's the West's lesson that we inflict on ourselves." After the witness completes this part of her testimony, as if to confirm this analysis, Falaï states to his friend, "Death is good." Later, we see a sequence from a film, titled *Death in Timbuktu*, being shown on television while young children watch raptly, laughing. Featuring an absurdist plot in which cowboys shoot and kill each other for no reason, murdering a woman while her young child looks on, its setting in the streets of a town echoes the courtyard-as-courtroom, the only difference being that the courtroom represents legal rather than extrajudicial killing (even as the moral calculations used to justify the killing effectively remain the same).

Yet these death-oriented practices of looking are not the only ones. Many shots show people looking at the witnesses providing testimony, at each other, at the people who go about their daily lives in the courtyard, or off into the distance as they listen to the trial proceedings—sometimes nodding in affirmation and support, sometimes prompted into deep thought of their own. Their attentive presence is perhaps the organizing thematic feature of this film, as it describes a relational space in which imperial geopolitics do not define all. Two key scenes movingly highlight this. The first takes place right before the title screen, at the end of an establishing sequence; here we see a witness, Zegué Bemba, gain entry into the courtyard and present himself before the chief judge. Bemba, via a translator, is informed that it's not yet his turn to speak; Bemba lingers for a few minutes though, noting that "Words are something. . . . They can seize you in your heart. It's bad if you keep them inside." In a second scene, toward the end of the film, he returns, standing up from the audience right after the chief lawyer for the defense, Rapaport, has given his closing argument. Once again speaking out of turn, Bemba interrupts the proceedings by acting as a griot. Notably, Bemba's speech here is not in French, the language of the court, but rather in Bambara; and not only does no one translate, it is not subtitled (unlike almost all of the rest of the dialogue). In this long and deeply affecting scene, we witness many people witnessing him, silently watching and reflecting, some of them crying. This is, to be sure, a very different silence than the kind that is imposed, even as it highlights what cannot be heard and who cannot be seen by the law even when it is stated loudly and clearly by a living, breathing, and very present person, because it breaks open the aesthetic and indeed ethical order on which juridical knowledge is founded. The terms of this order are laid out in lurid detail by Rapaport as the chief lawyer for International Financial Institutions. After spending the trial blaming the plaintiffs for the harm his own clients have done to them, Rapaport makes an appeal for humanity to come together as a single global community to address "common threats" to its existence, namely, global warming, nuclear weapons, and terrorism—and he argues that development and its (ostensible) alleviation of poverty is central to this project.

I begin with this extended discussion of *Bamako* because it so brilliantly traces the intricate intertwining of modern humanitarianism with genocidalism. As Rapaport invokes the welfare of humanity as a means to deny the realities of the witnesses for African Society, and ultimately to suggest that their suffering is necessary to the preservation of humanity writ large, his argumentative logic epitomizes the particular relationship to death that, I argue, invests modern humanitarianism. This relationship is one of management and ownership, an attempt to determine who dies, under what circumstances, and what that death means, by claiming the right to intervene on behalf of humanity as a whole. *Humanity's Ruins* exposes humanitarianism's founding on an explicitly Eurocentric, white-ascendant conceptualization of humanity that was produced within and for the purposes of the specifically Western project of conquest. As such, humanitarianism is not simply the convenient cover for neo-imperial governance, which is the argument that many extant analyses of humanitarianism ultimately structure their critique upon. Rather, it is animated by and expressive of a fundamentally genocidal aesthetic and ethical order that itself predates, and has created the conditions for, Western imperial governance in the wake of World War II and in the ensuing long Cold War/post–Cold War era. In its contemporary iterations, humanitarianism is not exclusively engaged in and propagated by social actors who could be described as paradigmatic Western subjects or as inhabiting the space of the West. Nonetheless, and precisely because its use is not confined to actors with specific identities, humanitarianism can be described as a Western discourse. I refer to the "Western" because it historically precedes other ways of indexing shifting geopolitical configurations (First/Second/Third World, or Global North/

Global South), for the humanity that modern humanitarianism takes as its object was formed along with "the West" itself. Humanitarianism's mobilization by variously situated actors within changing geopolitical relationships of power demonstrates its continued attachment to genocidal figurings of racialized humanity, even as its differential and shifting use speaks to the ungroundedness of race itself.

I compose my inquiry in this book by tracing the lineaments of the aesthetics of ruination that structures humanitarian logics, cultural objects, and political projects. I invoke aesthetics in terms of the particular characteristics of the humanitarian cultural and media texts I take up and the sensory experiences that engaging with them produces, as well as in the particular sense that political philosopher Jacques Rancière describes, that is, aesthetics as the "distribution of the sensible" that orders perception and the organization and assumed placement of the members of a given political community.[2] My analysis along these lines is about how the aesthetics of humanitarian discourses—characterized by a sensorial archive of devastation and a genocidal management of onto-political grouphood—produce a humanity whose identity can only be realized through actual and imagined eradication. In other words, the genocidal project of *extermination* comes to be aligned with the *survival* of humanity in a variety of contemporary discourses and projects that are predicated on humanitarian ideals and ethics. Fear of extinction and the presumed need to ensure humanity's endurance has long been intertwined with the presumed necessity of the eradication of some human beings to the realization of humanity's ostensible essence. In modern humanitarianism, this longer-lived and intense preoccupation with the possibility of civilization's (indeed, humanity's) decay and downfall finds new sustenance and inspiration in the advent of massively destructive events and technologies, and new capacities for the assertion of its own will in the same. Ultimately, I am interested in the current resurgence of a variety of imaginings of humanity's end—through nuclear warfare, runaway environmental devastation, advanced capitalism, or artificial intelligence—and how humanitarian ideals have become a predominant means through which to mobilize arguments for humanity's survival, arguments that are constructed on a heavily militarized and deeply violent repertoire of logics, ethics, and affects. It is telling, to say the least, that these imaginings simultaneously ignore the histories of devastation and world-ending faced by, and instrumentalize as agency-deprived figures of ultimate suffering, those peoples who have been subject to the eradicatory drive of Western imperial conquest. Those who are authorized to tell the story of humanity's possible end and to propose how "we" might save ourselves betray a fascination with destruction, such that it becomes difficult to distinguish between the false sense of mastery provided by the effort to save humanity and by the tools of destruction themselves.

In order to consider the many and various sites where meaning about humanitarianism is produced and humanitarian projects are undertaken, I read broadly, across a variety of textual genres—fiction film and documentary, news stories, organization websites, popular essays, scholarly writings. Reading in this way, we can see how humanitarianism is formed as a multiplicity of codes, discourses, and institutions: as a moral imperative, a legal concept, an informatics, a visual order, and a tool for making a variety of different political claims. I attempt to trace the ebb and flow of their coherence with each other and the radical disagreements that well up in the spaces between these texts and articulations, to acknowledge the violent force of that coherence, and to attend to the possibilities opened up by those disagreements. Often invoked apparently unintentionally, genocidal aspirations appear in diverse humanitarian discourses and projects, and seem in many contexts to have overdetermined the possibilities for thinking about humanity. It is for this reason that I take the broadly defined media landscape of humanitarianism as my archive, because such an approach perhaps allows a reckoning with the various and subtle ways in which many of us are called into humanitarianism's work, and what we may do to refuse to participate in that work.

In the rest of the introduction to the book, I situate humanitarianism within the historical context of post–World War II geopolitical reorganization and the rise of human rights frameworks and laws, looking at how humanitarianism reappropriates and reproduces a longer-lived understanding of humanity born and sustained in the heart of the Western imperial project, and illuminating the violent forms of knowledge production that underlie the equally violent actions often done in the name of humanitarianism. I engage critical scholarship on the rise of human rights instruments, policies, and broader discourses in the long Cold War/post–Cold War era and their centrality to the reconfiguring and reassertion of imperial modes of governance and warfare in response to unfolding anti-colonial movements. In this, I consider what the framework of biopolitics/necropolitics offers in terms of illuminating the relationship between human rights and warfare, as well as what I am identifying as the genocidal formation of "humanity" that defines the content and character of modern humanitarian projects and discourses. Diverting the concept of genocide away from its common use to diagnose the putative expression of racial/ethnic hatred, I instead understand it as an assertion of the specific form the onto-political order of humanity "should" take, which I argue opens up the interpretive possibility for a more thorough inquiry into how humanitarian discourses conceive of the very makeup of the world (indeed, the universe, existence, and nonexistence), often in deeply troubling ways that might not be readily apparent.

To establish my contention regarding the genocidal underpinnings of modern humanitarianism's conceptualization of humanity, I unearth and explicate what I argue are its two major defining conceptual formations: "humanity as a whole" and "human suffering." While there is an increasingly substantial body of scholarship that offers serious historically grounded critiques of various humanitarian endeavors' expression of violence against those humans whose suffering they claim to have an interest in alleviating, there is as of yet not much sustained inquiry into the thought apparatus that simultaneously gives rise to and is remade by humanitarian projects and discourses. "Humanity as a whole" and "human suffering" emerge as conjoined concepts across a variety of cultural texts, producing "humanity" as an ostensibly internally coherent category. Making a differentially defined category (that is, any category) *appear* to be internally coherent requires unceasing effort. Given the impossibility of "humanity's" internal coherence, violence is the outcome of the imperialist/racist drive to achieve the illusion of that coherence. What surfaces from my reading of these texts is that humanitarianism has been mobilized to manage this problem of humanity's conception, that is, its fundamental failure as an internally coherent, self-same category. Those who threaten to expose this failure—either by presenting the possibility of a variety of different humanities, by "inappropriately" claiming to be part of humanity and/or to be able to define humanity writ large, or by refusing to recognize humanity as a valid category—become the targets of this management. Within this targeting, humanitarian modes of knowledge production align with neo-imperial warfare in their emphasis on totality and control.

I am thus deeply concerned about the iron grip that humanitarian logics now seem to have on social justice projects in general and, more specifically, on endeavors to put an end to warfare. Indeed, the paucity of the humanitarian epistemological and ethical tool kit for an anti-war project—a project which I hold near and dear—and the dire need for something else describe the origins and aims of this book. As I discuss later, "humanity as a whole" and "human suffering" produce a conceptualization of humanity as defined by vulnerability, and this vulnerable humanity appears in explicitly racist/civilizationist war ethics, reckonings with the threat caused by human-induced climate change, and feminist anti-violence efforts alike. The recognition of human individuals' shared exposure to vulnerability has been increasingly taken up for the new anti-violence ethical possibilities it seems to offer. But it is this very idea that also continues to form the core justification for the genocidal use of atomic bombs and the maintenance of nuclear weapons arsenals with world-destroying potential. It is in this conception of humanity as essentially vulnerable that, I will argue, humanitarian investments in protection and preservation come into alignment with genocidal aspirations.

Postcolonial feminist cultural theorists provide incisive analyses of the kinds of epistemological and ethical technologies that I see as comprising the aesthetics of ruination. While this book is not solely about feminism, it takes feminist modes of inquiry to be essential to understanding humanitarianism as a Western imperial formation that proliferates racisms anew, in particular through the genocidal notion of humanity it both relies upon and reproduces. I align with scholars who argue that processes of racialization and the targeting of racialized communities and polities are less about designating some humans as not full or real humans, and more about the convoluted and contradictory processes of recognition that define humanity. In other words, I do not pursue the kind of argument that attempts to rectify a false distinction between the human and nonhuman; rather, I analyze the workings of what I see as the pervasive attempt to enforce a synonymy between human being and humanity. It is precisely the shifting relationships of various racialized groups to humanity, and the very necessity for these relationships to never reach a point of clear and precise definition, that renders the category of humanity ever-vulnerable to dissolution. A major contention of *Humanity's Ruins* is that modern humanitarianism takes the forestalling of this dissolution as its main project—often by any means necessary. Its abiding, brutal, and profound antagonism toward the possibility—much less desirability—of the nonhierarchical, noninstrumentalized, and noncoherent *simultaneous* existence of various different forms of human life shows up in many places. It feels like it cannot help itself. Thus, in picking my way through humanitarianism's cultural landscape of death and decay, I attempt to refuse to follow the defined path it lays out. If I myself linger in the debris, it is in the interest of dismantling and rearranging the reality constructed by the architecture of the ruins.[3] Indeed, because the humanitarian discourses I examine in this book are oriented toward the preservation of a given social structure, I am not interested so much in assessing the accuracy of humanitarian discourses as I am in disrupting their very ordering of reality. It is in the interest of disruption, then, that I turn toward these authors, attempting to think alongside and with them about the relationship between humanity and violence in a way that humanitarian discourses cannot seem to do without reverting to severely compromised lines of argumentation and logics.

Human Rights and a Genocidal Humanity

What happens when we understand humanitarianism not just as a practice of alleviating human suffering, but rather as central to Western and Global North neocolonial governance and militarism? To address this question, I take up an exploration of humanitarianism's role in post–World War II geopolitics from the perspective of two lines of scholarly inquiry: critical histories of the development of human rights, and the theoretical construct of biopolitics/necropolitics. I seek to show that the institutionalization of human rights is a primary way in which humanitarian principles have become central to the authorizing of Western, Global North, colonial, and imperial forms of governance (including military interventions, development, economic policies, peacekeeping missions, etc.) in the wake of World War II. I also seek to show how the development of modern humanitarian principles is indebted to a longer-lived, genocidal configuration of humanity; inextricably connected to the Western project of colonialism, humanist epistemology and ethics serve as the supporting structure for a hegemonic post–World War II vision of a global humanitarian order.

Rather than continuing to uphold the common definition of human rights as a set of values or principles, one important body of scholarship helps to shift our frame of reference by redefining it as a moral/juridical/political technology for codifying neocolonialism in the face of ongoing successful anti-colonial liberation movements. This work moves against a pervasive discourse according to which the atrocities witnessed during World War II led to some kind of elevated consciousness of the universal nature of human suffering and of the need for ways to mitigate future suffering. This is precisely the narrative that authorized calls for world governance (headed by the United States and/or select Western nations) and led to the founding of the United Nations.[4] This is not to say that Western and Global North actors have been the sole agents of human rights laws, policies, and paradigms. Authors like Balakrishnan Rajagopal and Sylvanna Falcón insist on the need to attend to the fact that the continued development of international political and economic institutions has been driven by multiple, dynamic Third World, Fourth World, and Global South justice movements.[5] Indeed, this was exactly why in and around World War II, the UN and allied institutions were established—because of these movements' strength and insistence on being involved in the UN itself, even as this institution proved too resistant to change to allow radicalization efforts to succeed.[6] For this reason, a definition of human rights like Inderpal Grewal's, as a "regime of truth" that has come to shape a variety of everyday cultural practices, acts of moral reckoning, and relationships characterized by governmentality—related to but extending well beyond the realms of law and politics proper[7]—is useful for contending with its broad reach, deep entrenchment, and the serious complexities it poses to any negotiation of access to resources and justice.

Randall Williams illustrates the rise of human rights as this seemingly inescapable regime of truth by focusing on how it serves as a primary means of managing authoritative uses of violence and, indeed, as "the privileged epistemic form for political violence"[8] in the current geopolitical context. Given its emergence "as a key concept in the discourse of the postwar international with the passage of the Universal Declaration of Human Rights (adopted December 10, 1948),"[9] human rights principles and legal instruments became a way to delegitimate and attempt to suppress a variety of anti-imperial movements.[10] As Rajagopal reveals, human rights doctrine developed as a reiteration of rather than a break with colonial-era laws that criminalized anti-colonial movements;[11] thus, "though it is commonly (mis)understood to be a pacifist philosophy . . . human rights discourse imposes obligations upon the state to use violence in order to secure basic rights—such as rights to life, personal liberty, physical security, equality, freedom of religion, or 'compulsory' education."[12] Talal Asad adds that with the drafting of the Universal Declaration of Human Rights, "the universal character of the rights-bearing person is made the responsibility of sovereign states," thus effecting "a direct convergence between 'the rule of law' and social justice" and *necessitating* that violence be committed against certain people in the name of the humanity of other people.[13] What is at stake here is not just the use of the authority of the law to uphold powerful interests in the name of human rights, but more insidiously, the multiple ways in which individuals and groups must prove their humanity—specifically, Asad implies, through the demonstration of adherence to the law and to the Christian emancipatory mandates that invest a presumptively secular political and juridical apparatus.[14]

That human rights principles necessarily involve hierarchical differentiation is a core tenet of a body of feminist scholarship that treats these principles as a primary mechanism through which gender norms and gender-based exploitation have been proliferated and codified in the post–World War II era, having particularly deleterious outcomes for women. Examining human rights' inception within the UN, what Sylvanna M. Falcón reveals is that the UN's formal structures for addressing gender inequality, for example the Commission on the Status of Women and the Committee on the Elimination of Discrimination Against Women, have been sites for promulgating the hegemonic feminisms that are premised on a monolithic womanhood and a willful neglect of anti-colonial and anti-racist analyses of power.[15] The global reach of human rights as a paradigm informing, and demanded of, feminist work is of deep concern in many senses. The very fact that, according to Inderpal Grewal, "gender was stabilized through practices articulated as human rights violations essentially linked to gender, for example widespread domestic violence or the vulnerability to rape for women by militarized or nationalist power"[16] is a problem because of the centrality of particular codifications of gender, especially the gender binary, to hegemonic definitions of humanity. Moreover, the hailing of "women" by human rights discourses has been a key imperial militarist tactic in the post–Cold War era. In an analysis of how women are invoked as signifiers within the representational landscape of post-9/11 politics, Leela Fernandes argues that the fact that the so-called war on terror has been persistently framed as a war for human rights has serious implications for "a global, international, and transnational feminist human rights approach," which has no choice but to "navigate within the representational terrain" of this war.[17] The representational terrain created by the militarized apparatus of human rights has had a variety of insidious effects. Examining the role of gendering in the latest iterations of what they refer to as accumulation by dispossession via "debt-based financing to the global South from the global North,"[18] Christine Keating, Claire Rasmussen, and Pooja Rishi show how the attempt to empower women through various development schemes that intensify global capitalism's reach ultimately relies on an abject predation upon these very women. In other words, human rights is the profoundly cynical mechanism through which the recognition of *some* women as deserving human compassion is used to fold them into imperial warfare, neocolonial extractivism, and indeed genocidally inspired projects.

These studies lead me to consider the very development of human rights as biopolitically/necropolitically motivated, and as such as indebted to the formation of the modern conception of humanity within a fundamentally genocidal worldview well before World War II. The understanding that the deaths of some humans have been made vital for other humans is, of course, central to the scholarship on biopolitics and necropolitics, which sees the former—a form of governmentality focused on the management of the biological characteristics of a population (including the active cultivation of certain forms of life)—as part of the same construct as the latter. Bringing to light some of the inadequacies of Michel Foucault's formulation of biopower, Achille Mbembe's famous articulation of the concept of necropolitics has inspired wide-ranging scholarship arguing that the intertwining of biopolitics and necropolitics is foundational to Western colonialism, chattel slavery, and empire.[19] While Mbembe's work has been widely used to analyze the operations of power in an array of contexts, I would like to emphasize his less-remarked-upon argument that in Western thought and politics, humanity is defined by the capacity to master death itself. Rerendering European political philosophy as animated not by the principles of reason and freedom but rather by death, Mbembe shows that the subject of this philosophy achieves his humanity by imposing death on others,[20] and it is thus that "terror and killing become the means of realizing the already known telos of history."[21] Apart from the act of killing, the other means of attempting to achieve a mastery of death is through the creation of "*deathworlds*, new and unique forms of social existence in which vast populations are subjected to conditions of life conferring upon them the status of *living dead*."[22] What Mbembe is highlighting here is a social scenography of devastation, the production and (attempted) orchestration of which is a principal means for the assertion of onto-political sovereignty on the part of the Western subject of humanity.

In his crucial work on the West's abiding investment in racist/colonialist destruction, Sven Lindqvist further illuminates the kind of logical bind animating a thought system that has organized itself around death—and the terroristic coping mechanisms that have been the result. In arguing that extermination forms the very "core of European thought,"[23] Lindqvist insists that humanism relies on the concept and practice of extermination,[24] and he demonstrates this reliance by tracing the codevelopment of humanism and extermination within the context of evolutionary theory. He provocatively suggests that the dread and horror produced by evolutionary theory's introduction of the possibility of human extinction was managed by the racist codification of extinction as a biological inevitability for some humans but not for humanity—indeed, by the idea that that inevitability was a prerequisite for humanity's survival.²⁵ Extinction not only served as the alibi for extermination practices, but came to be seen as a mercy, an end to the suffering of those humans whose very existence was seen as being defined by it.²⁶ Thus extermination became a way to attempt to master death, materializing as "fact" the premise of extinction as a process naturally suffered by a subset of humans. For Lindqvist, the posing and answering of the grand question "What is it that makes us into human beings?"²⁷ by the naturalists, psychologists, anthropologists, and medical men credited with defining modern Euro-American thought—Freud, Darwin, Durkheim, Lévi-Strauss—was thus premised on genocide.

Mbembe and Lindqvist suggest the necessity of understanding genocide as both more expansive and more essential to Western epistemologies and ethics than it is sometimes characterized as being, as do influential genocide studies scholars Patrick Wolfe and Omer Bartov, who have worked diligently to illuminate genocide's embeddedness in the Western/European imperial project and in its social structure. In his famous article "Settler Colonialism and the Elimination of the Native," Wolfe's specific interest is to elaborate on the various forms that the logic of elimination takes within settler colonialism as "a specific social formation,"²⁸ with genocide as one particular expression of the logic of elimination that characterizes settler colonialism broadly speaking.²⁹ Refusing to parse different "forms" of genocide as a way to describe systematized elimination in varying contexts—which would risk qualifying the genocide of Native peoples as a particular type and thus characterizing it as less consequential than the Holocaust (as the implied founding event defining what genocide is)³⁰—Wolfe insists on an understanding of genocide as not confinable to discrete events but rather as imbued in the political and social orders characterizing settler colonialism.³¹ Bartov also considers the saturated presence of genocidalism within the social order in another context, namely Europe in and around World Wars I and II and indeed in the continuing aftermath of the Holocaust. For Bartov, genocide is a core feature of modernity, and in its horrific development in the event of the Holocaust it refined the much longer-lived fear of extinction (as revealed by Lindqvist) into a technologically advanced practice of what Bartov names as industrialized killing. As Bartov puts it, "the organizers of the killing, and those who supplied the scientific rationale and know-how for extermination, were all members of an elite that perceived itself as taking part in a heroic, self-sacrificing venture aimed at the salvation of humanity from an array of Satanic forces threatening it with extinction."³² While Bartov's focus is such that he does not consider the legal and political apparatuses and social and moral conditioning through which Western nations attempted to justify colonial horrors and no doubt instilled the capacity for mass murder, I note the importance of his analysis of genocide's key role in defining "humanity" as vulnerable to extinction and as requiring preservation by any means necessary.

Crucially, Wolfe also points our attention toward the fact that genocidal practices and logics do not just seek to eradicate individuals within (predefined) groups, but rather to define, adjudicate, and eradicate the possibility of certain grouphoods:

> The etymology of "genocide" combines the senses of killing and grouphood. "Group" is more than a purely numerical designation. *Genos* refers to a denominate group with a membership that persists through time.... It is not simply a random collectivity.... Thus genocide has been achieved by means of summary mass murder ... in the frontier massacring of Indigenous peoples, in the Holocaust, and in Rwanda. But there can be summary mass murder without genocide, as in the case of 9/11, and there can be genocide without summary mass murder, as in the case of the continuing post-frontier destruction, in whole and in part, of Indigenous *genoi*.... The question of degree is not the definitional issue.[33]

Genocide is not necessarily about eliminating every member of a particular group, but rather eliminating the very notion of a people as a people: "the containment of Indian groups within Euroamerican society that culminated in the end of the frontier produced a range of ongoing complementary strategies whose common intention was the destruction of heterodox forms of Indian grouphood. In the post–World War II climate of civil rights, these strategies were reinforced by the policies of termination and relocation, held out as liberating individual Indians from the thralldom of the tribe."[34] In other words, in attempting to ensure a particular ordering of the political world at the levels of identity and ontology, genocide seeks not only to destroy, but to produce a specific onto-political architecture in the ruins of that destruction. This is to say that genocide aims at a certain kind of productivity, insofar as it imbues and structures sociality and the dynamics of relationality, and relies on the proliferation of discursive scenes of humanity's supposed presence (scenes that are heavily reliant on a grammar of devastation).

To that end, I propose that genocidalism is a defining characteristic of contemporary humanitarianism's aesthetics of ruination. Earlier, I invoked

Jacques Rancière's notion of the distribution of the sensible, which he describes as "an 'aesthetics' at the core of politics," where aesthetics is "the system of *a priori* forms determining what presents itself to sense experience. It is a delimitation of spaces and times, of the visible and the invisible, of speech and noise, that simultaneously determines the place and the stakes of politics as a form of experience."[35] This "primary aesthetics" provides a basis for inquiry into the aesthetic characteristics of specific artistic practices and whether and how they might "intervene" in a given distribution of the sensible. Because the relationship between sense perception and its interpretation or intelligibility within a given distribution of the sensible necessarily describes "a form of hierarchy among sentient beings,"[36] aesthetics is vital to the reorganization of and reorientation to the given social order that is the essence of true politics. Rancière's analysis as developed over the course of many works centers a distinction between the police and politics; the former includes "the set of procedures whereby the aggregation and consent of collectivities is achieved, the organization of powers, the distribution of places and roles, and the systems for legitimizing this distribution,"[37] while politics unsettles and rearranges the police distribution of the sensible. Crucially, politics is only possible through the assertion of what is perceived as excessive to the human social order yet is in fact fundamental to it—an "equality of anyone and everyone";[38] it happens when those who have no right within the prevailing order to speak or to describe themselves as part of a community nonetheless claim that they do have a part in that community, that they *are* that community.[39] Likewise, "politics ceases . . . wherever the whole of the community is reduced to the sum of its parts with nothing left over."[40] To truly engage politics, then, is to invoke disagreement as a fundamental and, crucially, irresolvable disruption in the nature of human social reality.

Rancière sees the current and frequent invocation of humanity as the ur-subject of a consensus-based global political system as in service to a project of radical depoliticization. Describing consensus as "one of the master terms of our time,"[41] he articulates a deep concern regarding its deployment to preserve the existing social order at all costs:

> Some interpret it as the global agreement of governing and opposition parties over the great national interests. Others see it more broadly as a new style of government that gives precedence to discussion and negotiation to resolve conflicts. Consensus, however, means a lot more—properly understood it signifies a mode of symbolic

structuration of the community that empties out the political core that constitutes it, namely dissension. A *political* community is indeed a community that is structurally divided, not divided between diverging interest groups and opinions, but divided in relation to itself. A political "people" is never the same thing as the sum of a population. It is always a form of supplementary symbolism in relation to any counting of the population and of its parts.[42]

Consensus is a kind of totalizing and infinite effort to secure humanity against the forms of grouphood that, through the lens of consensus, can only be seen as existentially threatening in their excessivity to humanity itself.[43] In this, Rancière has much to offer the critique of a widespread and entrenched mode of thought according to which humanitarian ethical considerations—how to best help a target population, how to discern who is in need and deserving of help in the first place, how to prioritize the distribution of limited resources so as to provide maximal relief for the most intense suffering—are seen as requiring a fundamental ideological agreement about the interest of the greater good that transcends and hence obliterates different understandings of reality. In a 2006 article, "The Ethical Turn of Aesthetics and Politics," he describes the post-9/11 Euro-American sociopolitical landscape as a flattened and featureless one in which consensus defines the foundation and end goal of (putatively) ethical action. Rancière defines "ethics" here as "the kind of thinking which establishes the identity between an environment, a way of being and a principle of action,"[44] and argues that it is the presumption of a necessary and complete synonymy of what is perceived as right and what is perceived as reality[45] that produces the kind of ethics that advocates for humanitarian warfare—that is, warfare the purpose of which is to achieve a sociopolitical community in which there are no distinctions or divisions. Conceived as an undivided whole, such a community requires a kind of radical exclusion that, terrifyingly, registers as no exclusion at all.

Following Rancière, we could say that in the reality created by a genocidal distribution of the sensible, a basic essentialism creates an orderly alignment of biological/cultural identities with political positions, and determines who is recognized as part of humanity (and what their "proper" place in it is). Indeed, humanitarian efforts to understand and restore societies that have experienced genocide tend to reinforce this distribution of the sensible. As Mahmood Mamdani reveals in his inquiry into the Rwandan genocide, the standard ways in which such events are critically analyzed are themselves indebted to the same colonial logics that created the very conditions for those events, and that persist in widespread and deeply entrenched sociological epistemologies about ethnic and cultural distinctions that supposedly inexorably lead to violence. For Mamdani, it is only possible to understand what happened in Rwanda—the fact that so many members of a society participated in the most brutal and intimate forms of violence, in the sort of killing that is "hard work"[46]—by breaking with the typical explanations given.[47] These typical explanations rely on the Western colonialist construction of ethnic and racial groupings, which are in turn seen as essentially determinative of one's worldview; as Mamdani puts it, they tend to "*naturalize* political difference as a simple and unproblematic reflection of cultural and biological difference."[48] For Dylan Rodríguez too, writing in regard to the long US imperial relationship with the Philippines, "the conventions of empirical social science do not offer an adequate methodological lens"[49] to understand and contend with either the true scale of genocidal destruction enacted by the United States or the lasting implications of the fact that "the process of genocidal conquest was utterly *labor intensive*"[50] in the massive violence required to create a new version of onto-political reality. Genocide cannot be understood here as a discrete historical event located simply in the past, as the logical outcome of the encounter with difference, or as based in an antiquated racism that has since been transcended; rather, Rodríguez sees "the ongoing inscription of racist genocide *as the condition of possibility for* the Filipino's sustained presence in (and proximity to) the United States."[51]

What I am naming "humanity's ruins" is this socio-onto-political order in which genocide regulates the distribution of the sensible via an intensive labor that many everyday people have been and continue to be engaged in. This labor takes many forms, including the consumption of scholarship, media, and news, through which many of us—albeit, and crucially so, in various and often incommensurate ways—participate in the production of humanitarian discourse and indeed the construction of a humanitarian ethos. The architecture of humanity's ruins is premised on the achievement of an ostensibly consensual organization of bodies, subjects, and roles—although this desired consensus is at best only ever extremely tenuous. Indeed, the definition of "ruin" is itself internally contradictory, as "that which remains" of a "complete loss." This tension, between the potentiality of a complete loss and the desire to nonetheless secure some kind of remainder in the aftermath of such loss, animates humanitarian renderings of the projects of alleviating human suffering and ensuring human survival. Ruins have an architecture, one that appears to allow for the destroyed structure (whether physical or social) to have some relation to what came before, a predeterminable meaning. Its usefulness for facilitating a knowledge project defined by control and guaranteeing some kind of continued presence for a predefined humanity is also what makes it such an attractive trope for genocidal regimes (as I will discuss later). In the next section, I will elaborate on the two core concepts of contemporary humanitarian ethics—humanity as a whole and human suffering—and the particular imagining of the human world they produce, so that I can then return to a further explanation of how the aesthetics of ruination manifest in a variety of discourses and media forms.

Humanity as a Whole and Human Suffering

The entry for "humanitarian" in its adjectival form in the *Oxford English Dictionary* highlights the two intertwined conceptual formations—humanity as a whole, and human suffering—that vitalize humanitarian ethics: "2.a. Concerned with humanity as a whole; *spec.* seeking to promote human welfare as a primary or pre-eminent good; acting, or disposed to act, on this basis rather than for pragmatic or strategic reasons. . . . 2.b. Designating an event or situation which causes or involves (widespread) human suffering, *esp.* one which requires the provision of aid or support on a large scale."[52] An understanding of humanity as defined by and for itself, with no remainder or outside, is suggested by the definition of "whole": "complete, undivided, total"; "lacking no part, element, or essential characteristic; having its entire extent or magnitude; perfect, complete."[53] And suffering, while implicitly posited as a fundamental and defining feature of human existence, gestures toward unequal and potentially hierarchical delineations internally and externally defining humanity in the invocation of taken-for-granted processes of discernment and definition—namely, about what counts as human suffering, how the necessity of aid is determined as a particular response to suffering, and indeed who should provide that aid and in what form and to whom.

Histories and examinations of humanitarianism take up these two conceptual formations to varying degrees—though to my knowledge, there has been no systematic inquiry into them and their relationship to each other, or into their association with a genocidal understanding of humanity. Scholarship problematizing the universalism that humanitarianism presumes and requires does not exactly critique the formation of humanity as a "whole," but it does importantly emphasize the serious problems with the idea that there are fundamental shared qualities that define all humans and that can serve as the basis for humanitarian work. As Julietta Hua explains so clearly, universalism relies on the demarcation of essential hierarchies in order to define humanity:

> The modern regime of power established in the Enlightenment and post-Enlightenment projects that sought to explain the nature of man and his difference from things, animals, and slaves posited the notion of humanity as universally defined by his capacity to reason, his ability to exist as self-conscious, and his recognition of the rule of law.... As the philosophers of man reasoned about those attributes distinguishing man, they were most concerned with describing the conditions around them: the condition of Europe.... The writing of this subject as the model of humanity envisioned this subject as universal—a standard against which all other consciousnesses and subjectivities could be measured.[54]

The violence of universalism is not just due to the fact that it refuses to recognize and appreciate difference, but is also due to what wholeness demands: dominance, ownership, and the (attempted) eradication of other ways of being human that would threaten the illusion of wholeness. Sylvia Wynter elaborates on this violence further in her description and indictment of the "overrepresentation of Man,"[55] in which the particular "Western bourgeois" conception of the human is posited as synonymous with humanity as a whole. She emphasizes the fact that this understanding of humanity is parochial, its very claim to totality indicative of a fundamental failure to see its own locality.[56] In this, she flips the normative racist script according to which some humans are too enthralled by the particularities of their own identities and socialities to have a conception of or commitment to humankind as a unified whole. But more than this, Wynter argues that what she calls the secular "liberation" that led to the rise of Man made the dehumanizing and domination of other humans into a logical necessity, given secularism's institution of the idea of a homogeneous and universal natural order. "The West would therefore remain unable, from then on, to conceive of an Other to what it calls human.... All other modes of being human would instead have to be seen not as the alternative modes of being human that they are 'out there,' but adaptively, as the lack of the West's ontologically absolute self-description."[57] The concerted, forceful, and never-complete *work* of realizing a hierarchy of humanity is evident in the philosophical machinations and material brutalities—indeed, the various forms of suffering—required to reproduce the universalist human subject.[58]

As such, what are the stakes and effects of humanitarian invocations of suffering? Based on what kinds of discourses, beliefs, and ideologies are certain events designated as involving "(widespread) human suffering" and requiring "aid or support on a large scale," and what kinds of actions does such designation enable? Who is understood as unable to alleviate their own suffering (much less that of others) and thus as requiring aid? Conversely, who is seen as causing such suffering and thus as requiring management and/or punishment—and as being dangers to a humanitarian world order? And what kinds of methods and aims of social justice, or liberation, or freedom, are made invisible or illegible by the understanding of suffering advanced under the mantle of humanitarianism? One of the first issues that arises in considering these questions regards the very recognition of suffering, as such recognition has been central to the institutions of genocidally aimed settler colonialism, imperialism, and chattel slavery. Discussing the writings of John Rankin, a white man who arrived at a critique of slavery by imagining himself and his loved ones in the place of the enslaved, Saidiya Hartman considers how in his expression of empathy, "Rankin must supplant the black captive in order to give expression to black suffering."[59] Not only does empathy serve to produce a white-ascendant form of subjectivity, it also undergirds the authority of the white-ascendant state. Indeed, in her rereading of *Heart of Darkness*, Neda Atanasoski reveals how colonizers' self-critique, in the form of the call to "recognize a common and universal humanity against which the excesses of imperial subjugation must be condemned,"[60] has long been part and parcel of the ongoing project of US empire. And Miriam Ticktin sheds crucial light on this phenomenon in the current moment, in relation to the French government's implementation of special humanitarian measures to admit certain and very few migrants, based on the official recognition of particular forms of suffering—namely, those that would not require a questioning of the operation and legitimacy of the French state.[61] In this sense, the very work of the humanitarian project to alleviate suffering is to construct the figure of the deserving recipient of aid, that is, the "victim."

Offering a critical genealogy of the rise of what she calls a "transnational regime of care," Ticktin expresses a concern with the centrality of this figure of the victim to "the new doctrine of the responsibility to protect [which] merges the benevolent responsibility to intervene in times of suffering with a right to employ force."[62] Insofar as the victim is aligned with the side of the good and the moral via their depoliticization, then conversely, those who are not legible as such "morally and ethically untainted" actors, or who refuse such positioning, can be characterized as immoral and unethical.[63] As targets of Western militarism are charged with committing inhuman forms of violence, then "fighting to bring inhuman geographies into the fold of historical progress, humanitarian wars against terror, or atrocity, are regarded as a sacrifice necessary to humanize the world."[64] It is in these zones designated for the commission of not only legitimate but necessary violence that humanitarian "action based on the moral imperative and grounded in benevolence and compassion"[65] reaches its terroristic apogee. Not only does suffering—both as an analytic category and as a presumed state of being—supplant other ways of resisting and experiences of socially sanctioned violence; moreover, the legible indicators of suffering of those who are in fact the targets of oppression/legitimized violence get grossly distorted to signify entirely the opposite, that is, that they are not the targets of oppression.

This use of suffering is investigated by scholars who look at how, at the sites of the most concentrated military operations, humanitarian principles come into synonymy with ongoing orchestrations of terror. Here, care *is* violence, operating as one type of "state force" on the minds, bodies, and hearts of its targets.[66] Treating Guantánamo as a palimpsest of US imperialisms, Neel Ahuja revisits the early-1990s incarceration of HIV-positive Haitian refugees there, "the world's first HIV concentration camp."[67] This camp, where people were made to live in—as they also rebelled against—horrific conditions, was described by the United States government as humanitarian, as protecting the lives of the imprisoned. For Ahuja, the fact that this characterization was at best cynical "does not mean that the state was incorrect to associate it with the practice of humanitarianism."[68] "Caring" for these people was a way to justify the supposed need for a military response to disease threats, which in turn became its own justification for the ongoing colonial/imperial state project of securitization.[69] Ahuja reveals how the vitality of humanitarianism itself—as a discourse, as something debated and as evolving through this debate—is produced by the deadly conditions of the camp:

> The open-air prison camps repeatedly constructed as emergency detention facilities at Guantánamo accelerated the biological precarity of those quarantined through practices of concentration, deprivation, and exposure, making normative political contestation

over camp life most often centered on whether the camp accomplishes the simple biological provision of life itself. . . . This very situation of deprivation quickly makes the camp into a site of contestation and reform, an emergent space of humanitarian intervention and the introduction of new disciplines of care. As such, the camp has an intimate if conflicted relationship to the expansion of liberal humanism under empire.[70]

This description speaks poignantly and urgently to just this situation in another context—Israel's occupation of Palestine. As Palestine is subject to continuing radical control and destruction, the resultant extreme "biological precarity" of the people living there has become the object of focus of humanitarian arguments and efforts.[71] In a kind of horrific tautology, the Israeli state itself has mobilized that synonymy of "Palestine" with "humanitarian disaster zone" to retroactively justify the continuing occupation. Jasbir Puar reveals how this invocation of humanitarianism has a precise aim: to turn the politics of the occupied—of survival, of living, of anti-occupation, of resistance, of freedom—into an impropriety.[72] Suffering becomes the ultimate trap, a setup, as in this context it will inevitably be taken by the occupying force as a sign that its violence is moral, just, and necessary.

This should lead us to critically consider the stakes of humanitarian invocations of suffering in social justice approaches to ending racist statecraft and imperialist warfare. For example, Judith Butler has developed a widely popular argument that locates the problem of war in the refusal to acknowledge all humans' equal capacity to experience suffering: "Those we kill are not quite human, and not quite alive, which means that we do not feel the same horror and outrage over the loss of their lives as we do over the loss of those lives that bear national or religious similarity to our own."[73] As I will assert in a more detailed argument about Butler's larger body of work and the related work of other thinkers later in the book, to posit that the way to end war is to achieve a shift in consciousness that will allow for a recognition of all humans' humanity—based in the recognition of the shared experience of suffering—is to promote an understanding of humanity as an internally coherent category. The internal difference that in fact defines humanity (as indeed any category is defined) must thus be externalized, projected outside in a kind of faux maneuver whose inevitable failure is proven by the fact that it needs to be reiterated again and again. "Humanity" is not simply an exclusionary category, but is dependent upon both an internal differentiation (of distinct kinds of humans and human qualities) *and* an indistinction from other things in the world, both of which inexorably point to the non-self-sameness of humanity. As Denise Ferreira da Silva argues, the establishment of "distinct kinds of human beings, namely, the self-determined subject and its outer-determined others"[74] could only be achieved "by tying certain bodily and mental configurations to different global regions: the subject of transparency, for whom universal reason is an interior guide, and subjects of affectability, for whom universal reason remains an exterior ruler."[75] But there is a founding paradox here, as the supposedly self-determining "transparent I" must appeal to the exterior in order to establish itself as such: "without the idea of exterior things, the mind's distinguishing attribute, interiority, cannot be articulated."[76] This is what Jacques Derrida's concept of *différance* captures, "the transparent (interior/temporal) I as an effect of differentiation or relationality, of the symbolic regimen where 'being and meaning' emerge always already in exteriority and violence, out of the erasure of other (im)possible beings and meanings."[77]

For Ferreira da Silva, this violence through which the "transparent I" is established has serious implications for how racial oppression, and emancipation from it, are commonly understood. Because fully achieved humanity is configured as the "transparent I" within the kinds of anti-racist arguments that treat race as primarily an essentialist construct, racial oppression is often conceived as the natural outcome of what are coded as pre-given differences. This is evident in the prevailing "view of subjection (domination or oppression) as exclusion from universality resulting from unbecoming sociohistorical (cultural or historical) strategies motivated by physical (sexual or racial) traits."[78] The answer to subjection as exclusion is figured as inclusion, but as Ferreira da Silva shows, the problem of racialized subjection cannot be solved by being recognized as fully human. Precisely because "it is always already the exclusive attribute of a transparent I, the racial subaltern's desire for emancipation, for inclusion in the dominant (white Anglo-Saxon society), is fundamentally a desire for self-obliteration."[79] In other words, the presumed need for inclusion within humanity that is the common humanitarian response to the problem of imperial/racist warfare relies on an implicit and obfuscated obliteration of the other-than-white racialized subject.

This obliteration manifests in humanitarian discourses as a demand imposed upon those polities positioned in the lower reaches of the geopolitical distribution of power and authority. In the realm of international governance, the mandate to adhere to human rights and to prove a commitment to a universal conception of humanity has been a key strategy for severely restricting what are seen as legitimate modes of resistance to oppression.[80]

This demand—to demonstrate a consciousness of and an orientation toward humanity as a whole—becomes a death sentence, due to the institutionalized and predefined failure of certain groups of humans to meet this demand. If, to reiterate a key claim of Wynter's, the Western/Eurocentric conception of humanity produces its putative universalism by eliding its actual parochialism, the latter must be projected onto various others. Across a great variety of humanitarian discursive and textual sites, parochialism is located again and again within certain subsets of humans: people engaged in socialities and/or polities referred to as tribes; Indigenous and/or Fourth World peoples; villagers in various parts of the so-called Third World and/or Global South; those living in poverty; and so-called Muslim extremists, among others. Placeholders for the local, the narrow, and the limited in view, these peoples are figured as what humanity must come to exist beyond. How that beyond is achieved is what concerns me. Often, it is through the instrumentalization and use of such peoples as figures in a scenography of a disaster that is posited as in *humanity's* imminent or possible future. Their actual and/or figurative disappearance, their violently enforced figuring as divested from futurity, is what enables a reflection on the possibilities for the preservation of a whole human community. Here, genocidal actions, ideologies, and fantasies of disappearance serve to actively produce humanity as well as that which humanity cannot abide.

Planned Ruins: Vulnerability and the Aesthetics of Ruination

The investment in defining humanity as an internally coherent, self-same category is manifest in the commonly invoked humanitarian trope of vulnerability. This trope has found purchase in a wide range of epistemic contexts as a primary means to characterize specific populations in relation to their exposure to threat and to the need for care, and as such it cuts across blatantly imperialist/racist and progressive discourses alike, charting the many indistinctions of humanitarian and war ethics.[81] Within scholarship specifically devoted to questions of social justice, vulnerability appears in a variety of roles: as a hermeneutic, a way to explain the phenomenon of individual and societal investments in violence; as the central concept of a theory of social positioning and relationality; and to name a state of being that is ostensibly characteristic of human existence. An attunement to humans' shared experience of vulnerability is meant to provide a new way of being with each other, of accessing and engaging ethical responsibility toward those who may be (perceived as) profoundly different from oneself. On this understanding, the capacity to know and act from the personal experience of vulnerability becomes a goal and a virtue, as it is deemed to offer a way to understand others' similar experiences of vulnerability and thus to not perpetuate harm.

But the act of defining humanity on the basis of a characteristic and fundamental vulnerability has a longer and deeply disturbing history. In regard to the formation of Western biopolitical epistemologies in the nineteenth century, Kyla Schuller's work reveals the conceptual and material history of vulnerability's racialization as a feature of a whitened ontology. Schuller reminds us that "the subject is constructed in Western philosophy *as a highly vulnerable* entity, for it is wholly dependent on sensory impressions from the environment for its own self-development and acquisition of knowledge."[82] It was precisely this understanding of the civilized subject as uniquely vulnerable that was expressed in the concept of impressibility, the capacity to receive and be affected by sense impressions generated by appropriately managed interactions with external objects.[83] Sentimentalism was what allowed for this appropriate engagement with the external world, "by cultivating the ability to respond to sensory stimulations on the basis of emotional reflection, rather than instinctive reflex. Together, impressibility and sentimentalism distinguished civilized bodies as receptive to their milieu and able to discipline their sensory susceptibility and as such in possession of life and vitality that required protection from the threat posed by primitive bodies deemed to be impulsive and insensate, incapable of evolutionary change."[84] As Schuller goes on to argue so persuasively about the capacity of impressibility ascribed to civilized subjects, "affect ... depends on the notion of impaired relationality as its constitutive outside."[85] This understanding of affect has also undergirded the characterization of colonized peoples racialized as other-than-white as actively threatening to a humanity conceived of as vulnerable. I would add that the ostensible qualities of the white civilized subject are also the qualities so often ascribed to the modern humanitarian subject: morally attuned to their own suffering and the suffering of others, able to emotionally process and respond to that suffering in an appropriate way, and possessed of a sensory and intellectual awareness oriented by and aligned with the particular distribution of the sensible that characterizes a whitened and civilized social order.

Perhaps more than any other, the event of the invention of nuclear weapons technology has been used to reproduce the trope of a vulnerable humanity whose continued existence can only be ensured through the development of a universal consciousness of threat, which will then be the basis for the elimination of that threat—a threat that is characterized as certain other human beings. This is strikingly apparent in the instrumentalization of the atomic bombing of Hiroshima and Nagasaki for the purposes of ostensible world peace. Lisa Yoneyama writes about this in relationship to Hiroshima in particular, brilliantly showing how bombing produces a particular kind of knowledge that not only informs humanitarian arguments for peace, but becomes formative of the experiences of those it targets:

> Almost without exception, the survivors' accounts include the distance they were located from the hypocenter, precisely given in meters or kilometers, at the instant of the bomb's explosion. The witnesses' memories are mediated by the visual image of a city map on which the by now familiar concentric circles, radiating outward and measuring distance from the hypocenter, have been superimposed. . . .
>
> At the same time, the image of concentric circles radiating outward over a map of the city replicates the vision of the pilots who dropped the bomb and inspected its aftermath. The power of the bombsight to objectify, determine, and name everything that survived beneath it was such that hardly anyone has been able to narrate postnuclear Hiroshima from outside this perspective. This gaze from above, a transcendental sight, was forever inscribed on the landscape and came to condition any subsequent attempt to represent the incident. It has also subsumed survivors' diverse experiences and subjectivities under the universal and anonymous identity of *hibakusha* [bomb survivor].[86]

This use of the atomic bomb on civilians has played a central role in producing a modern aesthetics of ruination, in which the most radical violence is codified as necessary to preserve humanity. In his indictment of the "necroeconomy" that undergirds international law's humanitarianism,[87] Eyal Weizman details the ideological machinations set in motion by this conceptualization of massively destructive nuclear technology as definitively humanitarian. Tracing the logics of the conceptual apparatus of the "lesser evil" used to justify Global North/Western military actions as supposedly necessary for the prevention of "greater evils," he notes that "in one of its more macabre moments it was suggested that the atomic bombings of Hiroshima might also be tolerated under the defence of the lesser evil. Faced with a humanitarian A-bomb, one might wonder what, in fact, might come under the definition of a greater evil."⁸⁸ The abject absurdity of the lesser/greater evil principle and its expression in the legal precept of proportionality is expressed in a variety of forms: a "death ratio," the number of civilians expected to be killed in a military strike, as determinant of whether the strike is justifiable; a mathematical formula, developed from an equation measuring molecular entropy, used to calculate the likelihood of an organization collapsing if a certain number of its members are assassinated; the measurement of the potential proportion of harm to civilians versus harm to soldiers.⁸⁹

Here we arrive at a characteristic feature of genocidal humanitarianism: The process of making meaning about, of evaluating the severity and degree of purposefulness of destruction, is appropriated from those who face its severest effects in service of humanity as a whole. In other words, destructive capacity itself, and control over what that destruction *means*, has come to be seen as the required foundation for a developed understanding of humanity, of the unique capacities and potentials that define it. This kind of thinking achieved a particularly bizarre refinement in Nazi Germany: Albert Speer, the Nazi Party's chief architect *and* planner of total war (war without destructive limits, which explicitly aims for the devastation of civilian centers), imagined that the very goal of civilized architecture was to leave behind ruins—ones of the sort that would be immediately recognizable to humans of the future as the remains of an advanced civilization. About Speer, Paul Virilio notes the following:

> For Speer, the architect had a cinematic function similar to that of the military commander—namely, the capacity to determine in a building *what is permanent and what is impermanent.* In the last analysis, he argued, to construct a building is to foresee the way in which it will be destroyed, and thus to secure ruins which, thousands of years later, "will inspire as many heroic thoughts as the models of Antiquity do today." In the same year Hitler and Speer, no doubt impatient to imagine the future décor of the tragedy on which they were working, ordered the demolition of the centre of Berlin. Before becoming a battlefield, it was to be a premature field of ruins.⁹⁰

In the chapter of his memoir titled "Architectural Megalomania," Speer explains that it was in observing the rusted remains of a streetcar depot being demolished to make way for the construction of his first major commission under Hitler—a huge stone amphitheater—that it occurred to him that "buildings of modern construction were poorly suited to form that 'bridge of tradition' to future generations which Hitler was calling for."[91] Speer's answer to this problem, his "theory of ruin value," proposed that "by using special materials and by applying certain principles of statics, we should be able to build structures which even in a state of decay, after hundreds or ... thousands of years would more or less resemble Roman models."[92] Speer's theory of ruin value thus articulated not simply a fantasy of permanence but also a management of the very process of decay, of impermanence itself. To wit, he had "a romantic drawing prepared" of the proposed building, depicting it "after generations of neglect, overgrown with ivy, its columns fallen, the walls crumbling here and there, but the outlines still clearly recognizable," which prompted Hitler to order that all important buildings were to be constructed according to this theory.[93]

The theory of ruin value exemplifies how the project of securing humanity against disappearance is conceived as necessitating genocide: In the construction of planned ruins, the ability and willingness to wage total war is made into the sign and definition of humanity's presence. But more than this, total war becomes the very means of ensuring the transmission of humanity's legacy into the future by controlling the meaning to be made about humanity's end. Thus humanity's ruins—exemplified by Speer's "romantic" crumbling amphitheater, an enclosed circle devoid of human life, empty seats bearing witness to nothing human—have a strange and impossible architecture. They index a humanity whose self-coherence could only be achieved through the eradication of all those who might dare to disrupt its desired order and to expose the impossibility of its attainment of self-definition. But such radical homogeneity requires nothing less than ultimate destruction; the hidden message of humanity's former presence that the ruins carry into the future would have no one to receive it. In this sense, a major effect of the imagining of humanity's end in the humanitarian mode, where the goal is to save humanity, is to quite literally destroy the possibility of disagreement, that is, to mandate a fundamentally depoliticizing approach to the response to human suffering that ultimately necessitates utter devastation as the price of epistemological certainty and ontological stability. I would suggest, then, that humanitarian discourses of ruin are not just about a sort of responsible expression of horror at the world-targeting technologies developed during twentieth-century warfare, but also a longer-lived project in which knowledge of and about violence is claimed over and against the "unknowing" state of those who have been made to experience its severest effects. The condition of possibility for the concept of the ruin is a cosmology in which "the end" can and must be defined, by and in the name of a humanity characterized by its capacity to *document and understand* vulnerability, over and against those who are seen as simply *being* ontologically vulnerable. Humanitarianism's grammar of anti-violence critique is structured around the treatment of the targets of violence as symbolic supply for the subject's intellectual engagement with the problem of how to save humanity as a whole.

Indeed, the aesthetics of ruination is founded in massive Western colonial/imperial violence against peoples across the globe as a grim historical continuity that those of us here and now are located firmly within. I am interested in how deeply and variously this aesthetics permeates a variety of media forms and fields, the distribution of the sensible it produces, how it orders our understandings of reality, and how it calls so many of us into its production. It is from postcolonial cultural studies' critical inquiry into the relationship between media, aesthetics, and colonialism as an onto-social-political project to fix the world into a hierarchical arrangement of being that I draw my discussion and analysis of specific material, epistemic, and affective technologies that constitute the aesthetics of ruination. In the scholarly and popular texts and cultural objects that I take up in this book, the following technologies emerge as especially common, cutting across the otherwise disparate interests, points of view, and approaches that make up the diverse landscape of humanitarian discursive production: the privileging of militarized visual knowledge systems that figure seeing *as* the capacity for destruction; the alignment of documentary and ethnographic modes of knowledge production with eradication; the narrativizing of human extinction due to the contemporary threats of environmental devastation and nuclear warfare via racialized imperial tropes and logics; the symbolics of poverty as a central concept and condition of the post–World War II project of development; and the hermeneutic functions of systemized violence that produces visible wounding. While each of these technologies has been critically analyzed in its own right, I am interested in how they work synergistically within humanitarian texts, projects, and discourses to produce a profoundly violent ethics where it is perhaps least expected. Indeed, by looking at a variety of media, I engage humanitarianism not as a specific set of acts by a circumscribed set of social actors, but rather as the very warp and weft of the socio-onto-political order in which many of us are in some way enmeshed.

As scholars such as Lisa Cartwright, Rey Chow, Akira Mizuta Lippitt, Jonathan Mirzoeff, and Fatimah Tobing Rony (to name a few) have shown, vision has held a privileged place within Western imperial epistemes as the sense best capable of demonstrating the supposedly heightened knowledge capacities of "civilized" human societies.[94] Postcolonial and critical military studies scholars have also made much of the historical and epistemic concurrence of the development of advanced photographic and motion picture technologies and airplane technology during the age of high imperialism; both have been imagined to grant those using them the reassurance of their own physical safety, technical and moral precision, intellectual superiority, and godlike powers of perception. Paul Virilio charts this concurrence in the development of high-capacity weaponry (like machine guns) and serial photographic technology, with designs for the latter directly inspired by the former,[95] while Caren Kaplan traces the alignment of aerial visual technologies with militarized modes of perception further back in history, to the development of military cartography, balloon aerostation, and building-sized panoramic paintings in the eighteenth and early nineteenth centuries, revealing how thoroughly it has infiltrated common understandings of human reality in general: "This view 'from the heavens' has powered various representations of not only terrain and individual communities but the Western, modern state as a political institution.... By the twentieth century, the concept of a universal, all-seeing perspective became thoroughly incorporated into colonial, state, and military modes of organization, management, and planning."[96] Within the specific conjunction of human flight and visual sensing technologies, the project of destruction came into alignment with the drive toward totalizing knowledge. Reflecting on the synonymizing of the supposedly unique powers of visual perception with the capacity for massive, horrific destruction on a scale not previously possible, Virilio notes this paradigmatic articulation: "'If I had to sum up current thinking on precision missiles and saturation weaponry in a single sentence,' said W. J. Perry, a former US Under-Secretary of State for Defense, 'I'd put it like this: once you can see the target, you can expect to destroy it.'"[97]

To this discussion, Ronak Kapadia adds the concern that current aerial sensing and warfare technologies efface the variety of other-than-visual sensations, experiences, and modes of living that the "US global security state"[98] both produces and relies upon for the continuation and justification of warfare. He notes that it is the alignment of visual technologies and discourses with an ostensible epistemic mastery that should prompt us to ask, "What do the people on the ground who are targeted by the so-called signature strikes of the drone age see, think, feel, and sense when they encounter this swarm in the dystopian here and now? How have early twenty-first-century technologies of aerial warfare and remote surveillance disordered and rearranged people's collective sense of place, space, and community across the expanding scenes of American warfare in South and West Asia, North and West Africa, and the Greater Middle East?"[99] Here, Kapadia asks after the experience of inhabiting the deadly ground on which humanity's ruins are being constructed and the sensibilities it enforces and those it makes difficult or impossible to access, revealing some of the multiple tactics employed to produce an aesthetics of ruination. For example, the use of the "double-tap" method in drone warfare (in which the same target will be hit multiple times in quick succession) has the effect not only of inducing an experience of constant, intense fear, but of "disaggregating" groups of people from each other as it "disorganizes and destroys communal bonds."[100] I would argue that such violent alterations of the structures and sensibilities of human life become the material and epistemological fodder for humanitarian subjectivity and ethics.

Theorist and filmmaker Fatimah Tobing Rony exposes the history of ethnography as precisely such violent consumption in her short video *On Cannibalism*, a commentary on the experience of her development of the "third eye," the capacity to see how one is being seen within a racist/imperialist sociopolitical order. The video covers the history of ethnographic visual technologies—chrono-photography, films, live ethnographic displays, museum dioramas—using overlaid images that emphasize the material and epistemic violences of ethnography's grammar of cultural knowledge. When at the end of the video Rony intones, "I haven't yet learned how to see. I haven't yet begun to believe," I take her to be pointing out that Western imperial modes of perception are not natural (despite the constant and forceful repetition of their supposed naturalness) but must be learned, an acknowledgment of seeing as destructive in ways less overt but no less dangerous than military targeting, an ironic jab at common understandings of who is presumed capable of seeing, and perhaps also a commentary on the conditions that give rise to the third eye and what they require of those who have the third eye experience.[101] The images of skeletons and dismembered body parts with putatively scientific labels highlights the synonymy of ethnographic documentation with the project of eradication. Trinh T. Minh-ha's classic and still crucial works on ethnography thematize this as well—the ethnographic project's consuming desire for total knowledge drives a project of complete capture and incorporation, aiming for the "skin, flesh, and bone" and indeed the soul of the ethnographic subject, the very "'*marrow* of native life.'"[102] I understand both Rony and Trinh as offering commentary on the impossible onto-philosophy of imperial ethnography, which seeks to establish a form of literal and figurative cannibalism in which the consumer accrues presence and sovereignty over the consumed, in some sense attempting the impossible task of escaping death. In this, we can trace the alliance between documentation and eradication back to well before the advent of planes and photographic/motion picture technology, locating it as a fundamental feature of the Western imperial episteme.

The extractivism that is at the heart of the project of development can also be understood as a kind of cannibalism or eradication, a vampirism, which precisely through extraction defines humanity as the achievement of civilizational advancement beyond poverty—that is, beyond dependence and lack. Indeed, Balakrishnan Rajagopal argues that in the wake of World War II, development became the new "ideology of governance"[103] for Western states and institutions rearticulating their authority in the face of rapid decolonization and Third World liberation movements. According to Rajagopal, "the discovery of poverty emerged as a working principle of the process whereby the domain of interaction between the West and the non-West was defined."[104] Here, Rajagopal names poverty not as a preexisting material reality but rather as a conceptual invention that would become a primary way in which the necessity for humanitarian intervention would be articulated and the extractivism of the post–World War II economic order would be elided.[105] Insofar as "*the objective of poverty reduction provided the moral, the humanitarian dimension*" to the creation of the Bretton Woods institutions (those UN-backed institutions of the current global economic order) "*as 'development' institutions,*"[106] humanitarianism becomes mercenary. Offering a similar line of inquiry into the concept of poverty, Sylvia Wynter indicts the definition of Man as "*Homo oeconomicus*" and its particular other, the poor and more especially the "underdeveloped."[107] For Wynter, *Homo oeconomicus* imposes a specific form of memory, a memory of human history as evolution and progress, where humanity expresses itself in its highest form by mastering "natural scarcity" through "material redemption," or the "unending production of wealth."[108] The underdeveloped are, of course, unable to achieve this mastery.[109] This articulates with the common portrayal of the "underdeveloped" as having an improper relationship to the plethora of objects produced under advanced racial capitalism; often cast as fetishistic enthrallment, I see this characterization of the relationship to objects as a reiteration of the supposed dependency of those peoples subject to development, a kind of sublation of the vast project of *taking* that brings those objects into existence, and indeed the voiding of an array of differential cosmologies and modes of human life.

A similar kind of onto-socio-political absenting is also effected by torture and wounding. While the instrumentalization of images of suffering for the purpose of justifying Western humanitarian military interventions has been very well analyzed across a broad array of scholarship, I am particularly interested in the specific functions of acts of wounding themselves, as well as of the circulation of images and narratives of certain kinds of physical and psychological wounds within humanitarian reckonings with warfare. Wounding and indeed torture serve not just to inflict harm and suffering, but also to create bodies and subjects and solidify social positions, and serve as modes of racialization, gendering, sexualization, and indeed of defining humanity. I recall here how Hortense Spillers positions chattel slavery as the founding event of the modern Western episteme specifically due to its employment of torture: Spillers argues that it was the torture of enslaved people that enabled the territorialization of the white American body and the putative consolidation of the same's subjectivity.[110] And while posed in regard to the particular situation of the postcolony, Achille Mbembe's notion of "death-worlds"[111]—involving the production of grievously wounded bodies "in the form of human shapes that are alive, to be sure, but whose bodily integrity has been replaced by pieces, fragments, folds, even immense wounds that are difficult to close"[112]—is helpful in understanding some of the perhaps less-obvious functions of the circulation of media displaying injured subjects. Mbembe posits that the function of these wounded bodies "is to keep before the eyes of the victim—and of the people around him or her—the morbid spectacle of severing."[113] Following Talal Asad's argument that torture is a main technique of the so-called war on terror for producing "the terrorist" as an ostensibly real and socially legible category of person, I would add that such wounded bodies also serve a pedagogical and a hermeneutic function,[114] impressing upon us that some people are especially ontologically vulnerable and that others of us—we humanitarians—have the duty to witness and make sense of this vulnerability for the sake of humanity.

How does one live with and in the aftermath of violence and continuing violence, committed and/or made sense of for humanitarian purposes, while dismantling the distinction between those who merely experience suffering and those who truly understand it? I read Rony as speaking to this question in her recent development of the concept of the fourth eye. Here, she references the experience and position of the young daughter of Philando Castile's partner, as she watches her mother confront Castile's murderers:

> When the mother sees herself and her boyfriend Philando being seen by the police officer as black, and therefore vulnerable to violence and death, she is seeing her situation with a third eye.
>
> The fourth eye witnesses that constitution of the third eye. The fourth eye not only sees that the emperor has no clothes, she sees that everyone is pretending that the emperor does have clothes. The fourth eye is profoundly collective: an inclusive "we," a communal "I," a black daughter comforting—and observing—her mother and how she constitutes herself in the face of police violence and a nation's visual biopolitics. The fourth eye requires us to be both the patient and the doctor: the patient who has to constantly explain to the doctor what the psychic trauma is and what is required to heal from that.[115]

In theorizing the fourth eye as communal, Rony shows that the humanitarian distribution of the sensible does not have a monopoly on reality, that a form of relationality that does not conform itself to the terms of humanity is already being lived. Here, the sense of "we" and indeed of "I" is formed via the witnessing of the radical lack at the center of what passes for given reality. Rony's invocation of the patient who must teach the doctor also points toward a foundational critique of humanitarianism's regime of care, which cannot offer healing or indeed anything other than a continuation of violence. Over and against this regime of care, I invoke Jinah Kim's exploration of the experience that she calls "postcolonial grief." Using the concept of the postcolonial to name "the complex processes through which decolonization is deferred after formal colonialism ends," she draws attention to "the productive nature of unresolved or unresolvable grief" in the face of this continuing deferral.[116] Kim is interested in the "insurgent" qualities of postcolonial grief, its capacity for remembering that colonialism is not over and for enacting an antiteleology in which "what is to come does not have to be defined solely by what was lost."[117] Working from Frantz Fanon, she argues that "the idea that subjects under colonialism can be healed is itself a colonizing idea.... Healing prepares the colonizer to wield violence for the state, and for the colonized to accept being terrorized as a regular state of being."[118] The commitment to holding on to grief, to resisting the alleged resolution of healing, keeps us attuned to the ways in which anti-colonial critique has at times itself been enacted as a form of overcoming, control, or mastery.[119] Perhaps insisting on holding on to grief is a way of practicing survival and enacting the fourth eye as a communal project in the name of forms of grouphood that are decidedly and importantly not folded under humanity.

Alongside particular material practices of racism and racial capitalism, genocidalism lives within the discursive, the affective, the imaginary. It drives cultural and political meaning-making, even where it does not show up as an actively articulated aim. We could say that it is an object both repressed and desired, feared and fantasized over, characterized as an inevitability only to be cathected onto others who end up figurally and literally bearing its brunt. Perhaps, too, this is precisely because the very notion of a discrete population is the illusory product of the idea that it could be completely and finally eradicated. The means through which a population is defined are constitutionally imperfect; genocide is always bound to fail to live up to its own terms of articulation. But beyond that, genocide is a self-negating project on the grandest of scales: were it to actually achieve the total eradication of human difference to preserve actual/real humanity, humanity in fact would no longer be able to define itself. It would cease to exist, too. It is this founding paradox, and the desperate attempt to cover it over, that I seek to elucidate in this book—by turning toward thinkers who, like Kim, insist on the irresolvability of the problem of humanity's demise.

Chapter Overview

In the first part of the book, chapters 1 and 2, I trace the role of nuclear weapons technology in the reconfiguring of a racialized conception of humanity around and after World War II. Chapter 1 takes on the ethical ramifications of the absurd fact that nuclear weaponry has come to be considered a paradigmatically humanitarian technology. Rendered as both a signal achievement of exceptional human capacities and as a primary means for ensuring world peace, I argue that "the bomb" has been mobilized to produce a post–World War II humanitarian ethics of what historian John Dower has called "idealistic annihilation"—"whereby demonstrating the appalling destructiveness of an atomic bomb on real, human targets" has been rendered as necessary for securing the survival of humanity.[120] Here, I look at how the humanity envisioned by various acts of meaning-making about the bomb (news stories, films, scientific reports, press releases, political science, philosophy) is also taken up and reproduced within a perhaps unlikely location: the discourse on the Anthropocene. I consider the stakes of the appearance of bomb ethics in this other register, namely in the form of the characterization of humanity as fundamentally vulnerable and as achieving a global cohesiveness through its exposure to the possibility of species-ending peril. The concept of the Anthropocene has become incredibly popular and is referenced in a diverse array of contexts, with many authors finding it a useful way to quickly index climate catastrophe produced by human actions. My focus is not on critiquing this particular use of the "Anthropocene," but rather on the concerning patterns that emerge from a critical reading of those texts that invoke the Anthropocene as a specifically philosophical concept. On my reading, as the predominant hegemonic discourse of human survival of our time, the discourse on the Anthropocene epitomizes the epistemological maneuvers through which some people are prescribed the state of ontological vulnerability so that others can make meaning about the vulnerability of humanity as a whole.

Working from the premise established in chapter 1 that Anthropocene discourse trades in imperialist precepts, in chapter 2 I look to how two films provide crucial alternatives to Anthropocene discourse itself. Kidlat Tahimik's *Mababangong Bangungot* and Souleymane Cissé's *Yeelen* are two highly regarded works deeply engaged in a critical postcolonialism that has always understood the perils to humanity of an imperial world order. Precisely because of their different contexts, engaging these works together honors the rich genealogies of transnational critical engagement with humanitarianism. Breaking with the tendency to read such films by using what is taken to be their national and/or cultural contexts (the Philippines and Mali/West Africa) as a primary guide, I highlight what they offer in the way of alternative genealogies of the role of bomb ethics within the post–World War II humanitarian management of so-called postcolonies. Focusing in particular on Tahimik's thematization of what he calls "overdevelopment," Cissé's indictment of nuclear colonialism, and their shared critique of the time frame of progress, I consider what these two films offer in the way of an alternative to the imperial conquest aesthetics of a humanism that is fundamentally premised upon a civilizationist/racist rendering of humanity's past and future, which Anthropocene discourse itself often reproduces.

In the second half of the book, I turn toward an examination of contemporary instantiations of genocidalism and the aesthetics of ruination within several different humanitarian projects and discursive sites. In chapter 3, I look at the circulation of figures of injured women from Muslim-majority nations subject to US military incursion as a key site for the reproduction of humanitarian aims as imperial aims. I focus in particular on cultural texts depicting women who have been subject to face-altering gendered violence as in need of rehabilitation: the Academy Award–winning 2011 documentary *Saving Face*, which features Pakistani women who have been the targets of acid attacks; and popular media portrayals of Aesha Mohammadzai, an Afghan woman who became famous after being featured on a 2010 *Time* magazine cover with her facial injuries on full display. Feminist scholars have tended to focus their critiques of such texts on the treatment of the women they depict as non-agentic objects of empathetic recuperation. I offer a different analysis here, focusing on the specific functions of the long-standing, explicit violence targeted at women in societies subject to Western imperialism. Thus, my inquiry in this chapter is focused not on the failure to fully implement humanitarian ideals in the mediatization of suffering, but on the necessity of violence to the production of the humanitarian subject and to the codification of a humanitarian distribution of the sensible. In other words, the circulation of representations of these women demonstrates the reliance of humanitarianism on suffering in a way that exceeds its usefulness for a project of putative care. In its propagation of the expectation that the targets of such imperial racism move on and relinquish any resentment they may hold against their aggressors in the interest of achieving racial peace, the humanitarian media I look at in this chapter are, I argue, a main mechanism for the simultaneous elision and justification of the intense and ongoing targeting of Muslim women and girls by counterinsurgency and counterterrorism tactics.

Beginning in the 2000s and early 2010s, a reconceptualization of the Amazon rainforest as both the product and remains of extensive precolonial civilizations (rather than a wilderness that never sustained large human societies) has coincided with a taking up of so-called uncontacted tribes as the objects of widespread public fascination. Coffee table books about jungle explorations and scientific articles about the terraforming that created the Amazon forest circulate alongside *National Geographic* articles and NGO press releases about how the remaining descendants of what is often described as a vanished civilization are on the brink of dying out. Indeed, a key characteristic of arguments and efforts to help uncontacted tribes to live is their portrayal as degraded, almost dead, or already vanished. In chapter 4, I consider the implications of uncontacted peoples' figurality in discourses focused on the larger fate of humanity in the midst of climate crisis and global capitalist entrenchment. Across a variety of discursive locations, these peoples continue to serve as ciphers for the depredations wrought by technological and civilizational advancement, rendered largely in relation to absence and as having lost the knowledge of their own past—thus requiring others, namely those with the self-designated capacity to understand the history of humanity writ large, to tell it. This, in turn, contributes to the conceptualization of the Amazon itself as a ruin, its remaining people rendered into objects of philosophical use for understanding how humanity as a whole can escape extinction. The production of media featuring the uncontacted has continued apace, as studies declaring the possibility that the Amazon itself has reached a tipping point of no return due to environmental destruction have recently come to cohere with an increasingly intensive mediatization of the Amazon as a war zone, in which it is proposed that only increased security efforts can stave off the ravages wrought by those humans presumed to have no sense of responsibility to humanity writ large. Even though these uncontacted peoples are not the targets of explicit military actions, the way in which they are figured supports the alignment of humanitarianism with securitization regimes that mobilize gender, sexual, and cultural deviance as indicators of inhumanity.

In chapter 5 I return to the concept of vulnerability, this time in order to consider its use in recent feminist philosophical work on how to achieve an end to warfare. I am curious about and, ultimately, concerned by some of this literature's tendency to emphasize individual openness to a shared human experience of vulnerability as the key to redirecting those psychological impulses that are posited as the basic cause of Western imperial war. I do take seriously what I understand as the call being made by these scholars: to grapple with the interface between institutions and individuals, and to offer deep inquiry into bringing about new modes of relationality. Yet insofar as some writers presume a kind of undifferentiated, universal human experience, they not only miss an opportunity to break with the model of vulnerable humanity born in nuclear humanitarianism (as explored in chapter 1); they also reiterate the very philosophical and discursive technologies of warfare and militarism that they aim to move past. Indeed, a variety of inquiries have been made by anti-racist and anti-colonial feminist scholars into whether humanity can admit everyone—and whether that admittance is desirable or viable. Crucially, in their critical assessments of and efforts to think beyond humanism and human-centrism, these scholars articulate a variety of incommensurable understandings of the human and humanity. As such, I engage this work for its critical insights into the problems of understanding humanity as vulnerable, and propose that it offers a conceptualization of humanity as differential—a humanity that is internally defined by difference and that can thus never be self-same. Reading their engagements as necessarily multiplicitous and as irreducible to each other, I argue that, read alongside each other, they offer possibilities for an anti-war ethics that is not premised on a shared conceptualization of humanity.

Finally, in the coda, I return to the inquiry into bomb ethics undertaken in the first part of the book, this time in light of the argument I make in chapter 5 regarding the possibilities for a feminist anti-war ethics that is not rooted in humanitarianism, but that treats suffering and disposability as experiences and states of being that should not be instrumentalized for the purposes of making meaning or ascribing value in the name of humanity. As it came time to offer concluding thoughts about this project, I found myself thinking once again about Jinah Kim's contention that within a context of oppression, the expectation to heal serves as a means to enforce the acceptance of "being terrorized as a regular state of being."[121] Countering bomb ethics might involve living with and within the break rather than repairing it, as suggested by Ocean Vuong in his invocation of fracture as a technique for refusing to embody suffering for the humanitarian subject to make meaning about. Reading hegemonic discourses of how to solve the inherent problems of nuclear waste storage as symptomatic of the desire for (and as epitomizing the impossibility of) humanity's mastery over its own end—such that these storage facilities are imagined as a type of planned ruins—I consider Vuong's invocation of debris as an aesthetic mode that disrupts genocidal humanitarianism's distribution of the sensible.

1

Bomb Ethics

VULNERABLE HUMANITY IN THE ANTHROPOCENE

> Visualizing hell on earth does not preclude finding it attractive. It may even invite drawing closer.
>
> —John W. Dower, *Cultures of War*

Doom Time

For the past several years, the Science and Security Board of the *Bulletin of the Atomic Scientists* has been moving the hands of its famous Doomsday Clock steadily closer to midnight, signaling an especially vulnerable position for humanity. The *Bulletin* was founded in 1945 by a group of individuals who had worked on the Manhattan Project, as a means to offer public commentary on the nature of the threat this new weapons technology posed, and to that end they introduced the Doomsday Clock in June 1947.[1] A paradigmatic editorial from its early days calls for US scientists to participate in the development of a world government and lead members of the public to "the same conclusion—that political likes or dislikes must be subordinated to the urgent common cause of establishing, within this generation, a community of mankind under enforceable law."[2] On January 26, 2017, in response to Donald Trump's inauguration as president of the United States, the Board set the Clock at two and a half minutes before midnight, closer than it had been in sixty-four years;³ two members of the group, Lawrence M. Krauss and David Titley, expressed an intensifying sense of urgency around the issues of global warming and nuclear weapons proliferation in the midst of the shifting geopolitics that Trump's election both signaled and produced.⁴ Since then, the Board has progressively set the clock closer to midnight.⁵ The editor's note prefacing the January 2020 statement declares that "the Clock has become a universally recognized indicator of the world's vulnerability to catastrophe from nuclear weapons, climate change, and new technologies emerging in other domains."⁶ Written as a letter addressed to "leaders and citizens of the world," the statement explains that "we move the Clock toward midnight because the means by which political leaders had previously managed these potentially civilization-ending dangers are themselves being dismantled or undermined, without a realistic effort to replace them with new or better management regimes. In effect, the international political infrastructure for controlling existential risk is degrading, leaving the world in a situation of high and rising threat."⁷ And explaining its decision in 2023 to move the Clock's hands to 90 seconds to midnight—"the closest to global catastrophe it has ever been"—the Science and Security Board emphasized the invasion of Ukraine and again highlighted the twin threats of climate and nuclear catastrophe while attributing the potential for both to the "eroding norms of international conduct."⁸

I am grappling with what it means that most of us humans alive now have lived our whole time on Earth marked by this world clock, and how one's very sense of the Earth and one's place on it is ordered by this technology for marking humanity's time. In treating the development and use of nuclear weaponry as a singular event—a paradigmatically human technological achievement that has the unique capacity to enact total devastation—the Doomsday Clock itself serves a totalizing function, appealing to and defining a humanity that can be addressed as a single entity. It enacts an iteration of world time that arguably recapitulates the global spatialization of human history that was foundational to Western colonialism and that made the material substance of the Earth an expression of teleology, locating certain places and peoples in humanity's past—what Johannes Fabian has famously called the "denial of coevalness."⁹ Indeed, the Clock is a means to quite explicitly assert a global political order of which humanity is the subject; while it might seem to include every human being in its sweep, its constitution of *humanity* as an object of concern and preservation, when put under a little pressure, divulges a reliance on constitutive exclusions and abjections. In fact and of course, the very existence of the Clock is predicated on the obvious doomsday event of the bombing of Hiroshima and Nagasaki. And the Clock takes figural inspiration from, while simultaneously radically eliding, the many doomsday scenarios coextensive with the event of nuclear technology development. This raises the question of how social technologies for naming and managing the potentiality of humanity's end, like the Doomsday Clock, work and for whom: how they call for a response, how they call to some of us and not others, what visions of human community they effect and rely upon, and who they name as being part of humanity.

This chapter considers one of those social technologies: the nuclear bomb. The development and use of the bomb by the United States against Japanese civilians are frequently referred to as driven by humanitarian motivations (the facetious argument for which is that the bomb ended the war earlier and saved lives), as inaugurating a new consciousness of both humanity's fragility and humanity's potential, and as pinnacles of civilizational achievement definitional of nothing less than the essence of what it means to be human. The concept of "ground zero," first used publicly in relation to the atomic bombing of Hiroshima,[10] exemplifies this understanding of the bomb's relationship to humanity: Ground zero is a site of both radical destruction and origin. The terrorizing nature of this concept is its predication of humanity's futurity on the space-clearing project of genocide. If the latter statement appears immoderate, consider Rey Chow's point that "even today, some of the most educated, scientifically knowledgeable members of U.S. society continue to believe that the atomic bomb was the best way to terminate the hostilities."[11] This belief persists despite the serious questioning of the dominant version of historical events commonly used to explain how the decision to use the bomb was made, well-established evidence that the humanitarian narrative was, to cite Lisa Yoneyama, "fabricated ex post facto,"[12] and the explicit racism that attended US military involvement in the Pacific arena and made the use of the bomb possible.[13] The bomb's exterminating capacity was always already the reason for its development and use.[14] According to the peculiar humanitarianism that underlies the hegemonic story of the bomb, certain deaths were and are necessary to preserve humanity as a whole. This common interpretation of the first and only intentional use of the bomb to kill civilians expresses the principle of "'idealistic annihilation,' whereby demonstrating the appalling destructiveness of an atomic bomb on real, human targets was rationalized as essential to preventing future war, or at the very least future nuclear war."[15] One spectator of the Trinity test—the first atomic bomb explosion in history—observed that the true nature of the bomb's destructive effects could only be fully understood in one way: "'It had to be witnessed to be realized.'"[16] In other words, the mechanism through which idealistic annihilation achieves its purported aims is by transferring the authority for determining what genocidal destruction *means* from those who are on its receiving end to those who enact it. This ideology of the necessity of genocidality's spectacular demonstration was itself arguably founded on what Traci Brynne Voyles conceptualizes as *wastelanding*. In a study of the continuity of settler colonialism and the nuclear weapons industry in the lives of the Diné, Voyles invokes wastelanding as a process whereby Indigenous peoples' lands are figuratively and materially emptied of value and meaning and, simultaneously, made subject to the destruction of extractivism.[17] The wasteland is a "floating signifier" that "flexibly (floatingly) marks different objects, landscapes, and bodies."[18] Their lands, labor, and lives treated as absent and void even as they have been made the foundation of nuclearity's material and discursive presence, "the Diné were rendered spectacularly mundane, or perhaps mundane spectacle; they became the collective object of a larger narrative that was predicated, ultimately, on their death."[19]

What I investigate in this chapter is the mobilization of the bomb to produce an ethics in which idealistic annihilation serves as a centrifocal force, seemingly drawing humanitarian thinking toward it relentlessly, and the extension of that same sort of peculiar humanitarian ethics in other registers. The rendering of humanity as fundamentally vulnerable, as achieving singularity and globality through a universal exposure to the possibility of imminent peril, has become axiomatic within humanitarian discourses broadly speaking. Interestingly, the *Oxford English Dictionary*'s entry for the adjective "vulnerable" illuminates a slippage that seems to be foundational to this appeal to a vulnerable humanity.[20] Definition 2.a., "that may be wounded; susceptible of receiving wounds or physical injury," suggests an ontological condition that could be extended to any living being. Definition 2.b. suggests a more particular exposure that is not just a condition of being but a willful targeting on the part of some actor: "*figurative*. Open to attack or injury of a non-physical nature; *esp.*, offering an opening to the attacks of raillery, criticism, calumny, etc." Under the mantle of bomb ethics, a particular instance of targeting is arrogated as evidence of a global ontological condition: The bomb's victims substantiate the danger that nuclear weapons technology poses to humanity writ large, and so their suffering is appropriated by humanity as its own potential future state, offering the possibility for humanity to not destroy itself through the same means.

This vulnerable humanity has also been mobilized in other intellectual and political arenas as of late, perhaps most importantly in the discourse on the Anthropocene. For some of those engaged in the debate about whether we have entered a new geological epoch distinguished by the advent of humanity as the major force changing the environment and the very geology of the Earth—the Anthropocene—and, if so, where to locate its beginning, the development and use of nuclear weapons is an appealing originary marker. Nuclear weapons explosions have left a measurable signature in the form of fallout across the globe, and the momentousness of the development of nuclear technology serves to index a cascade of other human-generated changes to the environment that will have a long life in the geological record. But more than this, the discourse on the Anthropocene shares with bomb ethics a preoccupation with humanity as a whole, a humanity whose differentiality is serially elided as actually experienced devastation becomes the figurative sustenance for a vulnerable humanity. Akin to the monumentalizing of the bomb as a fundamental turning point in humanity's understanding of itself, the Anthropocene also names a kind of crisis in understanding. Many writers comment on the scale of threat in the Anthropocene and the barriers to human comprehension it presents. And for some, it also has a kind of active disordering effect on the human mind. This betrays a deep anxiety about the potential for a radical rupture in what is posited as an essential feature of humanity: the successful transmission of knowledge and consciousness considered proper to and definitional of humanity across the depths of history. While there is incredible variety within what I am naming the discourse on the Anthropocene, including a significant strain of internal critique, this critique tends to focus its attention on the specific historical events and processes that are posited as characteristic of the Anthropocene, and on arguing for a different set of such events and processes other than the prevailing ones. My own interest has more to do with investigating the work to which the very idea of the Anthropocene is put when it is taken up as an object of philosophical reflection. In the amnesia of the historical geopolitical conditions that have led to the problem of world-ending ecological catastrophe in the first place—that is, Global North and Western militarism that originated in the heart of conquest (colonialism/chattel slavery/imperialism)—that is a feature of many of its constituent texts, the discourse on the Anthropocene becomes a primary site for the seemingly paradoxical alignment of a genocidally infused conceptualization of humanity with the effort to save humanity from impending doom.

While the vulnerability of humanity is often claimed as a new and more useful paradigm for humanitarianism to follow, one that holds promise for humanity's survival and perhaps even for world peace, bomb ethics demonstrates its centrality to genocidal thinking, policies, and projects. In account after account of what the bomb means for humanity, and indeed of what the Anthropocene means for humanity, the fear of humanity's imagined end resolves into a scene of failure and dissolution of knowledge and indeed of meaning itself. As discussed in the introduction to this book, the notion of a global humanity that could achieve a consciousness of itself through the realization and mitigation of threats to its existence precisely as a whole—including through genocidal elimination—is not new. The immediate context of the creation of the Doomsday Clock, and its creators' call for a "community of mankind under enforceable law," was a sense of Western vulnerability in the face of ongoing anti-colonial rejections of such law. Now, in the current moment (of perpetual warfare since the time of that call, of colonialism and imperialism, of changing and intensifying forms of securitization), what are the effects of naming the bomb as a singular event aiding the development of a new consciousness of global humanity? What kind of human life is imagined as under threat and hence as needing to be preserved? Conversely, which human deaths have failed to register as of significance to humanity as a whole—have, in other words, been treated as non-events in the history of humanity—even as they have been constitutive of it? And for whom and in what contexts are genocidal actions and imaginings purposed for a totalizing vision of humanity's continued presence on Earth?

I address these questions first by examining the discursive construction of the use of the bomb as a humanitarian act, specifically in the appropriation of the suffering of its targets by humanity as a whole. The act of nuclear bombing has become an aesthetic event, proliferated as a cultural experience available in a variety of outlets and aimed specifically at spectators hailed as humanity's protectors; visually witnessing this act is meant to instill a consciousness of humanity's precarity and thus a will to not allow humanity to destroy itself. I note the particularity of what witnessing for humanity means in this context, and who is considered capable of witnessing: Those whose labor and lives enabled the production of uranium in multiple colonialist contexts,[21] whose homelands make up the "geography of sacrifice" wrought by imperial militarism across the globe,[22] and who experienced the bomb in the most immediate of ways by being among those targeted for annihilation, have been explicitly rendered as non-witnesses or as limited witnesses. The grandiose inflation of the development and use of nuclear weapons technology to the status of securing humanity's continued presence, as well as the pinnacle of scientific knowledge and indeed the end point of its teleological raison d'être, is fundamentally reliant upon such foreclosure. After considering this cultural life of the bomb, I then turn toward the discourse on the Anthropocene and its production of a vulnerable humanity, reading it as indebted to and replicative of the long intellectual genealogy of Western empire in its articulation of what is ultimately the intensely racialized fear of humanity bringing about its own end. In the humanitarianization of the bomb and in the discourse on the Anthropocene alike, we can see the manifestation of a sclerosis and stasis at the heart of humanity's being. At the end of the chapter, I invoke a recent example of a call for the American public to educate themselves in the continued potential of nuclear annihilation in order to consider how bomb ethics requires subjects of humanity to cultivate particular sensibilities regarding nuclearity, specifically ones characterized by the concordance of perception and reason. These sensibilities demanded by and necessarily experienced as a function of nuclearity themselves presume the necessity of destruction for the production of humanitarian consciousness. While the humanity that is the subject of bomb ethics is meant to encounter nuclearity in the register of the philosophical and the speculative, there has been an active obscuration of the many other forms of encounter by those who mine and process uranium, live downwind of test sites, have themselves been bombed, and/or live in the midst of radioactive contamination.

The Bomb

"In the whole of history, no single force has cast a greater terror over all mankind than the Atom. Since Hiroshima, the image of final catastrophe has seized on the minds and hearts of men. The Atom has so heightened the desperate problems of a world in turmoil that it seems to have fused them all together into one single universal issue: can an atomic holocaust somehow be avoided?"[23] These words, published in 1963 by the first and former chairman of the Atomic Energy Commission, David E. Lilienthal, are indicative of the heightened and even grandiose rhetoric that quickly became a naturalized feature of bomb discourse: The terrible force of the bomb, it is claimed, has exercised an almost religious hold on the consciousness of humanity, inexorably sweeping up other more individualized troubles into one monumental threat. Demonstrating the enduring nature of this discourse, the recent PBS documentary *The Bomb* (2015), released in the seventieth anniversary year of the bombing of Hiroshima and Nagasaki, presents its titular subject as an event defining and defined by humanity.[24] Both the voice-over narration and the various interviewees who appear in the film repeatedly reiterate this framing. In its opening sequences, quick cuts between dramatic explosions, experts' sound bites, and footage from different moments in the historical period covered by the film create a visceral experience of this supposed power of the bomb to reconfigure the very landscape of knowledge and meaning. The Trinity test is described as "where the modern era started." Likened to the discovery of fire, the bomb is said to constitute a "dividing line between everything that came before and everything that follows." One interviewee states that "for the first time in human history, we now were capable of our own destruction, as a species," another that "this was a millennial change in human affairs; everyone was at risk." This avowal of a new form of consciousness enabled by the capacity for self-destruction, and of a risk that everyone was supposedly equally exposed to, is linked in these opening scenes to the ways of seeing enabled by new filmic technologies: *The Bomb* is described as offering footage enhanced through "state of the art restoration," so that "we can see the incredible power of this device in a new way." To demonstrate, wipes reveal how original footage of explosions appears after using these techniques. Indeed, the new images are spectacular, incredibly detailed, vibrant, and alive. The footage is often beautiful in its way, particularly the close-up shots of the Trinity test, where one small part of the massive fireball appears in the frame as swirling bright colors, shifting light and shadow. Viewing these images, one is invited to imagine oneself in the place of those who might in the future experience, in Lilienthal's words, an "atomic holocaust," becoming part of the global humanity that is its supposed target. This invitation has arguably become a hallmark of visual media on nuclearity; in the 2023 film *Oppenheimer*, for example, any visual presentation of the devastation wrought by nuclear weaponry is glaringly absent save for the very end, and it appears only in the future tense at that, with imagery of the Earth being set ablaze in a nuclear conflagration (which, presumably, *Oppenheimer* itself is supposed to warn humanity against). One might question to whom this kind of visual experience is addressed and, indeed, to whom it is available; and in the case of those to whom it is not, what that means for their status within the onto-political formation of humanity.

This understanding of the bomb as a singular event, one that has inexorably led to a new human species consciousness, has long been axiomatic. Historian Paul Boyer reveals that the appropriation of terror away from

1.1   Evidence of humanity's destructive capacity: the ruined city in the aftermath of the atomic bomb. (Rushmoore Denooyer and Krik Wilfinger, dirs., *The Bomb*, 2015. Screen capture.)

those who had directly experienced the violence of the bomb was almost immediate, as the possible future scenario of the United States facing nuclear devastation was played out over and over.[25] US media "quickly transmuted the devastation of Hiroshima into visions of American cities in smoldering ruins, and millions of Americans soon made the imaginative leap.... Sole possessors and users of a devastating new instrument of mass destruction, Americans envisioned themselves not as a potential threat to other peoples, but as potential victims."[26] Indeed, in their 1955 essay "The Peril of Universal Death," Albert Einstein and Bertrand Russell positioned themselves "not as members of this or that nation, continent, or creed, but as human beings, members of the species Man, whose continued existence is in doubt," in order to draw attention to the danger of the recently developed thermonuclear weapons: "It is understood that the new bombs are more powerful than the old, and that, while one A-bomb could obliterate Hiroshima, one H-bomb could obliterate the largest cities, such as London, New York, and Moscow."[27] For many, it was not simply all human beings who were newly in danger, but more urgently, a humanity conceived as such through having achieved so-called advanced civilization. This is apparent both in more subtle references (e.g., Einstein and Russell's "largest cities") and in more explicit considerations of what the bomb meant for civilization. For Joseph Rotblat, who left the Manhattan Project and became a proponent of the elimination of nuclear weapons (and a Nobel Peace Prize recipient), World War II itself was distinctive and unprecedented because it was "a war in which the survival of basic civilized values was at stake."[28] Journalist and one-time editor of the *Washington Post* Felix Morley was concerned about the moral and spiritual losses for members of Western societies attendant upon the use of the bomb, going so far as to say that Hiroshima cost "us" more than it did the Japanese as it led to an unmooring from civilization's values.[29]

Such critiques of the use of the bomb share a logic with arguments for its justification, which were explicit in their call to use a demonstration of the capability of massive, instantaneous atrocity on Japanese civilians in order to ensure world peace. J. Robert Oppenheimer argued for the use of the bomb on Japan as a demonstration to Russia and to safeguard geopolitical stability after the war; Arthur Compton, another physicist who did work for the Manhattan Project, argued that a real demonstration of the terrible effect of an actual bomb strike was necessary to the maintenance of a future peace.[30] Compton, Oppenheimer, and the other members of the Science Panel of the Interim Committee that advised the US president wrote in June 1945 that "we can propose no technical demonstration likely to bring an end to the war; we see no acceptable alternative to direct military use."[31] The understanding of the bomb as coextensive with the very essence of humanity's highest, most civilized expression would almost seem to necessitate such conclusions about the need to use it. In a remarkable account of the Trinity test, journalist William L. Laurence epitomizes this understanding of the use of the bomb:

> The big boom came about one hundred seconds after the great flash—the first cry of a newborn world. It brought the silent, motionless silhouettes [of observers] to life, gave them a voice. A loud cry filled the air. The little groups that had hitherto stood rooted to the earth like desert plants broke into a dance—the rhythm of primitive man dancing at one of his fire festivals at the coming of spring. They clapped their hands as they leaped from the ground—earthbound man symbolizing the birth of a new force that for the first time gives man means to free himself from the gravitational pull of the earth that holds him down.
>
> The dance of the primitive man lasted but a few seconds, during which an evolutionary period of about 10,000 years had been telescoped. Primitive man was metamorphosed into modern man—

shaking hands, slapping his fellow on the back, all laughing like happy children.³²

In critiques and justifications alike, the bomb became humanitarian in its potential as a tool—whether literal or figurative—to prevent possible future suffering of a humanity conceived as newly vulnerable. Indeed, this perception and assertion of humanity's vulnerability on the part of those who had enacted brutal destruction would continue through the so-called Cold War. For example, Michael Nacht's *The Age of Vulnerability: Threats to the Nuclear Stalemate* comments on the tense, precarious relations between the United States and the Soviet Union during the 1980s; he notes "the sense of vulnerability—the capacity to be wounded—that the introduction of nuclear weapons has caused in our time" and goes on to argue that "the 'nuclear stalemate' has served us well despite its inherent dangers and that we should try to preserve it."³³ Here, recognition of vulnerability is explicitly named as necessary to humanity's continued existence. Indeed, deterrence—the paradoxical doctrine according to which the very possession of nuclear weapons is treated as the means to prevent their use—relies on the notion of a universal consciousness of humanity-in-peril that the development of nuclear weaponry ostensibly leads to.

This treatment of the use of the bomb as an unprecedented event, in which vulnerability is transferred onto humanity as a whole, relies on four interconnected, violent discursive operations, which I elaborate on in the rest of this section of the chapter. First is the use of some people's suffering and death for the purpose of producing a consciousness of humanity's vulnerability, and more specifically, a consciousness developed by the cultivation of particular experiences and sensibilities and the barring of others. Second is the use of the event of bombing to attempt to attain a mastery of knowledge, through the production of data about the dangerous effects of the bomb. Third is the imposition of social, psychic, and political demands on those who did experience and survive that event, namely, to participate in the cultural production of the bomb as a peace-instituting technology. And fourth is the rewriting of imperialist geopolitical history effected by the characterization of the bomb as a singular event. As I seek to demonstrate, these ways of reckoning with the bomb ultimately efface the drive for global governance that characterized both pre– and post–World War II statecraft on the part of Western nations, and the continued positioning of colonized and other racialized subjects as figurally and materially necessary to, but not having a part in, the survival of a vulnerable humanity.

The nuclear bombing of Hiroshima and Nagasaki enacted a double disappearance of the people in those two cities who actually experienced the end of their worlds. The "men" implicitly referenced by Lilienthal, whose "minds and hearts" have been grabbed and held by the "image of final catastrophe," are most certainly not those who were incinerated, or whose bodies succumbed to the effects of radiation. Whatever the bomb's immediate victims experienced is gone, along with them. This exposes the tragically literal nature of the documentary *The Bomb*'s characterization of the first Bikini Atoll test (a year after Hiroshima/Nagasaki) as the "first nuclear explosion to be witnessed by the public," for it was surely not the first such explosion to be seen or experienced by civilians as it was happening. Rather, it was the first such explosion to be openly made available for viewing as such by US citizens who, furthermore, had been informed ahead of time about—and thus, ostensibly, "knew"—what they were seeing. Those who did experience and survive the bombing of Hiroshima and Nagasaki were positioned as limited witnesses, as much because their experience of the bomb did not index a knowledge of this new technology as for their questionable ability to serve as archetypes for a universal humanity. Both the disappearance of the bomb's immediate victims and the limited witnessing of its survivors contributed to the appropriation of vulnerability by those who meted out this particular devastation.

Reflecting on the power to inflict suffering on enemies in warfare, Hugh Gusterson remarks that "the very limit of this power is the ability of the powerful to make the human bodies of the Other completely disappear."[34] The disappearance of war casualties from the media,[35] as well as the more literal disappearance aspired to by racist war projects, provides the raw material for the production of information of the sort that can be applied to humanity writ large. Not only did US scientists work "to turn the dead and injured bodies of the Japanese into bodies of data,"[36] they extended this necropolitical meaning-making in experiments involving the deliberate exposure of test subjects to radioactive material, thus using "mutilated human and animal bodies, reincarnated as bodies of data, to help display the military power of those who control nuclear weapons and to certify the realism of the elaborate scenarios about hypothetical nuclear attacks."[37] The Japanese were not the only ones subjected to disappearance via knowledge produced about but not for them. Reflecting on the US Division of Public Health Services's early-1950s studies of uranium mine and mill workers, which documented the known effects of radiation exposure even as this knowledge was not shared with the workers themselves, Voyles suggests that these studies are best understood as one manifestation of a larger "culture of experimentation" that characterized the colonial/imperial restructuring of entire geographies—including "Los Alamos, the Marshall Islands, the Japanese cities of Hiroshima and Nagasaki, labs across the country, and certainly the Colorado Plateau uranium districts"—and the transformed embodiments of humans and other living beings within them.[38]

Akira Mizuta Lippit similarly reflects on this synergy of knowledge and devastation, as expressed in the bomb's physical effects on humans. The bomb did not simply ravage human lives; rather it—like the X-ray photography technology that was its antecedent—"recorded the destruction of its object," creating an "archive of annihilation."[39] The bombs dropped on Hiroshima and Nagasaki acted as cameras, their terrific heat and light creating images on bodies and streets and buildings. Some of these images were of people killed almost immediately[40]—as Richard B. Frank has put it, "at or near the speed of light, passing from being to nothingness faster than any human physiology can register."[41] So the work of the bomb takes on absurdist connotations, as it is conceived and used in the project of recording absence—a project founded in an impossible ambition of totality, of "absolute visibility and total transparency."[42] Recognition of that impossibility is sublimated via the trope of nuclear war itself. Lippit, reading Derrida, suggests that "the fable of nuclear war (the story of a possible history yet to come) serves as the limit against which the archive survives."[43] In other words, the discursive figure of a war that could destroy humanity, leaving absolutely no trace, in fact defines the substance of what it is that might be lost—that is, humanity itself. The *trope* of nuclear annihilation is the other of the archive of knowledge proper to humanity, the outside that makes that archive possible. Reproduced over and over, this trope indexes something that has not yet happened, but the prospect of which helps to define what and who constitutes humanity. In that sense, the people who have actually experienced nuclear annihilation serve as the material ground for a tropology of humanity's precariousness, as they could never be within the humanity that is defined by not yet having faced nuclear war.

Those who were not immediately disappeared by the bombing of Nagasaki and Hiroshima, the survivors, have been expected to serve as a different kind of material ground through their participation in a particular kind of witnessing. Due to censorship by both the US and the Japanese governments, survivors' experiences have been sublimated to the "moral imperative" of acting as witnesses to an event that was "conceptualized not as a cataclysmic horror but as a rebirth that allowed its victims to find meaning in the quest for a future world without wars."[44] Ran Zwigenberg writes eloquently about the imposition of this role of moral witness, where survivors of the bomb could either take on the distinctly public activity of witnessing—strictly adhering to the discursive codes dictated by the new cultural trope of the "survivor-witness," transforming their experience into an attestation of the relevance of the bomb for a global humanity—or in effect be silenced.[45] Kenzaburo Oé, Nobel Prize–winning author, writes about the implications for those who have been made to serve in that capacity:

> For my part, I have a kind of nightmare about trusting in human strength, or in humanism.... My nightmare stems from a suspicion that a certain "trust in human strength," or "humanism," flashed across the minds of the American intellectuals who decided upon the project that concluded with the dropping of the atomic bomb on Hiroshima. That "humanism" ran as follows: If this absolutely lethal bomb is dropped on Hiroshima, a scientifically predictable hell will result. But the hell will not be so thoroughly disastrous as to wipe out, once and for all, all that is good in human society.... There are, after all, people in Hiroshima who will make the hell as humane as they possibly can.[46]

Oé draws attention most incisively to the *work* that the targets of this horror were expected to do for this "paradoxical humanism,"[47] which was to provide evidence for the goodness and worthiness of humanity, the necessity of saving humanity. "The people of Hiroshima *went to work* at once to restore human society in the aftermath of this great atomic 'flood.' They were concerned to salvage their own lives, but in the process they also salvaged the souls of the people who had brought the atomic bomb."[48] In this case, recovering one's own life was/is inevitably doing this larger work for humanity; the question of choice in the matter becomes burdened.

Indeed, Lisa Yoneyama argues that as "Hiroshima" in particular has come to signify both the need for and possibility of so-called world peace, "the subject of remembering the bombing of Hiroshima, the instance that simulates a panhuman eschatology, is therefore humanity, the omnipresent and universal subject that transcends all particular locations and differences"; she writes movingly about what it means for survivors to be simultaneously hailed as witnesses and deleted as individuals in the interest of creating this universal subject of humanity.[49] The identity of hibakusha, survivor of the bomb,[50] has been simultaneously imposed, taken on, inhabited with complexity and skepticism, and/or refused by the individuals it claims to name. Even as some have felt called to share their experiences, the position of hibakusha can be reductionist, for "in antinuclear campaigns, survivors' testimonial accounts have tended to be conflated with the specific political end of preventing future nuclear devastation. Through their involvement in oppositional politics, the survivors' subjectivities—their ideas concerning the reasons for existence and suffering, the objectives of life and death, the meanings of survival, and the purpose of their narrative practices—also came to be contained by their identity as *hibakusha*."[51] In those instances in which the experience of the bomb is shared in the interest of preventing its future use, the narrative conventions of such remembering reveal the impossibility of what bomb ethics wants, that is, to redeem the bombing by forcing it to mean the same thing to everyone everywhere: "the moment the storyteller desires his or her testimony to be heard as a prophecy, or as a possible future event, the past event is relentlessly made allegorical, undermining faithfulness to the original occasion and the impulse toward mimetic representation. The remembered event is dislodged from the past and transfigured into a future happening in a fictive timespace. Hence, the survivors' testimonial practices traverse and confound the conventional course of time in standard historiography, which extends linearly from the past into the present and future."[52] The resistance of survivors' testimonies, stories, and memories to epistemological and affective confinements is also important because of its troubling of the mobilization of Japanese civilian suffering to cover over Japan's own history of colonizing violence. Yoneyama points out that the portrayal of the bombings as an event for humanity "enabled Japanese memories of atomic victimization to fuse with those of the victims of their own aggressions and racism."[53] This flattening of the complexities of geopolitics via racialization was and is necessary to the rendering of the event of the bombing as completely detached from colonialism. It has also effected a curious kind of containment—one that arguably underlies the specific strategy of containment as it names Western and especially US efforts to control the production of nuclear weapons—in which "Hiroshima," and in particular its Atomic Bomb Dome, a peace memorial that preserves and encloses bomb ruins, "obscures other contemporary realities: namely, that the nuclear horror may in fact be present everywhere outside this museumized site, that the world may be thoroughly contaminated by nuclear weapons."[54]

The ideological strategy of containment also shows up in the common understanding of the bombing of Hiroshima and Nagasaki as unprecedented military events. Zwigenberg understands the rise of the survivor-witness for humanity as a response to a loss of faith in modernity and progress: "Witnessing entered into the gaping hole that Auschwitz and Hiroshima blew in our paradigms of knowledge and our self-confidence as a civilization."[55] In this, he echoes many other commentators on the bomb, for whom its first and only use as an act of war against civilians was somehow unprecedented and thus unfathomable, fundamentally resistant to understanding. But as Lee Kennett notes, the bomb's use was in fact utterly predictable and vulgarly instrumentalist, if situated within the longer history of the use of conventional bombs against civilians.[56] For many, the event of Hiroshima/Nagasaki was very much to be expected—the people upon whom total war had already been waged, both within the confines of what is frequently thought of as World War II proper and in the context of the other issue subtending that war, namely, the reconfiguration of geopolitics in the midst of decolonizing/anti-colonial movements. In total war, the killing of civilians is conceived not as collateral damage, but as an explicit goal. During World War II, this was codified as a central feature of warfare, in the guise of "strategic bombing"; as H. Bruce Franklin puts it, civilian populations came under the gaze of military strategy "as 'industrial targets' (cities), 'transportation centers' (cities), 'communication complexes' (cities), and 'nerve centers' or 'vital centers' (cities)."[57] In the European context, total war came into practice gradually, authorized by the theory that the new technology of aerial bombing could enact such complete devastation that it would destroy the morale of an enemy people.[58] Of course, the explicit targeting of civilians had long been practiced against colonized peoples in the form of conventional bombing campaigns meant to preemptively break the wills of their targets, or to simply clear an easy path for domination by way of abject extermination.[59] If colonized civilian populations were not euphemized as "communication complexes" or "vital centers," it was because "the rules of so-called civilized warfare tentatively adopted by the industrial nations of course did not apply to the 'pacification' of colonial peoples, who posed no apparent threat to turn conflict with their colonizers into mutual suicide."[60] In the realm of military strategy and ethics, then, the use of the atomic bomb was an act of continuity rather than a historical break. Aerial bombing of places and peoples subject to Western imperial rule was an explicit, widespread, and (needless to say) devastating strategy that arguably informed debates about the ethics of using such a strategy on denizens of the metropoles themselves.[61] And the atomic bombing of Hiroshima and Nagasaki was specifically planned as one part of the larger and, by that point, mostly completed project of destroying Japan: These two cities were declared off-limits by US military command "'so that they wouldn't already be over-bombed'" and the destructive effects of the new atomic technology could be more accurately studied.[62]

It is the historical fact of this routine that fundamentally calls into question the claim that the use of the atomic bomb was unfortunate but necessary, or that it somehow led to a new understanding of the sanctity of human life. Contra the standard narrative, it appears that World War II did not effect a grand rupture in the empathic capacity of those in power for those subject to their imperial pursuits. Rather, I argue, it brought to fruition, and justified the continuation of, genocidal killing in the name of humanity. The continuity between what came before and what came after the bomb is elided by the fact that large-scale events of human death—planned or not—prior to and after the event of Hiroshima/Nagasaki have not been conceived as indicative of a threat to humanity writ large. For example, even the United States' strategic conventional bombing campaign targeting most of Japan's population centers during World War II, the horrific deaths of hundreds of thousands of people in firestorms explicitly engineered to destroy entire cities and most of the people in them at once, is not discussed as an event of world consciousness-changing proportions. As such, the common understanding of the bomb cordons off these othered losses, effectively positioning them in a time before the grand rupture in human history that it supposedly inaugurated. As it turns out, the idea of a nuclear weapon powerful enough to destroy cities, that could put an end to future war by demonstrating the terrifying effects of radiation on human bodies and the civilizational supremacy of the West, was conceived long before 1945 and well outside the confines of scientific inquiry proper.[63] These scenarios were on offer in popular novels, as in *The Vanishing Fleets* (1908), in which Britain and the United States ensure Japan's surrender and, later, a global prohibition on war with the development of radioactive airplanes known as "peacemakers"; or in *The Man Who Rocked the Earth* (1915), in which an atomic superweapon is developed by a man named Pax, who demonstrates its power by using it to destroy the Atlas Mountains (and many African peoples), thus instilling a new desire for peace among the warring states of Europe; or in *The Orphan of Space, A Tale of Downfall* (1926), in which "western civilization is saved by an atomic spaceship" that annihilates Russia and China.[64] H. G. Wells's 1914 novel *The World Set Free*, about an atomic bomb, reportedly helped to inspire physicist

Leo Szilard's development of the idea of the nuclear chain reaction and the nuclear reactor.[65] Thus was the dream of many of the key players in the war, "the dream of a superweapon that brings peace,"[66] foretold by long-standing imperial fantasies.[67] Thus, rather than the inevitable end product of techno-scientific evolution, the bomb was predicted and even called for by a broad cultural imaginary and established military practices fixated on the annihilation of non-European peoples. In this sense, it was simply an even more brutal expression of imperial/racialized warfare, one of the functions of which has been to define civilization through specific practices that mark and thereby produce the enemy body as uncivilized.[68]

While not exactly the inculcation of a US-ruled global government, the establishment of the United Nations in 1945 laid the groundwork for continued projects of destruction in the name of humanity. If, following Rajagopal, in the aftermath of World War II a new "apparatus of management" for a rapidly decolonizing world arose in the form of the UN-directed project of development,[69] then the outright slaughter of colonized and formerly colonized peoples who dared to seek their equal place in the new world order became the shadow side of humanitarian law. As "atoms for peace" was promulgated as a method for spreading the civilizational wonders of nuclear energy across the globe (while maintaining nuclear weapons technology in the hands of a few), millions of people were bombed into oblivion by conventional weapons.[70] What Hugh Gusterson refers to as "nuclear orientalism"—"an entrenched discourse on nuclear proliferation that has played an important role in structuring the Third World, and our relation to it, in the Western imagination"[71]—thus represents the instrumentalization of anti-proliferation for the purposes of simultaneously eliding and justifying imperialist asymmetric warfare through nonnuclear means. Designating the Non-Proliferation Treaty of 1970 as a key event in the division of the world "into nations that can be trusted with nuclear weapons and those that cannot," Gusterson argues that "the treaty has become the legal anchor for a global nuclear regime that is increasingly legitimated in Western public discourse in racialized terms."[72] This racialization is expressed through a litany of strained characterizations of Third World psychology: Supposed Third World desires for nuclear weapons technology are ascribed to "desperation," "incivility," irresponsibility, or "a narcissistic desire for self-aggrandizement."[73] Such characterizations support the idea that deterrence will break down if nuclear weapons are acquired by these nations, because their leaders and peoples are ultimately incapable of preserving the interests of humanity as a whole.[74]

Conversely, this suggests that the doctrine of deterrence, and the principle of mutual assured destruction upon which it rests—the main justification for a state of affairs in which only a few major world powers possess nuclear weapons arsenals—also is thought of as representing the achievement of an enlightened, civilized mindset. The principle of mutual assured destruction arose after the invention of thermonuclear weaponry, a putative advancement from the original atomic bomb in the sense that it made survival of a nuclear attack no longer plausible.[75] It assumes that full knowledge of the unsurvivability of nuclear warfare, for those with advanced reasoning capabilities, will lead to its prevention. Hence deterrence, according to which the development of a deadly arsenal supposedly provides the assurance of mutual destruction and, thus, peace. This characterization of the humane West as the proper location of responsibility for humanity's well-being is one explicit way in which the source of the potential for the destruction of human civilization is shifted onto the so-called Third World, Islam, the Middle East, and other figures of barbarous inhumanity. Gusterson suggests that this has an explicitly instrumentalist purpose: to make invisible "the continuity between Third World countries' nuclear deprivation and other systematic patterns of deprivation in the underdeveloped world *in order to inhibit a massive north-south confrontation.*"[76]

Bomb ethics is thus dependent upon a horrifically ironic reversal, in which humanity is equated with Western civilization is equated with target for obliteration. What might at first look like a strange shuttling on the part of the archetypally Western subject of humanity between the subject of power, mastery, and reason on the one hand, and the subject of vulnerability on the other, is in fact an act of grand and terrible appropriation, in which the status of survivor is taken on by those who claim to be able to speak for humanity as a whole. To put it bluntly, the ascription of the identity of survivor to humanity writ large was made possible through killing, much of which was genocidal in aim (if not in effect). Those who were killed, whether quickly or slowly, have been made into test subjects for the Anthropocene, examples of what could happen to humanity but not fully allowed as having a part in that humanity themselves. So, while I find it difficult to argue with the claim of many anti-proliferation arguments, that "for the sake of humanity . . . we must get rid of all nuclear weapons,"[77] I also note that it would be a very different thing to say that we need to do so from a primary commitment to those who have already suffered and died because of nuclear technologies.

The Anthropocene

While the broad-based anxiety over a possible nuclear holocaust has in many ways faded since the end of the Cold War, the notion of an essentially vulnerable humanity expressed in bomb discourse continues. The ascription of vulnerability, and hence of survivor status, to humanity as a whole is indeed central to the concept of the Anthropocene and the wealth of reflection it has generated. Widely taken up to address the human-induced catastrophe of global warming and climate change, the concept of the Anthropocene was initially proposed as a potential new addition to the geological timescale, marking a new epoch succeeding the Holocene (which began 11,700 years ago).[78] While in March 2024 the International Commission on Stratigraphy—the organization that sets and names the demarcations of the Earth's history on the International Geologic Time Scale—ratified a vote to not officially recognize the Anthropocene as our current epoch, debates about its scope and application persist even as it has already been put to use to index the scale of human impact on the very geology of the Earth.[79]

I am troubled by the ways in which the use of the Anthropocene as a scientific concept, facilitating practices of measurement and knowledge transmission, comes into contact with more philosophical reflections on the nature of humanity. In many contexts, and despite other divergences in its use, the "Anthropocene" is invoked to name a rupture in human knowledge and capability, a "completely novel situation"[80] of rapid global environmental and climate change described as unprecedented within the lifetime of the human species, with long-lasting effects the exact nature of which is essentially unpredictable. Critiques of the concept often focus on its universalism and/or the inadequacy of the word itself to accurately relay the origins and complexities of human-influenced Earth processes. It has been widely noted that the Anthropocene is often invoked in a way that implies that all humans are equally culpable for environmental disaster and asserts a Euro-American/Western-centric epistemological and ethical perspective, failing to consider the deep and profound inequalities through which disaster is produced and comes to have outsize effects on some much more than others.[81] As Zoe Todd puts it, "not all humans are equally implicated in the forces that created the disasters driving contemporary human-environmental crises, and I argue that not all humans are equally invited into the conceptual spaces where these disasters are theorized or responses to disaster formulated."[82] Salar Mameni highlights what is at stake here in terms of what and whose kind of knowledge is indexed and elided by the "Anthropocene" as a conceptual apparatus, noting that "the scientific designation of the Anthropocene at the turn of the century presented ... geopolitical events in geological terms as migrant and Indigenous laborers and activists across the globe protested land appropriation, extractive economies, and the toxic landscapes enabled and supported by corporate war machines."[83] Precisely for this reason, some scholars invoke the Anthropocene by way of resignifying it from the standpoint of non-Euro-American/Western-centric epistemologies, ethics, and cosmologies; Kyle Whyte, Zoe Todd, and others engage it from within the framework of Indigenous-centered environmental studies and justice work, proposing critiques of the tendency to characterize climate change rather than colonialism as the agent of destruction and harm, as well as of the common characterization of the transition from the Holocene to the Anthropocene as a movement from stability to unprecedented change.[84] Others have proposed names other than the "Anthropocene" in order to more accurately name the origins of and solutions to the urgent issue of environmental devastation—for example, the Capitalocene, or Mameni's Terracene, which blends an emphasis on the racial military/imperial terror that is both the reason for and effect of ecologies of extractivist devastation with a shift in perspective to those who are the main targets of this terror.[85]

Thinking alongside these critiques, but taking an approach that has a somewhat different focus, I am concerned with the political and ethical claims about humanity being reproduced within the discourse on the Anthropocene, not just as an exclusionary category but as one fundamentally conceived in racial and genocidal terms.[86] Mameni's crucial observation that "the Anthropocene must be interrogated from the vantage point of the war on terror because of the historical coincidence of the two terminologies in the early 2000s as frameworks for understanding a new world order"[87] moves in the direction I seek to go in here, given that much of the discourse on the Anthropocene elides the fundamental relationship between environmental destruction and the infrastructure and ideology of warfare. The issue here is not only the posture of innocence that Kathryn Yusoff diagnoses in the Anthropocenic "claim that humanity has failed to understand the violent repercussions of colonialism, industrialization, or capitalist modes of production."[88] Rather, as Axelle Karera puts it, "Anthropocene thinking has generally been unable to yield a sustained critique of the racist origins of global warming capable, in turn, of exposing the limits of its desire to rethink—to 'revamp' perhaps—the concept of the 'human.'"[89] Few authors who engage in an otherwise critical consideration of the work of the concept of the Anthropocene do so in a way that addresses this problem of the very desire to retain, even if by rethinking, "humanity" itself.[90] Yet, insofar as much of the discourse on the Anthropocene describes a humanity confronted for the first time with its own radical vulnerability, I argue that it is implicated in genocidal humanitarianism's distribution of the sensible.

The exact nature of this vulnerability is most frequently articulated as involving the breakdown of the transmission of the culture and knowledge that are understood as constituting humanity's defining character. "Civilization," if not figured as the only form of life that is under threat, is nevertheless often taken up as the implicit object of primary concern. As Jeremy Davies puts it, "the birth of the Anthropocene is the death of the Holocene epoch, the epoch of 'civilization.' . . . Human civilization has existed only in the Holocene so far, and no one knows what will happen to it once that setting is replaced by another."[91] I am interested in the work done both by the articulation of this threat and by attempts to imagine how it could be mitigated. These include calls for a kind of interdisciplinary unification of knowledge toward the common goal of species survival, an essential and sweeping change in humanity's perception of its relationship to the Earth, and an attempt at reassurance that some trace of humanity's time on Earth will be recorded in the geological record for imagined beings in the distant future to discern.[92] The widespread appearance of variations on the word "derange" within writing on the nature of human vulnerability in the Anthropocene is notable. More than just a disruption or interference in the status quo, "derangement" carries the colloquial sense of psychological breakdown. Indeed, proposals for how to measure and mark the Anthropocene often come into alignment with ethical claims regarding what form human sociality needs to take now, and knowing about the Anthropocene is thought to ensure against the ultimate threat that it poses, the breakdown of humanity's very understanding of itself as such. In these ways, the discourse on the Anthropocene frequently deploys the concept of crisis as a means of making claims about history, where history is conceived as coextensive with humanity. As Janet Roitman argues, crisis as "an omnipresent sign in almost all forms of narrative today . . . is a non-locus from which to claim access to both history and knowledge of history. In other words, crisis is mobilized in narrative constructions to mark out or to designate 'moments of truth': it is taken to be a means to access historical truth, and even a means to think 'history' itself."[93] For writers on the Anthropocene, the designation of the current moment as one of derangement thus articulates both a fear of humanity's dissolution—whether by species extinction or by the survival of humans who have no sense of humanity as a whole—and a reassertion of humanity's presence.

One strand of Anthropocenic inquiry focuses on an exceedingly detailed, careful consideration of what specific kind of stratigraphic marker both meets the scientific criteria for a geological event horizon and could be visible to a hypothetical geologist in the future. As Simon L. Lewis and Mark A. Maslin put it, "the case for a new epoch appears reasonable.... The impacts of human activity will probably be observable in the geological stratigraphic record for millions of years into the future, which suggests that a new epoch has begun."[94] The preferred markers for divisions on the geological timescale are those that offer "unambiguous geologic signals of human activity that are synchronous around the globe."[95] The notion of time as linear is called up to render history as an empirical reality materialized in the very rocks of the Earth, the one record of humanity about which it can be said with certainty that it will be available in the far future. Indeed, the geological timescale itself has been characterized as "'one of the great achievements of humanity.'"[96] Thus, quite apart from an intellectually neutral way of discerning information that is supposedly already there, the concept of the Anthropocene emerges in the wake of a profoundly interested version of history; it supports, in the words of Christophe Bonneuil and Jean-Baptiste Fressoz, "an authorized narrative of the Earth ... a narrative that makes the management of the Earth system a new object of knowledge and government."[97]

I am taken by Bonneuil and Fressoz's point that this making of the Earth into an object under the sign of the Anthropocene owes much to warfare and the knowledge systems generated for and by military applications "such as cybernetics, followed by general systems theory, which claims to be applicable to all domains: every object of study from organisms to machines, cities to ecosystems, is broken down into discrete elements whose interactions and overall behaviour can then be analysed. Cybernetics, game theory and operational research became *the* privileged means of analysing situations, managing complex systems and rationalizing action, whether it was the Korean War, city planning, the management of health care or the whole Earth."[98] This acknowledgment of militarized ways of knowing, rare in the general literature on the Anthropocene, offers a crucial means to critically question the selection of two of the dates that have been proposed for the Anthropocene's beginning, for in each instance the event in question conjoins Western imperialist-induced mass death with measurement accuracy. These two proposed dates are 1610 and 1952,[99] respectively coinciding with the initial holocaust visited upon the civilizations of what are now known as the Americas upon contact with Europeans, and fallout from the detonation of nuclear weapons. The original proposers of the 1610 date, Lewis and Maslin, chose it because of a corresponding global dip in the atmospheric carbon dioxide level, caused by the reforesting of previously cultivated land in the Americas in the wake of the deaths of some 50 million people.[100] They favor it not only because it indexes other key environmental and geological transitions, but also because it corresponds with what they call "the beginning of the modern 'world-system.'"[101] Alternatively, Colin Waters and coauthors recommend 1952, the beginning of intensive nuclear weapons testing and the global spread of nuclear fallout. In their words, the "signature of weapons testing coincides with a range of human-driven changes that have produced stratigraphic signals that indicate a dramatic shift in the Earth system around the mid-20th century, which in total may be considered the distinctive feature of the Anthropocene."[102] In regard to 1610, Yusoff argues that the very choice of the date reinstantiates the Western white supremacist ordering of global geography: "This 'Orbis spike' of systematic murder marks the instigation of Global-World-Space (an understanding of the world as a global entity that is open to the conquest of the entirety of its spatialized and subjective relations)."[103] This conquest geography, I would argue, founds the set of spatial and geopolitical relations that describe the aesthetics of ruination, in which humanity as a whole claims for itself those events of destruction whose full implications were suffered by specific groups of people.

The Anthropocene's humanity is often thought of not just as vulnerable itself, but as responsible for a "vulnerable earth"—a responsibility that requires "a 'radical' change in perspective and action."[104] According to such assessments, differences among humans—and, more specifically, what are couched as unnecessary and inappropriate attachments to these differences—are largely a barrier to bringing about this radical change. Roy Scranton's writing exemplifies this vision of human difference codified under the sign of the Anthropocene. A veteran of the war on terror who has channeled that experience into writings on how militarized Western culture constructs and reflects on death, Scranton opens his book *Learning to Die in the Anthropocene: Reflections on the End of a Civilization* with the following line: "Driving into Iraq in 2003 felt like driving into the future"; he continues, asserting that "with 'shock and awe,' the US military had unleashed the end of the world on a city of six million—a city about the same size as Houston or Washington, D.C."[105] In language that could be borrowed directly from common portrayals of the aftermath of the bombing of Hiroshima and Nagasaki, Iraq's (supposed) present becomes humanity's future. The problem here is not a derision of or failure to fully recognize Iraqis' suffering, for Scranton expresses much empathy along these lines. Rather, the problem is a discursive and affective milieu in which it makes sense to set the scene for a book-length meditation on the possible end of Western civilization with a kind of apocalypse already experienced by those against whom that civilization has long defined itself. The quality and character of that civilization becomes evident in another telling passage: "Carbon-fueled capitalism has given rise to a truly marvelous liberal multiculturalism, but if we are to survive its death throes, tolerance must mature into conservation and synthesis, grounded in a faith in human community *existing beyond any parochial identity, local time, or single place*."[106] Not only does this effectively erase different socialities and modes of living, it also suggests that they are dangerous to humanity and must be dealt with accordingly—for Scranton, likely by being subsumed under the more general category of humanity.

Something else happens—or rather, does not happen—in Scranton's call to form a new human community that is characteristic of most such calls: There is rarely, if ever, a turn toward the various forms of human life that have been and are being lived against, alongside, and in spite of the particular one that is now ostensibly in the midst of dying. For Scranton, "learning to die as an individual means letting go of our predispositions and fear. Learning to die as a civilization means letting go of this particular way of life and its ideas of identity, freedom, success, and progress"; both kinds of learning require "the humanist thinker."[107] And while letting go is provided as the answer to the question of how humanity can survive, that letting go of (a) civilization is the object of melancholy. Where a gesture is made toward ways of knowing that are not part of the broadly Western canon, it is to incorporate particular cultural objects (for example, the *Bhagavad-Gita*) into the narrow category of humanist thinking. In this context, "learning to die" takes on terrible connotations. For some have been consigned to deaths from which there was nothing at all to be learned, other than the reiteration of the fact that power sometimes takes the form of an infinitely deep hole. Some deaths register as little more than an event facilitating someone else's pedagogy. Some have been put to death in a way explicitly designed to produce a total and abject fear that cannot be overcome. And many deaths have served the purpose of shoring up freedom, success, and progress.

I do not want to single out Scranton, however. For many such writers, who are keenly aware of the profoundly inequitable ravages of capitalism and colonialism on different human communities, turn toward the transcendence of difference in seeking new ways to imagine humanity. In two articles on global climate change and the challenges it poses to the very idea of humanity, Dipesh Chakrabarty takes on what he sees as the key problem of the sheer inadequacy of existing concepts and methods for the task at hand. For Chakrabarty, "the ideas about the human that usually sustain the discipline of history but also the analytic strategies that postcolonial and postimperial historians have deployed in the last two decades in response to the postwar scenario of decolonization and globalization"[108] cannot sufficiently address the fact that humanity (as he understands it) exists and acts on a scale it never has before. He reads climate change as presenting an unprecedented encounter with "our own limits," precisely because as a geological force "there is no 'humanity' that can act as a self-aware agent."[109] In other words, humanity acts upon the Earth as a species, but no individual human can have the experience of being a species as such; humanity's species effects on the global environment are thus necessarily disjoined from, and cannot be accounted for by, the old theories of human agency predicated on the individual.[110] Chakrabarty sees this new state of humanity as a kind of universalism that yet cannot be experienced as such.[111] While he notes the importance of questioning (and even refusing) a notion of universalism as arising out of a kind of essence or teleology, he also argues that "climate change poses for us a question of a human collectivity, an us, pointing to a figure of the universal that escapes our capacity to experience the world. It is more like a universal that arises from a shared sense of a catastrophe."[112] This is where he ends the first article. In the next one, published several years later, he articulates more directly what kind of problem-solving approach such a "shared sense of catastrophe" might lead to. Here, he calls both for a more complex understanding of what the human is, and a kind of movement past intra-human (what Chakrabarty calls "anthropological") difference. The latter, it would seem, no longer matters anyhow if human agency has transcended the sphere of being-based agency to become something larger than the sum of its parts: "The fact that the crisis of climate change will be routed through all our 'anthropological differences' can only mean that, however anthropogenic the current global warming may be in its origins, there is no corresponding 'humanity' that in its oneness can act as a political agent. . . . Precisely because there is no single rational solution, there is the need to struggle to make our way in hitherto uncharted ways—

and hence through arguments and disagreements—toward something like what Latour calls 'the progressive composition of a common world.'"[113] But this understanding of human difference is difficult to distinguish from the one that locates trouble-causing difference only within certain populations. Chakrabarty's argument circles back to the commonly invoked one about the Anthropocene, that it, by virtue of presenting unprecedented material constraints to human life, also demands an unprecedented shift in thinking and meaning-making on the part of humanity as a whole: "Today, it is precisely the 'survival of the species' on a 'world-wide scale' that is largely in question. All progressive political thought, including postcolonial criticism, will have to register this profound change in the human condition."[114] It is thus not clear to me that a shared sense of catastrophe is indeed a fundamentally different or new kind of universal, for it seems to both index a singular human condition and mandate a particular mode of approaching the challenges of the Anthropocene.

Thus, even in arguments that forward a critique of the transcendental, unifying aspirations of certain invocations of the Anthropocene, another kind of archetypal human subject reemerges, in the form of an argument regarding the limits of the human mind to either perceive or fully comprehend something as large and complex as global environmental catastrophe. For example, Timothy Clark critiques those who would use the Anthropocene to mark "the emergence of the human species per se as a different form of 'transpersonal agency,'" an agency founded in "a new, potentially redemptive, form of human identity, based on self-recognition as a species."[115] Like Chakrabarty, Clark is skeptical of existing modes of understanding humanity, particularly those that presume that the main problem at stake in addressing the Anthropocene is making sure that enough people know enough about the challenges of ecological devastation. For Clark, limited understanding is not the main problem—it is, rather, that no full understanding of the Anthropocene is possible.[116] For "the Anthropocene also manifests itself in new kinds of psychic affects and a destabilization of norms as to the serious and the trivial. Global environmental issues such as climate change entail the implication of the broadest effects in the smallest day-to-day phenomena, juxtaposing the trivial and the catastrophic in ways that can be deranging or paralyzing—for what can *I* do?"[117] To this array of psychic manifestations Clark gives the name of "Anthropocene disorder," "a feeling of a break-down in the sense of proportion and of propriety when making judgements."[118] The sheer scale on which the Anthropocene exists as an event makes it not only resistant to understanding, but also actively deranging; that is, it exposes the vulnerability of the human mind. I would note here that, if we follow those authors who insist that the Anthropocene's environmental catastrophes are the direct product of very conscious decisions to enact and maintain the racist instrumentalization of human beings, the notion of Anthropocene disorder reads as an alibi; in this sense, the appropriation of the suffering of some by humanity writ large in order to constitute it as a whole operates as a grand abdication of responsibility.

Amitav Ghosh also sees the Anthropocene as presenting unprecedented challenges to human conceptual capacity. His approach is to focus on how it pressures the limits of current dominant cultural forms (namely literature, and especially the novel) as it works through "forces of unthinkable magnitude that create unbearably intimate connections over vast gaps in time and space."[119] He imagines humans in the future looking back to our present and naming it "the Great Derangement," a time when we found ourselves incapable of acknowledging or confronting reality.[120] Yet the geography of Ghosh's vulnerable Earth is shaped first and foremost by empire, and as he points out, "the discourse around the Anthropocene, and climate matters generally, remains largely Eurocentric."[121] This is, in part, what I take Ghosh to be referring to when he invokes "derangement": the willful failure to acknowledge that the basic promise of modernity—that the good life means having what the materially wealthy have, and that everyone can one day have this life—is a lie. The power and privilege differentials upon which the imperial world order is founded are precisely what cannot be confronted or changed using the cultural and intellectual models of the Anthropocene.[122] This, it seems to me, is the most provocative and indeed useful rendering of what is deranged and deranging about the so-called Anthropocene: not that it is too big for the human mind to handle, but that the geopolitical violences and modes of governance that created it also make humanity itself a perhaps irredeemable category. In this sense, Ghosh exposes the tendency of Anthropocene discourse to posit the Anthropocene as offering the possibility of redemption—or as Karera puts it, "the opportunity to finally dispose of the solipsistic Cartesian individual for a future eco-oriented humanity acutely aware of its 'geo' co-constitution with other forms of earthly entities."[123] The implication of Karera's critique is that conceiving of the Anthropocene as redemptive not only abjures the necessity of a "systematic analysis of environmental violence unleashed along racial lines," but also indicates and enacts a need and even a desire for racist violence: "one finds that the apocalyptic catastrophe anticipated by the Anthropocene is, strangely, both considered comforting and ethically welcomed."[124] Given that the defining characteristics of the Anthropocene era are a direct product of such violence, the welcoming of it as a chance to reconfigure human consciousness is at best a willful failure to contend with the historical and ongoing fact of genocidalism, and at worst treats it as the necessary condition for an ethical turn.

This discursive move toward redemption is the same move made by bomb ethics. Indeed, what many texts on the Anthropocene conjure is a humanity facing its own limits, the possibility of its end, the terror and derangement of a death without meaning or solace or remainder, *for the first time*. When Roy Scranton writes that "learning to die means to let go,"[125] I cannot help but think about the fact that letting go is a controlled, willful, planned action. It is not about a grief that takes you without warning, or waking up day after day to confront a loss so total that your body and face no longer feel or look to you like your own, or not waking up at all. These other, more terrifying manifestations of death peek from behind the heavy curtain of knowledge and meaning produced by many accounts of the Anthropocene. Speaking about the need to preserve something of human culture through the cataclysm to come, Scranton notes "the futility of life without memory. . . . Papyrus rots, paper burns, museums get sacked, hard drives crash."[126] It is this vulnerability of memory to obliteration that threatens the possibility of "the human soul coming to know itself in its mortality."[127] But the obliteration of memory seems inevitable, even (and perhaps especially) on a strict stratigraphic reckoning. As Davies points out, "looking back over a distance of a hundred million years, geologists are hard pressed to distinguish dates more precisely than to the nearest hundred thousand years or so"; thus in the far future, "the manufacture of Aurignacian flint tools and the building of the Burj Khalifa in Dubai would look more or less simultaneous. . . . The beginning—the 'base'—of the new interval might just be a single human event layer."[128] In the record that geology will make, human history, it seems, will be flattened into one moment, making current markers of putative civilizational advancement profoundly moot. That possibility has long been circulated through the representational schemas of empire. Indeed, certain populations are imagined as already living a life without memory, and hence as ultimately incapable of being part of humanity writ large. But if anything here is precarious, it is that very definition of humanity, for if humanity is defined by the continued possibility of long memory, then it is indeed surely (and always was) doomed.

For some authors of the Anthropocene, this inevitability is not an object of distress so much as an indication that the idea of a singular, enduring, self-same humanity was never to be invested in. For Timothy Morton, the distinctive feature of the Anthropocene is its introduction of "gigantic nonhuman beings—radioactive materials, global warming, the very script of the layers in Earth's crust," which he calls hyperobjects, "objects that are massively distributed in time and space relative to humans."[129] Such hyperobjects give the lie to any affectation of humanity's presence: "Nuclear materials like other hyperobjects are so massively distributed in time and space that they end the idea that time is a neutral container that is outside the physical universe. This idea is discovered always already to have depended upon a stable (human) vantage point.... Likewise geologic time, emerging for humans since the advent of modernity, is an abyss whose reality becomes increasingly uncanny, not less, the more scientific instruments are able to probe it. Knowledge ceases to be demystification, if it ever was."[130] In naming what are elsewhere taken to be pinnacle achievements that define humanity as in fact bringing that humanity into question, humanity is once again defined as vulnerable through an intellectual maneuver that looks a lot like the simultaneous neglect and appropriation of differential violences. Another way to say this is that I am not convinced that it is either useful or relevant to think of nuclear materials as "hyperobjects" when you have had a bomb dropped on you, or when the lands that are your home harbor the radioactive remainders of legal uranium mining or illegally dumped nuclear waste, or when you are contending with the quite immediate and material effects of having lived downwind from a test site. The human beings who have been and still are forced to contend with the very intimate and very local terrors of nuclearity thus get written out of the humanity that is ostensibly experiencing the "end [of] the idea that time is a neutral container." And as humanity is identified once again with a very particular cosmology, other cosmologies in which, say, demystification of the universe is not the point (or possible) and being human has never been conceived as offering a stable vantage point, are positioned in a time before humanity's realization of both its scientific capacities and the ultimate limits of those capacities. Thus, while Morton is not anxious about the fact that hyperobjects resist human attempts at knowledge production, the conception of nuclear materials as hyperobjects also belies their development and their use, by humans, for very specific purposes.

Nuclear material may elude human attempts at control, but humans certainly made it, and indeed these two facts seem to be why, in debates over where to set the Anthropocene's starting point, the year 1610 sometimes loses out. As Yusoff points out, for the Anthropocene Working Group, "the biostratigraphic signal from colonizing the Americas remains incompletely documented."[131] Yusoff adds further context: "According to the AWG, the geochemical residue from the Trinity atomic device at Alamogordo, New Mexico, detonated on July 16, 1945, is the start of the Global Standard Stratigraphic Age.... Plutonium (^{239,240}Pu) is suggested as a good trace due to its ability to absorb into clays and organic compounds within marine sediments and because of its mostly artificial radionuclide suite, with a half-life of 24,110 years, that will be detectable in sedimentary deposits for some 100,000 years into the future."[132] Indeed, before the International Commission on Stratigraphy's vote to not recognize the Anthropocene as our new and current epoch, the Anthropocene Working Group sought to codify the choice to set the beginning of the Anthropocene in the mid-twentieth century by proposing Crawford Lake in Ontario, Canada, as its golden spike location (a stratigraphic reference point that marks the beginning of a geological time period); the mud at the bottom of this deep lake includes markers of humanity in the form of "sharp changes in plutonium and radiocarbon from nuclear detonations, and in fly ash from accelerated burning of fossil fuels."[133] What are the implications of this effort to establish the most accurate, global, and long-lived signal alighting upon a technology whose main definitional feature is its capacity to exterminate life in general, even while a known event of genocidal proportions is characterized as incompletely documented? The features of nuclear materiality that make it resistant to human mastery are also what seem to make it so attractive to scientists of the Anthropocene. Nuclear matter's own agentic properties—which are by definition fundamentally destructive ones—are also taken to be a sign of its humanness. Given that within the confines of a racist Western episteme being human has been defined on the basis of an agency/non-agency binary,[134] we could also say that the conception of nuclear materiality as in the realm of hyperobjects has actually been central to the project of racialized scientific mastery under the mantle of the Anthropocene.

A Community of Deterrence

The Lawrence Livermore National Laboratory (LLNL), engaged in a long project of restoring, digitizing, and declassifying films of atmospheric nuclear bomb tests conducted by the US military between 1945 and 1962, made many available for public viewing via its YouTube account in 2017 and 2018. An article announcing this event includes commentary from the head of the project, Dr. Gregory D. Spriggs, explaining the reason for creating a publicly accessible archive: "'We hope that we would never have to use a nuclear weapon ever again,' he said. 'I think that if we capture the history of this and show what the force of these weapons are and how much devastation they can wreak, then maybe people will be reluctant to use them.'"[135] Also cited is the need to study the shock waves produced by nuclear bombs using recently developed technologies, so as to increase the accuracy of data produced by computer modeling on the likely effects of potential nuclear attacks (since atmospheric testing has all but ceased). On the LLNL's YouTube site, each of these declassified films is accompanied by a contextualizing caption that echoes Anthropocene fears of a severed connection to humanity's epistemological legacy, explaining that as these films "sat idle, scattered across the country in high-security vaults," "the film material itself was slowly decomposing, bringing the data they contained to the brink of being lost forever."[136] These films are short and soundless, many consist of a single take on a stationary camera, and in many of them the framing of the shot makes it difficult to discern the scale and impact of, or even what, one is viewing. Rather than impressing upon me either the devastation possible with the use of nuclear weapons or some clearer knowledge of how they work, these films by and large presented an aesthetic experience of distanced and detached viewing. I know from the title screen at the beginning of each film that these tests were conducted at the Nevada Test Site, but from the act of viewing I get little sense of the material realities of these events. Two of the Operation Dominic films I watched show a round glowing ball appear in the middle of the sky and then hang there for some seconds or minutes;[137] in another, a white light taking up the whole frame collapses into a small ball that then turns into what looks like a jellyfish.[138] The one film that induced dread in me focuses on what happens at ground level of a detonation that slowly raises an incredible mass of earth, rocks, and trees into the sky and then continues to expand, the cloud of violated matter and life spreading out toward the camera and eventually taking up the whole frame, moving slowly and getting close enough to afford me the time to sit with the terrible devastation no doubt experienced by countless beings in this event.[139]

This call for the US public to renew their investment in the project of deterrence puts me in mind of the words of one observer of the Trinity test, mentioned earlier in this chapter: "'It had to be witnessed to be realized.'"[140] I saw this call to witness articulated yet again most recently when, like many other denizens of the United States, I saw *Oppenheimer* in the summer of 2023, which I experienced as depressingly reiterative of

1.2   Nuclear destruction as aesthetic experience: A declassified film presents a bomb explosion as a sparkly, softly glowing ball hanging above the clouds. ("Operation Dominic–Housatonic 120256," Lawrence Livermore National Laboratory, YouTube, March 20, 2018. Screen capture.)

the baldly terroristic idea that murder is necessary for the establishment of world peace for a vulnerable humanity. This lesson is offered in a pivotal scene in the film: Oppenheimer appears and asserts himself in the middle of a meeting being held by other scientists at Los Alamos, who are discussing the fact that it would be unethical to actually use their new creation on human beings, given that the Allies were on the verge of winning the war. Oppenheimer interrupts, disagreeing, stating that they as a group know what such weapons could do given their understanding of "theory," but that others do not have that understanding and thus will need to witness its actual use. His colleagues look, listen, nod, as if inexorably drawn to his logic, now seemingly the only logic possible. And on this logic, genocidal destruction—thematized by the film's omission of the historical fact of the calculated drive to destroy Japan—is the unfortunate but necessary moral fodder for the development of humanity's understanding of its own vulnerability to destruction. Notably, we are treated to footage of the Trinity test, but no depiction of the horrors enacted by the actual bombing of Hiroshima and Nagasaki. I take it that the call to witness by viewing sanitized, contained, and visually pleasing footage of bomb explosions rather than the well-documented effects of nuclear technologies on actual people is instrumental to the conflation of achieved comprehension (realization) with the visual experience of the original event of the nuclear bomb detonation (witnessing). For this conflation only works if one ignores the realities—material, physical, epistemic, and otherwise—of the bomb, which cannot be defined either as a singular event, or as having effects only in its detonation, or as *mattering* only or even mostly in the realm of the visual. Nuclear weapons production in and of itself relies on death and destruction, the toxification of the land and air and water and various life forms, as does nuclear weapons testing, the legacy of which in the geographical space of the United States itself has been (to put it charitably) publicly elided. Indeed, the manufactured silence regarding the effects of nuclear weapons production and fallout produced by atmospheric testing on people in the United States is a constitutive feature of the doctrine of deterrence. For how else could the call be made for the US public to watch videos of bomb tests in order to understand the dangers of nuclear warfare *to themselves*? Given the history of the use of US citizens and denizens as test subjects, in multiple senses,[141] to describe as facetious the need to study the effects of nuclear weapons using visual technologies and computer modeling would be generous.

The particular sensibility that is meant to define one's viewing and understanding of these films—a reasoned, rational fear produced by the experience of seeing the document of an actual event, followed by the desire to act in the interest not just of oneself but of humanity—is premised on a presumed unity of perceptible sensation and sound judgment (a kind of conjoining of the different meanings of "sensible").[142] But the particular materialities of nuclear weapons (mining, processing, emissions, waste, fallout, heat, light, radiation) do not necessarily work that way. Jake Kosek writes about this in regard to Los Alamos and the people who live near it:

> Radiation is a strange beast. It is undetectable by our senses. Discerning its nature requires special equipment and training and privileged access. Its shape and form—its very existence—require an act of faith that is corroborated by its violent effects on heredity and flesh....
>
> Living next to a deeply secretive, historically deceptive nuclear research complex that produces a highly volatile, mobile, odorless, tasteless, invisible substance that is unimaginably enduring and deadly in its toxicity blurs the traditional boundaries between material and imaginary. The very essence of an object changes meanings: a dust cloud from the east, smoke from Los Alamos, firewood,

drinking water, an elk steak, all become haunted by possibilities of what is not perceptively present but always a threat. What makes sense in a context where senses are useless?[143]

If the senses are useless for determining the presence and movements of radiation, then the focus on something, anything, that they are useful for—seeing a blast, feeling shock waves—becomes a means to publicly and officially elide the incapacities of the sensible, to conceal and control what is known about the ongoing depredations wrought by nuclear technologies, those that are not sensible. For it is profoundly unclear of what use would be a highly detailed knowledge of the exact intricacies by which modern thermonuclear weaponry achieves ultimate physical destruction. Ironically, then, deterrence relies on a series of invisibilities, silencings, and not-knowings.

The notion of a humanity that is characterized primarily by its vulnerability also relies on and demands such a nuclear sensibility, where the perception of the precarity of humanity as a whole supposedly leads to an ability to judiciously determine one's part in and responsibility to that humanity. Nuclear sensibility thus operates as a demand, to engage certain texts and beliefs and discourses, to negotiate certain kinds of feelings and determine what actions they lead to in specific ways. I hope for my own readings of and movements between different textual and discursive spaces and genres to enact a defiance of the modes of sensibility that define generic forms, yielding a more expansive set of possibilities for the different "genres" of the human that do and could exist (to reference Sylvia Wynter). Some of these possibilities might take form within those places and lives that cannot be conceived as anything other than useful objects within the discursive space delineated by bomb ethics. To refer back to the John Dower quotation that begins this chapter, the envisioning of hell on earth only works by making some actually live in its presence: These people have had no need to imagine its future emergence or to draw it closer, for that hell is here and now, coextensive with even if not defining of their own lives. One of the subjects of the next chapter, Kidlat Tahimik's film *Mababangong Bangungot* evokes this in its very title (which is most frequently translated as *The Perfumed Nightmare*). The nightmare in question is progress, and the film tracks the main character Kidlat's process of coming to an awareness of the genocidal logics undergirding projects of ostensibly peaceful advancement, against the backdrop of the US space program and its simultaneous support and effacement of violent US imperial projects during the so-called Cold War. Yet Kidlat's realization of the landscape of modernity as no longer beautiful but rather hellish is also what leads him to the inhabitation and embodiment of a different kind of possibility for human life. The purpose of the other film I look at in the next chapter, *Yeelen*, is not to visualize hell per se, but it does evoke the post-apocalyptic hellscapes of Hollywood visual fantasy—rock, desert, sun, silence—reinvesting spaces commonly rendered as empty and dead with a different symbolism entirely, one of danger and vitality, possibility and plenitude, secret knowledges and extra-human forces. The viewer has most likely already in some sense seen the places to which *Yeelen*'s main character, Nianankoro, travels, for *Yeelen* was shot in some of the same locations as have been used to render alien landscapes in science fiction films, most famously *Star Wars* (in which, of course, a distant humanity is rendered in the universalist tones of whiteness and British and American accents). Indeed, *Yeelen* stages a seemingly familiar narrative in a seemingly familiar setting, yet precisely in doing so makes different claims on humanity than those for which they have so often been used. These two films offer vitally important reflections on, critiques of, and varied approaches to witnessing, to the possibilities and profound limits of understanding the bomb by watching it, ones that I might dare say create possibilities for an antinuclear ethic that is also non-humanitarian, possibilities for present and future human community not premised on the bad-faith nihilism of deterrence.

2

Postcolonial Histories of the Bomb

DIFFERENTIAL TEMPORALITIES OF DESTRUCTION IN KIDLAT TAHIMIK'S *MABABANGONG BANGUNGOT* AND SOULEYMANE CISSÉ'S *YEELEN*

> Man himself is inside knowledge. He comes to this world within knowledge and he can only master a part of it. The film is concerned with this small part that man is able to control. I ask the spectator to be careful with the small knowledge that he had; to think about the consequence of knowledge before engaging in creative activity. . . . Knowledge . . . contains man; knowledge is a totality which includes man.
>
> –Souleymane Cissé, "Souleymane Cissé's Light on Africa"

Overdevelopment in the Time of Nuclear Colonialism

Toward the end of "Postcolonial Studies and the Challenge of Climate Change," a key entry in the discourse on the Anthropocene, Dipesh Chakrabarty declares "that in an age when the forces of globalization intersect with those of global warming, the idea of the human needs to be stretched beyond where postcolonial thought advanced it."[1] Under the heading of the "postcolonial," Chakrabarty places what are on his view two inadequate understandings of the human: the human as a collectivity of like individuals who should all have the same access to rights and resources, and the critique of this latter understanding of the human as positing a self-same subject.[2] The implication is that neither of these understandings is up to the task of addressing the ostensibly new challenges presented by the Anthropocene. For Chakrabarty, climate change "calls us to visions of the human that neither rights talk nor the critique of the subject ever contemplated," and while "the science and politics of climate change have not rendered these moves irrelevant or unnecessary . . . they have become insufficient as analytical strategies."[3] But what if we were instead to understand "postcolonial thought" in a more capacious way, hence opening to question the very diagnosis of what the challenges of this time are, and indeed of what is meant by "this time"? While Chakrabarty's interest is, to be sure, to offer a means of reckoning with humanity's responsibility for global warming and climate disaster that is appropriately complex, he also posits the challenge of climate change as a type of historically specific crisis of human knowledge in the sense that Janet Roitman identifies, that is, where crisis is itself assumed to be "an object of empirical knowledge. The grounds for such knowledge are left unexamined: crisis is a condition of human history and human affairs."[4] While Chakrabarty articulates a concern about the limits of humanism, a humanist view of history and knowledge arguably shows up in the conceptual framework he forwards, especially in the appeal to the notion of a reality (crisis as a "condition of human history and human affairs") that has yet to be met with the correct kind of analysis. The "unexamined ground" of this argument is a reduction and parochializing of postcolonial thought, its location in the past, and its diagnosis as incapable of contending with the reality taken to define the current state of crisis. Indeed, Chakrabarty's declaration has the perhaps unintended effect of making postcolonial thought seem to be one self-coherent thing, and charging it with exactly the kind of limited view that self-designated representatives of humanity have used to claim the right of representation over and against a variety of tribes, villages, "underdeveloped" nations, stateless peoples, and other such conclaves—that is, those who have been instrumentalized precisely for the purpose of constituting a humanity in whose future they themselves have no part other than a figural one. As the discourse on the Anthropocene imagines the human-imperiling problems of the here and now as requiring an ostensibly new set of rationalities and sensibilities, it also renders the long-standing and complex genealogies of anti-colonial and anti-racist thought as one point on its geologic/human timescale, a point in the past and somewhere outside of humanity's fold.

In response, I offer a different kind of thought challenge—a challenge to revisit older work, work that does not claim to be addressing the Anthropocene per se but that has long understood the perils of an imperial world order underwritten by the onto-political formation of humanity and seemingly hell-bent on destruction via a global war industry as the expression of mankind's fulfilled destiny. This is what I hope to do in this chapter, by thinking with two films that engage in and with what I would describe as postcolonial thought: Kidlat Tahimik's *Mababangong Bangungot* (1977) and Souleymane Cissé's *Yeelen* (1987), two highly regarded works by filmmakers who are well known on the international film festival circuit and to scholars of postcolonial cinemas. *Mababangong Bangungot*, most often translated as *The Perfumed Nightmare*,[5] is Tahimik's first film, and perhaps still his most widely known. Centered on the character Kidlat (played by Tahimik himself), the film follows him from his home village of Balian in the Philippines, where he works as a jeepney driver, to Paris with a character known as the American. The American, who has built a gumball machine empire, brings Kidlat with him as his driver and gumball machine refiller, with the promise that he will eventually take Kidlat to America and hence to the place of his dreams, Cape Canaveral (as Kidlat idolizes the US space program). Significantly, he never makes it there, as in Paris the originally naïve Kidlat experiences an awakening to the predations on which the very idea of progress relies. The film ends with him flying back to Balian in a vehicle improvised from a trash incinerator, powered by his own breath. *Mababangong Bangungot*'s much-remarked-upon "low-tech" qualities—shot on 16 mm film, it does not employ sync sound, and it features footage from happened-upon events rather than fully blocked-out scenes—have, for some critics, seemingly obscured its formal and intellectual complexities, prompting readings that equate the exigencies of material under-resourcing with the limitation rather than the expansion of artistic possibility (and in this way, against Tahimik's own understanding of the filmmaking process). Conversely, *Yeelen* (Brightness or Light) is widely regarded as a work of aesthetic and technical mastery—it won a prize at Cannes in 1987[6]—and yet the critical emphasis on these qualities has also covered over the kinds of ethical and political engagements that it offers. By most accounts a film set well in the past in and around what is now the nation of Mali,[7] *Yeelen* follows the protagonist Nianankoro Diarra in his efforts to initially evade and then confront his father, Soma, a powerful member of the Komo society of blacksmiths and spiritual workers, who seeks to destroy his son in a misbegotten effort to maintain his own power. After receiving a prophecy from his uncle Djigui, Nianankoro challenges Soma, and both are killed in a cataclysm that remakes the world, with the film's final scene portraying Nianankoro's son and the son's mother, Attu, as the survivors connecting this new world to the old one. Theories about the exact historical moment it depicts vary: Suggestions include the thirteenth century, sometime earlier than that (before Islam had become the dominant religion in the area), or the eighteenth/nineteenth centuries given parallels to the Diarra dynasty of that time.[8] Yet, that the film's penultimate scene involves a catastrophic explosion that emits a blinding light and transforms the landscape into a desert—very much like a nuclear bomb detonation—suggests that the film is not meant to simply represent a particular time in the past.

On my reading, these films offer many possibilities for a refusal of the discourse on the Anthropocene and the particular reality it presumes and posits, a reality structured by the aesthetics of ruination. In understanding Tahimik and Cissé as entering into conversations and theorizing about the sociopolitical and ethical stakes of humanity's racialized and civilizationist formation, I assert a principled break with the tendency to situate the meaning these films have to offer within what is taken to be their national and/or cultural contexts. This is not to say that those contexts are unimportant, but rather that I take up these films in order to offer a different way to engage with cultural and intellectual forms that (and, indeed, thinkers who) are predominantly not thought of as theorizing for, about, and/or against humanity. Ethnographic and culturalist readings dominate the critical response to *Mababangong Bangungot* and *Yeelen* despite the fact that both filmmakers have explicitly articulated other possibilities for understanding these works. By his own account, one of Cissé's intentions in making *Yeelen* was to directly counter a Eurocentric ethnographic gaze;[9] Tahimik sees his work in *Mababangong Bangungot* and other films as in part an engagement with the conceptual and ontological status of the "Third World";[10] and as I will explore in more detail later in this chapter, both have described their films as enacting a transformation of consciousness rather than as being primarily representations of cultural realities. Many critical engagements with these two films do not engage with such possibilities in a sustained way, in what I take to be a sign of the deep entrenchment and persistence of the ethnographic as a hermeneutic. As one especially egregious example, Werner Herzog—who has arguably built his filmmaking career as a project of theorizing what it means to be human—has described Tahimik's work as "primitive."[11] Other prevailing readings of this film are similarly routed through the ethnographic even as they reject Herzog's brand of racist logic: Scholars tend to frame their analyses of *Mababangong Bangungot* by characterizing it as semi-autobiographical (the perhaps dominant reading), as ironic documentary (as I first encountered the film, in a documentary history course), or as critically ethnographic.[12] Similarly, many engagements with *Yeelen* share the assumption that it more or less reliably conveys a set of cultural truths, or to put it in the pithy terms of one review, that it is "based on myths from Mali."[13]

Yet, just as Tahimik and Cissé refuse to concede to the terms of ethnographic/culturalist realism, so can—and should—we spectators. I suggest that these films can be understood as reflections on and critical engagements with realism as a form that is implicated in genocidalism and its fantasy of a humanity defined by the internal characteristic of consensus, within which relationships between individual humans are defined by a singular and total understanding of reality. Another way to say this is that realism is a key technique of the aesthetics of ruination. The realist mode locates human bodies in political space by suturing culture to ontology and thus by fixing the range and kinds of meanings that can be understood as being produced by individuals with particular bodily forms and geopolitical locations. As Lindiwe Dovey notes, this mode constitutes a set of aesthetic, formal, and narrative norms that have come to define the genre of world cinema, especially in its ordering of the world as exhibition.[14] In suggesting that *Yeelen* can be read as working against this ordering of the world via its "turn to the resolutely local and specific,"[15] I take Dovey to be referring to a kind of locality that resists the presumption of transparency, accessibility, and totality of meaning that a taxonomic ordering of the world claims to make available. This is a different form of locality than that offered by culturalist realism and its aesthetic of authenticity—one that stakes a claim on and to humanity precisely from a radically specific location and, in doing so, reveals the eradicatory processes and aspirations that define humanitarianism's distribution of the sensible. The radically local articulations that I see both films as engaging in erupt from what is supposed to be the flat, featureless plain of humanity's order, punctuating that putative totality.

Likewise, and contra Chakrabarty, I see the postcolonial as offering the possibility of a necessary reordering of our sense of place and time in its interruption of the long-lived rendering of world human geography according to the temporality of progress, which is to say, the temporality of genocide.

What Fabian diagnosed as the denial of coevalness is both a denial of presence in the here and now and a mechanism for relegating difference to another place and time,[16] and thus for belying humanity's constitutive differentiality. This is the aporia at the heart of the civilizationist project, that is, its reliance on the very notion of difference as temporal distancing—as Roitman points out, of a fundamental difference between the past and the future as "necessary to transformation"[17]—for the achievement of humanity's sovereign presence. My interest in the framework of the postcolonial, then, is in its capacity to articulate a differential concept and experience of temporality. It can emphasize the importance of maintaining a vigilance toward claims to having surpassed the colonial, while simultaneously articulating a commitment to knowing that there have been and must still be cosmologies and ways of being that exist in radical difference to the colonial: the "post" does both of these things at the same time, suggesting that the conceptual rubric of the "colonial" itself is to be, always, troubled, precisely because it is not selfsame. Indeed, I understand the "post" to name the space and time of the colonial as palimpsestic, circular, iterative, rather than linear or teleological; the project of colonization has always been resisted, fought against, undermined, and thus forced to remain forever incomplete and unsuccessful.

Both *Yeelen* and *Mababangong Bangungot* not only forward critiques of the destructive and genocidal logics of progress, but articulate antiteleological temporalities in their grappling with the violence wrought by Cold War neo-imperialism in postcolonial contexts. To this end, both Cissé and Tahimik take on the practice of what might be called critical fabulation as described by Fatimah Tobing Rony in her reflection on the specific possibilities film provides for this practice:

> Film is a perfect medium for critical fabulation because of its special relationship with time, reality, and realism. Born of the trace of what is recorded by the camera, the shutter opens, and what is fixed on the emulsification of the film is what passed or stood in front of the camera shutter, a ghostly trace. These imprints, these recordings, these traces, are then compiled, stitched, sutured together by an editor, to create an apparently organic beast that is actually inherently full of gaps and holes. . . . Finally, the film that gets seen is not the one that the filmmaker makes, but the one that catalyzes and provokes the memory-scape of images, experiences, and sounds that make up the viewers' unconscious. Filmmakers can excite that combination and transform it, not merely by changing subject matter and narratives,

but by triggering different temporal and spatial limits of the mind, by configuring new subjectivities.[18]

Rony's connection of "time, reality, and realism" speaks to the technical features of the filmic medium as it interacts with human sensory capacities, which features can be used either to participate in the elision of or to bring pointed attention to how what one is perceiving is produced as such. Film can either present (an ostensible) reality or it can draw attention to the compositional features of realism—and if the latter, it can also do something more, including perhaps allow us to see the uneven knowledge terrains and nonlinear temporalities that actually make up the grand narratives of human history as driven by a logic of progress, advancement, cause-and-effect, control. Both films do this something more, offering critical engagements with the post–World War II/Cold War management of postcolonies by presenting the progress-oriented projects of development and nuclear colonialism as aesthetic projects, that is, as being characterized by particular aesthetic features but also, beyond this, as inducing particular sensibilities and as ordering what is perceptible as reality.

If *Mababangong Bangungot* is less explicitly concerned with the bomb per se than it is with the implications of the space race for peoples subject to Western empire, its main object of critique—a humanity defined by genocidal practices and logics—is arguably born of what in the previous chapter I dubbed bomb ethics. The vision of humanity achieving its ultimate capacities by breaking free of the confines of the Earth to travel to the moon and beyond is revealed to rely on destruction; the extolling of America's triumphs in space served to morally sanitize its murderous projects in the Philippines, Korea, and Vietnam and to conceal its extraction of resources and labor from the Global South under the guise of development. If, as Jodi Kim argues, the United States' "genocidal war of conquest in the Philippines" was a historical and conceptual suture point between its colonial/imperial targeting of Native Americans and of Vietnam,[19] this legacy did not end after the Philippines gained independence in 1946 even as its relationship to the United States took on new forms, including development schemes and the "rule of globalized capital through the comprador/oligarchic elite."[20] Indeed, *Mababangong Bangungot* was made in the midst of what E. San Juan Jr. calls the "refeudalization" of the Philippines, as the policies of international economic institutions became the bridge across which millions of people from the Philippines have traveled across the globe—to work under conditions of cheapened labor.[21] These are also the conditions under which the character Kidlat himself is able to travel. Demonstrating a critical eye for the empty promises made by the humanitarian-driven IMF, World Bank, Western-based NGOs, and successive Filipino governments, *Mababangong Bangungot* is finely attuned to the process that Tahimik has come to refer to as "'overdevelopment': the compulsory production of unnecessary goods."[22] The important critique of racial/imperial capitalism and resource extraction commonly articulated in the concept of underdevelopment is radicalized here by Tahimik's notion of overdevelopment, and in *Mababangong Bangungot*, the reliance of the ideology of development on a simultaneous proliferation of things and institutionalized disappearance of people is thematized in relation to the US space program. The ironies of a society that would spare no expense to put "whitey on the moon"[23] while neglecting the most basic needs of so many people were certainly not lost on critics of racism at the height of the space program.

Yeelen also intervenes in humanity's definitional aspiration toward technological control of the natural world, in part by making strange the standard accounts of humanity's knowledge of its own history. It does this in part by weaving together cultural references from disparate historical and geographical settings, arguably alluding to elements of both the Sundiata Epic (based on the story of the founder of the Mali empire in the 1200s) and *Star Wars* (some of which was filmed in the same area of the continent). Ralph Austen notes that in Cissé's rendering, "secret Mande knowledge is akin to a 'force' that strongly resembles modern technology."[24] The fact that *Yeelen* looks and reads simultaneously like the precolonial past *and* like a science fiction future *and* like commentary on nuclear colonialism opens up the potential to read this film as questioning standard chronologies of civilizational progress.[25] Indeed, the nuclear bomb–like explosion that occurs in its penultimate scene, along with the shots of a desert landscape at the end of the film, evoke the complex Cold War political milieu of the 1960s. France engaged in atmospheric nuclear weapons testing in this part of the world,[26] and its testing program in southern Algeria, from 1960 to 1966, resulted in "significant environmental contamination in North Africa, particularly high in desert sand."[27] This became a flash point early on for various geopolitical interests, as both the United States and the Soviet Union sought to distance themselves from France in order to maintain ties with Third World nations, especially with the rise of the Non-Aligned Movement and the Pan-African Movement with their challenges to Western and Soviet nuclear weapons proliferation.[28] This was, of course, also a decade of major decolonization in Africa, the decade that saw the establishment of an independent Malian state (1960) and the military coup that installed Moussa Traoré as president (1968). It was precisely during this time, in the 1960s, that Cissé studied filmmaking in Moscow.[29] Indeed, many of this generation of African filmmakers completed their formal training in the Soviet Union through sponsorship programs; and in nations that were formerly French colonies, this was the first time when Black African filmmaking as an established practice became possible (given French censorship prior to decolonization).[30] The continuation of France's nuclear weapons program after the Cold War, in the face of what have been couched as new threats to Western Europe,[31] speaks to the continuities of the use and portrayal of North and West African locales under the regime of nuclear colonialism. Watching the film in the current moment, some thirty-five years after its release, becomes important in a new way as the landscape and geopolitical position of this part of Africa is reconfigured yet again, now via war on terror neo-imperial aspirations: The US Air Force has recently built a drone base in the desert near Agadez in Niger, to expand its efforts to fight so-called Islamic terrorism in the area.[32] Among residents near the new base, "rumors circulated that the dozens of dump trucks rumbling in and out of the heavily defended front gates each day were secretly stealing valuable uranium, for which the region is renowned."[33] Of course, such rumors about US military efforts are dead right about many things: the killing of civilians, the extractivism, the maintenance of a weapons arsenal with world-destroying capabilities, the twinning of secrecy and surveillance.

The drone base is a kind of archetypal embodiment of the aesthetics of ruination in architectural form: a monument to humanity's endurance through the mark left by its unique talent for engineered destruction, built by the extractivism that is the project of (over)development, dedicated to the process of wastelanding in the name of the effort to save humanity from terrorism. The idiom of suffering that this aesthetics of ruination produces—that of the denizen of the underdeveloped world, from whose abjection humanity writ large might learn how to live—is precisely what both films reject as they dare to offer postcolonial imaginings of other possibilities for humanity's survival.

Progress Is a Ghost: *Mababangong Bangungot*

Mababangong Bangungot begins with the character Kidlat excitedly sharing his work as the founding president of his village's fan club dedicated to Wernher von Braun, an architect of the US space program. By the end of the film, he composes a resignation from the club in which he states, "I declare myself independent from those who would build bridges to the stars." Here he refers to one of the key tropes of the film, the bridge, and throws into question its use as a positive metaphor for human progress. The film's narrative arc thus begins with Kidlat articulating himself in relation to humanity writ large through the logic of Cold War US civilizationism (the advancement of humanity through the conquering of new frontiers—i.e., warfare), and then enacting a disarticulation from that humanity and a movement "back" to the local. The declaration of independence could be read as a gesture toward a general anti-colonialism, but also as a refusal to play a role in the composition of humanity in its hegemonic form.[34] I find the possibility of such refusal to be particularly interesting when considering the relationship between the particularities of Kidlat Tahimik's life story and the work that the film itself is doing. Tahimik earned an MBA from the Wharton School at the University of Pennsylvania, and had a career in Paris as an economist for the Organization for Economic Cooperation and Development, only after which he learned to make films.[35] Significantly, he did not take the Tagalog name Kidlat Tahimik until after making *Mababangong Bangungot*. That Tahimik himself plays a villager, using a name that he would assume in real life only after the film was completed, takes on added weight given that the character Kidlat is, as many commentators have noted, portrayed as very naïve for the majority of the film. Many readings of the film are scaffolded around this issue of the relationship between the character Kidlat and the person Tahimik, and what Kidlat's naïveté means for whether *Mababangong Bangungot* can be described as a politically aware anti-colonial work. And a good number of them respond directly to Fredric Jameson's deeply controversial chapter on the film, "'Art Naïf' and the Admixture of Worlds." In opening his analysis by positioning *Mababangong Bangungot* in relation to "Third-World cinema," Jameson simultaneously problematizes the generalizations commonly made about this category and locates Tahimik's work largely outside of it, sidelining an exploration of the film's politics in favor of reading it alongside arthouse favorites like Godard and Tarkovsky.[36] Yet as San Juan has suggested, it is also entirely possible to understand Tahimik's work as theorizing the material and cultural mechanisms through which that very work will inevitably be seen; as San Juan puts it, "Tahimik precisely questions even the terms of Western art-historical discourse which frames the intelligibility of this essay, a problem of which I am fully aware."[37] What this suggests is that the writing of the character Kidlat as initially naïve is politically purposeful, and that Kidlat's naïveté is specifically of anti-racist and anti-colonial analytics and movements.

Tahimik's own narration of how he came to take his name describes a dual process, one characterized by both self-making and responding to a sort of external call: Noting that he first used it publicly when queried about how to credit the film for its showing at the Berlin Film Festival, he also describes seeking a new name because he had no say in the granting of his given one (Eric de Guia), and that in the process of editing the film "I became the person Kidlat Tahimik or that person I made in the footage became me." Translating Kidlat as "lightning" and Tahimik as "quiet," he remarks, "I was discovering the roots of my own contradiction."[38] He goes on to discuss his renaming as "how I slay the father," a reckoning with the ways his own sense of identity has been shaped by the official US policy toward the Philippines of "benevolent assimilation"[39] and that policy's horrific cultural violence. As this phrase is transmuted into the much more truthful "benevolent assassination" through a "mistake" in pronunciation that Tahimik's son makes,[40] the violence through which Tahimik's own subject position is formed is revealed. So too is a possible reading of the character of Kidlat that is somewhat askew from the typical ones—a reading that highlights the structured impossibility of a nonviolent representation or recognition of the Third World[41] subject as such. My reading of the character Kidlat thus highlights the film's gestures toward such foundational and continuing violence, over and against critics' tendency to focus on the emotional sincerity of Tahimik's work, its funniness, and its evident sensibility of tenderness. Such framings tend to prioritize those features of the film that seem to transmit a truth underneath the semblance of parody of the kind of life and experience represented in the person of Kidlat, and thus overlook the complexities of the film as a work about and of self-formation with a narrative structure that spirals and doubles back, offering a fundamental challenge to the whole idea of progress and the realist cultural forms it relies upon. In other words, I propose a more cutting and complex interpretation of Kidlat's naïveté as being in the service of caricature—that is, a profoundly non-naïve performance of naïveté. Such a reading allows us to see what I believe Tahimik is drawing attention to: the limited conditions of legibility for a Third World subject, because so often, to be recognized as such a subject is, in effect, to be slotted into the position of caricature, no matter how one would otherwise choose to represent oneself.

It is precisely as a caricature of a caricature that through the character of Kidlat, Tahimik himself is able to enact what Christopher Pavsek has insightfully called a "'politics of mis-pronunciation,'" according to which "the proper stance toward 'aid' and 'development politics,' NGO munificence and IMF demands for structural adjustment, is not to translate them into local idiom . . . but instead to mis-pronounce them 'properly,' so to speak . . . to re-render them *so that they speak their truth content in their own language*. 'Benevolent assimilation' becomes not its Filipino equivalent, but rather the English term for its actuality: benevolent assassination."[42] It is thus in the performance of a mispronunciation, ostensibly a naïve act that is in fact calculated and prescient, that the genocidal reality of the cultural system enabling Kidlat Tahimik's very entry into the category of world cinema is revealed. In *Mababangong Bangungot*, it is the mispronunciation of the word "mankind" that, I argue, is key to the work of the film in both offering a serious analysis of imperial and postcolonial state violence and pointing to other forms of human life and community. The Third World subject's claim to represent mankind is structurally impossible, and yet precisely because of this, something else happens in that claiming, a gesture toward a position outside of the enforced one that is not graspable within the terms of its grammar. In "Cups of Gas Filmmaking vs. Full Tank-cum-Credit Card Fillmaking," Tahimik takes on the name of "Third World" for his approach in a way that both acknowledges the realities of material distribution and infrastructure access that structures the First World–Third World distinction, and questions more simplistic uses of "Third World" to describe a particular ethos, aesthetic, or culture. He is ultimately less interested in parsing the details of this distinction and more interested in what possibilities are opened up when one is not beholden to the value system of capital: "Time is money. My lack of resources can become a blessing because my time frame escapes this deadline obsession, and allows me to discover motifs. The film becomes an interaction between me and the cosmos."[43] Indeed, in the interviews and writings of his that I have encountered, Tahimik emphasizes this notion of time again and again. I want to connect this to my reading of *Mababangong Bangungot* as offering a critique of the devastation of the progress model of humanity's history—the genocidally aimed actions and death and deadlines it relies on—and an attempted reconfiguring of humanity against progress.

 The deadly serious joke that forms the central conceit of the film is Kidlat's minor obsession with Wernher von Braun, a fraught figure of US ascendancy. I have found no readings of the film that do more than mention Kidlat's veneration of von Braun as a simple plot point—so I linger on this, to see what happens. Von Braun was a NASA engineer who worked on the pioneering Apollo missions, and who also took an active role in popularizing the US space program and the importance of manned space missions.[44] But von Braun had also been a member of the Nazi Party, and he was instrumental in the German military project to develop the V-2 rocket, the first ballistic missile. This groundbreaking technology was first and foremost a technology of murder of genocidal proportions: Germany used its V-2s against London and Paris, and concentration camp internees were often worked to death to excavate tunnels for and to build the rockets.[45] It was precisely for the knowledge of such technology that he was then brought to the United States (along with other scientists) after the war, given US citizenship, and integrated into the US militarized technocracy. But even without knowledge of von Braun's Nazi past, it is evident that the lauding of such technology's capacity to secure the civilizational triumph of humanity is complicit with more blatantly murderous projects and aspirations for Western-based world governance. For von Braun also worked on ballistic missile technology for the US Army, and proposed space stations as a kind of superweapon, a way for the United States to "dominate space" and in so doing, to enforce world peace.[46] A novel he wrote, *Mars Project*, envisioned the achievement of human technological capacity as premised on the genocide of Asian peoples in particular: In the novel, "seventy passengers go to Mars in ten spaceships after the West defeats the East with atomic bombs dropped from an orbiting space station."[47] Wayne Biddle suggests that von Braun's repeated claim that "what he had really been doing all along was developing the means to travel into outer space"[48] largely served to justify his work on a technology whose sole purpose was to kill, especially given that so many of his visions for manned space travel were fantastical and even preposterous.[49] Indeed, *Mababangong Bangungot* highlights the twisted intricacies of the space program as a cultural technology for attempting to involve Third and Fourth World subjects in the justification of their own extermination. That von Braun is the object of Kidlat's admiration—and not, say, one of the astronauts, especially given that it is Kidlat's dream to travel to the United States in order to become one—suggests that the film offers a deeper interrogation of the long history of empire and its particular expression during the Cold War era than many readings allow.

Mababangong Bangungot, from the beginning, stresses the reliance of progress on death. An extended opening sequence of about seven minutes introduces this thematic with the trope of the bridge. The story of Kidlat's own life begins with the story of the bridge, and the bridge also makes his village accessible to the encroaching forces of empire, signaling its entry onto the world stage of humanity. It is precisely this telling of the history of the village, and of why the human beings who inhabit it matter, that Kidlat will come to repudiate by the end of the film. In the opening sequence, the bridge into Balian becomes a loaded metaphor of ongoing imperialism and postcolonial governmentality, in the guise of a seemingly quaint story of one young man's aspirations to leave his village for something bigger and better. A Tagalog voice-over narration by Tahimik begins quietly in the background, as an English translation is spoken over it and at higher volume, also by Tahimik, in the voice of the character Kidlat. He explains that the bridge was originally built of bamboo, which was destroyed by the Spanish in the service of building a "better" bridge, which American military engineers later tried to widen; the bridge is now "used by the leaders who promote discipline and uniformity" (a reference to the Marcos regime[50]), and "is used also by the followers. It is our bridge of life." This narrative is recited over several scenes of the bridge in use, including most importantly by Kidlat himself, who appears three different times pulling a jeepney (a leftover US Army vehicle reconstructed as a taxi) at three different stages in his own life: trying to cross the bridge "alone" for the first time at age three; trying to cross the bridge again "by myself" at age four; and third, in the present, with the declaration "today I am still trying to make that final crossing to freedom. I am Kidlat Tahimik. I choose my vehicle, and I can cross all bridges." But each jeepney is bigger than the last, and the third time Kidlat especially struggles to pull it at its full size; these visuals sit uneasily next to Kidlat's claims of access to the freedoms of choice and movement. Further troubling the invocation of the bridge as a figure of "life" are the ensuing images of a funeral procession and Kidlat's discussion of another kind of bridge "out of the village," the one he says that his grandfather took after spending his life building bamboo huts. This other bridge, which is implied to be death, is something that Kidlat then admits to relying on in his work as a jeepney driver (ferrying people to and from church). The progress represented by the bridge, and by Kidlat's embrace of entrepreneurialism through his work as a jeepney driver, is thus clearly possible only through the kinds of death that are the outcome of military and capitalist violence.

Moreover, in the mapping of his own life narrative onto that of the bridge and the historical events it represents, Kidlat performs the civilizationist trope of recapitulationist theory, in which the development of an individual person serves as a synecdoche for species development—or to put it more directly, according to which "the childhood of the white race was a counterpart to primitivism or savagery on the evolutionary scale, while adults of 'inferior' groups were at the mental or emotional level of white male children or adolescents."[51] In his aspirations and the incapacities they ultimately reveal, Kidlat thus embodies both the desire to fulfill his own potential by enacting those feats that ostensibly express the essence of what it is to be human, and the throwback to another time who serves to negatively define humanity's highest potential. He is, in other words, a caricature of the archetypal subject produced by developmentalism: He himself desires development, and yet it is intimated that he may never achieve it (as he represents the failure that developmentalism relies on in spite of itself).[52] Precisely as caricature, Kidlat gestures toward the bizarre, disturbing, and ridiculous elements of American white-ascendant masculinity: the boyhood spent lusting after white beauty queens and the conquest of space, the achievement of manhood predicated on the utterly illusory claim to be self-fashioning, the strange synchrony between Christian religiosity and militaristic techno-rationalism.

This opening sets the tone for the rest of the film, in which it is made clear that only a willed ignorance of the historical and conceptual relationship between progress and genocide could produce such an optimistic view of humanity's technological capacities: Bridges are invoked by Kidlat over and over as symbols of possibility and human achievement, and the jeepney his means of eventually accessing the vehicle of his dreams, the rocket to space. Indeed, the sequence that begins after the title card has Kidlat sleeping and, it is implied, dreaming of the objects of "his" desire. Shots of a white carabao—which will come to represent both the mystique of a devastating American cultural imperialism and the anesthetizing power of Kidlat's own desires for such Americanness—appear interspersed with shots of the "Evolution of the Filipino Flag" and Miss Universe posters adorning the walls of Kidlat's home, while a Voice of America radio program plays. Kidlat wakes up, declares (in voice-over) "Good morning, darling of my life," and kisses the picture of Miss Universe 1974. Not just another example of the infiltration of Western culture, this is perhaps more importantly a comment on the differentiation, inequality, and ultimately white ascendancy that the notion of a universal humanity relies upon: The Miss Universe 1974 pageant was held in Manila, but Miss Universe 1974 herself was white. In one shot in this sequence, Kidlat cuts out Miss Universe's picture and puts it in a double frame next to an image of the Virgin Mary, which evokes the racist trope of peoples subject to colonialism comporting themselves toward Western cultural objects in an ignorant way, while also subtly suggesting that the generally accepted forms of relationship to these two figures are not so different after all.

The direct invocation of sexuality I also read as a very knowing reference to the racialized sexual dynamics of Western imperialism, as the ridiculousness of Kidlat's gesture is compounded by the fact that he is a Filipino man openly expressing desire for a white woman. Whether coded as effeminate and not possibly desirable to such a woman or as hypersexual and hence dangerous to white racial purity—depending on the context[53]—the brown man's desire for the white woman is both naturalized and treated as absurd. Kidlat thus begins the film wanting things he neither needs nor has any socially sanctioned right to; he is desire without the taming apparatus of conscience. As a caricature of a caricature, he references those Eurocentric thought systems, like psychoanalysis, which have "systematically encoded race as a question of sexual development."[54] As David Eng points out in his brilliant reading of Freud, the latter premised the possibility of advanced human community on proper individual sexual development; the sublimation of immediately experienced and improper sexual desire through the psychological mechanisms of "conscience and guilt" is what, according to Freud, allows the very "emergence of the social sphere."[55] Kidlat himself both desires and identifies with what a white-ascendant masculinity would deem as proper objects, yet his encoded racial difference exposes the constitutive exclusions of such a model. So it seems significant that this caricature of the white supremacist construction of brown male sexuality is the immediate prelude to the introduction of Kidlat's main object of enthrallment, Wernher von Braun. Kidlat's desire for Miss Universe is quickly transferred to an identification with von Braun, yet the frisson of improper desire remains. I think it is precisely this desire that is potentially disruptive of the triumphal narrative of humanity achieving technological supremacy through rationalism. As the Voice of America touts a book titled *Man's Conquest of Space* while Kidlat busies himself with Miss Universe's picture, the fantasies, narcissism, and base yearnings driving the space race—as well as the cultural role of the US space program in codifying the very notion of mankind—are alluded to.[56] And when Kidlat muses, "Dear Voice of America, Where can I get an autographed picture of Wernher von Braun?," the figural synchrony of the images of the Virgin Mary, Miss Universe, and von Braun suggests that idolatry was always at the heart of the rocket engineer's fame.

Kidlat goes on to compose a letter to the Voice of America: "Dear Mr. Voice of America, Since I have my transistor radio, I listen to you every day. However in 1969, during the Apollo moon landing, I had no radio then. What were the first words your great American astronauts first said when they landed on the moon? Can you please play it for me? Yours truly,

Kidlat Tahimik, President of the Wernher von Braun fan club of Balian."
This letter is composed with a wink and a nod, for the question could not
really be asked without knowledge of those famous words. Kidlat later reads
the letter he receives in response to the other members of the fan club: "In
answer to your question, 'That's one small step for man, one giant leap for
mankind.'" While much of Kidlat's voice-over and dialogue in English is
meant to sound not fully in command—through the performance of mispronunciations, or syntax that is slightly out of order—his reading of these especially famous words is notably slow and labored. Both "giant" and "mankind"
are explicitly "mispronounced," the latter doubly so. "Giant" becomes "gee-
ant," suggesting the reduction of a supposedly momentous event to nothing at
all ("gee-ant" doesn't mean anything in English). Kidlat particularly struggles
with "mankind," stumbling over it several times, initially pronouncing it as
"monkey"[57] before finally getting it right, or so he thinks, as he triumphantly
pronounces the word as "mankind" with a short "i" and repeats the sentence
one final time with surety: "One gee-ant leap for mankînd." As Harrod Suarez
notes, the first mispronunciation of "mankind" arguably indexes the use of
"monkey" as "a racial slur that has been directed at Filipina/os in colonial as
well as anticolonial propaganda during the Spanish-American war, and later
during the colonial period."[58] It is thus born not of ignorance but of a deep
knowledge of the exterminating violence of "mankind's" supposedly inclusive
definitional sweep.[59] Kidlat's caricatured ignorance also reveals something
about the tenuous hold of humanity on its supposedly distinguishing and
distinctive features. For "monkeys" (chimpanzees) were sent into space
before humans, used as test subjects for humanity's conquest of the new
frontier;[60] chimpanzees thus were figured both as central to humanity's
achievement of its full potential and as beings whose *proximity* to humankind was precisely what made them expendable.

Through the teachings of his mother and family friend Kaya, Kidlat's original ignorance serves as the vehicle for a pedagogy that situates knowledge
of colonialism, the postcolonial era, and the global machinations of capital
squarely within the socialities of precisely those people who are rendered as
parochial by those systems. Upon hearing that Kidlat will be traveling with
the American, Kidlat's mother invokes his father in order to offer her son
a cautionary lesson: He was a man who was "fascinated by the white man's
mind" (like Kidlat himself), and who met his fate after being taken in by the
United States' false promise of freedom. In a story recalling the history of the
Philippine Revolution against the Spanish (1896–98), the Spanish-American
War (1898), and the ensuing purchase and annexation of the Philippines by

the United States, and later the Filipino-American War (1899–1902), Kidlat's mother tells of his father being a "happy taxi driver" until the day when "a smiling stranger gave him a rifle, the bridge to your freedom, your vehicle to freedom. 'We will help you with your revolution against the Spanish tyrants,' said the smiling Americano." She continues the story by noting that "as he sang the sweet song of victory, the Americans were buying us in Paris." Kidlat's father was then killed by American soldiers for trying to enter Manila, or "trespassing on US property," according to the official military report on his death. Kidlat's mother then gives Kidlat a small horse figurine, which she has carved from his father's rifle; later it is affixed to the hood of his jeepney. Kaya then offers to tell Kidlat the "real" story of his father's death, claiming that the official military story is not the "true" story: "He did not need his rifle. Your father took a deep breath. He blew with a fury that knocked the guard down, stronger than the winds of Amok mountain, Kidlat. Fifty more Americans fell before they finally stopped your father. Kidlat, when the typhoon blows off its cocoon, the butterfly embraces the sun. The sleeping typhoon must learn to blow again." I do not take these stories to be a veneration of the father figure, but rather complex commentaries on nationalism and the mythologizing of the past, opening paths for questioning the gender dynamics of both colonial and postcolonial societies rather than imposing a valorized masculinity.[61] As Dixon and Zonn point out, it is Kidlat's mother who offers perhaps the most complex and knowing explanation of the codependent machinations of empire and capital: It is she "who tells the story of how the Americans came to wield such economic and political influence in the Philippines through the fable of Kidlat's father," and not Kaya.[62] Indeed, in *Mababangong Bangungot* it is men who are invested in grand narratives of an illusory freedom. Women, in the figures of Kidlat's mother and sister, and in the Parisian market vendor Lola, are the ones who contend with the craft of survival and who articulate clear analyses of unequal social positioning.

Kaya serves a crucial role in the scene that immediately follows the one featuring stories of Kidlat's father, in which Kidlat narrates his experience of "the day that I became a man" in a circumcision procedural, in which the white carabao figures heavily. This is the second time in the film that the white carabao is the subject of conversation. The first time, Kidlat goes to ask Kaya about the significance of the white carabao that keeps appearing in his dreams, asking, "Kaya, why is the eye of the white carabao so cold?" Kaya replies, "The white carabao is rare. It is born against nature. The white carabao is beautiful, but inside it's cold and aggressive.

One day, Kidlat, you will understand that the beauty of the white carabao is like the sweetness of the chewing gum the American soldiers gave you." Later, the circumcision scene opens with Kidlat remarking to Kaya, "I now recall I first saw the white carabao somewhere here, many years ago, on the day that I became a man." This is a long scene that includes footage of actual circumcisions being performed in a forest clearing, in which Kidlat narrates a cryptic and unnerving story in voice-over about his own experience. He states, "I was no hero," and "while they were hammering at me, I could not take my eyes off a strange, leafless tree." The camera pans down this tree, stopping on a wooden carved carabao sticking out of a hole, after which there is a cut to a hand-drawn graphic of a white carabao's head and eye. Kidlat says in voice-over, "the white carabao stared so coldly, I felt no pain." Pavsek suggests the following reading of this scene: "the carabao, already marked as stand-in for U.S. culture, provides a welcome, if haunting and suspicious, anesthetic for Kidlat at a moment of intense bodily pain. . . . The figure of the carabao posits then yet another function for commodity culture that supplements and reinforces its role as a force of violence and disruption of native culture—that of anesthesia, the false amelioration of the experience of pain."[63] I would add that the white carabao works not only as a stand-in for US culture, but also as an externalized figure of Kidlat's own desires, that is, his interest in "the white man's mind," which Kidlat spends much of the first part of the film equating with the most fundamental features of his own identity. Along these lines, I note that the carabao is arguably a palimpsest, not just a symbol of US culture but a signifier of the tangled complexities of cultural objects, identities, and selves forged in the midst of empire. In this key moment where Kidlat enters into society as an adult, he experiences a kind of splitting of the self, a fraught experience that yet later on allows a critical distancing from the relay of looks he is subject to and that subjectivizes him. The *narration* of his circumcision as a prior event can be read as a third eye/fourth eye act in Fatimah Tobing Rony's sense, according to which the capacity to see how one is being seen allows an ontological repositioning of oneself against the deadening white gaze, in concert with a "we" that understands the reality of (rather than the compromised sense of reality created by) the social technology of racialized looking.[64] Indeed, Kidlat introduces this story by addressing it to Kaya, indicating that it is the product of Kidlat's further reflections on Kaya's teachings rather than a rote rendering of a circumscribed past event, and that Kidlat's relationship with Kaya has already afforded an escape from the capture of the carabao's cold stare.

As Kidlat travels to Paris, we encounter the devastation wrought by progress in the form of concrete, supermarkets, and an abundance of trash. Kidlat spends his days traversing the city, filling gumball machines, and coming to know the erasures necessary to building so many bridges: Kidlat writes to his mother, "Do you know Paris has twenty-six bridges? Why can't we have progress like this?" Kidlat is initially fascinated with Paris's bridges and buildings in particular, and frequently juxtaposes them to the technology of the bamboo hut. Yet even as he marvels at the wonders of this heart of empire, the contradictions of his position become more apparent and the tone of the film becomes more menacing. He makes friends with Lola, who sells eggs at a local market, and learns that she will soon be put out of business by the new supermarket being constructed across the street. When Kidlat shares with her the story of the wooden horse, she remarks, "Ah Kidlat, your mother is wise to know a simple tribute is more powerful than the giant monuments of our civilization." Here we see a brief shot of a white-cloaked figure standing at the edge of a forest, perhaps invoking the many deaths on which civilization has relied (including Kidlat's father's) as well as foreshadowing Kaya's claim later in the film that "progress is a ghost." Or perhaps this is the ghost of the forest that, as Kaya later reveals in a letter to Kidlat, will soon be destroyed. Such non-diegetic shots puncture the smooth surface of Kidlat's chronicling of the civilizationist advancement ostensibly expressed and embodied in the very architecture of Paris itself, and impress themselves with increasing insistence on Kidlat's consciousness.

Non-diegetic shots of bamboo structures and urban construction also appear just before Kidlat admires the Church of Humanity,[65] the inscription on which he reads aloud: "Religion de l'Humanité: L'Amour pour Principe et l'Ordre pour Base, le Progrès pour But" (The religion of humanity: love as principle, order as basis, progress as end).[66] This motto, encapsulating French philosopher Auguste Comte's (1798–1857) understanding of positivism as a thought movement in which science would guide politics, suggests an evolutionary view of human society and indeed progress as the very definition of humanity.[67] Kidlat grapples with what this means: Even after Kaya tells him about the rampant destruction of forests near his home, Kidlat responds, "'quiet strength of bamboo.' That is why we have no progress! Kaya, you still refuse to see why bamboo art is doomed to extinction. I am living in a tower that is five hundred years old, and it will survive another five hundred typhoons and earthquakes. Kaya, you cannot build rocket ships from bamboo." We hear a countdown to blastoff and Kidlat's tower shakes and rumbles, in a seeming homage to the Viking I landing on Mars. Bamboo is supposedly not civilized because, in addition to its racialized associations, bamboo is more visibly subject to the alterations of time: A bamboo house degrades more quickly than stone or concrete, providing no lasting mark or evidence of the people who built it, unlike the planned ruins of Western civilizationism. As Kidlat points out, it is the sign of extinction. The structures that Kidlat comes to refer to as "super chimneys," giant incinerators described by the American as "an extra service of the supermarket," seem to serve as a caricaturized manifestation of this concept of planned ruins and the actual deaths it relies upon. Marveling at their size, Kidlat calculates that thirty people could live in each of the ten super chimneys, exclaiming, "that's half of my village!" This imagining of Filipino villagers living inside of incinerators evokes deep figural resonances: with Nazi concentration camps; with American fire-bombing of whole cities of people living in flammable structures; with the long history of colonized peoples being figured as human waste, whose inevitable end could be "humanely" hastened through planned destruction. The super chimneys also look not unlike the Apollo spacecraft, and moreover are reminiscent of nuclear power plants, suggesting the destructiveness of both technologies and indeed their own finitude despite the desperate attempts to render them as securing humanity's future.[68]

But it is not long after this that Kidlat is shown trapped inside some sort of structure, climbing wooden slats and looking out, and indeed this is the pivotal moment when the full weight of what he has learned comes to bear on his consciousness. As the American prepares to travel to the United States and take Kidlat with him as promised, Kidlat balks: "If the small chimneys work, why the super chimneys? If the small markets work, why supermarkets? If small airplanes work, why super flying machines?" The American's friends begin to arrive for a farewell party, "men more godly than your Wernher von Braun," according to the American, as depicted by found footage of white dignitaries intercut with people who look to be Filipino actors wearing white people masks. The sense of menace grows as Kidlat articulates a full awareness of his use as the object against which the very concept and entity of "America" might be defined. "Why is everybody staring at me? I feel I am becoming smaller." Kidlat then blows them away with his own breath, as we hear Kaya's voice intoning the refrain repeated several times in the course of the film: "When the typhoon blows off its cocoon, the butterfly embraces the sun."

In the final minutes of the film, the relatively clear narrative through line gives way to surrealism, and Kaya's repeated voice-over reminders about the strength of the typhoon interarticulate with Kidlat's redefinition of self and reassembled view of reality. A close-up shot of the horse figurine carved from his father's rifle shows it traveling, perhaps on the hood of the jeepney, past ruined buildings. As this shot continues, we hear Kidlat in voice-over assert a form of self-determination that both recalls and rewrites the one that began the film: "This is the last will and testament of Kidlat Tahimik, and a declaration of independence. I, Kidlat Tahimik, of my own free will, hereby resign as the president of the Wernher von Braun club, and relinquish all rights and duties as president and founder of the club. Furthermore, I totally resign my membership in the club. This resignation is absolute, irrevocable, and is effective now. I declare myself independent from those who would build bridges to the stars." Reminiscent of the legalese that is foundational to imperialist notions of both individual and state sovereignty, Kidlat's last will and testament assumes the form but not the content of such texts: instead of declaring rights over anything, Kidlat enacts a renunciation of such rights. He then climbs into a super chimney, which flies away powered by Kidlat's breath. After a shot of Kidlat looking out the window, we then see images from in and around Balian, though it is never made explicit whether Kidlat is physically traveling there in the super chimney, and *Mababangong Bangungot* ends by establishing an oblique viewpoint that cannot definitively be identified as Kidlat's. In the last scene of the film proper, taken from outside Kidlat's mother's bamboo-construction home, we see her look out of her window (in an echo of Kidlat looking out of the super chimney), before she lowers its shade. It seems fitting that the film concludes with this image of impermanence, the bamboo hut, which finds a kind of human life and view in the relinquishment of any particular claims on the future. Midway through his stay in Paris, before his political awakening, Kidlat hears from Kaya: "The ghost of progress has visited us. Dear Kidlat, how are you? Do you remember the forest where you became a man? The government razed down the trees to make way for a new highway for tourists. Who will stop this madness?" If progress is a ghost, then it is not of the future but from the past, what remains of something that once was alive but is no longer. It is an entity with intentions and commitments of its own, ones that are perhaps bitter and vengeful. If progress is a ghost, we need a new view of human life that is not sublimated to humanity's survival.

2.1   Traveling through ruined Paris before heading back home. In the foreground is the horse figurine carved from Kidlat's father's rifle. (Kidlat Tahimik, dir., *Mababangong Bangungot*, 1977. Screen capture.)

Memories of Future Catastrophe: *Yeelen*

If the very process of making *Mababangong Bangungot* changed Tahimik's conception of himself in a way that is articulated in the film's examination and relinquishment of the Western imperial formation of humanity, something similar could be said for *Yeelen*. Cissé explains that making *Yeelen* "'was a discovery of a new thing that I knew existed but which I had not experienced in real life. And discovering the ritual scenes was like taking part in the activities; it was like an initiation for me.'"⁶⁹ This suggests that *Yeelen* is less a representation of knowledge to which Cissé already had some kind of access than it is an intricate enactment of learning, of shifting identity, and of a complex politics.⁷⁰ Rather than a more or less accurate portrayal of Mande culture prior to Western imperialism, *Yeelen* can be understood as bringing attention to the tropes that define the aesthetic technology of realism and then doing something else with them. Cissé is explicit about

POSTCOLONIAL HISTORIES OF THE BOMB   99

the fact that his filming of contemporary Komo practitioners did not result in an "authentic" rendering of their practices; the man who plays Soma Diarra (Niamanto Sanogo) notes that the practices they demonstrate "are merely a 'version' of the real thing, which 'resembles' the *komo*."[71] In this sense, the elements of Mande culture portrayed in *Yeelen*—for example, the ideographs that open the film, and the development and use of special powers by the Komo society—are perhaps more importantly seen as being repurposed here to create a new history, new ideas, new practices and interpretations. That Cissé's other films directly address power, politics, and violence in postcolonial Mali[72] also suggests that such a reading of *Yeelen* is possible, as does an established critical tradition that refuses to locate the meaning of such a film in its ostensible "cultural illustrations of 'authenticity.'"[73] In the words of Alexie Tcheuyap, we might instead read for how "postcolonial narratives turn to myth and epic in order to search for *new meanings*."[74]

This adds yet another layer to the discussion about whether or not *Yeelen* participates in a reinscription of "Africa" for an audience desiring the experience of precontact authenticity, given the fraught histories and circumstances of African filmmaking. For some, films like *Yeelen* have "represented a regression, from urgent (mostly urban) political issues, to a less confrontational aestheticizing and exoticizing rural Africa for 'Western' consumption."[75] Certainly, *Yeelen* is not set in a modern city, and the aesthetic beauty of the landscapes traversed by the protagonist Nianankoro are a key feature of the film. But this is also a question of reading. What if *Yeelen* is read not as engaging throwback naturalism but rather as, for example, rendering a seemingly premodern landscape in a science fiction mode? Taiwo Adetunji Osinubi considers the possibility for cinematic engagements with science fiction to render "African postcolonial time" in new ways, such that "the circulation of postulated African futures fosters reflexive corrective narratives to estranged African communities 'connecting' in the commons of the dream."[76] While Osinubi discusses films that posit "near-future" temporalities, I like the possibilities he opens up for also engaging with *Yeelen*, particularly in terms of its rendering of a commons that is possible as such precisely because of the ambiguity of its temporal location. Putting *Yeelen* into conversation with other films that share a commitment to "replacing historical accuracy and rationality with an alternative epistemological apparatus," Tcheuyap argues that "it is the hegemony of rationality that is in itself challenged by these films."[77] For peoples who have been subject to the violence of colonialism, slavery, and neo-imperial globalism, a rational, teleological rendering of history might in fact serve to imply that such violence was and is an inevitability. Conversely, *Yeelen* provokes us to consider that the prediction of future catastrophe might seem magical only within the context of a racist imperial order that wants to render the targets of its violence as unknowing victims of a putatively natural process of dying out; that in Djigui's prophecy *Yeelen* stages the prediction of an event, namely chattel slavery, that we already know of from a vantage point in the future of the film's own time frame, suggests that it can be read as purposely deconstructing a standard account of history, wresting it away from its typical authors. The version of humanity *Yeelen* calls into question— humanity as defined by a sovereignty achieved through destruction and killing—is arguably one of Sylvia Wynter's items of chief concern in her analysis of Man as *Homo oeconomicus*, whose putative mastery is achieved via the remembering of humanity's history as a narrative of civilizational advancement. Importantly, Wynter suggests that Africa holds a particular place in this configuration of humanity, that as "the extreme form of the 'native Other' to *Man* . . . no other continent must as prescriptively find itself enslaved to the unending global production of poverty which is the necessary underside of the this-worldly goal of *Material Redemption* from *Natural Scarcity*."[78] Following Wynter along these lines, we can understand *Yeelen* as a reworking of human memory against the formation of Man, from the specific location of Africa, through a double refusal: the refusal of a teleological narrative about the relationship between Mali's (or West Africa's) past and present, and, relatedly, through a refusal to claim mastery of knowledge.

Yeelen arguably works to refigure not just the history but also the geography of this part of the world, imbuing the land with different and new meanings, ones not proper to the common renderings of African landscapes by Western cinema, Cold War political configurations, or indeed the postcolonial Malian state. Cissé reappropriates many familiar visions of West and Northwest Africa, makes them strange, and puts them to new work: the landscapes of the Sahel and the Maghreb rendered as alien in just post-Vietnam scenes of humanity's future à la Hollywood; nuclear apocalypse; Black African cultural practices presented through the framework of authenticity. While it has often been commented upon that *Yeelen* had to be set in a premodern era because a contemporary setting would have made its critique of modern Malian politics more explicit and hence been a danger to Cissé—especially given that Cissé worked for the government producing films[79]—the film's complex rendering of geographical and geopolitical locale cannot be reduced to simple allegory. As Cissé himself puts it, *Yeelen* "'is a profoundly political work in which you have to get beyond the surface of the image.'"⁸⁰ Along these lines, Osinubi's argument allows a reading of the supernatural features of *Yeelen*'s storyline and aesthetic as just such a political engagement, as he discusses in relation to other films that "scrutinise the surface of social reality through explorations of the occulted, the invisible or the pervasiveness of 'hidden' forces that structure the realities of Africans.... The films portray politics and political discourse as subterranean forces; social structural relations are presented as spatial relations symbolically anchored in the SF city."⁸¹ In *Yeelen*, these spatial relations are not located in the science fiction city but nonetheless are present in the vast landscape Nianankoro traverses while encountering various different peoples, peoples whose particular relations to place become important features of his learning and essential to his arrival at the final encounter with his father, and there are sacred locations, cleansing waters, meanings to be found in termite mounds and trees.

Against realism, then, *Yeelen* offers a syncretic and palimpsestic rendering of this part of the world through multiply resonant and competing discourses that have a differential relationship to each other. In this way, I read the film as engaging with the devastating consequences of humanity's formation as selfsame and hence necessarily eradicatory. Interestingly, Cissé asserts a notion of human universality that, I argue, has the potential to reconfigure humanity—or at the least, to expose the terms of its composition—insofar as it positions Africa as centrally located within worldwide human life and concerns: "'It is a film in search of man's mysterious side. It evokes a number of African themes which may be universal. The lethal clash between a father and his son, this desire to kill.... Why reach the point of wanting to kill one's own flesh and blood?... Africa has a wealth of knowledge which can help humanity to advance.'"⁸² This particular articulation of universality is, crucially, grounded in an understanding of what I would describe as human incapacity. The title of the film, translatable as "Brightness" or "The Light," is visually referenced in relation to material processes of destruction and re-creation that transcend human capacities to fully understand or exert power over. Indeed, Cissé speaks of the relationship between the film's title and the thematic of the impossibility of human *possession* of knowledge:

> If "light" is our guide to knowledge, we must know how to use it the right way; we must know how to control it. Man is possessed by this anguish; the anguish to know, to be in control of a knowledge, and

to avoid the dangers of possessing a knowledge which contains the potential of destroying him. Man does not know the limits of science. We know how to create, but we do not know how to protect ourselves from our creations. So I posit the problem in apocalyptic terms in the film. Knowledge is built and consolidated by one generation, it is destroyed by another, and recreated by a new generation. This is the universal aspect of the film; it does not address the Bambara alone; it is for everybody. . . . I will go further and say that man himself is inside knowledge. He comes to this world within knowledge and he can only master a part of it. The film is concerned with this small part that man is able to control. I ask the spectator to be careful with the small knowledge that he had; to think about the consequence of knowledge before engaging in creative activity. . . . Knowledge . . . contains man; knowledge is a totality which includes man.[83]

It is difficult for me to not read Cissé's words in relation to the devastating egomania that produced nuclear technology. Indeed, the very first shot of the film is of the sun—which is, after all, a giant nuclear reactor—in its immensity and power, a huge burning sphere on the horizon, slowly ascending. It also suggests Soma's hubris, as this shot is a prelude to a scene in which Soma attempts to bring about nothing less than utter catastrophe in the effort to find his son. Causing a sacrificial rooster and then a nearby tree to burst into flame and addressing himself to Mari (god of the Earth),[84] Soma calls for destruction of the physical being of the world: "Dry the lakes, burn the trees. . . . Break it all . . . break the sky, break the earth. . . . Destroy towns and buildings, find Nianankoro for me." The "brightness" invoked here is less about illumination and more about burning, a violent process of transmogrification, one that is invoked only with uncontrollable results.

The main action of the film is preceded by a spare, eerie score and a black screen, on which appear several ideographs and their Bambara translation in succession. This translation, rendered as "Goniya Tâ Dyè fla," is subtitled in English as "Heat makes fire and the two worlds, earth and sky, exist through light." Then, on the same black screen, there appear several paragraphs written in French, with English subtitles that are themselves reductive and do not include all of what is being stated in the French paragraphs above them: "For the Bambara, the Komo is divine knowledge. It is taught by 'signs.' It covers all forms of knowledge and life. The Kore is the 7th and final Bambara initiation society. Its symbol is the holy vulture, bird of space and knowledge. Its emblem is a wooden horse, symbol of the human spirit.

Its scepter, a carved board called Kore wing. Kolonkalanni, a magic pylon, is used to find lost things, and to expose and punish thieves, traitors, and perjurers. The Kore wing and the magic pylon have been used in Mali for centuries." The progression of translations in this opening sequence invites a close reading and consideration. A bit of information is given—just enough to prepare the audience for the appearance and importance of the Wing of Koré and Kolonkalanni—but this is framed in a way that suggests a larger knowledge is being withheld. Thus, whose voice this represents, if anyone's at all, is an important question. Austen makes a convincing case that *Yeelen* purveys elements of Eurocentric anthropological accounts, as for example, "the texts and graphic signs at the beginning of the film do echo classic, and much-disputed, French texts on these subjects. . . . French anthropologists have . . . influenced a range of Mande intellectuals and artists."[85] Austen also questions "the representation of Kore (in the opening titles) as 'the seventh and final Bambara initiation society.' This concept of a universal Bambara initiation practice, arranged in a systemic hierarchy was formulated in the 1950s by the anthropologist Dominique Zahan. More recent studies indicate a much more varied and changing set of societies (called jow) across the Bamana landscape."[86] While the kind of withholding that Cissé himself as filmmaker engages in here could be troubled, there is also another withholding happening in this film, one that Cissé does not control and that also impacts the work of the film's opening. As noted previously, the Komo practitioners involved and portrayed in *Yeelen* presented something *resembling* the Komo. Knowing this leads to a different possible reading of the film's opening sequence, as providing something that is less like a cultural primer and more like an epistemic break.

Indeed, a key feature of *Yeelen*'s aesthetic and form are such epistemic breaks, which serve to introduce antiteleological renderings of time that engage the spectator in the experience of human incapacity. Apart from the opening sequence, there are at least four other ways in which such epistemic breaks appear in *Yeelen*: the structuring of the plot; the use of non-diegetic sequences and quick, subtly rendered shifts in time frame; the penultimate scene of Nianankoro's and Soma's deadly encounter, and its aftermath as shown in the final scene of the film; and Nianankoro's meeting with his uncle Djigui Diarra as a key event in the narrative, in which Djigui shares prophecies about the Diarra family's future. While the plot structure appears on the surface to be fairly linear, a more careful consideration reveals that it is actually organized by a series of spatial and temporal dislocations and circularities. It begins with Nianankoro seeing the image of his uncle Bafing in the water held by a calabash; Bafing is coming for him under the direction of Soma, accompanied by two attendants who are carrying the magic pylon. However, Nianankoro then refers to the fact that it is his father who is pursuing him, and indeed in several following scenes it is Soma who we see pursuing Nianankoro (also with the magic pylon but a different set of attendants); only quite a bit later does it switch back to Bafing, and then back again to Soma later on. Nianankoro's mother decides that he must leave to protect himself and find Djigui, to whom he must give the eye of Koré (a crystal) to be placed in the Wing of Koré. Through much of the film, Bafing and Soma continue the pursuit that puts Nianankoro's story into motion, yet Bafing and Soma always arrive belatedly, to find Nianankoro no longer where he was. Ultimately, the narrative line has Nianankoro simultaneously fleeing from and heading toward his father, resulting in a confrontation that (we will find out) has been foretold. Bafing's appearance is in part a function of the fact that Cissé had to change the script mid-shoot when the actor originally hired to play Soma, Ibrahima Saar, passed away; Cissé wanted to keep his scenes, in tribute to this well-loved actor, and so included Saar as the new character Bafing.[87] Yet this particular feature of the film also articulates with those others that, together, make *Yeelen* a meditation on nonlinear temporalities.

Stefanson refers to such "time warp" elements of the film in regard to the depiction of Soma's involvement with the Komo society, and to two non-diegetic sequences near the beginning and end of the film.[88] In the scene roughly in the middle of *Yeelen*, in which Soma gathers with other members of the Komo in a forest clearing to receive support for his pursuit of Nianankoro, the very last shot must be set in a different time frame than the rest of the scene—for suddenly, the statue of a seated man is holding the Wing of Koré, which it was not earlier in the scene and indeed could not have been, given that within the diegesis the Wing of Koré is in the possession of Djigui. Pointing out this easily missed and subtle shift, Stefanson argues that it indicates the "sacrilegious" nature of Soma and his supporters, as contrasted with another time when the Komo used their powers for peaceful and good ends.[89] Stefanson has a similar reading of two non-diegetic sequences in which a young boy leads a goat into the forest clearing and ties it to the same seated statue holding the Wing of Koré; for Stefanson, the goat indicates a proper sacrifice, one that would be done for Nianankoro's initiation by his father, if Soma were invested in good rather than evil.[90]

But I am also interested in the importance of these sequences as interruptions in the narrative in ways that go above and beyond their thematic content. Indeed, careful attention is required in certain sequences, as shifts in time and space are rendered quickly and with subtlety. The very opening scene includes one of these; while non-diegetic, its shot structure interweaves it into the scene in which it is embedded, which itself unfolds out of sequence. In this opening scene, we see the sun rise, then the sacrificial rooster on fire. There is then a cut to the child leading the goat into the forest clearing; after he ties the goat to the statue, the camera focuses on the Wing of Koré, beginning with the eye of Koré and then panning down the Wing to the statue's head, which appears to be bleeding and which also holds a crystal like the eye of Koré. Then we return to the rooster, whose blood is similarly running down the pylon; we see it burst into flames again, as Soma calls for the power to destroy his son; and the scene ends with Soma wrapping the magic pylon in a cloth. The sequence featuring the boy cannot be taking place within the time frame of the scene in which it is embedded, for it is in the very next scene that Nianankoro is given the eye from the Wing of Koré by his mother to take to Djigui. The boy leading the goat appears again in the penultimate scene of the film, Nianankoro's and Soma's confrontation. As the camera pans up the magic pylon, a disembodied voice decries Soma's actions: "Soma, your ancestors were priests of the Koma [sic], but for centuries, they've misused their powers. I've left only ruin in my wake. I've been faithful to the Diarras. Now it's over. Your lust for revenge, your contempt and hate of humanity have gone too far. I'm going to disappear. You won't survive, Soma, for you are one of those who use their power only for evil and injustice." We then see the boy leading the goat to the statue (though this is a different take from the scene that appears earlier in the film). After cutting back to the scene of the confrontation, as Soma and Nianankoro stand facing each other, there is then another cut to several shots of a water buffalo moving toward the camera. Soma's face fades into a shot of an elephant's face, Nianankoro's into a lion's. As we hear the sounds of the rooster sacrifice from the beginning of the film, the crystal in the magic pylon and the eye of Koré both begin to emit a bright light that then engulfs the screen, as Soma and Nianankoro fall to their knees and the sound of a shattering explosion rises.

The non-diegetic sequence of the boy leading the goat, here again, seems to reference the inappropriateness of Soma's use of his powers, and its dire consequences. So the appearance of these two very similar sequences, first during Soma's initial call for the power to destroy his son and then again during the final confrontation in which Soma attempts to do just that, does provide structure to the narrative—just thematically and aes-

2.2   Attu and Nianankoro's son crosses a sand dune into the new, unknown world created by the nuclear explosion-like catastrophe that annihilated his father and grandfather. (Souleymane Cissé, dir., *Yeelen*, 1987. Screen capture.)

thetically, rather than temporally. Moreover, the fact that the same actor plays both this boy and Attu and Nianankoro's son means that these sequences could be set in the future, after the events chronicled by the film. I propose that what is important here is precisely the ambiguity of this sequence's temporal setting. Indeed, the film's very last scene resists narrative closure, and it too features the young boy. Attu and Nianankoro's son unearths two large eggs (which may signify Soma and Nianankoro),[91] leaves one and takes the other to Attu; Attu then gives the child Nianankoro's robe, she takes the egg and sets it down in front of the Wing of Koré, which she picks up, and then walks over to her son in order to present him with it; they walk off together, and in the final shot we see the boy walking with the robe and the Wing of Koré along the ridge of a sand dune. This complex sequence certainly suggests the continued existence of Nianankoro's legacy, but it is Attu and the child who remain and who are the only indication of the form and character of this new world, which is otherwise not revealed except for a seemingly endless expanse of sand.

The end of *Yeelen* suggests a radically transformed world and the possibility of something new, with the death of the tyrant father and the survival of Attu and her son by Nianankoro. While many have noted Soma's defeat, the various possibilities of what and how Nianankoro's death signifies have been less frequently explored. Perhaps Nianankoro's actions are a kind of sacrifice, but I think the end of the film resists any sort of moral triumphalism. Soma's claims that Nianankoro is a thief—that he deviously obtained knowledge of the Komo that he should not yet have had access to, given his age—appear to have a truth to them (even if Soma also has his own desires for inappropriate power),[92] given that in the course of the film Nianankoro also succumbs to and is used by the knowledge and supernatural powers that are not his (or anyone's) to claim. During his journey, Nianankoro earns the trust of a village king by using his powers to defend the village from an attack. The king then asks Nianankoro to cure one of the women he is married to, Attu, of infertility. Nianankoro does this while committing the ethical breach of sleeping with Attu (and, thus, ending her infertility by impregnating her himself); in the lead-up to this unseen act, as Nianankoro effects the cure, the dreamlike qualities of the scene suggest that the same power through which Nianankoro works the cure is also working on him. So while he does not intentionally use his knowledge to cause harm, his example demonstrates the impossibility of human mastery over those forces that transcend us. As Cissé himself says, "it is not a dated film; it is based on the evolution of human beings and their cultures. It is because of this that the end of the film takes place without any commentary. If people stop at problems of tradition or such, it means they did not understand the film."[93] Perhaps, then, we can see *Yeelen* as also being about the consequences of invoking tradition in order to wield control over the future. Unlike the ordered, planned ruins that could easily transmit knowledge of the past to a hypothetical advanced future society, in *Yeelen* catastrophe creates something other, undetermined by humans. To use Cissé's words, knowledge will effect its own world-making, with or without man.

I conclude my discussion of *Yeelen*, perhaps appropriately, a little out of order, with a scene that occurs just prior to the final sequences of the film. Before Soma and Nianankoro's confrontation, Nianankoro meets his uncle Djigui, who offers a prophecy:

> Your wife is pregnant. The child will shine. It's a boy, and predestined to be a bright star. Yet, what I foresee promises nothing good for the Bambaras. The country's future hangs by a thread. Listen closely to what I say, and remember it like a sacred rite. Since the dawn of time, the Diarras have been the placenta and umbilical cord of the Bambara people. For a long time, our family has been cursed. I don't know why. My mind is tormented for my death is near, and I don't see who, after me, can interpret that curse. That worries me. But last night I

saw a bright light cross the sky and stop before me. It said "Djigui, the threat hovering over the Bambaras will strike the country, but spare your family." That restored my hope. In the same dream, I was also told this: "Your descendants will undergo a great change. They'll be slaves, and deny their race and faith." All upheavals are full of hope. The woes I saw in my dream will be turned to the Bambaras' advantage. I also see that many peoples will covet our country. I think one can die without ceasing to exist. Life and death are like scales laid one upon another. My child, do you know why I was separated from my twin Soma? One day I asked my father to reveal to us the secrets of the Komo so that all might profit from the knowledge. Your grandfather, in a rage, rushed into his room and came out with the Wing of Koré. Its brightness dazzled me. I could see nothing but shadows. So I left the country, blind. Only your mother knows my story.

We see here direct references to specific future events that we know will come to pass (slavery, the Diarra dynasty of the eighteenth and nineteenth centuries),[94] as well as more generalized references to a variety of events including, presumably, the spread of Islam, Western empire, development, the Global North's various extractive predations, and postcolonial power struggles ("many peoples will covet our country"). But Djigui's prophecy is not about perfect vision. Much of what he says requires creative interpretation, and the details of the dangers to come are not elaborated upon. Moreover, the end of the prophecy includes a cautionary tale about Djigui's own former desire for greater knowledge, which could still be seen as an act of hubris, despite his good intentions. While the knowledge that Djigui has been presented with might have been passed down through Nianankoro, given the latter's death (and indeed the catastrophe) soon after this scene, that possibility seems to have been shattered. In this sense, the prophecy is a different way of telling time and understanding history, serving to demonstrate human incapacity in the face of knowledge. Watching the film, the spectator bears witness to the prophecy, only to see the possibility for the transmission of the knowledge it contains fail. Humanity's vulnerability is not something to be overcome, but the basis for a radical humility in the face of the knowledge that precedes us and brings us into being. As with *Mababangong Bangungot*, *Yeelen* finds the human precisely in humanity's incapacity to determine its future. The attempt to make a particular claim on the future is deadening; humans get to be, get to survive, in spite of our attempts to define the precise nature of that humanity and its future.

Against the discourse on the Anthropocene and its romance with a renewed universalism—which is necessarily predicated on a civilizationist rendering of human history as a teleological narrative driven by technological advancement—*Yeelen* and *Mababangong Bangungot* offer antiteleological, anti-colonial temporalities that reveal the parochialist mentality out of which emerge those forms of massive violence done in the name of humanity. Indeed, the act of rejecting progress is central to both films, whether that be Kidlat's revocation of his membership in the Wernher von Braun fan club (and hence mankind) and his repurposing of a super chimney not to advance but to move back home, or the voiding of Soma's power and concomitant reconfiguration of humanity's relationship to knowledge and history. Thus, if the Anthropocene is a theory of catastrophe expressed in passive voice, from the vantage point of a singular humanity, these films reveal what that theoretical posture of innocence so flimsily conceals: the entanglement of the Anthropocenic rendering of humanity with what are ultimately the racist and genocidal foundations and aims of colonialism and imperialism. Progress is a ghost; teleology is an impossibility.

3

Converting Absences into Signs

THE WAR ON TERROR AND THE HUMANITARIAN NECESSITY OF VIOLENCE

> What might it mean to seriously contend with humanitarianism itself as a hollow ideal?
>
> —Neda Atanasoski, *Humanitarian Violence*

Wounded Muslim Women and the Aesthetics of Faciality

When the United States withdrew its remaining troops from Afghanistan in 2021, it was perhaps inevitable that news and public commentaries about this event would anchor their analyses to the trope of "Afghan women," especially as it became clear that the Taliban would regain the control they had attained prior to the 2001 invasion. Some simply characterized the withdrawal as the end of two decades of protections and improvements, while perhaps also directly calling upon the US government to continue to guard the human rights of Afghan women and girls.[1] Others expressed solidarity with Afghan women and focused attention on human rights violations that would continue to be committed against them by the Taliban, while cautioning against the potential remobilization of the gendered discourse of rescue that was a key feature of the justification for the 2001 invasion.[2] An article by Dr. Sima Samar, the former deputy president and minister of women's affairs for Afghanistan and chair of the Afghanistan

Independent Human Rights Commission, which appeared in *Ms.* magazine in August 2021, epitomizes the deeper continuities between these different approaches, both of which used the framework of human rights to figure Afghan women first and foremost as suffering victimization by the Taliban—and, thus, drew their reasoning and motive force from an entrenched synonymy of US imperial military endeavors and humanitarianism. Samar gives a brief history of the United States' fluctuating interests in Afghanistan, specifically its abandonment of humanitarian responsibilities, leading to the initial rise of the Taliban in the 1990s. Here, the 2001 invasion, though not named as such (the reference to this event is oblique, as in "since the Taliban regime fell in 2001"), is implicitly aligned with the upholding of human rights, as Samar goes on to assert that since that time, "women and girls—with leadership of Afghan human rights defenders and women's rights leaders from the U.S. and the international community—have made substantial gains in all spheres."[3] Samar states that "the protection of human rights and the achievements of the past two decades is a shared responsibility of the United States, the international community and human rights advocates," and she issues a call for these actors to take up an array of action points, from offering aid, to using international legal structures to help protect those targeted by the Taliban, to the utilization of the United States' "leverage" with Pakistan to get the Taliban to negotiate. Samar concludes by invoking the United States' geopolitical position as adjudicator of global justice, arguing that "in addition to the devastation that would be faced by Afghan women and girls and ethnic minorities, the return of the Taliban would cause the U.S. to lose credibility on the global stage, risk a resurgence of threats to the U.S. from terrorists, and accelerate the drug trade that finances the Taliban."

Rather than focusing on Samar's call as a singular object of critique, I wish to draw attention to it as a manifestation of a desperate situation in which it might seem as if the only way to avert suffering of disastrous proportions is to keep an occupying military force in place. As such, it demonstrates that the predominant question that long drove the general media coverage of the possibility of US withdrawal—should the United States leave Afghanistan or not?—itself presumed that militarism does not preclude humanitarianism. This presumption is, horrifically if unsurprisingly, not wrong. In her history of the United States' development of a humanitarian approach to its militaristic endeavors in a context of post-socialism, Neda Atanasoski argues that the loss of the war in Vietnam was instrumentalized to produce the United States as a humanitarian actor. When "told as a story of moral shock"[4] the commission of atrocities during that "failed" war became a means to assert the development of a more humanitarian ethical system that would guide American politics and sentiment. Thus, for Atanasoski, "cultural criticisms of imperial brutality and excess are not apart from but rather constitutive of future imperial projects."[5] This co-constitution of violence and a moral system based on the alleviation of suffering is revealed by Laleh Khalili to be the defining feature of what she calls liberal counterinsurgency warfare. Khalili focuses specifically on confinement, often in the form of the "mass incarceration of civilian populations,"[6] which is used in asymmetric colonial/imperial warfare in concert with social science–informed tactics that would be recognized as humanitarian in approach and aim. She notes that "it is precisely the processes of intensive 'reform,' cultural interventionism, and social engineering that makes these carceral programs such carriers of liberal intent."[7] This is illustrated by the US military's use of so-called Female Engagement Teams in Afghanistan, whose purpose was the "'non-lethal targeting of the human terrain' to 'enable systemic collection of information from the female population in a culturally respectful manner to facilitate building confidence with the Afghan population'"; under these conditions, as Khalili puts it so lucidly, "provision of aid to women becomes a tactical act."[8] This helps to explain why so much of the coverage about what has happened in Afghanistan after the withdrawal reiterates Afghan women's perilous protesting of the Taliban at the steepest of costs, while implying that their desire for freedom is a result of their *occupier's* humanitarianism.

We can see the withdrawal, then, as a continuation of the process through which "failed" military endeavors become the moral fodder for the cultivation of an imperial humanitarian ethos. Indeed, the emphasis on withdrawal as an event obfuscates a lot. As Khalili puts it, the claim that "'we don't want to stay' . . . is unpersuasive not because it is untrue—yes, the United States probably does not want to establish permanent structures of direct rule overseas—but because in effect, population-centric counterinsurgency produces these structures of rules, through its persistent focus on civilians."[9] In this chapter, I look at a set of media texts and cultural objects that deploy the figure of the wounded Muslim woman, the production and circulation of which, I argue, serves as a population-centric counterinsurgency tactic—one that, moreover, has contributed to the ongoing enactment of eradicatory violence in the name of humanity. Originally circulating during the height of the US occupation of Afghanistan and at a formative moment in the constitution of what is sometimes referred to as

"Af-Pak" as "an extreme topography of counterterrorism,"[10] these diverse texts presented well-publicized cases of women in and from Afghanistan and Pakistan who had experienced intimate partner and familial violence resulting in grievous wounds to their faces. In 2010, *Time* magazine featured what became an instantly famous cover photo of Aesha Mohammadzai,[11] an Afghan woman who survived an attack by her husband and in-laws; her story was followed in a variety of media outlets for the next several years, as she was brought to the United States for treatment and eventually adopted by a new family. And the documentary *Saving Face*, directed by Daniel Junge and Sharmeen Obaid-Chinoy (2011), which follows the efforts of a cosmetic surgeon to aid Pakistani women who have been the targets of acid attacks, was distributed by HBO and won an Academy Award in 2012. Many of us will be unsurprised by the appearance of these women's images and stories as objects of humanitarian meaning-making, given the continuing circulation of the figure of the (presumptively) Muslim woman's face through the networks of war machines and imperial discourses.[12] Clustered around 2010–14, these particular media texts and the discussions about them indexed the synonymy of the United States' imperial aspirations and its claim to be savior of the world, a decade into the war on terror, which was from the beginning explicitly framed as humanitarian and which has relied on the continued and intensifying assertion of the United States' security interest in countering gender-based violence.[13]

In a rich body of work, feminist scholars have interrogated the ways in which the figure of the suffering Muslim woman has been deployed for the purposes of suturing imperial warfare to humanitarianism; as these scholars note, this figure often appears in the form of the victim of what is rendered as patriarchal domestic (familial/spousal) abuse, who is characterized as deserving of sympathy and portrayed in ways that emphasize her supposed vulnerability and lack of agency.[14] In many feminist diagnoses of the problems with such depictions, the main questions posed have to do with whether they accurately represent the nature and extent of the portrayed subjects' suffering, whether particular instances of ostensibly benevolent recognition of suffering are compromised by infelicity, inadequacy, and/or instrumentalization for the purposes of statecraft, and whether the assumed approaches to ending suffering are in fact effective. For example, writing about the proliferation of images of "unveiled" Iraqi women upon the event of the US invasion, Judith Butler asks, "where is the loss in that face? And where is the suffering over war? . . . We saw and heard through that face no vocalization of grief or agony, no sense of the precariousness of life."[15]

Butler thus invokes the acknowledgment of suffering as a key feature of a feminist ethical critique of those supposed liberation projects that are actually imperial/military ones. Wendy Hesford centers the question of suffering in a different way, focusing on the spectacle as a process of (questionable) inclusion supported by images of suffering that mostly function to elicit empathy and recognition: "I use the term *human rights spectacle* to refer to the incorporation of subjects (individuals, communities, nations) through imaging technologies and discourses of vision and violation into the normative frameworks of a human rights internationalism based on United Nations (UN) documents and treaties."[16] Opening her book with what she sees as the archetypal example of young Afghan women whose faces frequent the campaign materials of human rights organizations and mass media, Hesford notes that "the Afghan girl has become a symbol of American charity and compassion—a representation that rests on the narrative configuration of the girl refugee as a deserving victim in need of rescue, and on the familiar dualism of tradition and modernity—intended to champion human rights within the framework of Western liberation."[17] And characterizing empathy as "experiencing what the other is suffering and *becoming* the sufferer," Sherene Razack sees empathic expression as a central action in the process of constituting a humanitarian consciousness; Razack's concern is that empathy "involves a consumption of the other, and thus the other's obliteration."[18] For both Hesford and Razack, the problem of human rights instruments and humanitarian projects is that they promote a dynamic where these women's own responses to, feelings about, and actions regarding their suffering become important only insofar as they are visible to and can be made to be about the authority of humanitarian law and consciousness itself.

While this set of problems must be engaged, I follow a different line of inquiry in this chapter. I propose that it is not necessarily the case that the designation of innocent victims deserving of care and the promotion of an empathetic response in the viewer are the primary effects of the texts I analyze here. Rather, I detect in them an invitation to blame the victim—an indication of the purposes of the wound above and beyond the garnering of empathy. In a discussion of the United States' destruction and then occupation of Japan during and after World War II, Camilla Griggers notes that the censorship of images of that horrific devastation (most particularly its effects on actual, individual people) coincided with a deployment of the woman's face as a key visual signifier meant to promote a new cultural and social order in occupied Japan.[19] Here Griggers explores the concept of faciality as "a system of signs organizing a zone of perceptibility and intelligibility for the socially constructed subject. As such, the face neutralizes, channels, and polices minoritarian forms and substances of expression. For this reason, Deleuze and Guattari write that 'the face is a politics,' because it is on the face that the limits and thresholds determining (im)proper conductions among signs and meanings are charted."[20] In regard to whether any particular individual's face will be perceived as appropriately aligning signs with meanings, the following questions might be posed: "Does the individual face conform to socially intelligible limits? Are its deviations intelligible? Does it *pass*?"[21] Considered as a function of the technology of social meaning that is faciality, the circulation of the injured faces of Afghan and Pakistani women coheres with long-standing knowledge claims about Muslim gender identity and Islam's refusal to allow women to be agents of their own destinies, thus channeling horrified and outraged responses to violence toward the very societies subjected to US military oppression. However, in line with that same tradition, it also appeals to the idea that these women themselves are in some sense culpable for the violence done to them, due to their continued adherence to a religion that has been codified as oppressive, and to their failure to achieve the normative standards for autonomous agentic subjectivity even when offered the opportunity to do so.[22]

Indexing the commission of unjust violence, the presumptively Muslim woman's wounded face serves as a key sign in the logical relay that begins with the identification of an instance of suffering and ends with the injunction to prevent future suffering by enacting humanitarian violence. As such, its repeated invocation aids in the production of a putative social reality in which Muslim women of color suffer harm almost exclusively at the hands of patriarchal and atavistic followers of Islam—and not due to the US state's racist/gendered counterinsurgency tactics in its global war on terror (both inside and outside the space of the US itself). Jasbir Puar crucially reminded us earlier in the war on terror that women most assuredly have been and are being detained, tortured, sexually assaulted, and put to death by occupying forces and military aggressors, while little evidence of this fact is widely available.[23] It is, in other words, an open secret that those who are portrayed as having the most to gain from military intervention are being systematically targeted for violence by their supposed saviors. This can be seen as one expression of what Ronak Kapadia describes as an "interplay between transparency and opacity—a contrasting relation that is part of the same visual and discursive field."[24] Kapadia argues that even as one of the main sources of the United States' power is its widely *known* investment in surveillance and intelligence practices, it must continue "officially denying that which everyone already knows to be true"[25] in order to authorize itself as democratic and just: "On the one hand, the state attempts to map racialized 'Muslim' populations and innovate surveillance and intelligence-gathering procedures. On the other, it is distinguished by a persistent disavowal of imperial violence and attempts to disappear the corporeality of its wars through 'black sites,' redactions, so-called touchless torture, denials of civilian deaths during drone attacks, and manifold unseen technologies of secrecy and terror that define the violence of the counterinsurgent state."[26] I would offer that this strategy, of insisting upon the truth of what everyone knows to be untrue, attempts at the finer level of the human psyche and heart to break down targeted peoples' trust in their own sense of reality, and at the broader level of the social to make it very clear who it is who gets to set the terms of what constitutes reality. This strategy—which is, to be clear, not just about a control over which among a range of different experiences and views get to be publicly voiced and validated, but about a control over the very nature of existence—is core to the establishment of the particular distribution of the sensible that is the ultimate project of the war on terror.

Thus, my own inquiry in this chapter is focused not on the failure to fully implement humanitarian ideals in the mediatization of these individual women's suffering, but on the necessity of violence to the production of the humanitarian subject and to the codification of a humanitarian distribution of the sensible. The implied blameworthiness of these women—a key aesthetic and narrative feature of the media about them, in terms of the sensibilities they play upon and attempt to invoke, and how they position these women in regard to a larger humanity—emerges as an attempt to not only obfuscate the explicit targeting for violence and death of women like them, but also to make them serve as the kind of sufferers over and against whom the humanitarian subject is able to cultivate her own capacities to understand the causes and effects of violence, how to properly address that violence, and thus how to restore and preserve the geopolitical order and the forms of relationality that characterize it. The media I look at in this chapter come into line with a long-lived and deeply entrenched set of US counterinsurgency practices aimed at women of color, with the war on terror as one of many arenas of their enactment.[27] Structured around the narrative conceit of the humanitarian provision of facial reconstructive surgery for the women in question and the pervasive, demanding assumption that these women's faces must and will be transmuted yet again—this time, in accordance with the logics of faciality—the texts in question share the conviction that facial restoration is necessary for the individual woman's rehabilitation and entry into a gender-equal geopolitical scene that is portrayed as having been made possible by their very suffering and the pedagogical uses to which humanitarians have put it. In this, they betray the larger purpose of such attempts to identify and alleviate suffering: the formation of a humanity defined by its members' shared understanding of the larger meaning of the suffering experienced by those who are figured as constitutively lacking in that capacity. Indeed, the minutiae of attempts at restoration are dwelled on, while those women who have little interest in them, or who "fail" at healing and moving on, or who undergo restorative procedures but understand them in ways that are more complex than or run counter to the logic of rehabilitation, become objects of terribly intense scrutiny, suspicion, and valuation.[28] As I intend to show, it is when the women in question do speak back to the many epistemological, ethical, and emotional demands being made of them—by engaging in behaviors that are identified and dwelled on as inappropriate, ignorant, and/or pathological—that they are treated with the most intense discursive violence.

In the next section of this chapter I build the foundation for my close reading of the cultural objects in question by considering what Talal Asad's theorization of torture as a hermeneutic—which produces a distinction between so-called just and unjust violence based on the putative characteristics of the "terrorist" psyche—offers a critical analysis of the explicitly feminist efforts made around the beginning of the war on terror to codify "gender violence" as an internationally understood knowledge object that could be the basis for moral cultivation and juridical action, specifically on the part of the UN and its allied institutions. Arguably, this effort had complicated effects, some of which cohered with and amplified the explicitly violent modes of knowledge production of the war on terror. These effects include the suppression of the recognition of counterinsurgency violence specifically against women in zones of racist imperialist warfare, and the constitution of Muslim women of color as a certain kind of subject, vulnerable to gender violence but neither willing nor able to articulate a broader ethical commitment based on the vulnerability of humanity writ large.

Torture and the Humanitarian Necessity of Violence

A key means of uniting war and humanitarianism has been the continued production of "Islamic terrorism" as an object of knowledge in the post-9/11 context. Tracing the tautological movement of those arguments that assert a distinction between terrorism and war in order to authorize the latter over and against the former, Talal Asad notes that they tend to locate that distinction in the qualities of the terrorist's psyche, given that the terrorist supposedly has different motives for committing violence and is differently affected by that commission than the non-terrorist soldier. But in his critical reading of political philosopher Michael Walzer's book *Arguing About War*, Asad points out how unstable the foundation of this distinction is, given that the supposedly superior moral capacity of the civilized wager of war is in fact made possible by a base cruelty: "Walzer himself proposed that when liberals act immorally in the conduct of collective violence against enemies, this 'leaves guilt behind, as a recognition of the enormity of what we have done and a commitment not to make our actions into an easy precedent for the future.' What he does not say, of course, is that the guilt may be accompanied by deep resentment against those whom one has wronged."[29] According to the ideology of just warfare exemplified by Walzer, guilt indexes a deeply fixed moral sensibility that preexists and remains after the immorally violent act—so the act may be wrong, but what really matters is the ability to know and feel that it was wrong. In obfuscating the possible presence of resentment toward those one has wronged, guilt as both affective experience and juridical measure thus serves as the central mechanism through which just warfare is authorized contra terrorism. We can see this in the common legal defense used to refute culpability for human rights violations, the claim of non-intentionality. As Eyal Weizman explains it, "juridical categories of 'necessity' and 'proportionality'"[30] define the killing of civilians as legal when that killing is a purportedly "unintentional" consequence of an otherwise legal military action or when it meets the bar set by "the lesser evil principle" of ostensibly causing less loss and suffering than some alternative.[31] Asad adds that "if state killing is authorized on the basis of due proportionality and military necessity (as humanitarian law requires of conduct in war), and if the question of what is proportional or necessary cannot be determined without regard to overall war aims as well as military strategy (there are always war aims in every war), every kind of forceful means can be—and is—used in war on that basis, including the destruction of civilians and the terrorizing of entire populations."[32]

What this suggests is that the claim of non-intentionality is underwritten by another even more insidious claim: that the very ability to distinguish right from wrong justifies any act, and that the violent act is in fact necessary for the creation of the very conditions for moral uprightness to be achieved, via a process of learning how to discern which kinds of violence are just and which are not. In other words, not only is the commission of military violence seen as legitimate under certain conditions, it is also posited as the foundation for the cultivation of liberal civilizational paradigms. Conversely, an act of violence becomes indefensible, terroristic, when it is committed by an actor who does not have the capacity for such discernment. Thus, the putative psychological event of non-intentionality must be evidenced by its opposite, that is, the terrorist's incapacity for such reasoning; it is the terrorist's psyche onto which is projected the civilized soldier's sublated resentment and desire to kill. Asad makes a persuasive case that torture is the main method through which the terrorist psyche, as object of knowledge, is produced. Torture constructs "terrorists" as fundamentally duplicitous, as impeding the natural flow of meaning: Terrorists are "people engaged in conspiracies," people who are driven by "secret motives."[33] Torture thus represents "an official suspicion about meaning"; it "converts absences into signs,"[34] uncovering those meanings concealed by the terrorist's deceptive nature.[35] The tortured subject's physical form is meant to express and provide access to an inner truth of devastation, which in turn is meant to provide the antithetical ground for the healthy psychic development of those who gaze upon it. In this way, injury—visible on the body, expressed in deteriorated mental health, or claimed via speech-acts—functions as a sign indicating *not* that one has been harmed, but rather that one is a "terrorist" whose injury is instrumental to the larger humanitarian project of ensuring the freedom of the world from terror. In other words, torture produces bodies and subjects who then become the tautologically achieved evidence for torture's necessity.[36] And, given the centrality of "just" violence to the production and enforcement of humanitarian laws and codes,[37] torture can be said to condition the emergence of the humanitarian subject, who is defined by the capacity for the moral discernment of the appropriate use of violence.

Following Asad, torture aims to produce a kind of fraught vulnerability in the Muslim subject and as the core component of Muslim subjectivity, which serves as a resource for the development of humanitarian consciousness and ethics and yet is also dangerous, given that it is the kind of vulnerability understood to make one a potential enemy of humanity. As authors studying the production of "Muslim" as a racialized category have argued, the induction and inscription of specifically sexualized and gendered vulnerability have been central to this production. Such vulnerability is (supposedly) manifest not only in queerness or gender anormativity but also in morphology.³⁸ On Salar Mameni's account, Muslim ontology is figured as a vulnerability to specific kinds of violation that are presumed to have an essential relation to specific kinds of bodily forms. Their own rereading of Alexander Weheliye's rereading of the figure of the "Muselmann"—a name for Nazi concentration camp denizens who were subjected to extreme bodily deprivation—in Giorgio Agamben's work,³⁹ highlights what the name of this figure can tell us about the political functions of the "Muslim body in pain," which Mameni describes as a "Dermopolitics," "the politics of an emaciated body reduced to skin, a skin hanging loose from its skeleton, whose shape, whose outlines, whose bending silhouette and enfolded contours determine its racial status within the camp. Here is an instance where 'Islam' is not a religious category, but a racial one, attributed to an emaciated and abject body reduced to its skin."⁴⁰ Crucially, as Junaid Rana argues, "Muslim" as a racial identifier came into formation precisely as a highly ambiguous category of identity. In tracing the complex history of this formation within a Western imperial episteme that has operated with a shifting set of determinations for what supposedly constitutes race in the first place, Rana notes that in the war on terror, "'the Muslim' emerged as a category of race that was policed through narratives of migration, diaspora, criminality, and terror," and as such reconstituted Muslim raciality as encompassing a differently expansive set of signifiers.⁴¹ This no doubt allowed the targeting of many individuals above and beyond practitioners of Islam, but also perhaps further entrenched the view of the Muslim body as inherently deceptive and thus as requiring the hermeneutic application of violence.

I highlight these particular qualities that are deemed to be the markers of racial Muslimhood—hyper-passivity, flesh reconfigured by the failure of functional control, a body folded over, in stasis, in the wrong place, signifying ontological uncertainty—because they at once suggest something about the gendering that is also a feature of Muslim racialization, are reiterated within some self-described feminist renderings of Muslim womanhood, and demonstrate the recursivity of torture and other forms of counterinsurgency violence in the production of legible Muslim subjects. This entanglement of repetitive violence with the material and discursive production of Muslim subjectivity comes to bear as an exceedingly complicated element of feminist efforts to systematize knowledge of violence against women and/ or gendered violence. Here, the thorough enmeshment of feminist thought and activism with UN-related initiatives, the epistemic drive to catalog, manage, and codify, and the expectation to engage humanitarian logics to achieve political/juridical/intellectual recognition become evident in the particular forms of vulnerability that Muslim women are expected to embody. Within broader efforts to name and address gendered violence as a global phenomenon, and more targeted efforts to recognize and prosecute wartime violence against women through an international juridical apparatus, Muslim womanhood is produced as at once uniquely vulnerable to violence understood as domestic and patriarchal, prone to collusion with violence coded as terroristic, and as incompatible with the gendered norms that define human rights and indeed humanity.

Several scholars have pointed to the 1990s and early 2000s as a historical turning point for feminist-inspired articulations of humanitarian ethics and political projects, which came to invest heavily in focusing on sexualized gendered violence against women. In her detailed intellectual historical account of the governmentalization of "the questions of violence posed by feminist movements"[42] that is a feature of the women's rights as human rights framework, Inderpal Grewal describes how the identification of domestic abuse as a global, cross-cultural phenomenon aligned with other kinds of gendered human rights abuses has operated to stabilize both the category of "women" and the notion of gender itself.[43] On Grewal's reading, this discourse produced the idea that "what differentiated the female body was the violence wreaked on it. This violence constructed the body as stable and essential, despite articulations of 'cultural' differences which could be overcome by education and through transnational connectivities."[44] In an important critique of the basic assumption of the women's rights as human rights framework that "nonliberal cultures of non-Western states are incorrigibly patriarchal," Ranjoo Seodu Herr dismantles the allied assumption that because some feminists in the Global South agree with this framing that it "is compatible with cultural pluralism, as it seems to accommodate the perspectives of women in the Global South."[45] As she points out, such accommodation is often not the interest of feminist arguments made in the name of women's rights, which might very well be invested in a characterization of Global South women who do not automatically embrace liberalism as suffering from false consciousness and internalized oppression.[46]

Bolstering this characterization was the alignment of "violence against women" as an object of knowledge and intervention with the project of development and, specifically, the couching of violence against women as a barrier to development. As Laura Hyun Yi Kang explains in regard to one illustrative document commissioned by the UN Development Fund for Women, the "assertion of a temporal lag in the proper recognition of gendered injury between *industrialized* and *developing* countries" has played upon explicitly racist and civilizationist notions of societal decay and progress.⁴⁷ Kang goes on to muse about the question of "how did and does the spectacle of the beaten, violated female body in pain complement and enliven the simultaneously proliferating ledgers of numbers, indices, percentages, and rankings" that measure social progress according to development logics?⁴⁸ In this, she crucially points to the necessary role that gendered violence against women would seem to play for precisely those projects that claim to want to eliminate it. Indeed, Dana Olwan's work suggests that the feminist conceptual formation of "domestic violence"—as a global phenomenon requiring intervention on the part of international juridical and governance entities—owes much to the identification of terrorism, such that domestic violence is conceived as akin to and even attributable to terroristic violence.⁴⁹

Insofar as the adjudication of war crimes is a key mechanism through which certain forms of military violence are authorized over and against others, this codification of sexualized gendered violence against women as an object of knowledge has come to play its own part in the sanctioning of asymmetric warfare, especially in its conceptualization as a crime against humanity; I note the serious implications of the fact that this development occurred on the eve of the global war on terror. For Rana Jaleel, the common rendering of gendered violence within the wars in Bosnia and Herzegovina in the early 1990s and in Rwanda in 1994 as the manifestation of ethnic differences/hatred—expressed in the new conceptual formation of "genocidal rape"—while driven by "an uneasy and contradictory amalgam of feminisms,"⁵⁰ resulted in the reassertion of the "reality" of the common global exposure of women to patriarchal violence. But it simultaneously gave its backing to the idea that particular regions/populations/cultures are especially prone to such violence and require the governance of humanitarian law; this is what Jaleel refers to as the "racialization of mass rape."⁵¹ Thus, the definition of rape as an atrocity crime established by the International Criminal Tribunal for the Former Yugoslavia and the International Criminal Tribunal for Rwanda—"so named as 'the most serious crimes against humankind' due to the belief that 'the acts associated with them affect the core dignity of human beings'"⁵²—became a way to reassert the predictable conflation of other-than-Western/European culture with violence against humanity writ large.

The concurrent development of interest in identifying and adjudicating so-called honor crimes as a specific form of gendered violence speaks to the long-standing and continuing invocation of the figure of the Muslim woman in Western aspirations toward defining and defending humanity. Olwan notes that the first UN resolution directly regarding honor crimes, passed in December 2001, "called on member nation-states to fulfill their obligations to international human rights treaties and to develop specific and multidimensional strategies to 'prevent and eliminate crimes against women committed in the name of honour.'"[53] While the conceptual formation of the honor crime has not cohered into a single, shared definition, and indeed reports and scholarship on this phenomenon do not necessarily refer directly to Islam, its presumptive application is very often to individuals, cultures, and societies identified as Muslim;[54] indeed, its legibility as a conceptual formation is arguably at least partly indebted to the identification of a racialized "Muslim culture" as especially violently patriarchal.[55] The distinction of gender-based violence and honor-related violence is at once specious and the horrifically logical outcome of a kind of feminist knowledge production that has been caught up in the exigencies of militarized and racialist state and international governance. As Olwan puts it, the invocation of honor-based violence in such governance policies and discourses—for example, in former US President Donald Trump's Executive Order 13769, "Protecting the Nation from Foreign Terrorist Entry into the United States"—"puts into use a 'coded' language that traffics in racial associations between certain forms of gender-based violence and terror."[56] Given Asad's argument regarding the production of the terrorist as object of knowledge, this is perhaps not surprising, but the implications of ascribing gender-based violence to "terrorist culture"/the "terrorist psyche" are serious and disturbing. In effect, it authorizes and calls for counterinsurgency violence (including against Muslim women of color) as a means to oppose gender-based violence, which effectively precludes an understanding of counterinsurgency and asymmetric warfare violence *as* in fact gender-based violence.

Looking specifically at the establishment of the International Criminal Tribunal for the Former Yugoslavia, Atanasoski also notes that feminists used this forum to quickly establish a new use of human rights frameworks to analyze sexual violence—in this case, specifically against Bosnian Muslim women—and to frame wartime gendered violence against women as a crime against humanity. However, as Atanasoski crucially argues, the capacity of the ICTY's proceedings to establish "crimes against women" as "war crimes"[57] has been predicated on a racialization of Bosnian Muslim women as white and their portrayal "as secular, modern, and European in contrast to dominant conceptions of Muslim women in the Middle East."[58] In this case, "although the Muslim woman was the hypervisible raped victim of war, as an unraced and secularized woman, she was able to stand for a universalized victim (woman) without particular religious or ethnic attachments."[59] The definition of "gendered violence" operating here is predicated on the absent presence of the figure of the Muslim woman of color, a fact that became incredibly useful in the construction of a justification for the war on terror. As Paul Amar points out, "in the year 2000, the UN Security Council passed Resolution 1325 on 'Women, Peace, and Security,' designed to assure the inclusion of women in military-humanitarian deployments and to legalize international armed interventions in response to rape, femicide, and sexual violence in situations of armed conflict, as well as in the context of peacekeeping operations.... In May 2003, UNSCR 1325 was cited in the preamble to UNSCR 1483, which authorized the US invasion of Iraq."[60] As such, the establishment of gendered violence against women as a category of crimes against humanity has itself become a predominant means of "acting on and enacting unequal sovereignties in the name of producing a common humanity."[61] This is how it could become the case that, while by the 2000s "the UN had formally acknowledged rape and other forms of sexual violence as a collective security interest,"[62] this exact form of violence as enacted by war on terror military forces would not be perceivable as such.

Not only can Muslim women in the greater Middle East/South Asia clearly not serve as archetypal victims of gendered war violence; additionally, the constitution of these women as objects of punishment is key to the conceptualization of imperial/asymmetric warfare as a project of a racially enlightened society seeking to establish justice on the broader scale of humanity. By invoking its supposed achievement of "racial pluralism to rationalize its militarism and interventionism as a technology of freedom,"[63] the United States could position itself in inaugurating the war on terror as both protector of (the right kind of) Muslims and, through the use of legitimate violence, guardian against an Islam characterized as prone to being used for anti-civilizational/anti-multicultural purposes.[64] Pressed into service as evidence of the endemic intolerance of gender equality supposedly characterizing Islam, against which the United States has positioned its own genocidal militarism as racial/gender enlightenment in the defense of humanity, these women's wounds signify the saving presence of humanitarian ethics, the global terror state's monopoly on knowledge and its concomitant capacity and right to do anything to anyone, *and* that the wounded deserved what they got.[65]

Afghanistan, "PTSDland"

As has been noted by others, the headline that accompanied the famous cover photograph of Aesha Mohammadzai on the August 9, 2010, issue of *Time* magazine—"What Happens If We Leave Afghanistan"—pointedly did not conclude with a question mark, confidently asserting a direct interpretive relation between the violence done to the young woman and the kind of response required.[66] The appearance of the tagline "Inside: Joe Klein on the Challenge in Pakistan" directly above the familiar *Time* magazine logo on that same cover serves as further indication that Mohammadzai's face was, from the beginning, made to serve as the justification for both contemporary and potential future military action in areas not confined to Afghanistan, and to facilitate an ongoing national reckoning on the question of what constitutes the moral use of military force. Indeed, Klein's piece characterized Afghanistan as a "sideshow" in comparison to the "national-security concern" posed by Pakistan,[67] and the events of the intervening span of time since those words were published certainly suggest that the details of the end of the United States' longest war to date are ancillary to the ongoing figural centrality of Muslim women to US empire. Arguably, the very intelligibility of Mohammadzai's face was predicated on and fixed by its use for the purpose of making such larger claims. Indeed, even some who expressed concerns about the *Time* article and its particular viewpoint on US foreign policy read Mohammadzai's face as indexing Afghan society's fundamental corruption. In an op-ed piece for the *Nation* magazine, Ann Jones criticized the *Time* headline and some other journalistic accounts of Mohammadzai's story for what was, in her view, the erroneous claim that the Taliban was responsible for the violence against Mohammadzai and for the major problems facing Afghanistan. Yet Jones's piece not only continued to make Mohammadzai the occasion for commentary on US military ventures, it also participated in the characterization of Afghanistan as "fundamentalist (and fundamentally misogynist)," a "fact" that she implied would not change whether or not the United States continued to occupy it.[68] This particular mode of *critique* of US militarism, in its deployment of the figure of the Muslim woman for the same purposes as the target of its critique—that is, as an object of knowledge who facilitates the author's and a wider public's own engagement with morality—stands as an example not of the misuse of humanitarian principles but of their formation and operationalization within a thoroughly militarized episteme.

Before the appearance of the *Time* piece, the story of the attack on Mohammadzai and her discovery and treatment by the US military and the organization Women for Afghan Women appeared in 2009 in the online magazine *The Daily Beast*, in an article by Gayle Tzemach Lemmon titled "An Unspeakable Crime."[69] Mohammadzai is given the pseudonym "Nadia" here. The one-sentence synopsis of the story that appears under the title positions it under the larger issue of an "epidemic" of domestic violence in Afghanistan, and the story itself begins with the viewpoint of Dr. Jeff Lewis, a US Air Force major and the head of the medical team who first treated "Nadia." Lewis's viewpoint serves as the framing conceit for the rest of the piece, and it is Lewis's own self-professed shock at seeing "Nadia" for the first time and the emotional process of surmounting that shock in order to attend to her medical needs that serves as the interpretive grounding for the young woman's own story. Lewis is quoted as saying, "'I have never seen anyone do something like this before to another person,'" and Lemmon then shares that "Nadia's injuries were among the most shocking Lewis, a veteran of two tours in Iraq, could remember seeing." That the Lewis quotation appears twice in the piece suggests that it is meant to emphasize the horrifying though culturally symptomatic nature of this young woman's violation: Mohammadzai's story, repeated many times over in a variety of outlets, is that she was forced into marriage with a member of the Taliban as a teenager, then abused by her husband and in-laws, who also inflicted the wounds for which she became famous (in retribution for an attempt she made to escape her abusers). Yet it also enforces an epistemological stance in which empirical evidence must be present and channeled through the eyes of particular individuals. According to this logic, if it has not been seen by a certain kind of witness—here, one who understands the systemic problem of domestic violence and can contextualize a particular incident within this larger framework—it does not exist as a phenomenon. Indeed, the characterization of these kinds of injuries as ranking among the "most shocking" observed by Lewis does double duty in eliding the socially sanctioned and state-sponsored violences enacted on women in the space of the United States, and rationalizing the violences committed by US forces.

Lewis's assertion might also be read as implying that people who do this to each other are not, in fact, people. The violent removal of "most of her nose and both ears" is the part of the crime against Mohammadzai that is referenced as "unspeakable," as beyond the comprehension of any person. That statement at one and the same time establishes warfare as a primary means through which the humanity of this young woman and those like her is documented and brought to the light of the world, *and* places her beyond the limits of humanity. That we do in fact know that people do this sort of thing to other people, and that some of us know that this sort of thing is done by the US military to people (including civilians, including women, including young Afghan women) is mitigated by the implication that only a nonperson would be able to make sense of such an image—if such images were even to be admitted to exist. There *is* an image that accompanies "An Unspeakable Crime," which appears at the top of the page before the text of the article, that is perhaps of the anonymous woman being discussed (although no descriptive caption accompanies it). It is blurry, pixilated. We see the figure from the side; she appears to be seated and hunched over, and her head and torso are draped and covered in a bright pink, semi-sheer cloth. In a way, it does not matter whether this is "Nadia" or someone else. What matters is the juxtaposition of this image with that of the author of the article, Gayle Tzemach Lemmon. The image of Lemmon is strictly of her face, in semi-profile and bearing a confident expression, whereas the image of the anonymous woman is all obscurity and shadows.

By the time Mohammadzai's own face appears on the cover of *Time*, the indistinct image has resolved into a very clear one, though rather than signifying the critical consciousness of authorial intent, this face is meant to index a bald empirical fact: what happens if "we leave" Afghanistan. According to that *Time* issue's feature story, Aryn Baker's "Afghan Women and the Return of the Taliban," the human rights of women would no longer be enforced because those rights were being ensured only by virtue of the United States' military presence. Imagining a post-American Afghanistan, Baker responds to plans for an appeasement of some members of the Taliban by noting that "the Taliban leadership has not yet shown any inclination to reconcile with Karzai's government. But a program to reintegrate into society so-called 10-dollar Talibs—low-level insurgents who fight for cash or over local grievances—is already in place.... Reintegrating low-level Taliban could mean that men like those who ordered and carried out Aisha's [Mohammadzai's] punishment would be eligible for the training and employment opportunities paid for by international donors—without having to account for their actions."[70] What was disturbing to Baker was not only that women would be subject to violence, but also that international aid could be used contrary to its original purposes by those who are nameless and untraceable, the anonymous "low-level Taliban," those who escape the knowledge and control of the United States as an occupying power. This worry was and is most assuredly not Baker's alone, but rather an animating feature of humanitarian warfare. In the wake of the 2021 troop withdrawal, in which Biden's declaration of the moral choice of bringing an end to a war coincided with the implementation of economic sanctions upon the Taliban's takeover, the breakdown in the reigning system for justifying global resource and wealth extractivism produced a certain anxiety: "As the country edges to the brink of collapse, the international community is scrambling to resolve a politically and legally fraught dilemma: How can it meet its humanitarian obligations without bolstering the new regime or putting money directly into the Taliban's hands?"[71] Recalling Asad's commentary on the use of torture, this anxiety can also be understood as being about the possibility that there are unknown subjects exceeding the terms of the attempted governance of discourse about Muslim-majority societies. In this context, Mohammadzai's wounded face serves as a key link in a ruthless interpretive chain, providing in a single glance immediate evidence of the terrorist's/Taliban's lack of conscience as well as of the continuing necessity of the war on terror (in its shifting forms and manifestations) as the only conscientious choice possible.

The potential for Mohammadzai's own deliberate participation in the flow of meaning enabled by the instrumentalization of her face could not be allowed, perhaps because it would interrupt her face's status as an uncomplicated sign; while others used her image and story to produce justifications for US military endeavors, her own efforts at meaning-making were pathologized. In the CNN story "Saving Aesha," journalist Jessica Ravitz makes it a point to note that Mohammadzai, despite supposedly enjoying a life of supposed safety in the United States, searched for images of other severed bodies (namely, victims of the Taliban) on the internet in what is described as a compulsive manner. The treatment of this particular activity is indicative of the portrayal of Mohammadzai in general: Her assumed failure to adapt is remarked upon over and over, such that the failure itself is paraded as an unclosed psychic wound of sorts. Countless others have looked upon images of her wounds—perhaps compulsively and/or obsessively, yet in privacy and without remark—and indeed such looking is often assumed to be a key practice in the cultivation of a humanitarian consciousness. But Mohammadzai's own looking was carefully tracked, recorded, and ultimately ascribed to mental instability, even as there was an expectation for her to articulate her own humanitarian commitments (as I will discuss in further detail below). Even Mohammadzai's relationship to her own image was scrutinized: "The organization's [Women for Afghan Women] decision to allow *Time* to photograph Aesha in 2010 was calculated and deliberate. The group wanted to influence the conversation about U.S. troop withdrawals, and Aesha was its best chance.... They acknowledged that putting her out there publicly served an initial purpose. But with all the challenges Aesha faced, they said, fame was a distraction. They rolled their eyes when noting how quickly she learned to love the spotlight.... Now, among her pastimes: She Googles herself."[72] A practice that would be taken as a sign of worldliness, self-fashioning, and responsible life management when enacted by another is quickly converted into a symptom of dangerous narcissism in reference to Mohammadzai.

The tracking of and commentary upon Mohammadzai's engagements with the discourse of the war on terror (including media featuring herself) is arguably aligned with US state surveillance practices, and in this sense produces what Sunaina Marr Maira calls "surveillance effects," or the "social and cultural registers through which surveillance becomes a part of daily life—normalized, even as it is resisted"[73] for "those who are constructed as racialized and gendered objects of permanent surveillance."[74] Maira describes the resulting "normalization of surveillance among its objects (not to mention its agents)" as having a "strategic effect,"[75] which in this case includes detracting attention away from the obsessive nature of others' portrayals of Mohammadzai, foreclosing any acknowledgment of while mitigating the disruption posed by the various forms of meaning-making and feeling she herself engages in. Ravitz's account, for example, reads as an insurmountably long list of character flaws: Mohammadzai's moods are reported to shift "impulsively"; her refusal to wear her prosthetic nose becomes an occasion for comment, and she is declared emotionally incapable of handling reconstructive surgery; her delight in acquiring sparkly shoes is ascribed to poor money-management skills. According to Ravitz, Mohammadzai was diagnosed with both post-traumatic stress disorder and borderline personality disorder, and while she notes that the latter has an unclear etiology, she also claims that it is what is responsible for Mohammadzai's "volatile behavior and black-and-white thinking."[76] Mohammadzai's diagnoses are not seen as a facet of her experience to be handled with any care, much less considered as meaningful adaptations to a world full of violence; rather, they are cavalierly instrumentalized for what are at best ethically dubious interpretive purposes. The invocation of Mohammadzai's diagnoses suggests that the answer to "what happens if we leave Afghanistan" is overdetermined from the beginning: The cycle of traumatic injury and action will repeat without interruption, and the natural tendencies of the

Afghan psyche will, in the absence of reconditioning, be allowed to express themselves. In retrospect, from the vantage point of the current moment, this reads not just as an argument to continue occupation but also as the preemptive self-absolution of the occupier—a pinning of the violences wrought on Afghanistan onto Afghans themselves and, in particular, their failure to concede to "social engineering"[77] efforts—such that the US leaving simply becomes another expression of Afghan society's intransigence.

Mimi Thi Nguyen's critical analysis of "the refugee condition as an object of biomedical study"[78] illuminates the longer history of such territorialization of racist/imperialist military violence onto the pathologized individual psyche, where the psychic wound becomes evidence of the racialized subject's natural vulnerability to breakdown and of the idea that the United States has something to offer (freedom, healing, safety) those people made refugees by its own wars. Looking more specifically at the figure of the refugee in the wake of the US war in Vietnam, Nguyen notes that within social and health science discourses, "it is not difficult to find statements imputing to the refugee the underdevelopment, or arrested development, of apperception, understanding, and reason,"[79] and the failure of "self-possession"[80] in the form of the loss of motive will and a learned helplessness. A similar use of the framework of "trauma as a form of biomedicine implicated in liberal structures of power"[81] is apparent in renderings of an Afghan society that, it is implied, has been fated to move inexorably toward its current state. In her article "PTSDland," Anna Badkhen invokes Mohammadzai as "the face of Afghanistan's spousal abuse,"[82] and poses the rhetorical question: "What happens when physical and emotional battlefields converge in a land whose people have been eking out an existence amid unending violence for generations? In such war-wrecked countries, the trademark symptoms of individual war trauma—depression, anguish, and hyper-aggression—leave whole populations envenomed with sectarian and ethnic mistrust, and with the certainty that only violence can end violence."[83] Being "war-wrecked" is implied to have become a sort of deep-seated characteristic of Afghanistan's people. The ideological understanding of violence being forwarded here—couched in the terms of medical and social science—is that it is a mental pathology, an essential feature of the occupied society. This, of course, might also be seen to imply that Afghanistan and its people draw violence upon themselves, and that violence is simply the natural response to those who appear violable. Badkhen's invocation of mistrust, as the inability and/or unwillingness to recognize and have confidence in others' humanity, infers an atavistic fear of cultural/racial difference. Locating the origin of such mistrust of religious and ethnic others within those who are commonly made to serve as the material evidence of difference itself reinforces the notion of US exceptionalism and its supposed regard for difference in the form of secularism and multiculturalism, which is also a key way in which violence committed in the name of the US state is washed of its racism and projected onto those who are characterized as living outside of "the frame of historical progress."[84]

Characterized as PTSDland, Afghanistan is imagined as culpable for its own breakdown; trauma becomes a feature of the country rooted in its very being and expressed in the unclosed wounds borne by those broken individuals who inhabit it. In speculating on what work is done by this characterization of the whole nation of Afghanistan as suffering from a psychological pathology, we might consider the numerous failures of the US occupation and indeed the failure that the troop withdrawal has represented to many. Raising concerns about the way human rights projects have used trauma as an analytic apparatus for theorizing violence, Wendy Hesford notes that "the U.S. occupation of Iraq has been viewed by some commentators and critics as traumatic repetition or, more specifically, the compulsive repetition of trauma as retribution: the United States, a nation traumatized by 9/11, invades and occupies another terrorized country (in this case, a country terrorized by Saddam Hussein). Paradoxically, trauma, which is most often represented as a break in narrative coherence, becomes history's metanarrative."[85] As historical metanarrative, trauma explains violence in essentialist terms, as a sort of self-perpetuating force beyond the reach of rationality and responsibility. Describing the US Centers for Disease Control and Prevention effort to study the effects of trauma on Afghan civilians—an effort that, I would note, coincided directly with US military presence there—Badkhen poses the question, "how does one help heal a country that has been forged in millennia of almost incessant conflict? There is no such thing as a Marshall Plan for the mind."[86] She thus suspends any acknowledgment of actual US military presence in order to focus on the individual pathology of the very targets of military violence, effectively portraying Afghan society as incapable of being helped. Jessica Ravitz expresses a similar sentiment when she states that "mental health isn't even a field of medicine where Aesha comes from."[87] Afghanistan thus becomes the object of study for the production of mental health knowledge, which, insofar as the US military and state are culpable for the trauma under study, can be understood as another expression of the meaning-making functions of counterinsurgency tactics like torture:

The US military invades and occupies, producing trauma in the occupied people, a psychological experience that is then studied to produce evidence of traumatizability. The reporting of Mohammadzai's response to the killing of Osama bin Laden—purported to be happiness, which is asserted given the fact that Mohammadzai stated "'Osama bin Laden crazy'"[88]—serves to posit killing as the prerequisite to healing, while also (with the diagnosis of bin Laden's "craziness") implying that mental illness makes one torturable and/or killable.

The moralizing discourse that surrounded Mohammadzai cruelly posited her behavior and her expressed understanding of her own experience as exceeding what would be considered a proper response given the nature of her life circumstances after coming to the United States. The implication at the time that she was unnaturally slow and potentially unable to heal from and live her life beyond trauma insistently located that trauma as properly in the past, foreclosing not only on the ongoing life that grief and loss tends to take on (indeed that is a basic feature of trauma) but also on any analysis of life within the bounds of the United States as itself potentially involving terroristic violence. And yet Mohammadzai seemed to become much less useful when the possibility of her being "saved"—or just choosing to lead a private life, or perhaps experiencing a range of emotions including happiness—became real. Putting the lie to the countless stories that claimed to be interested in her well-being but could not seem to stop making a case for its impossibility, the mass media coverage ends around the time when she began the grueling process of the surgical reconstruction of her nose (a process that, I would note, involves acts of fleshly alteration not as distinct from the original wounding as it might at first appear). The most recent substantial piece focused on Mohammadzai that I could find, from 2014, is a brief video about her nose reconstruction in a series titled "Patients of Courage" produced by the American Society of Plastic Surgeons (ASPS).[89] Interestingly, in revealing that Mohammadzai's reconstructive surgery was an intense, multistage process that took years to complete once initiated, the video reveals a quite different story about Mohammadzai's experience and capacities than that given in many other contemporaneous accounts. At the same time, the video also does not counter the expectation that the trauma survivor undergo a rehabilitative process.

As explained in the video, Mohammadzai was named a 2014 Patient of Courage by the ASPS "for her miraculous emotional and physical transformation." The video opens with still images of Mohammadzai's face and wounds, with her adoptive parent Mati Arsala explaining a bit about

Mohammadzai's backstory in voice-over. We also hear from her plastic surgeon, Lieutenant Colonel Kerry P. Latham of the Walter Reed National Military Medical Center, who speaks about why she nominated Mohammadzai for the award: "I haven't seen anyone change so dramatically in the two years that I've known her, not just physically . . . but emotionally, her outlook on life, her dedication to helping others. We felt a unique connection to her because all of us have been deployed to Afghanistan and could relay to her that we are familiar with her home country. And that made an immediate connection." We also hear, quite briefly, from Mohammadzai herself, who shares, "I want to learn more English. I want to show to other people, all people that women, girls are as strong as a man," after which Arsala, who is sitting next to her, expresses a desire to see countries in "that part of the world" embrace women as full community members. I want to be clear that, rather than scrutinizing the individual intent behind these expressions, I am asking after what work the video as a whole is doing within the larger context of the humanitarian warfare mediascape. I note the positioning of Mohammadzai as having a commitment to societal improvement, to humanitarianism, as a reason for being named a Patient of Courage but also for why her surgery matters. I can imagine many reasons to feel the desire/need to undergo the no doubt painful and in some ways dangerous process of reconstructive surgery on one's face, but those are obscured (and, frankly, never even acknowledged to exist) by the narrative framing of the surgery itself as an object about which to make some kind of larger meaning.

I also note Latham's expression of the idea that intimacy can happen under conditions of warfare, indeed that military occupation is a form of intimacy. I do not think Latham is wrong, which is precisely what I find to be so disturbing, because this is exactly how violence becomes humanitarian. The intimacy that the occupier imposes—an intimacy forged through surveillance, the most violent of epistemic practices, bodies coming into contact by way of rending and destroying, and weaponized care—is, via the repeated invocation of Afghan society as defined by the impossibility of appropriate, healthy, and nonviolent gendered relationships, made into an expression of connection. Mohammadzai's own particular experience of abuse and pain is, in essence, made to disappear, sublimated in favor of a narrative about Afghan society. We can see this disappearance as part of a larger pattern in which "Afghan Americans are invisibilized in the public sphere, including as U.S. imperial subjects" and "erased by a dominant discourse of humanitarianism that is deeply racialized."[90] Mohammadzai's face can be said to serve as the cathexis point for a variety of displaced beliefs and feelings, ones that are not mutually exclusive after all: the fate that Afghan men themselves are thought to deserve; the metonym for what "life behind the veil" is understood to be like; the oblique threat to support a white-ascendant/Western form of feminism unless you want this to happen to you, too; or the lesson undoubtedly taught to countless women by the US military itself, a fact that cannot be admitted too explicitly without risking the collapse of the logic of liberation through military intervention, but the effects of which can—and indeed must—still circulate in this other form.

Saving Face: Pakistan and the Law

In her brief piece on Sharmeen Obaid-Chinoy (co-director of *Saving Face*) for *Time* magazine's feature "The World's 100 Most Influential People: 2012," Angelina Jolie characterizes the Oscar-winning filmmaker as the conduit between "towns and villages in Pakistan" and "the world stage," facilitating an alignment between Pakistani women's everyday experiences, juridical expressions of Pakistani state authority, and the larger human world: "*Saving Face* depicts a Pakistan that is changing—one where ordinary people can stand up and make a difference and where marginalized communities can seek justice," writes Jolie, invoking the same understanding of what constitutes a progressive society that has been deployed by the United States to justify its own imperial authority and to describe the societies it is ostensibly attempting to craft through the means of the war on terror.[91] Jolie concludes with the injunction "I dare anyone to watch this film and not be moved to tears and inspired into action," thus prescribing a highly ritualized proper set of responses: the immediate, visceral response to the images of these women, and the emotional and intellectual response to the social conditions that led to their being harmed. As it gestures toward an implicitly natural instinct to turn away, it also predicates the capacity for humanitarian feeling and action on the cultivation of a psychological willpower that can overcome that initial reaction in the service of a commitment to a larger humanity. Any other response is, by default, inhuman (which, to be certain, is the suggestion made by the film about those who are defined as the perpetrators of the violence on display); "anyone" who watches and is not moved in the prescribed ways is implicitly not "anyone." It also denies other possible and perhaps likely responses, precisely those that cannot be admitted to under the auspices of a humanitarian mission: disinterest, gratification, schadenfreude, morbid curiosity, or resentful evaluation. Yet while tears and action are explicitly invited by the film itself, *Saving Face* arguably also appeals to and offers abundant means of experiencing these other sensibilities and emotions.

Jolie's characterization of Obaid-Chinoy was both prescient and performative, as in the ensuing decade her prolific documentary and journalistic work, largely focused on women's experiences of gendered violence in Pakistan, Afghanistan, and Canada, has continued to earn praise. This kind of portrayal of Obaid-Chinoy serves its own pedagogical function, instructing in what are implied to be the correct ways to engage with, feel in response to, and make meaning about her work. Both Obaid-Chinoy herself and writings about her frequently align her work with the law, assuming a clear and straightforward relationship between the project of bringing various forms of gendered violence to light and the project of bringing the powers of state recognition and punishment to bear on the problem of women's inequality. Named one of the 2012 "Women of the Year" by *Glamour*, Obaid-Chinoy is credited with fomenting the development of legal measures to address acid violence: "Thanks in large part to the film [*Saving Face*], perpetrators in Pakistan's largest province are now subject to much harsher punishment, and acid violence is classified as what it is: a form of terrorism."[92] A viewer's guide included with the DVD version of *Saving Face* frames the film as an occasion to learn about the realities of acid violence as a "worldwide human rights violation"[93] and to cultivate the skills and moral orientation of a women's human rights advocate. The section "Combating Acid Violence as a Crime" calls for laws "that adequately punish perpetrators of attacks and limit the easy availability of acid"[94] and specifically lists key documents and events in the post–World War II establishment of an international human rights legal and moral order. Not surprisingly, the phenomenon of acid violence is attributed to "weak rule of law, political corruption, cultural inequalities between genders and the availability of acids, such as Nitric or Sulphuric Acid used in manufacturing and processing cotton and rubber,"[95] appealing to widely circulating common knowledge about the places where acid violence is posited as most likely to happen (the greater Middle East, South Asia, and Southeast Asia) while also obliquely referencing a global extractivist economic order as the unquestioned state of things.[96]

I am interested in how this invocation of jurisprudence as a mechanism for both diagnosing the problem of gendered violence as patriarchal abuse at the site of the family, and remedying such violence through the restoration of women's voices (through the restoration of their faces), comes to bear on the geopolitical positioning of Pakistan in particular. The hunting down and killing of Osama bin Laden in Pakistan in 2011, the same year as the film's release, perhaps adds a particular symbolic weight to its documenting of the passage of the Acid Control and Acid Crime Prevention Act (also in 2011), coded as offering a pathway for Pakistani women to participate in the development of a global humanitarian consciousness and system of governance precisely through the identification of Pakistani men as proper objects of punishment. Saadia Toor offers an incisive critique of this phenomenon, particularly as the "very real gendered racial project at the heart of the War on Terror" is lent further support by "a new front of international feminists and human rights advocates [which] has emerged to challenge what they see as the international human rights community's inordinate focus on Muslim *men* as victims."[97] The characterization of Pakistan in the US news media as on its way toward, but as not yet having been able to throw off so-called radical Muslim elements highlights Pakistan's simultaneous proximity to and distinction from Afghanistan within the formation of Af-Pak. As with the coverage of Mohammadzai, *Saving Face* sutures individual women's worthiness to the nation-state's particular characteristics, flaws, and/or progress. In depicting acid violence as unjust violence born of backward cultural precepts, such legislation serves as evidence of both Pakistan's progress and Islam's atavism at the same time. And Pakistan as a law-governed nation-state is, likewise, established as simultaneously distinct from Afghanistan and incapable of asserting control over external and internal elements of cultural/political degradation on its own. There is also a complicity and at times indistinction between Pakistani state, "anti-state local security institutions" (or ASLSIS, like the Taliban),[98] and US military interests at work here, as Bina D'Costa points out in her examination of the public and political response to instances of ASLSIS' punishment of women. This is exemplified by a 2009 agreement made by the Pakistani government with the Taliban that allowed the latter to apply and enforce faith-based law in the northwestern region of Pakistan in return for peace; this agreement was, furthermore, backed by the United States "as an attempt to create a division between the Pakistani Taliban and the Al Qaeda-linked Taliban."[99] The point is that each of these actors, in their own way, position themselves as simultaneously saviors and punishers of women in their maneuvering for power, influence, and control with and against each other.

As Obaid-Chinoy has, since *Saving Face*, continued her work in a similar vein, more recently in regard to the phenomenon of honor killing[100]— winning another Academy Award for her 2015 documentary on this issue, *A*

Girl in the River: The Price of Forgiveness—these linear narratives of women who are wronged but may be granted the ability to move on through corrective state force are complicated and exceeded by their very reliance on examples of women who are imputed to be partially to blame for the violence done to them and, as such, come to serve as objects of punishment. *Saving Face* largely focuses on the experiences of two women, Zakia and Rukhsana, who are positioned as foils to each other. Zakia is portrayed as the clear success story, and she is the very first individual who appears in the film, which also ends with her, while Rukhsana is portrayed as remaining stuck, moving largely in ways that return her, both physically and emotionally, again and again to the scene of the crime. The narrative arc of Zakia's success maps her bid to prosecute her husband under the newly minted Acid Control and Acid Crime Prevention Act onto her willingness to pursue risky surgery and her embrace of a facial prosthesis, which is portrayed as allowing her to inhabit public spaces without covering her face. Like the texts on Mohammadzai, *Saving Face* also appeals to and draws from a very common set of understandings of gender roles and patriarchal violence—which are then presumed to require a very particular kind of response, spearheaded by human rights organizations working to implement human rights laws. Recognized and identified by these laws, the exemplary victim of violence is granted rights, but only with concomitant duties: She becomes responsible for her own healing and redemption. Likewise, the transformation of her face to make her engagement in the public sphere possible and acceptable is taken as both evidence of, and as helping to form, a healthy psyche and an understanding of her proper place within humanity. This is Zakia's story, as it is presented in the film, just as Rukhsana's story is presented as a brutalist rendering of the logic of faciality. For the deviations of Zakia's face to be intelligible, Rukhsana's cannot be. Rukhsana's face, in its failure to pass, is arguably transmuted just as much by the film as by the events that the film wants to document— from a feature of her own individual person (however *she* might define that) into a conduit for what I take to be a broader social judgment that some of the wronged deserve what they have gotten after all.

The framing device that sets the film's narrative into motion is the story of Dr. Mohammad Jawad, a London-based cosmetic surgeon who, as he tells it, has felt compelled to return to Pakistan after learning about what he calls "the violence in my homeland." We learn about Zakia's and Rukhsana's stories at his clinic, and their periodic visits for follow-up treatments serve as anchor points in the telling of their personal journeys—Zakia toward a self-described "new life," Rukhsana toward a continued daily existence with her abusive family by marriage and a surgery postponed due to pregnancy. Jawad is clearly meant to serve as a moral and political compass for the viewer and for the subjects of the film themselves, as he offers commentary on the situation in Pakistan to the camera, and encouragement and/or admonition to his patients. Toward the end of the film, he remarks, "In a way, I'm seeing my own face. Because I'm part of this society, and we share this disease. And I am doing my bit, but there is only so much I can do. Come and join the party." What this statement reveals is that, despite the explicit valuing of Zakia's story, Rukhsana's is also necessary to the humanitarian discourses that this film participates in and draws meaning from. Jawad needs the injured faces of these women to have access to his own "face"—his beliefs and precepts, his role in the larger social order, and his ethical orientation—and, by extension, so do the film's viewers in order to partake in humanitarian work themselves.

This invitation to "join the party" is set over and against figures who symbolize the inability and/or unwillingness to do so. Notable in this regard is Rukhsana's husband Yasir who, second to Jawad, gets the most on-screen time of any man in this film. The filmmakers ask Yasir whether he has ever abused Rukhsana, perhaps as a gesture toward documentary integrity and fairness, given that Rukhsana offers her own full account of having been attacked by her husband and sister-in-law with acid, then doused with gasoline and lit on fire. Yasir denies her account, suggesting (according to the English translation) that "one day she lost her mind and threw gasoline on herself." He further claims that in the hospital burn unit "99 percent of the women there have burned themselves alive." The viewer is clearly meant to approach this claim with profound skepticism, as is indicated by several close-up shots of burn marks on his hand, which he explains as being the result of trying to put out the fire that injured Rukhsana. Indeed, the statements themselves are, in the context of the film, meant to sound absurd. But read counter to how it is meant to be, this scene also conveys what is arguably the deeper logic of the film: The proof that must be rendered is that these women are worthy subjects, that they have not lost their minds, that they did not harm themselves, and that fault can be ascribed clearly and appropriately. Like other such texts, the attempt to provide evidence of these women's inner psychological states relies on establishing a bar for ethical conditioning and worthiness, one that some will inevitably fail to achieve—thus throwing that evidence into question, making its provision in and of itself a never-ending process.

Zakia's portrayed demeanor is one of quiet self-possession. She expresses the emotional and physical pain resulting from the violence done to her, but also confidence that the legal path she has chosen to follow (the prosecution of her husband under the new acid crime legislation) is the right one. On the other hand, composure appears to escape Rukhsana. She cries often, her voice constantly breaking into different registers, her descriptions of what has happened to her filled with anger, terror, grief, and a profound sense that there is little hope for things to change—she wants out of her life, but does not have the means to leave, and she does not pretend otherwise. Showing her raw edges and frayed nerves, Rukhsana makes it impossible to ignore the sheer complexity of her life and the irreparability of her injuries, thus in her own way rupturing the film's narrative movement toward resolution. While Zakia is shown in motion and engaging in the work of daily life (cooking, interacting with her children, engaging in various household tasks, walking in public), Rukhsana is largely not, suggesting that she is in stasis, emotionally, physically, and materially—even though it is also entirely possible to see her as engaged in an active process of contending with her experience, one that furthermore does not preclude a certain kind of moving on, as we will see later in the film. In a remarkable scene, she shows the filmmakers the room she has been relegated to in the family home; as the camera surveys the space, she explains, "This is where they burned me alive. My life was destroyed in this room." As we learn in a later scene set in the same space, the room has been sealed off from the rest of the family dwelling, according to Rukhsana, who is clearly in emotional agony as she explains that this has been her husband's and mother-in-law's way of keeping her from her own daughter. We have a sense of how excruciating this is given that, earlier in the film, Rukhsana had explained that she moved out for a period of time, but felt compelled to move back in and "make up" with her abusers. While Zakia is portrayed as having achieved a kind of psychological healing as manifested by her criminal complaint against her husband, and thus as able to function within the broader social institutions and modes of daily life that she inhabited before her experience of trauma, that Rukhsana keeps revisiting the site of her injury, both psychologically/emotionally and quite literally, is taken to indicate that she is not (yet) as capable of rehabilitation.

It seems telling that the occasion on which Rukhsana appears the most hopeful, the discovery that she is pregnant, is also an occasion for expressions of social sanctioning and reprimand by both Jawad and another medical professional. With incredulity and disdain, the latter asks her why she did not use birth control, in essence making her responsible for the abuse and its effects: "Don't you realize what happened to you could happen to your child as well?" It is difficult to think of a more cruel thing to say to her, yet the film plays it straight, letting it stand without comment. Later, Rukhsana herself explains, "My new baby will bring happiness back to me. I hope I have a boy, because a girl's future gets risky after marriage. I wouldn't want my daughter to face the same fate as me. In our society boys live well. Girls are often unhappy." Meant to indicate just how distorted her view of herself has supposedly become under the force of oppression—there is the strong implication in those admonitions that she does not understand just how terrible the abuse she has been made to endure has been, even as she seems to offer up direct evidence of pervasive gender inequality—her pregnancy is also portrayed as hindering her general progress because she must now wait until she has had her child before she can undergo facial surgery. There appears no space allowed in the film for Rukhsana's own view to stand unquestioned and unevaluated, despite her multiple expressions of great clarity about exactly what happened to her and why, and the choices available to her to contend with it. Indeed, *Saving Face* ends up, in spite of itself, revealing exactly what Rukhsana needs—economic and material support that she does not have to rely on others for—while willfully ignoring this fact by pathologizing her and quite literally creating the conditions for her punishment. In this sense, it is hard not to see the film as an alibi for the extractivist global economic system that relies on the reproduction of intensified inequalities along the lines of the gender binary.[101]

Early in *Saving Face*, Zakia declares, "I cannot bear people staring at my face," right before donning full face and head covering to walk in public. At the end of the film, after she has had her surgery and been fitted with a prosthesis, she is shown walking down the street, her face uncovered, while commenting on how much she has changed since the attack and how she is ready for her "new life." Meanwhile, we never see Rukhsana's face transformed. The last we see of her, she has just given birth and is informed she will need to wait six months for her surgery. Referencing the long-standing ideology that Muslim women's liberation can only be achieved via an emergence from facial invisibility and into faciality, the wounded face (and what it supposedly represents, i.e., a cultural tradition of patriarchal violence) is meant to be understood as the last barrier to these women's participation in civil society and a global human community. Here, it is perhaps no longer precisely the putatively face-obscuring veil that is presented as the problem, but the attempt of desperate reactionary men to cling to some semblance of control in a new world order where the project of women's empowerment is steadily prevailing. In a telling scene that is situated right in the middle of the film, amid Zakia's clear beginning-to-end trajectory, and which seems to further emphasize the portrayal of Rukhsana as being caught between competing forces, several women address a forum of supporters of the new acid crime legislation. Rukhsana herself speaks here, and states (according to the English translation), "even our own people do not recognize us anymore. This is such an injustice to us. Someone must stop these brutal people who made us into the living dead." Rukhsana's characterization of herself as a member of the "living dead" speaks all too clearly to the role of the unredeemed victim in the envisioning of a humanitarian world order; the living dead are relegated to permanent residence in a border zone where no movement is possible, a space of liminality that defines others' progress. In the context of the film's ideological framework, Rukhsana's comment appears to provide evidence that circumscribed forms of legal and social recognition are a requirement for having a life worth living, thus overriding other potential readings of her statement: Perhaps her own understanding of recognition is different from that which is codified in the very law to which her statement seems to appeal. Here and elsewhere, *Saving Face* approaches the topic of the law in a manifestly didactic way, staging a consideration and rejection of other potential methods for addressing the problem of acid violence. At several points in the film, different individuals propose a community-based reckoning with such crimes, in which the perpetrators would face the publicly meted-out justice of having acid thrown on them. As one man puts it, "if Islam permits it, why don't we use such punishment?" These suggestions are then characterized as impossible and ultimately unnecessary, thus implicitly positioning Islam and the law as opposed, a characterization that the film evidences by following the process through which the new acid crime law comes into being (the first person to be prosecuted under which is Zakia's husband). Whereas Zakia's emotions are portrayed as achieving coherence through their evolution beyond negativity as a result of her successful use of the law, Rukhsana's terror, pain, irreconcilable anger, *and* hope for a better life for her children remain raw and untempered and sit uncomfortably alongside each other (inappropriately so, as suggested by the film).

Ultimately, the film's viewers are invited to position themselves as Jawad does and as the filmmakers do: as outside of and unimplicated in the violence whose aftermath they are witnessing, and thus as those to whom such violence would never happen because they/we are ostensibly equipped to see it. The implication, of course, is that Zakia and Rukhsana were abused in part *because* they were not so equipped. The prioritizing of the face as the locus of what Spivak calls "voice-consciousness"[102]—the (supposedly) authentic expression of one's self-defined needs and interests—in liberal secularist models of human community sets the ethical and political standards according to which these women are judged, standards that they are held to most stringently and which some have always already failed. What is being demanded of these women in order to be intelligible social subjects is a pure communication of their individual freedom and agency, uncontaminated by the strictures of religion, society, or ideology. As we have seen in the cases of Rukhsana and Zakia, not only are some implicitly rendered as lacking such a consciousness to express, but the representation of those who are deemed so capable is often in the service of ventriloquizing an absent authority's own sovereign subjectivity (here, perhaps the law, the Pakistani state, and/or the US military), as indeed Spivak has pointed out in her still all-too-relevant critique of gestures toward "allowing" the oppressed subject to speak her own truth (a trope and a call to action that is, devastatingly, still in heavy circulation more than thirty-five years after "Can the Subaltern Speak?" was first published).[103] In this sense, these women are not exceptional, but rather are like many others who have struggled to have their faces identified as such despite possessing all of the requisite parts and forms: those people whose features have been subject to "scientific" measurement and deemed to fail the test of full humanity; those who dare to look back or away, who refuse to engage in normatively appropriate forms of looking; or those whose faces are not available for public gazing.

Instrumentalizing Resentment

The mediatization of Aesha Mohammadzai's, Zakia's, and Rukhsana's experiences exemplifies the exceedingly difficult demands made of the Muslim woman of color subject: She must at once index the irreparable and exceptional harm of Muslim patriarchy, and fulfill the promise of healing proffered by humanitarian law and order. She must support the appropriate use of the law as the only appropriate punisher of the perpetrator, and by way of this form of punishment she must see her way clear to a new life, a better future, forgiveness. This kind of mandate for victims of systematized violence to forgive and move on is a pervasive feature not just of popular humanitarian discourses, but also of formalized humanitarian processes of post-violence reconciliation, one that Thomas Brudholm's illuminating analysis of South Africa's Truth and Reconciliation Commission suggests needs to be seriously questioned: "Victims who cannot or will not abide with the call to forgive and reconcile are often pictured as 'prisoners of the past': traumatized, self-preoccupied, resentful, and vindictive. To be able to forgive or forget is generally taken to be morally and therapeutically superior to harboring resentment and other 'negative' emotions."[104] The characterization of resentment as unhealthy and even immoral when experienced and expressed by the victim surely serves several purposes: obscuring and facilitating the humanitarian's/military's own use of resentment to make them appear as the insulted party who deserves justice; characterizing the target of violence as having brought that violence on herself; and dismissing anticolonial and anti-racist movements as violent, intolerant disruptors of the social order. Any resentment such victims themselves may feel or express must be elided, attributed to individual deficiencies, and/or punished if it is not to disrupt the process through which the humanitarian's capacity for understanding and assessing the proper uses of violence can be cultivated. The victim's forgiveness is necessary because its withholding implicates the humanitarian subject herself in the violence, the experiences, and indeed the ontology that are ostensibly what distinguish the victim as such. As Mimi Thi Nguyen puts it, "an insistence on speaking as if the trespasses of the past are *still present*, which may include a desire for political agitation or retributive justice, precludes the victim and others whom he or she touches—those who shudder—from inhabiting history proper. Inassimilable and self-destructive, feelings such as anger or bitterness hence are equated with captivity, anachronism, and bondage."[105] To allow for resentment would, then, indict the very notion of humanity's teleological movement from primitivity to civilization that militarized humanitarianism promises to provide.

In one of her more recent films, the 2015 documentary *A Girl in the River: The Price of Forgiveness*, Obaid-Chinoy returns to the themes explored in *Saving Face*, in many ways replicating its form and argument while also interestingly raising—as I read it, unintentionally—a complex set of questions about what the law demands of those it claims to help and, conversely, how the demand for forgiveness exposes the constitutive violence of the sociopolitical order that the law takes as its mission to consolidate. Ultimately, in treating the specific form of forgiveness referenced in the title of the film as a barrier to the achievement of women's human rights, the film elides its own investment in demanding a certain kind of forgiveness on the part of the victim. Focusing this time on the phenomenon it identifies as honor killing, *A Girl in the River* features a young woman named Saba, whose father and uncle attempted to murder her and then left her for dead in a river following her elopement with her now-husband, whom they did not approve of her marrying. The narrative arc follows the hunt for Saba's father and uncle, their capture and imprisonment, and the question of whether and how justice will be served given what is revealed to have been a feature of Pakistani law at the time: the potential for the acquittal of someone charged with honor killing upon a formal declaration of forgiveness given by the victim or one of her family members.[106] As in *Saving Face*, we once again learn of the status of Pakistani law when it comes to gender violence crimes rendered as culturally specific and exceptionally heinous, hear from experts (a lawyer and a criminal investigator) about why the law needs to be changed for the sake of women's rights, and are given insight into the various differing views of members of Pakistani society about Islam, the law, and gender roles.[107] As it happens, Saba was shot in the face during her attempted murder, and when we first see Saba she is lying down on an exam table surrounded by medical professionals; we are then shown graphic images of her face (displayed on her doctor's phone) from shortly after being shot, with the doctor explaining that the wound "made it almost impossible to recognize anything." Yet unlike in *Saving Face*, being a good subject of women's rights law does not guarantee justice. The restoration of Saba's face as well as her faciality are demonstrated through her portrayal as having a strong, clear, and advanced view of what justice and healing look like: Initially she wishes for her father and uncle to never be released from prison, and in her words, "the world should see this— brothers, sisters, parents, uncles, and aunts. So this doesn't happen again." But she is in some ways blocked from moving on due to what are portrayed as the failures of the culture and the state of the law. Ultimately, after a council of neighborhood elders recommends that the two families come to a compromise and end the conflict with each other, Saba decides to make the official declaration of forgiveness that frees her father and uncle. Saba's lawyer, Asad Jamal, explains that he can understand her decision to do so as the most protective one for her, which he attributes to the fact that "our justice system is not strong enough to provide her security," and indeed Saba confirms later on, "Everyone knows that I forgave them for society's sake. . . . But in my heart, they are unforgiven."

However, there is some ambivalence around forgiveness here, much more than I think the film intends. The viewpoint that the audience seems meant to take on is that Saba's offer of forgiveness represents the backwardness of the legal system at that point; thus, insofar as *A Girl in the River* argues that tolerance, progress, and equality can be achieved through the proper advancement of the law, it can only do so by evading a deeper inquiry into the orienting of emotion and thought in the aftermath of violence that juridical processes of establishing justice always demand. If Saba's resentment of her father, uncle, and the legal system is allowed within the terms of the narrative and even to some extent drives it, it is because it is instrumentalized toward the project of juridical progress. Still, even as the fact that legal, rehabilitative, and reconciliatory processes require concessions on the part of the victim is elided by the framing narrative, it comes out in other ways, most especially in Saba's own complex rendering of her experience and her negotiation of the limited range of choices before her.[108]

For such instrumentalized figures of wrong, the price of forgiveness is, I would argue, to serve as evidence of the need for the gender norms that human rights discourses and humanitarian projects themselves often presume and impose—and sometimes, too, of their own incapacity to adhere to these norms. Either way, their experiences of violence are posited as necessary events in the constitution of a global humanity founded in an enlightened recognition of women's human rights, even as the discourse surrounding them manufactures and plays out an anxiety about whether certain women can or should themselves be rehabilitated into humanity. In this, they are expected to take on the impossible labor of reconciling a globe-spanning definition of womanhood with the need of that definition for a constitutive outside in the form of infinitely violable subjects. This is how the Muslim woman domestic abuse victim does double duty, as to-be-saved and to-be-punished at one and the same time, joining the work of humanitarian law and counterinsurgency together. The right kind of victim is law-abiding and clearly not culpable for the violence done to her or the hardship she faces, but even the right kind of victim is seen as ultimately unreliable, defined by her lack of agency and damaged state. She is thus an unstable figure to pin the securitizing hopes of a humanitarian international order upon: In short, she makes it difficult to convert absences into signs. It is thus not much of a stretch for the victim of violence to also be seen as the appropriate target of counterinsurgency, made into the ground for the attempted solidification of the knowledge project of the war on terror.

To close this chapter, I turn toward the case of Noor Salman as a paradigmatic figure of the violent contradictions that implicate certain framings of gendered violence with asymmetric warfare. Salman was married to Omar Mateen, who murdered forty-nine people at the Pulse nightclub in 2016; she was charged with terrorism for allegedly aiding Mateen in planning the attack as well as with obstructing justice, and was acquitted of both by a unanimous jury in 2018. To succeed, the prosecution would have needed to show not just that Salman knew about Mateen's plan, but that she had also actively aided in it; ultimately, it could do neither.[109] I am interested in this case not from a legal perspective but because of the way that discourses of US empire, racialized Islamophobia, the psychology of abuse, and gendered violence collided in the figure of Salman, who was ultimately rendered as unreliable not just as accused perpetrator of violence but also as known victim of violence. What led to Salman being viewed as a suspect and charged is surely a complex matter, but I do not think it is a stretch to imagine that the narration of Mateen's crime within the frame of US sexual exceptionalism potentially played a role here.[110] Given her presumed identity and relationship status, she could easily be slotted into the role of figuring the prejudice that US society has putatively advanced beyond and now has a duty to guard against. The fact that she had experienced abuse at the hands of Mateen is perhaps what (barely) saved her, but even then, the orientation toward the domestic abuse victim who has not left her abuser permanently is very often one of suspicion—a suspicion that, in Salman's case, was enhanced and juridically formalized by the positioning of Islam as a threat to the US state and culture. What are the ethical implications of the fact that a readily available feminist argument used in support of Salman was that "a woman living in a relationship defined by coercive control that is enforced through the threat of violence cannot realistically be held to the same standard of criminal liability as a person whose life is characterized by free choice," as argued by two domestic abuse victim advocates in advance of Salman's trial?[111] Demonstrating a constitutive problem that defines the framework of women's rights as human rights, it appears that Salman could only be seen as being on the right side of the law and of humanitarian civilization if she was rendered as having little or no agency and as herself ignorant, that is, ultimately lacking in the knowledge of Islam's supposed propensity for moral corruption.

While I have often witnessed victim-blaming being characterized as born of ignorance of the existence of gender inequality, I would suggest that the reality of it is dirtier and messier, more tangled up in the vicissitudes of emotional reckoning, than could be addressed by having more knowledge: Victim-blaming serves a function, which is to preserve the terms of the sociopolitical order as they already exist. Another way to put this is that it seems that it is easier to complete the destruction of the victim—to make of her refusal to forgive a dysfunction that must be eradicated—than to rupture the romance of community or to reckon with the kinds of losses that are not recoverable, the breaks that cannot ever be fixed. It is this difficult truth that those of us doing feminist work must address if we are to contend with how imperial forever war conditions our very relationality, and thus if we are to have any chance of bringing an end to warfare as the very state of human being.

4

Documentation as Eradication

THE AMAZON'S "UNCONTACTED TRIBES" AND THE
SECURITIZING OF HUMANITY

> Perhaps the indifferent native never has to say no. Perhaps the indifferent native simply wanders off.
>
> —Keguro Macharia, "On Being Area-Studied"

Battlefield Amazon

Midway through the "Jungles" episode of the BBC television series *Human Planet*, during a flyover shoot of the Amazon forest, the viewer is presented with indistinct images of a village and its presumptive inhabitants. The voice-over describes these images as "the very first aerial footage of an uncontacted community," contextualizing their importance within an international debate about the treatment of uncontacted peoples by further explaining that "there are some who want to deny that uncontacted tribes live here at all. The fight to protect these people depends upon proving and publicizing their existence." José Carlos Meirelles, the official from the National Indian Foundation of Brazil (Fundação Nacional do Indio, or FUNAI) who is leading the shoot, declares that "it's important for humanity [that] these people exist. They remind us it's possible to live in a different way. They're the last free people on the planet." Such explanations suggest that what is on offer to the spectator is an elevated act of viewing that transcends mere watching and becomes witnessing, where nothing less than the continued survival of humanity is at stake. The strangeness of the description of these people as free, given the contextual terms of their uncontacted status—many of the Amazonian uncontacted are descendants of, or are themselves, escapees from genocidal imperial/extractive capitalist incursions into the Amazon—signals the stakes of such a project, the erasures and violences it relies upon. In other words, what is in fact a tactic of surveillance is characterized as key to liberation, self-determination, and the preservation of human rights—another manifestation of militarism defining humanitarian ways of knowing.

Indeed, the contemporary discursive life of the Amazon is a case study in the profound entanglement of humanitarian efforts of preservation—of the environment, of the Earth, of humanity—with modern warfare. The now-common tropology in which the Amazon is situated as a key battleground in a war over the preservation of humanity's future features the uncontacted as a primary feature of this militarized terrain, if not exactly of the humanity imagined by its particular articulation of a desired future. Identified as an ecosystem whose health is necessary to the preservation of Earth's climate stability, the Amazon is also often described as a zone of exemplary criminality, as inexorably attracting the degraded impulses of people who have no commitment to humanity writ large, and thus as needing to be securitized to ensure its own and humanity's survival. The urgent call to stop the destruction of the forest is often expressed in the terms of a complicated metaphorics, with the desire for and possibility of preserving a biodiverse plenitude frequently rendered in the terms of barrenness and ruination. A piece in the *New York Times Magazine*, titled "The War for the Rainforest," depicts one of the Indigenous reserves established by FUNAI as a war zone where competing interests of a fractured Brazilian nation stake their claim on the Amazon. Settlers in the reserve who are depicted as the main threat to the uncontacted peoples there are described as inhabiting a "ragged village" on "denuded land": "Many residents are armed and all, it seems, are angry."[1] Meanwhile, the uncontacted peoples who are presumed to live there are figured largely as absent presences, fearful denizens rather than active shapers of the places where they live, "so furtive that they may not realize that they inhabit their own official preserve."[2] That what is presented as their secretive nature is connected to an imagined lack of understanding of their place in the world is, indeed, typical of portrayals of the uncontacted and suggests their figural necessity to the kind of worlding that is effected through the designation of the Amazon as crucial to humanity's fate.

Recent declarations that the Amazon forest may be close to ecosystem collapse frequently identify criminality as the main threat to its continued existence and advocate for securitization efforts utilizing the power of the military backed by humanitarian law. Upon opening the nonprofit Survival International's webpage on the Awá people of the Amazon, described as "Earth's Most Threatened Tribe," one is met with the following declaration: "Success! This webpage was launched in April 2012 for Survival's global campaign to save the Awá. Two years later, in April 2014, Survival, the Awá, and their supporters celebrated as the campaign scored an unprecedented victory when the Brazilian government sent in troops to expel the illegal loggers from Awá land."[3] Writing about the suspected murders of two champions of the Amazon, journalist Dom Phillips and former FUNAI employee Bruno Pereira, Robert Muggah states that "the ongoing investigation is exposing a veritable ecosystem of crime to the world," and that "Amazonian cities have a murder rate that is 40% higher than other Brazilian municipalities. As locals well know, danger multiplies under the forest canopy where state institutions are weak, and the rule of law falls short." Referring to the weakening of protections for Indigenous peoples and the environment alike, Muggah states that "this in turn is incentivizing loggers, miners and hunters to commit environmental crimes with potentially catastrophic implications. Today, the Amazon rainforest is perilously close to a tipping point with dire global consequences."[4] And contextualizing her discussion of Phillips and Pereira in relation to this problem of the tipping point, Eliane Brum argues that "the global community must respond swiftly and strongly" to the two men's disappearance in order to, in turn, ensure humanity's survival: "The 21st century's more protracted, harder-to-win wars are the ones unfolding this very minute all across our natural life support systems—the tropical forests and the oceans, which are this world's true centers. Unless we understand this, we may find it impossible to respond as urgently as needed to halt our race toward self-destruction. We need to fight for Dom Phillips and Bruno Pereira; when we do, we fight for all humankind."[5] A piece for the *New York Times* that includes video shot from the point of view of a passenger on a boat moving down the waterway that Phillips and Pereira themselves were on when they died, invites the reader/viewer to join this responsive global community by experiencing oneself as quite literally in the position of the journalist writing a book on "how to save the Amazon" (Phillips) and the defender of Indigenous rights (Pereira).[6] Here, individual lives and losses are sutured to the grand narrative of global warfare, as recently articulated in regard to the climate crisis as "World War Zero":[7] The standard, seemingly requisite invocation of the forest as a land of cultural and ecological riches ("the Amazon is crucial to slowing global warming, is overflowing with wildlife and natural resources and is home to isolated communities that preserve a culture and way of life largely forgotten to modernity") is followed by a still image of Pereira's gun from the perspective of the shooter, which he reportedly acquired because "'it's a pump-action, 12-gauge. . . . If you're going to be in the forest, then you need something more brute.'"[8]

As if specifically designed to illustrate what Nicholas Mirzoeff has dubbed a "post-panoptic visuality" according to which "anywhere may be the site for an insurgency, so everywhere needs to be watched from multiple locations,"[9] the situating of the media consumer as humanitarian actor, whose agency is facilitated by militarized technologies and ways of seeing, and indeed the use of violences of various sorts, is a defining feature of the texts that have brought so-called uncontacted peoples into broad international public view. The nonprofit organization Survival International has taken up the protection of the uncontacted as one of its main aims, with a substantial and highly aestheticized website and celebrity ambassadors like Gillian Anderson and Mark Rylance; the likely ethnic/cultural identities and living conditions of the uncontacted continue to be the focus of governmental and anthropological evaluation; and they have become the subjects of popular educational media outlets like the *Human Planet* television series, *National Geographic* magazine, and journalist Scott Wallace's well-publicized first-person account of an expedition in *The Unconquered: In Search of the Amazon's Last Uncontacted Tribes*, along with his ongoing, frequent news stories about their status. The uncontacted—groups of Indigenous peoples who have no sustained contact with others—cannot represent themselves on a public stage through the typical means, not only because their survival might rely on them remaining off of that stage, but also (and relatedly) because they choose not to. Considered in this light, the putatively objective descriptions of the sort offered by the "Jungles" episode of *Human Planet* begin to break down under their own figurative weight. As these people—being filmed without their consent—gesture at the plane agitatedly, with several appearing to take up bows and arrows, the voice-over's declaration that "using a stabilized zoom lens, it was possible to film from a kilometer away, minimizing disturbance" seems, in spite of itself, to draw attention to the concerning power dynamics at play here.

Such concerns are at times articulated in these texts, though mostly as a means to produce a kind of ethics premised on ostensibly resolvable questions, and indeed this has not mitigated but rather it seems proliferated the production and circulation of portrayals of the uncontacted. I understand the texts that I take up in this chapter as constituting a broad-based popular humanitarian project, one whose contours can be traced to reveal the emergence of genocidal humanitarianism in a discursive site that explicitly and directly appeals to and cultivates a transnational public invested in the survival of humanity. In the midst of the declaration of impending Anthropocenic ruin, the uncontacted have been slotted into the role of representing what happens after the apocalypse, when humans lose their sense of being part of humanity. While at times the uncontacted are simultaneously invoked as figures of a form of human life that retains a connection to ways of being beyond carbon-based capitalism, it is only insofar as they are presumed to lack consciousness of what they have to offer to humanity writ large. The intensification of the Amazon's figural importance is a recent feature of those common narrations of climate catastrophe which themselves arguably serve as an alibi for the devastations wrought by the imperial military industrial complex. Here, the Amazon becomes the figural terrain onto which are projected self-induced fears about the end of the human world, where a wild oscillation between the possibility that doom can be managed and the deeper fear that it cannot is repeated again and again. The emotional scenography of Anthropocene discourse is charted in the positioning of the uncontacted as figures of pity and projection, desire and repulsion, dread and excitement. Little acknowledgment of, much less engagement with, the complex colonial and imperial dynamics that are responsible for the geopolitical position that the uncontacted are in, and indeed for the continuing destruction of the Amazon forest, is evident here: Individuals engaging in criminalized economies and unhinged politicians are identified as the enemies of humanity rather than, say, carbon-based racial capitalism's drive toward ever-proliferating production, or US entities (including but not limited to the CIA and major corporations alike) providing support for coups and death squads in nations like Brazil to protect commercial interests.[10] At best, the recognition of empire and conquest comes in the form of a recursive insistence on invoking the uncontacted as relics of nearly completed genocide who have something to teach those of us hailed as part of humanity proper, as we are called to participate in the project of desperately contemplating how to defend against our own inevitable end.

Apart from considering the deeply disturbing implications of the entitlement and felt need to make uncontacted peoples *useful* as the foundation for an argument that they themselves deserve to survive, I aim to show that the imagining of humanity's end—an imagining that is itself a genocidal maneuver—is redeployed in the figuring of the Amazon's uncontacted peoples as both needing to be saved and as already gone, as remainders, living remnants of disappeared peoples. Indeed, that the effort to establish the need for their protection is predicated on generating copious evidence that they are almost dead/still barely here, suggests that it is not the actual end of humanity that is at stake here so much as the reliance upon Indigenous peoples for the production of artifacts of meaning about being human. The context for this production of meaning is what Macarena Gómez-Barris describes as a "permanent war against Indigenous populations,"[11] within which these peoples are subject to "extraction [that] operates through material and immaterial forms of converting Indigeneity into exchange value, where intellectual and spiritual resources are taken to produce new forms of colonial currency."[12] For Gómez-Barris, state juridical efforts to secure the rights of Indigenous peoples obfuscate the deep entanglement of putative environmental protection efforts with extractivism and indeed the continuation of colonial/neocolonial militarism. Thus, the gathering and dissemination of information verifying the existence of the uncontacted not only participates in and enables multiple forms of extraction, but can also be understood as the expression of what Paul Amar has identified as human-security governance, a conjoining of securitization and violence as an explicitly humanitarian project, specifically by nation-states like Brazil and Egypt in the so-called Global South seeking to exert a counter-hegemonic agency in a geopolitical scene dominated by Western and Global North actors. In such a context, the targets of securitized humanitarian governance are not so much holders of rights as they are "human-security products" who are seen as simultaneously threats to the social order and in need of protection.[13]

What makes the uncontacted idealized subjects of securitization-as-protection and objects of humanitarian affect is precisely that they can be made to appear as absent from the scene of meaning-making. Yet the fact that this is not entirely due to the choices made by those who claim to document them or the fact that the government officials tasked with their protection have a no-contact policy, but also to the uncontacted exercising a set of decisions that those circulating their images and stories have little or no access to, introduces an element of insecurity into the project of representing their presumed needs and interests. Moreover, presented as ignorant of and disconnected from the sense of being part of a larger human community, they are not unlike those figures of unauthorized violence who are rendered as having no commitment to humanity, thus with the presumption of their innocence always on the verge of tipping over into the possibility of their dangerousness. In this sense, the promotion of their survival seems to be predicated on the fact that they are small in number and seemingly pose no threat to the geopolitical order as currently configured—so long as they remain uncontacted and, furthermore, so long as they can continue to serve their designated role in completing the circuits of humanitarian exchange value. What the texts in question cannot seem to abide is, to cite Keguro Macharia, the "indifferent native"—the one who actively chooses to not acknowledge the presence of the journalist, activist, or government official tasked with their protection, to refuse both contact and participation in the work of reproducing a future for humanity in its hegemonic configuration.[14] Macharia notes that "this native haunts colonial archives and, if you check, recent NGO reports. This native fails to speak in the correct way. Chooses not to answer questions. Rarely shows up. Shows up when not expected. . . . Perhaps the indifferent native never has to say no. Perhaps the indifferent native simply wanders off."[15] The main work of the most common portrayals of the uncontacted could, in this sense, be said to be the attempted disappearance of the indifferent native who, in not engaging at all—not even to say no, to critique the hegemonic order, and/or to speak for oneself—disturbs the orchestration of presence and absence on which the humanitarian onto-socio-political order relies. Where recognition is itself a foundational mechanism of settler colonialism and conquest, and arguably of internationally administered human rights, refusal threatens to reveal the radical dishonesty of the imperial knowledge-making project.[16]

Looking beyond the rather flaccid and hasty invocations of the necessity to ensure the human rights of the uncontacted, and thus understanding them to instead be constituted as human-security products, it becomes possible to inquire into the implications of the documentation of their existence, specifically in regard to securitization's proclivity toward various forms of eradication. Indeed, the reiteration of absence becomes a site of epistemological, affective, and ethical plenitude for the producers of discourse on uncontacted peoples. The repeated refrain that the uncontacted must be documented in order to survive, even as they are largely rendered in ghostly form as already gone or nearly so, demonstrates the cannibalizing mode of a humanitarianism that of necessity relies on a variety of differentiated forms of human life in order to constitute humanity. The essence of a people who by their very designation must remain *ostensibly* silent seems to be the required raw material for the production of preferred definitions of what it means to be human—a destruction and taking in of the other's body in order to sustain the life of humanity. Pursuing an analysis of the synergistic effects of documentation and eradication, I track the movements of three themes that appear across texts focused on the uncontacted: first, the imagining of the Amazon as the ruins of a civilization rendered as gone, in the past; second, the perception of encounter with the objects of modern life as fundamentally degrading to the Indigenous psyche; and third, the reproduction of gender as a site of trouble for the achievement of a globe-encompassing human community. That the discourse on the uncontacted largely operates in seeming ignorance of or in outright contradistinction to the media projects that Indigenous peoples have been producing on their own behalf from the beginning is to be expected.[17] If the widespread practice of viewing, documenting, and displaying racialized peoples can be located squarely within a visual biopolitical project of whiteness seeking ascendancy through the deaths of others, we must also assume that those being looked at are absolutely looking back and, in doing so, profoundly shaping the very medium that operates on the erroneous presumption of control.[18] The humanitarian media consumer might not be able to perceive this, and certainly cannot know what the content of that return look (so to speak) is, which is precisely the point. Scholarly and political debates about Indigenous peoples of the Amazon have taken on a life of their own, and in that sense they operate through tragically ironic conditions of possibility: to be sustained, they rely on the continuing imperilment of exactly those people about whom they are so deeply concerned.[19] To counter this, we must think about looking differently, with an understanding that what one sees is not what is actually there.

"The Man of the Hole": The Amazon as Ruins

The practice of predicting particular racial groups' extinction due to the evolutionary laws seen as determining the progress of human history—which, as Lindqvist has argued, is not separable from the practice of extermination for the sake of humanity as a whole[20]—seems to have emerged once again in the representation of Indigenous peoples of the Amazon. As Lindqvist has also contended, such prediction has served not only as a moral technique for justifying imperialism's devastations, but also as a means to deny and attempt to guard against the realization that humanity itself might—in fact, will—go extinct.[21] As discussed in chapter 1, the development and use of the nuclear bomb has often been understood as a means to secure humanity against disappearance, as its capacity for creation through devastation is expressed in the concept of ground zero. The Amazon, too, is often figured as a sort of ground zero, a ruins that offers new knowledge for the sake of humanity's future, but only through the interpretive capacities of those who ostensibly know what they are looking at and what it means. Alongside a longer history of mounting evidence that significant portions of the Amazon's forest exist in their present forms due to precontact civilizations' practices of ecological management, more recent advancements in aerial photography, satellite imagery, and laser-guided remote sensing and Global Positioning System technologies have provided visual confirmation of large-scale precontact settlements and structures. Simultaneously, the Amazon has become the locus of renewed interest in archaeological projects and adventure tourism seeking to locate "lost cities."[22] While this challenges the long-lived understanding of the Amazon as only ever sustaining very small human communities who were more or less at the mercy of the jungle, nonetheless in many popular and scholarly accounts alike its peoples are imagined as inhabiting the ruins of their own bygone civilizations, and as having limited knowledge of their connection to that past. Unlike the planned ruins of genocidal fantasies about humanity's future, the Amazon's ruins are presumed not to be capable of securing a unified understanding of humanity's presence across time and space, perhaps especially because they have been portrayed as having only recently become discernible.[23] Indeed, William Balée identifies the concept of "missing destructiveness" as the key to explaining why those who study the Amazon have only recently entertained the possibility that it was produced by large, sophisticated societies.[24] The Amazon's rich biodiversity had for a long time been taken to be the mark of civilization's failure there;[25] because of the prevailing belief that destructiveness is a natural feature of humanity's presence, the absence of destruction has served to index the absence of humanity.

These old and new visual technologies being employed to map and understand the history of the Amazon and track the presence of uncontacted peoples cannot be either epistemically or materially disconnected from their imperial/extractivist/militarized applications. In her work on the use of drone technology in asymmetric warfare, Lisa Parks introduces the notion of a "targeted class" of people for whom "daily life is haunted by the specter of aerial monitoring and bombardment."[26] The uncontacted are not the direct targets of the global war on terror she has in mind, but I would argue that the distinction here is of degree rather than kind.

Parks articulates the need to "extend beyond Paul Virilio's important recognition of the technological fusion of the airplane, the camera, and the gun to include more careful consideration of the vertical fields—material resources (fuel, labor, lands, hardware, networks, data, sky, orbit) and hierarchies of command—that enable aerial restructuring of life on earth,"[27] and here I see a crucial reminder that the uncontacted are most certainly being subjected to such restructurings precisely in being characterized as mere grounded objects in the vertical field of vision. The perception of the Amazon as ruins is predicated on a particular mode of seeing and interpretation, one in which the visual is associated with immediacy and a security in/of the knowledge it ostensibly transmits. Mirzoeff's reminder that before "visuality" came to refer to "the totality of all visual images and devices" it was "an early nineteenth-century term meaning the visualization of history" helps us to understand the stakes of this latest rendering of the Amazon; because "what is being visualized is too substantial for any one person to see and is created from information, images, and ideas," the "ability to assemble a visualization manifests the authority of the visualizer."[28] For Mirzoeff, visuality is not just one particular mode of knowledge production but rather the very basis on which the claim to Western/imperial epistemic authority is built.[29] Access to, and the capacity to understand, the visual in this particular register are assumed to be lacking in the peoples of the Amazon themselves.[30]

Such invocations of the uncontacted as prototypical figures of putative visual, technological, and historical incapacity abound. In the book *Deep Jungle*, which offers a global history of human relationships with forests in a mode bridging the popular and the scholarly, Fred Pearce gives an account that epitomizes this trend. Pearce reports on the evolution in researchers' understanding of the Amazon as having supported major civilizations, while positing imperial conquest as all-determining and masterful, so that his critique of conquest itself serves to reiterate the colonialist tenet of Indigeneity as naturally inclined toward oblivion. Pearce places knowledge of humanity solely in the minds of Europeans in his description of what happened to these civilizations with the event of pandemics and conquest:

> It seems likely that while the farmers and ranchers and metal-makers and priests and scholars who must have made up these societies gave it all up to become hunters and gatherers, the European invaders and despoilers were barely aware of what was going on in front of their eyes. For American Indians, the arrival of Europeans had

a similar impact to what Europeans imagine might happen in the event of a nuclear holocaust. The primitive nature of some tribes still being "discovered" from time to time in the Amazon rainforests is due in large part to the arrival of Europeans. Likewise, much of the "virgin" forest of the basin may be regrowth following the exterminations of the conquerors. If anyone made the jungle and their "stone-age inhabitants," it was the Europeans.[31]

The claim that Europeans "made the jungle" serves a dual function: As soon as it gives credit for the existence of the forest to Indigenous peoples' technological capacities of ecological transformation and management, it takes it away, with the implication that current forest denizens have no knowledge of their own history, acknowledging their societies only in the past tense. Not even the trauma they experienced at the hands of the agents of colonization is theirs, for it is implied that the nuclear holocaust-like annihilation instituted a radical break between these people and their knowledge of themselves, a characterization given even more weight by the invocation of nuclear technology, which the people being imagined here are presumed not to know of. Destruction thus facilitates and becomes an indicator of the observer's own reclaimed and corrected knowledge of these peoples. In answer to the question "how did scientists get things so wrong for so long?," Pearce reiterates the notion of colonizers' ignorance, suggesting that by the end of the eighteenth century, "the forests then looked to many as if they had always been empty, even though many had only recently been emptied. And yet, even at that time, the most acute observers were aware of something different, that the forest inhabitants were not so much noble savages as the traumatized survivors of past societies."[32] Following many a postcolonial thinker, the other interpretation of how this happened does not have to do with the ignorance of the conquistadors (or the scientists for that matter) but rather with the epistemological mandates of the imperial visualization of history. In Pearce's account, how "scientists got things so wrong" in actuality—which would, from the perspective of a historically informed account of colonialist and imperialist forms of knowledge production, be because of the will to see conquered lands as always already empty of people—is made to disappear from the record.

Radicalizing Pearce's assertion, if the Europeans can be said to have "*made*" the jungle, it is as a figurative *wasteland*, a place whose discursive value for uplifting the capacities of civilized epistemology lies in its ostensible emptiness of meaning and form. Interestingly, this meaning of the word *jungle* has been arrived at via the convoluted routes of colonial appropriation: "1. In India, originally, as a native word, Waste or uncultivated ground (= 'forest' in the original sense); then, such land overgrown with brushwood, long grass, etc."[33] Definitions 1.b. ("A particular tract or piece of land so covered; esp. as the dwelling-place of wild beasts") and 2.a. ("A wild, tangled mass. Also, a place of bewildering complexity or confusion; . . . a scene of ruthless competition, struggle, or exploitation") remind us that the jungle represents the loss of humanity, a place where life is defined by its inhumanity. Understood as once cultivated and now again wasteland and the terrain on which the depredations of hate, violence, and unregulated capitalism define the limits of civilization, the Amazon is claimed for the purposes of an anxious lesson in the loss of knowledge of and connection to a larger sense of human purpose. According to their designated role in this scenario, the people who actually did create the Amazon are gone. Yet this eradicatory documentation of the Amazon and its peoples as nowhere is paradoxical by nature; their absence seemingly must be verified again and again, which both admits the necessity of their presence and, conversely, constructs the presence of those doing the documenting as its own kind of void (i.e., as predicated on and constituted by other peoples' absence).

This invocation of the presence of the uncontacted only to insist on their absence is indeed a structural feature of several of the more extensive projects of representing their plight, most especially the organization Survival International and the work of journalist Scott Wallace. In his book-length account of an expedition he joined, the purpose of which was to get close enough to a group of uncontacted people to be able to track their movements while also avoiding physical encounter, Wallace relates the charge of the emotional vacillation between the thrill of discovery and the potential of a horrible outcome in a story featuring Sydney Possuelo, the FUNAI representative leading the expedition:

> In a small clearing, several palm fronds were spread out on the ground beneath a large tree, some parallel to one another, others perpendicular, done with an intentionality that bespoke the hands of human beings. The leaves were brown, though not yet brittle. And they were indented lengthwise in the way a body leaves its mark in the mattress of a cheap motel. . . .[34]
>
> Possuelo peered out to some point far beyond the trees that encircled us, as though directing his gaze into a looking glass focused

across a great distance, aeons away. "These Indians are very close to the way Vespucci would have found them," he pronounced, his voice rapt with marvel and admiration. "They live from hunting, fishing, and gathering."

Encountering such *vestigios*—the vestiges of isolated tribes—was the lifeblood of Possuelo's work, and it was hard not to share his enthusiasm. If there was any such thing as time travel, this was about as close to it as you could get. Five hundred years of world history hadn't touched these people. Or if so, barely.[35]

In this scenario, the work of the humanitarian takes on substance, meaning, and willful aim through his engagement with vestiges: What animates and excites this kind of work is characterized not as the uncontacted peoples themselves so much as the traces that mark their absence. Their bodies register only insofar as they are vanished from non-spaces that merely demarcate the boundaries of the livable (the indented mattress in the cheap motel). Meanwhile, Possuelo's gaze traverses human history and penetrates through the obscurity of the jungle, as the old technology of the looking glass prefigures the clean(er) lines of sight offered by aerial photography. Here and elsewhere, the value of knowledge about the uncontacted is premised upon their nonappearance within the scene of its production, a scene forcibly constructed and conveyed through the humanitarian's gaze. A paradigmatic video available on the page of the Survival International website dedicated to the Awá people, titled "Uncontacted Forest," is a ten-second-long stationary shot of a small area of forest in which no humans are apparent.[36] Another video of uncontacted people released by FUNAI presents its subjects as quite literally fleeing from the scene: In it, members of an uncontacted group talk with each other as they walk through the forest, passing by FUNAI agents without noticing them at first, until they spot their observers and the group runs away, shouting and apparently afraid. The video offers the explanation that "under mounting siege from loggers and land invaders, the Indians shout 'Enemy!' and flee when they glimpse the FUNAI team."[37] Emphasizing the authority and greater knowledge of those behind the camera by explaining several times that while this area is dangerous for the uncontacted that the FUNAI agents "are there to protect them," the video forecloses the questions that arise when we remember that what the viewer is witnessing is a violation.

Addressing this ethical problem has been folded into and become a key feature of the discourse about the uncontacted, openly acknowledged in order to be quickly resolved through the accompanying claim of the necessity of this "lesser evil" to provide the evidence that will allow others to ensure their survival. In this regard, one man in particular—frequently described as "the last survivor of his people" or "the last of his tribe"—has long served as a central figure in media about the uncontacted, signifying both death and survival, trauma and resilience. With his whereabouts tracked by FUNAI for years, updates about him are frequently issued by Survival International. The organization's website at one point featured a video surveying the home of this man, which has since been taken down from the website but still appears on its YouTube channel. Despite the fact that, according to the explanation given in the video, this man "totally rejects any type of contact," the video team films his home down to the last detail. In one scene, a team member climbs into a hole in his dwelling. It is explained that "he is sometimes known only as 'the Man of the Hole' because of the big holes he digs either to trap animals or to hide in." As the grounds of his dwelling are portrayed in panorama, this last man is nowhere to be seen.[38] But more recently, what has been described as "stunning video footage" of this very man, taken by FUNAI agents, has been released. In this short video we see the man chopping a tree before he walks away, and it seems clear that he is being filmed without his knowledge.[39] The accompanying Survival International piece by Fiona Watson argues that the protection of the uncontacted and their lands would be impossible "if it weren't for footage like this, showing uncontacted people alive and flourishing."[40]

Characterizing the presence of uncontacted peoples as a kind of void—whether they are invoked as just not there, or their appearance on camera is taken to be unknown by the uncontacted themselves—serves a significant purpose in providing raw material for the humanitarian subject's moral development. Wallace's commentary on the video of the "man of the hole" as well as another one released by FUNAI around the same time that featured aerial drone footage of a group of uncontacted people is a case in point: "Both videos were taken without knowledge or consent of the subjects, raising ethical questions about their rights.... But FUNAI officials say they decided to release the images after a consensus was reached among veteran field agents to heighten awareness within Brazil and around the world of the existence of the isolated tribes and their increasingly precarious status."[41] Here, the fact of violence is acknowledged (albeit in a subdued way) precisely in order to instrumentalize that admission toward the putative protection of its targets. Interestingly, Wallace goes on to report on the long history of FUNAI's engagement with this man, suggesting that despite the fact that he "continues to shun direct contact with outsiders," "FUNAI's overtures appear to have engendered a certain level of trust . . . the man has signaled to patrols to avoid pitfalls he'd dug as defenses against intruders and to trap wild animals." Yet even with a history of ongoing indirect contact and the building of a limited relationship of sorts with this man—in other words, well over a decade (at that point) of moments of his assertion of his presence—he is still identified with the trope of the hole: "He also digs deep, narrow holes inside the palm-roofed huts he builds for himself as he wanders the reserve alone. . . . Officials remain perplexed by the excavations, but some believe they may be a vestige of his tribe's spiritual practices. Absent any knowledge of the tribe's name, officials came to refer to him simply as *o índio do buraco*, the man of the hole."[42]

The conclusion in these writings and others seems to be that to "let this man live in peace" (to cite the title of Watson's piece) requires a nonconsensual mode of relation, one that I dare say is arrived at by a certain kind of longing on the part of the humanitarian to have the relationship with this "last" man be about more than he himself has allowed. After all, the man's own communication with FUNAI agents seems to mainly involve pointing out the holes/pitfalls he has made, a form of recognition of his watchers that indexes their own (self-admitted) ignorance. If it is the vestigial nature of uncontacted life—dead leaves where a body once lay, an empty hole, a vacant forest clearing—that makes it most valuable, it seems this is at least in part because it allows the humanitarian to set the terms of relationality with the uncontacted. Indeed, the rendering of these peoples as exceptionally vulnerable to disappearance in turn allows the humanitarian claim to have made the right choice to not violate but, rather, to protect. However, the implication that the impulse to harm those who are vulnerable is a natural one also appears here, at once signaling the humanitarian's special capacities for civilized reasoning and empathy and, more subtly, suggesting the attractive pull of the possibility of violation. There is something about the repetition ad nauseam of these scenes of uncontacted people's fear of the unwelcome presence of cameras and those who wield them, of their resistance to what is couched as contact and their clear desire to not be watched or intruded upon, that, when you read and watch enough of this stuff, suggests that it is the very violence of these interactions that at least partly drives their incessant production. The aesthetics of this mode of documenting the uncontacted, in which ultimate violability characterizes their embodied, subjective, and territorial presence—where violability signals and registers as the product of a variety of losses and absences—also implicates humanitarian protectionism in layered settler colonial and imperial modes of positioning Indigenous peoples within politicized landscapes and political space. As where the uncontacted are and are not is mapped and defined, so is where they should and should not be.

A brutal set of material conditions thus defines the epistemological aftermath of the kind of data-gathering being enacted by efforts to document the uncontacted. The emphasis on providing the uncontacted with protection specifically from those operating outside of the extant systems for designating and adjudicating the boundaries of Indigenous lands serves to reify the authority of both the settler state and the geopolitical institutions and infrastructures that uphold it. As Maria Beatriz Correa Neves and Marco Antonio Calil Machado argue, Brazilian demarcation of Indigenous territory (territory that is still under the jurisdiction of the Brazilian nation-state) is fundamentally instrumentalist, serving to "redeem, institutionally" the horrors committed against Indigenous peoples.[43] Indeed, FUNAI, the government entity founded in 1967 that is responsible for demarcating and administering these lands and producing official knowledge about the peoples there, has an exceedingly fraught history, having directly participated in the Brazilian government's colonization of and ultimately genocidal actions in the Amazon.[44] In this sense, the common portrayal of FUNAI in the discourse on the uncontacted can also be seen as an effort at reauthorization through image-cleansing and the alliance with transnational popular humanitarianism and modes of governance, a reauthorization predicated upon data-gathering and social scientific knowledge production. Because "the authentication of an indigenous land can only succeed after an anthropological, scientific report,"[45] the very notion of "self-demarcation" on the part of Indigenous peoples themselves is rendered null and void.[46] The humanitarian subject has a key role to play in such processes of actively denying self-demarcation, not just discursively or juridically but as that denial registers in the sensory experience of the expedition member, the camera-holder, and the viewer of images and indeed for the uncontacted themselves. This involves, at the least, a repeated violation of boundaries and the imposition of a state of being in which survival is predicated on fear, which is operationalized via the humanitarian's own experience of physical and ethical risk followed by potential catharsis and, if nothing else, the surety of satisfaction that comes from being on the side of good. While scenes of uncontacted absence are treated as existing prior to their documentation, they are produced and enforced by the very presence of those doing the documenting, a fact that highlights the profound ambiguity of what is understood to constitute contact proper—a conversation that I will take up in more detail in the next section.

Proper Objects: The "Lure of 'Things'" and the Pedagogy of Violence

For the organizations and texts in question, "contact" seems to mean a type of physical proximity that allows for all parties in the encounter to look at each other with the unaided eye, as well as for the transmission of pathogens. This concern about disease transferal to groups who do not have broad community-based immunity is, of course, of the greatest importance. Yet the ambiguities that quickly become apparent in this predominant understanding of what constitutes contact suggest a general disavowal of the effects of those projects that claim to represent the uncontacted without significantly impacting them. A keen nervousness about the possibility of such affectation—about the fact that contact is indeed happening despite the attempt to restrict its definition so that it appears that it is not—is, in the texts at hand, expressed and resolved through an extreme preoccupation with Indigenous peoples' relationship to objects, and in particular those that are seen as proper to what is deemed to be modern life. Objects are a rampant and ultimately uncontrollable source of potential contact, given their circulation as a result of the legacy of colonial encounter, prior efforts to contact the uncontacted, the incursions of capitalist and commercial projects, and indeed the current attempt to locate and save the uncontacted. The attention to objects—where and of what sort they are, who should and should not have them, whether they are being appropriately used—thus operates in a compensatory mode, effecting a narrative project of both geographical and moral location in the face of the quandaries opened up by the massively violent upheavals euphemized as "contact." It betrays an investment in theorizing Indigeneity via the positing of modern technologies as fundamentally corrupting and degrading.[47] And it is entirely predicated on a refusal to recognize the existence of, much less engage with, cosmologies that do not recognize objects in the way being imposed here.[48] Conversely, the preoccupation with the relationships that uncontacted peoples form with objects on the part of those who write about them reveals the contours of a Western imperial cosmology, in which objects are inanimate, of use, and exist primarily to define the capacities and humanity of their users.

The excessive cataloging of various degraded and degrading relationships to objects that is a hallmark of the discourse on the uncontacted reinforces a distribution of the sensible predicated on a human/object divide, in which the relationship to so-called objects (defined as other-than-human and supposedly insensate presences) determines whether one is recognized as having a part in humanity as an onto-political formation, and conversely in which the assertion of forms of relationality that do not abide by this sensibility is taken as the sign of one's inhumanity. In the context of a consideration of Indigenous political thought and practice in the Andes that has sought to protect land precisely by insisting on just such a relationality (specifically, with nature), Marisol de la Cadena notes the invocation of entities known as "earth-beings"—entities that would be seen as mere objects of the natural world in the Western-originated political tradition, for example, mountains—as sentient actors within the political realm. Crucially, she argues that the practice of positioning earth-beings as political actors cannot be read simply as an invocation and reinforcement of "ethnic politics," because in fact it poses another order of being that does not adhere to the racialized arrangement of bodies under modes of governance predicated on a hierarchization of different human forms.[49] As de la Cadena puts it, "nature—what it is, what it does—is not an 'apolitical' entity as we have learned to think. Rather, its constitution as ontologically distinct is at the heart of the antagonism that continues to exclude 'indigenous beliefs' from conventional politics—with the idea of 'beliefs' working to occlude the exclusion, or setting the internal limits ... to the ontological construction of politics."[50] Thus, my interest here is not in showing that the uncontacted might also experience and invoke the presence of earth-beings were they to have the chance and desire to articulate themselves in relation to a broader political realm, but rather that the obsessive policing of Indigenous relationality to objects serves the desperate function of attempting to eradicate the kind of disagreement that would offer a radically different notion of the very nature of reality. The reduction of objects to mere insensate items for human use in turn facilitates the figural use of Indigeneity as an object of evaluation in the reestablishment of an ontological order in which self-control, mastery, and above all independence are what secure humanity's presence.

In one especially disturbing example of the typical kind of reference to objects in debates over what to do about the uncontacted, conservation scientist John Terborgh, in his review of Scott Wallace's book, attributes the failure of the Brazilian government's former policy of Indigenous assimilation to the inability of Indigenous people to form a proper relationship to objects, and more specifically, the kinds of objects that owe their existence to capitalist mass production (which Terborgh refers to as "things"): "The Indians' culture of survival that had served them so well prior to their encounter with Western society had little relevance or value afterward. The lure of 'things' (including alcohol) was irresistible and led to dependencies.... Exploited by settlers and unscrupulous merchants, and with little prospect of achieving a level of prosperity, independence, and self-respect that would have carried them over the cultural divide into real assimilation, many indigenous communities became trapped in a state of demoralization and profound cultural poverty."[51] For Terborgh, "real" assimilation is the only humane approach to the uncontacted due to the inevitability of the encroachment of things as well as to the "vastly richer existence" offered by the "modern world."[52] Even as he admits that such assimilation programs are "abysmal," for Terborgh they are nonetheless necessary alternatives to the "social ostracism, demoralization, and alcoholism [that] comprise the barren netherworld between cultural states."[53] This is a disturbingly racist account of Indigenous lifeways, not just because Indigenous being is reduced to "survival" but because this is the kind of humanitarianism that envisions humanity's presence as requiring certain forms of elimination: According to Terborgh, Indigenous suffering should be alleviated, but to do so requires providing Indigenous people with the means to transition away from their own ways of being. Here, inclusion within humanity as a whole is on offer, but only at the price of the extermination of entire cosmologies. The language of entrapment, stasis, and in-betweenness that Terborgh uses to describe Indigenous placement in the onto-socio-political order also conceives of such being nowhere real—nowhere that matters—as defined by sheer lack and loss. The desire for and possession of things effect a kind of hollowing out or evacuation of meaning, place, and self, invoking Indigenous life as a hollow that needs to be filled but will unavoidably be destroyed in the filling. Ways of life other than the one on offer here (i.e., the one Terborgh names as "modern") can only be imagined as a radical impossibility on these terms.

Indeed, already-contacted Amazonian peoples are the implied denizens of Terborgh's "netherworld" of cultural oblivion—a world that must be charted by the non-Indigenous humanitarian. This rendering of Indigeneity is not unique to Terborgh; it has a long and deep history, and it shows up elsewhere, including the writings of those who are staunchly opposed to assimilation. Thus, in Wallace's account of the expedition he accompanied, while Indigenous team members are employed for their knowledge of the forest and for their ability to better relate to any uncontacted people who might be encountered, they are also presumed to be more careless than the expedition organizers and leaders, less attentive to the gravity of their work and to its implications for humanity. Describing a near encounter with one uncontacted group, in which the team wanders into a recently occupied village, Wallace notes with concern that "half the expedition was parading through the houses, picking things up to examine like they were curios in an exotic boutique."[54] Wallace himself, though, proceeds to write about the homes and their contents in intimate detail, an act that in and of itself takes on particularly distressing connotations given that the village inhabitants had clearly fled very recently due to the approach of the expedition.[55] In a later scene, Wallace again responds with concern about Indigenous peoples' relationships with objects, this time upon realizing that a team member has spent his whole earnings from the expedition on a stereo, speculating that he "had been left to fend for himself in an alien world. He must have been bedazzled by the thump of the boom box's speakers, its flashing lights, and the promise it seemed to offer for good times to be had back home."[56] The stereo is presumed to be reduced to the status of a degrading thing in the hands of this man, rather than an instrument of creativity, political expression, or an enjoyment that should draw no scrutiny or indeed external meaning-making at all.

According to such accounts, the capacity of Indigenous people to maintain a commitment to their own moral sensibilities is precluded by the encounter with the objects of modern life: "Once a person *knows such things exist*, then that person and his entire community are irrevocably changed. . . . Dependency instantly demotes proud, confident, and independent people to a mendicant status that is pitiable to behold."[57] Terborgh's depiction of the mendicant here indicates a view of dependency as a moral failing rather than a condition of life that, even more, could be the basis for the ethical practice of the vow of poverty (a view that is inherent to the other prevailing definition of *mendicant*). There is a kind of tautology at work in his argument, which follows a logic that goes something like this: As humans they are atavistic, not capable of embodying the full potential of humanity, therefore their relationship to objects is marked not by mastery but by enthrallment and dependency, therefore when presented with modern objects they are made incapable of living full human lives. I suggest that, ultimately, this is an expression of the anxieties arising from the demands made of the subject by a social order in which to be fully human means to achieve supposed independence via mastery over various presences (other beings, objects, etc.) designated as the non-self. Within the confines of this order, and as noted by de la Cadena as discussed above, the environment is posited as a separate entity, which is what I take Balée to be pointing out when he remarks on the underlying assumptions driving many researchers' accounts of the Amazon as a product of Indigenous peoples' technologies: "Even if one grudgingly admits . . . that some indigenous Amazonian societies of the past may have managed their heritage of natural resources, their modern descendants, in this view, are inevitably to be drawn into the vortex of expanding Western society," especially by the "allure of . . . material abundance."[58]

There is a kind of ideological dishonesty going on here: The narrative of Indigenous dependence on modernity provides an alibi for the imperial predation of land and livelihood, while the prospect of uncontacted peoples' continued independence is lauded only insofar as it can be taken up as its own kind of object—that is, as an object of contemplation for the humanitarian tasked with ensuring humanity's future. Thus, the debate over what to do about/for the uncontacted tends to turn on the perception of their ability to use the land they inhabit to sustain themselves in health and, above all, independently. Here, Indigenous people are invoked as figures evacuated of interiority, used to ventriloquize a vision of racial hierarchy that is attributed to a subjectless and decontextualized "mindset": Wallace remarks that "the equating of primitive culture with backwardness has been so ingrained in the popular mind that even so-called civilized Indians on the lowest, most marginal rungs of society invariably believe themselves to be superior to their isolated brethren who remain in the bush. But Possuelo was calling that whole construct into question. The Arrow People were in no way inferior to any tribe. On the contrary! Their near-complete independence from the white man's world was to be admired, even emulated."[59] The uncontacted (the group referred to by outsiders as the "Arrow People") appear as a cipher for reflection on the humanitarian subject's own relationship to objects and to the environment. This is also apparent in another passage, in which Wallace muses on his own self-described "obsession" with getting to drink a Coke after spending an extended period in the forest:

> For all the illusions of freedom our society promotes, rarely do we have the chance to step outside it long enough to gain some distance. Beyond the fatuous talk about liberty and the price our founders paid for it, I wondered: How free were we if we'd become so dependent on the comforts produced by industry that we couldn't do without them? How free was I, that the first thing I wanted and had been craving for weeks was a sweet and fizzy caramel-colored

beverage that came in a bottle with a scarlet label and passed itself off as the Real Thing?

May the Arrow People never come to know it. As long as they had streams unsullied by mercury and sprawling woodlands rich with animals, they could remain beyond our reach, beyond the swirling vortex of consumer society and the machinery that manufactures our wants, creates our needs, serves us our ice-cold beer. May they never come to know the squalor of their brethren, not only in Brazil but all across the Americas, who have been sucked in, then spat out and left to wander dusty frontier streets or the hopeless, crack-infested subdivisions on the rez, filthy and destitute, the objects of scorn and derision.[60]

While Wallace's account shifts the focus of the concern about the lure of things to what we might call, following Kidlat Tahimik, the imperial enthrallment to overdevelopment, it is nonetheless also the case that the potential for the radical differences of their humanness requires the uncontacted to be absent from the scene of the very community of humanity they are supposedly necessary to the survival of. And "their brethren" occupy their own space of negation—not of absence, but of the destitute margin, demarcating through their "hopeless" ambulation the outskirts of human social order. The humanitarian subject's attachment to the fantasy of the "Real Thing" might put into question the supposed superiority of modern life, but at the same time, the claiming of the ability to pose that question and indeed to recognize real freedom is still articulated as the proper role of the humanitarian subject alone.

Thus is the humanitarian subject called to protect the freedom of the uncontacted, including by taking upon oneself the psychic burden of the "terror" of first contact. In an interesting passage, Wallace recounts the experiences of FUNAI scouts from before the implementation of the no-contact policy, when it was believed that controlled, planned contact was the best way to ensure the protection and survival of uncontacted peoples—an approach that, as Wallace describes it, had horrific results.[61] This story suggests that the experience of committing unintentional violence is necessary to the production of a humanitarian sensibility:

> For a number of *sertanistas* [FUNAI scouts], contact became not a triumph but a tragedy. Wellington Figueiredo notched eight "first contacts" of his own and had taken charge of the Department of

Isolated Indians during Possuelo's two-year reign as FUNAI president. Toward the end of his career, he'd come to be "terrified" by the prospect of first contact. On one expedition, a colleague suggested they should hide the Indians rather than contact them. He agreed. If only they could have. Contact left *sertanistas* as troubled and traumatized as combat veterans, having to contend not only with the spectacle of mass death, but also in some cases with the near-certain knowledge that they had been the bearers of the deadly illness.[62]

It was not only the mass die-offs that burdened the conscience of FUNAI agents. There were also countless cases of their own inadvertent bungling and insensitivity, moments they wished they could take back and do over again, things for which apologies were wholly inadequate.[63]

I draw attention to this passage not to minimize the violence of the acts described (indeed, Wallace's reflection upon them is important), but rather to suggest that it speaks directly to how the interanimation of documentation and destruction emerges as a structural feature of the very project to engage with the uncontacted in the most humanitarian way possible, such that the most well-intentioned of individuals cannot resolve or really even get a firm grasp on the legacies of imperial realities at play. No amount of recognition of one's relationship to power changes things for the better for the subjects of the humanitarian's protection. Indeed, it is the consistent turn toward the individual humanitarian consciousness as the site of such fantasized resolution in much of the discourse on the uncontacted that is so concerning, because it fundamentally obfuscates this reality. Thus violence, rather than being confronted as a material feature of the imperial onto-political order, becomes the humanitarian pedagogy par excellence—that is, the experience deemed necessary for transforming consciousness and effecting an ethical reorientation toward a greater good beyond the self. Another way to put this is that the invitation to participate in violence is another key mode in which the media-consuming public is meant to engage the humanitarian content of these texts.

The pedagogy of violence meets the fixation on objects in the convention of naming various different uncontacted groups according to their presumed weapon of choice, as, say, the "Arrow People" or the "Head-Bashers,"[64] thus aligning their very being with technologies (arrows and clubs) implied to be primitive. In this, the uncontacted are rendered as requiring protection through the humanitarian's use of advanced technologies, but also as having a proclivity toward the kind of barbarous violence that, it is implied, is both the sign and cause of their incapacity to understand and use civilized technology in support of either their own or humanity's cause. Thus their naming also participates in the desperate refusal to acknowledge that those same hands that hold bows and arrows could themselves hold cameras and know what to do with them, and indeed in the abject denial of the fact that Indigenous peoples—just like everyone else—have been using cameras from the very time of their invention.[65] Another way to say this is that the positioning of the camera as object denied to those it supposedly helps to protect enables "the deliberate erasure of indigenous ethnographic subjects as actual or potential participants in their own screen representations."[66] Given the insistence on locating the uncontacted in particular outside of the geographical, political, and ontological territory that is designated as that of humanity proper, the denial of the camera has functions that extend beyond the realm of visual representation to assert a more fundamental eradication of the very existence of uncontacted peoples' experiences, presence, ways of knowing, and modes of being.

To close this section of the chapter, I refer back to the *Human Planet* series as an archetypal deployment of the aesthetics of eradication that, yet, has not succeeded on its own terms. The synonymizing of the possession of the camera with both the capacity and the right to define humanity occurs during the opening and postscript sequences of each episode in the series: During the opening, an image of a human eye is superimposed over Earth as viewed from space, with the Earth situated in the eye's pupil, and during the postscript sequence the same image is used as the pupil fades out to be replaced by a camera lens. This is not a brown or a black eye—its iris is blue, green, gold, and amber—implying that the understanding of humanity that can only be achieved through a global vision (and quite literally the envisioning of the globe) is in fact not achievable by just anyone. This rather forceful assertion about who can and should exert control over the production of knowledge about what it means to be human was reiterated more recently in a different mode. The 2011 version of the *Human Planet* series has been pulled from distribution by the BBC, an act described as a response to having "been alerted to some editorial breaches" in the series,[67] one of which involved a staged scene of people in Papua New Guinea living in a treehouse.[68] While couched in the language of ethics and responsibility ("since this series was broadcast in 2011, we have strengthened our training for the BBC's Natural History Unit in editorial guidelines, standards and values"[69]), I would suggest that pulling the series betrays a concern about authority over knowledge production, as an act that obviates the need to seriously contend with the emptiness of the trope of cultural authenticity. The inaccuracies, potentially caused by editorial desires to produce a particular kind of product, undermine the authority of the producer and stand to disclose the agency of the people being filmed—and, additionally, to introduce the possibility that they could choose to represent themselves in purposely inaccurate ways, to not offer transparent views into their lives, thus using the camera for their own purposes after all.

Human-Security Governance and the Humanitarian Need for Recognition

In the annals of the uncontacted, alongside the violent relics, the terrified hole-dwellers, and the derelict drifters, we also have vigorous, if still imperiled, villagers who signify the possibility of humanity's survival. For Survival International's Fiona Watson, "uncontacted peoples are supreme conservationists with the lightest footprint on our planet: from the Amazon to the Chaco, they protect some of the world's last and most biodiverse forests. They have developed extraordinary skills and have unrivalled knowledge of their universe. Above all they are contemporary peoples who like any of us want to live well and in peace."[70] While not rendered in the same terms of absence as some other portrayals, the uncontacted here are nonetheless positioned along the demarcation lines of humanity (having the "lightest footprint," living in the "last" forests), even as they also serve another function, the cultivation of an expansive aesthetic/emotional experience. Portrayals of uncontacted life as defined by freedom and plenitude in particular fulfill this function. A 2016 *National Geographic* article provides such an experience of richness for the reader precisely by positing the uncontacted as such limit figures:

> Aerial photographs of an isolated tribe in the Brazilian rain forest are yielding a sensational new look at a Neolithic way of life that has all but disappeared from the face of the Earth.
>
> The high-resolution images, taken from a helicopter last week by Brazilian photographer Ricardo Stuckert, offer an unprecedented glimpse of a vibrant indigenous community living in complete isolation in the depths of the Amazon jungle. . . .
>
> "I felt like I was a painter in the last century," Stuckert said, describing his reaction to seeing the natives. "To think that in the

21st century, there are still people who have no contact with civilization, living like their ancestors did 20,000 years ago—it's a powerful emotion."

Stuckert's close-up photographs taken near Brazil's border with Peru show details about these Indians that had previously escaped the notice of experts, such as their use of elaborate body paint and the way they cut their hair. "We thought they all cut their hair in the same way," said José Carlos Meirelles, who has worked with and studied Brazil's indigenous tribes for more than 40 years. "Not true. You can see they have many different styles. Some look very punk."[71]

Declarations like Watson's in her characterization of the uncontacted as "contemporary peoples" seem hard-pressed to hold up against the forces of teleological thinking and ethnographic cataloging, which are on full display in the description of an Indigenous society as both unchanging and as having certain social practices that are surprisingly analogous to some "modern" ones. Indeed, both of the above-cited descriptions trade in a similar logic, one in which the freedom of uncontacted life is ascertained through the documentation of their appropriate use of their environment and thus their ability to sustain themselves—unlike their "dependent" Indigenous kin against whom they are so often juxtaposed. Still, the admission that pointed visual evidence of uncontacted individuals' differentiation from each other is surprising to some speaks to the role of all of this documentary material in the production of a generalized Indigeneity, where sclerotic race/ethnicity/culture is the presumed totality of Indigenous being. There is a whole aesthetic order compressed into the brief comment about haircuts, an order in which the incapacity and unwillingness to acknowledge the individuality of human beings is structured by a gendered racialization of legible ontology and subjectivity.

I thus assume it is not incidental that the twin projects of documenting different forms of humanness and defining the contours of humanity, as they are enacted in the discourse on the uncontacted, are imagined as largely by, for, and of men. It is certainly not surprising. Few women appear, for example, in *Human Planet* or *The Unconquered*, and much of the news coverage of the status of the uncontacted focuses almost exclusively on men. Where women do appear, it is largely to provide documentation for the state of "living well and in peace," which does the simultaneous work of employing the uncontacted (as epitomizing Indigeneity) as a fulcrum for a variable symbolics of human survival in the face of annihilation. Indeed, the one place where they are featured prominently is on the portions of the Survival International website featuring media purporting to explain the beliefs and lifeways of Indigenous Amazonian peoples in a popular ethnographic manner. Yet, precisely as preeminently ethnographic subjects, women serve as the entry point for ambiguity, making it unclear what the particular nature of uncontacted peoples' humanness might be. One main way in which women are made to serve as exemplars of cultural authenticity is through their imputed emotional and physical connection to nonhuman animals, which indeed constitutes a disproportionate amount of Survival International's ethnographic coverage of the people identified as the Awá.[72] The materials featuring their relationship with animals are notable both for how prominently they are featured on the website, and for the nature of their content—namely, the amount of attention devoted to women breastfeeding baby animals they have taken in as pets. Of the several available videos on the Awá, one focusing on pets is the only one in which women (rather than men) provide voice-over narration regarding the group's cultural practices. In this video, a woman explains in voice-over (translated into English subtitles) about their animals that "when they're older, they become independent and go back to the forest. Sometimes when we're out hunting, I'll see one of our pets and say, 'don't hunt it!' . . . My pet lives in the forest, and now it's going to make a family of its own."[73] This narration occurs over various different shots of women taking care of these pets, sometimes while also taking care of children. The website offers further elucidation: "The tribe are extraordinary pet keepers: most families have many more pets than people, from raccoon-like coatis to wild pigs and king vultures. But without question, monkeys are the Awá's favourites. . . . Although wild monkeys are an important source of food, once a baby has been brought into the family and breast fed, it will never be eaten. Even if it returns to the forest, the Awá will recognize it as *hanima*: part of the family."[74] The pedagogical presentation elides the use of a highly aestheticized rendering of gendered embodiment, in which the act of breastfeeding nonhuman animals is lingered over visually, while also being presented as the act defining the Awá's distinctive definition of family.

Even though these practices and relational formations are presented in a tone of impartial acceptance, the echoes of a variety of racializations produced by way of the human/nonhuman animal categorical divide resonate strongly here. The discourse of contagion originating in consumption of wild animals deemed to be improper (the "wet market," "bush meat," etc.) comes to mind, introducing the specter of disease transmission in the other direction upon the occasion of first contact and thus suggesting that the fear of spreading illness to those with no natural immunity is not the only one at work. Moreover, noting the long and violent history of the circulation and presumed availability for consumption of such images of women's bodies in racist imperialism, here we see such images put to similar use, though this time for the production of a humanitarian knowledge and ethical conditioning. Indeed, the vast archive of racist representations of Indigenous women includes many entries showcasing their conflation (and purported liaisons) with animals.[75] "The breast" in particular comes into view as an especially fraught aesthetic object, as simultaneously sustainer of human life, evidence of humans' dependence on each other, designator of gendered particularity (and thus of qualified humanity), and object of sexualization. That the Survival International materials focus on monkeys in particular is also significant in this regard. Monkeys and apes are uncanny, indexing the failure of categories to hold, and so their very resemblance to humans has often become an occasion to attempt to define their difference from humans. Other famous such primates come to mind here: the Giant of Karisimbi,[76] or King Kong. We know what happened to these quasi-analogues of humanity: They were shot and put on display (or vice versa), to consolidate and authorize the gender propriety of whiteness, to preserve for the benefit of humanity the knowledge of a primeval mode of life that was dying out as a necessary part of the process of civilizational advancement, to teach a terrible lesson regarding so-called miscegenation while simultaneously disclosing desire for it, and indeed to eliminate boundary confusion. Seen in this light, the images of breastfeeding could have multiple effects. They might serve as supposed evidence of gender as a transparently visible and fundamental feature of human bodies and experience. They might reinforce the presumed inability of these people to leave their own particular cultural enclave behind to comport themselves as citizens of a global humanity. Or they might introduce irresolvable questions about what and who that category of humanity can hold. The utter normalcy (constructed, of course) of the fact that child-rearing and family nurturing is women's work might reassure us that we are in the realm of a simple and clear moral code, while the cultural and indeed cosmological difference of this relational practice from those of its implied viewers might ensure the necessity of the distinction between the human and the nonhuman (and imply that some are less capable of discerning that distinction).

The implications of the potential work done by these portrayals go beyond questions of (mis)representation; ethnographic renditions of racialized/Indigenous culture are also mobilized for the purposes of securitization discourses and practices, in which targets of protection can simultaneously be figured as targets of management and regulation. Awá women may not be the direct focus of a specific securitization scheme, but their representation nonetheless constitutes one especially dense discursive nodal point for the making of meaning about humanity. On this note, I invoke Paul Amar's characterization of human-security governance projects that reinforce gender and sexual norms "in terms of security-sector struggles to discipline dangers and desires that mark the controlled boundary of the human."[77] Amar argues that human-security governance practices "emerged from the intersection of three processes: the militarization of urban social-control operations; the NGOization of transnational civil society and its adoption of humanitarian enforcement doctrines; and the designation, by transnational actors and UN agencies, of certain racialized, moralized, and sexualized problems as requiring new kinds of intervention"; while initially emerging in Global South milieus, they have "transferred to global human-development policy experts and UN institutions via particular encounters and in concrete contexts."[78] If we see the project to save the uncontacted as one of these encounter points, it becomes possible to situate their portrayal as aligned with Brazil's aspirations for greater geopolitical power (as a permanent member of the UN Security Council, as a leader of "the democratic Global South")[79] as well as a commitment to securitization-via-humanitarianism on the part of a broader set of international actors. In other words, the discourse on the uncontacted cannot help but have implications for state projects of humanitarian regulation (for example, in the Brazilian state's own redeployment of tropicalism) as well as for extra- and quasi-state, transnational, and international juridical ones.[80]

The implications of the instrumentalization of the uncontacted for the purposes of regulating the gendered/sexual/racial boundaries of human community are starkly illustrated in a recent story about "the last three known survivors of the Piripkura people"[81] of the Amazon forest. What begins as the story of a man named Tamandua and his uncle Pakyi and the ongoing attempts to ensure their protection unexpectedly shifts focus to offer a highly disturbing account of how Pakyi murdered his niece and nephew. Rita, Pakyi's sister and the third member of the Piripkura people, first appears in the narrative of the article as a subject of patriarchal violation. According to the article, "as one of the few women" left in her group when she was younger, she "was highly coveted," and after the father of her two children died, "Pakyi and her father propositioned her." Soon after Rita rejected their advances, Pakyi killed her two children. The rest of the article follows Rita and Jair Candor, a FUNAI agent, as they track the whereabouts of Tamandua and Pakyi over the course of years in an effort to prove that they are still alive and thus that their land should be protected. Tamandua, however, has recently disappeared because he doesn't want to be found, and the article ends with Rita declaring that "'we have to find him'" in order for there to be a chance for the Piripkura to survive. The ethical convolutions of this article are too complicated to trace in their entirety here, but I would point out several of the more alarming implications of this piece, which suggest that the taking up of the plight of the uncontacted is less about the well-being of the uncontacted themselves and more about instrumentalizing them for the purposes of demarcating the "controlled boundary of the human" (to refer back to Amar). The portrayal of the Piripkura strongly resonates with other portrayals of ostensibly patriarchal cultures that suture practices of gendered violence to racialized being. To put it bluntly, the article is organized such that it seems the reader is meant to get to the end of it and wonder whether the Piripkura have a right to survive, given their violent treatment of their own. That Rita herself serves in the role of arguing that they should only amplifies the usefulness of this piece for the humanitarian subject seeking to develop her own ethical consciousness by reflecting on an instance of terrible violence against clear innocents. Finally, the expectation that Tamandua should do what needs to be done to ensure the survival of his people—indeed, the broadcasting of this expectation to a vast international audience—is arguably and at the very least an expression of racialized sexual violence in and of itself.

Both Survival International's ethnographic materials on Awá women and the story of the Piripkura highlight the extent to which human-security demarcations and management of cultural deviance is expressed in the terms of international humanitarian norms regarding gender and the rights of women. Whether exemplified by the more benign practice of nourishing nonhuman animals from one's own body, or the clearly horrific practice of child murder, gendered forms of putative cultural difference operate as a powerful mechanism for adjudicating membership within humanity, as Ranjoo Seodu Herr points out when she argues that the "acceptance" of cultural pluralism has already been constituted as a foundational problem for humanitarianism, especially in its liberal feminist expressions.[82] In an international order in which the political/power trouble cathected onto gender and cultural difference is managed through the codification of women's rights as human rights, peoples like those identified as the Awá or Piripkura are folded into international governance regimes by being recognized as either prepared or not prepared to uphold such rights (and then rewarded or punished accordingly). As Herr goes on to point out, the formation of women's rights as human rights has also served as the basis for invalidating Indigenous expressions of ethical livelihood (by international legal bodies and indeed by non-Western/Global South states themselves) by seeming to provide evidence of their incapability of conceiving and enacting gender equality.[83]

Ultimately, the instrumentalization of the uncontacted for the ends of settler state and international governance practices serves to codify a humanitarian distribution of the sensible in which Indigenous peoples as a political body have no *admitted* part in humanity. It is precisely in the prescribed parochialism of their being—their supposed lack of capacity to develop and maintain a consciousness of humanity as a whole—that they are offered up for humanity's use. In this, the discourse on the uncontacted serves to support the notion of sovereignty and indeed state structures and thus to obfuscate Indigenous and anti-imperialist/anti-conquest theories and practices of other political and social forms. Jodi Melamed points out that the post–World War II geopolitical order is predicated on this very state of affairs: "The United Nations is an alliance of nation-states, the conditions of which, for many, required colonizing and displacing indigenous peoples. As Mohawk scholar Taiaiake Alfred reminds us: 'State sovereignty can only exist in the fabrication of a truth that excludes the indigenous voice. It is in fact antihistoric to claim that the state's legitimacy is based on the rule of law.' Insofar as the UN represents just global governance, it does so only as an amalgamation of nation-states whose sovereignty depends upon bracketing indigenous claims."[84] However, Alfred notes about his own work that it "reflects a basic sentiment within many indigenous communities: 'sovereignty' is inappropriate as a political objective for indigenous peoples" due to the location of political sovereignty within "unjust state structures."[85] So the bracketing and denial of Indigenous articulations of sociopolitical formations that work against unjust state structures facilitate the humanitarian claim to Indigeneity as raw material for the construction of its world order. As Melamed argues, "neoliberal multiculturalism is one of the most useful discourses functioning today to dispossess indigenous peoples of their lands and resources.... It justifies the removal of indigenous peoples from their lands by describing the entire world as the rightful potential property of global multicultural citizens. At the same time, it stigmatizes indigenous peoples as monocultural, unrealistic, doomed, chauvinistic, or 'tribal,' connoting a negative orientation to an exclusively defined group."⁸⁶ To see how this shows up in the discourse on the uncontacted, we need only look to one entry in the ongoing debate over whether or not the no-contact policy is serving uncontacted people: Kim R. Hill, who cowrote an editorial arguing for a reinstitution of controlled contact, has commented that "'all of the isolated tribes in the world are pretty much under the control of pathetically inept and corrupt Third World governments that are doing a piss-poor job of protecting them.'"⁸⁷ Here, "Third World" ineptitude is invoked as a means to hand over the very land and lives of the uncontacted to humanity.

Those who desire to preserve the uncontacted in their cultural particularity are thus faced with a logical quandary when the ideological demands of the synonymizing of particularity with parochialism present themselves. Wallace relates how during the expedition he joined, Sydney Possuelo "was also assembling a core of young men whom he could inculcate in the course of the journey with a new kind of pan-Indian consciousness. It was critical to involve the Indians in the protection of the reserve, to raise their awareness beyond the near horizon of tribal self-interest toward collective defense of their land and cultures."⁸⁸ But Possuelo also asserts that "'the only problem is that by the time you get the Indian to understand that, he's stopped being Indian.'"⁸⁹ Indigeneity is in this line of thinking counterposed to the development of a humanitarian consciousness, that is, the kind of consciousness required for envisioning the globe-encompassing community that could save humanity from extinction. Where the possibility of uncontacted agency is acknowledged, it is codified as a narcissistic collapse inward as opposed to the kind of physical and egoic movement outward that, it is implied, is required to sustain humanity: "Indigenous groups living in isolation are isolated because they choose to be. It's not for complete lack of contact, but precisely because previous experiences of contact with the outside world proved so negative."⁹⁰ What this does, ultimately, is to articulate a refusal to entertain two feared possibilities: that the uncontacted might eagerly join in the kind of intellectual and political work that would challenge state structures and perhaps international law itself; and that the uncontacted might continue to walk away, which would constitute its own kind of challenge. In either case, both the fear itself and the refusal to name it serve to ignore and hence invalidate such work already being done all along by Indigenous peoples. Indeed, I see this as the driving logic behind Possuelo's characterization of his work, which seems to sum up the general sentiment of the various projects to represent the uncontacted, when he declares, "'I fight for the human rights of those who do not even know that human rights exist.'"[91] Defining human rights in that way, as a sort of empirical object perceivable by anyone with a fully developed mind, enables a localizing, compression, and mapping of diverse processes of socially sanctioned violences such that they can be seemingly answered to with a single sentence. Similarly, the defense of the uncontacteds' right to remain so by invoking it as their choice both acknowledges their agency to some extent, and at the same time, in speaking for them, obscures the deeply complicated conditions that give rise to the contextual possibility of such a choice.

The discussion regarding uncontacted choice (whether they are enacting it, whether they know what they want, whether they should be allowed to live as they want) also belies what I would dare say is the humanitarian's *own* desire and, indeed, need for contact. This is perhaps the elephant in the room, the major force defining the discursive space of the plight of the uncontacted that can never be explicitly named: the reliance on the recognition given by the uncontacted to reiterate the humanitarian's presence, again and again. The drive to keep producing and disseminating visual evidence of the uncontacted, more than serving to prove they're still here, seems to also fulfill a need to assert that we humanitarians are still here, to make the uncontacted see those of us who are hailed as the consumers of these accounts and thus validate our own existence as such. In one telling section of *The Unconquered*, in which Wallace recounts getting very close to an uncontacted group, the likelihood that the expedition team is being watched by this group who they never see themselves is presented as thrilling in its danger. After Possuelo explains, "'they've been watching us. They've been just ahead of us, watching everything,'"[92] Wallace muses that it is "as though they'd developed a heightened suspicion of contact—refusing all gifts, spurning all overtures, fleeing deeper and deeper into the jungle. What would they do when they'd gone as far as they could go, when they felt they'd run out of room and could go no farther? Perhaps the Arrow People had just reached that point."[93] I read a kind of desire here in the imagining of being seen without being able to see—even if it's a violent desire that imagines the possibility of the subject's own death, a kind of recognition at the ultimate price—a desire that, in its expression, acts as an attempt to alleviate the prospect of the kind of death that has no witness.

The anxiety often expressed about the uncontacted, that "'they could disappear from the face of the Earth, and we wouldn't even know it,'"[94] is perhaps then also a reflection of the foundational anxiety of the self-appointed representatives of humanity, for whom the prospect of disappearance without remainder and without meaning is, ultimately, what must be managed. In the interest of such management, the potential disappearances (in their various forms) of the uncontacted must be made into a pedagogical event, so that in turn the Amazon can become a ground zero of humanitarian consciousness, a point of origin birthed of destruction. The possibilities that the outside world could be reconfigured by the uncontacted, or perhaps even treated by them as an object of indifference, seem too much for the humanitarian subject to bear. Here, in the longing for the recognition of the disappearing Native, we can see both another iteration of the appropriation of genocidally induced suffering for the enrichment of humanitarian consciousness, and the abyssal lack at the heart of humanity that by definition can never be filled.

5

A Differential Humanity

BEYOND THE NEW FEMINIST ETHICS OF VULNERABILITY

> Even walls tend to bind together those they separate, usually in a wretched form of the social bond.
>
> —Judith Butler, *The Force of Nonviolence*

Violence and the Vulnerable Subject

Sometime in the first several months of the recent Israeli invasion of Gaza, while I was listening to the radio, an official whose name I did not catch was offering commentary on the abject destruction and the terrorizing and murdering of Gazans (my description, definitely not the official's). This individual offered what is probably the most horrifying explanation of the invasion that I have heard, horrifying as much for the matter-of-fact tone with which it was delivered as for its content: that it is good for the people there, that it will lead to a better life for Gazans. I was left to sit with the implications of this distilled version of genocidal humanitarianism, and its illustration of how more blatantly racist and exterminatory reasons for enacting extreme violence can quickly come into alignment with seemingly more salutary ones. I continue to be struck by the grammar of the hegemonic renderings of what is happening there, which strain even the logics of humanitarian warfare past their breaking point; even to call it asymmetric warfare would be to grossly understate the power and authority of the Israeli state and military and overstate that of Palestine and Palestinians.[1] But then again, part of the point of arguing over the specifics of when and where war is necessary, what constitutes a war crime, and exactly what proportion of blame and guilt to lay at the feet of whom, is arguably to obscure a more basic operation of power: the instrumentalization of what is widely understood to be the extreme vulnerability of both Palestine and Palestinians as their fundamental, defining state of being, or in other words, the positing of the necessity of their violation as emanating from an ontological fact. The pedagogical function of the invasion and indeed its representation in countless discursive forms is to show that anything can, will, and should be done to Palestine—that, in other words, it is eminently vulnerable. This demonstrates the slippery and flexible nature of vulnerability in its instrumentalization for the commission of the most devastating violence.

It thus seems crucial to carefully examine the recent embrace of vulnerability within anti-oppressive projects, precisely in the midst of a pervasive ascription of vulnerability to the very peoples targeted by neo-imperial violence in the name of instilling a peaceful world order. In this new social justice–oriented vulnerability discourse, we see the conjoining of particular sensations/sensibilities with the political arrangement of social bodies. Here, vulnerable subjects—those who use their attunement to the ontological condition of vulnerability taken to be basic to all humans as the impetus to practice embracing that vulnerability—cultivate a sensibility of openness to exposure, specifically to the recognition of suffering in others and thus potentially in oneself, and the creation of an intimacy against an artificial separation, shielding, or distancing from others. This practice of being vulnerable is imagined to be allied with or even necessary to the development of a new ethics that could in turn effect a reworking of the political order, such that those who are especially targeted for socially sanctioned violence would be newly perceived as rightful full members of that order on the basis of their humanity. In other words, embracing vulnerability is imagined as the way for members of privileged groups to counteract the limiting effects on our perceptive capacities of the sensorial archive of devastation in which we are currently immersed, and to engage in new ethical sensibilities.

In a recent guest essay in the *New York Times*, Alex McElroy articulates an understanding of vulnerability that is paradigmatic of this discourse, bridging the registers of the popular and the scholarly, while also introducing an issue that is rarely discussed: the need to examine vulnerability's frequent invocation as an alibi for socially sanctioned forms of violence.

McElroy describes having felt hope about the rise of a new interest on the part of many men in practicing a vulnerability that explicitly involves "taking responsibility for their actions and feelings." But in the wake of the events of January 6, 2021, and other incidents signifying the increasing entrenchment of military-style racialized violence, McElroy notes, "my hope has begun to diminish as I've watched male vulnerability curdle into something toxic: Let's call it petulant vulnerability."[2] McElroy's description of vulnerability's susceptibility to use as a justification and refusal to take responsibility for violence and as a tool to enact emotional manipulation is compelling. They go on to distinguish this form of toxic vulnerability from true vulnerability, which, according to McElroy, "means accepting change, personal fallibility and the human condition of reliance on others, [whereas] petulant vulnerability feigns emotional fragility as a means of retaining power." While below I will suggest that making such a distinction between true and false vulnerability might not succeed in doing the work that it is meant to do, I believe that what is salient here is the point about power. The claim of the aggressor to be the actual victim of aggression will sound very familiar to anyone who has experienced abuse at the hands of another individual, an institution, or the state: The aggressor's appropriation of vulnerable status produces a dynamic in which the abused person is charged with and expected to take on ultimate responsibility for the abuse that they are targeted for, even as their experience is rendered wrong, immaterial, and void in the process. Being responsible for everything while being treated as nothing is an impossible position to inhabit—ontologically, psychologically, epistemologically, and ethically—which is the ultimate point of the abuse, that is, to annihilate the target. This is the most wretched of social bonds indeed, for the essential mechanism through which the abusive dynamic operates is the very mobilization of that bond to destroy the target's trust in her own sense of relationality.

By raising the question of power, McElroy begins to address a central and largely disregarded problem with the invocation of vulnerability as the basis of an anti-oppressive ethics, which is that the relationship between human experience and the possibility for ethical action that it describes is much more complex and fraught than is often allowed, given that the field of relationality is also the field of violence. In previous chapters I examined the messiness and murkiness of the discursive logics and affective states that characterize many of the extant reckonings with massive imperial military violence. As I have tried to show, it is entirely possible for recognition of another's humanity to elicit violent retaliation; for someone to be seen as both the victim of patriarchal violence and as to blame for that very violence; for protection to be conceived as punishment; for a life to be treated as grievable at the same time that the extermination of that life is seen as necessary. Vulnerability, either as a concept or as a state of being, is not itself free from these ugly complexities. Indeed, the notion of a vulnerable humanity that is a characteristic component of contemporary humanitarian discourses has often been used to describe a social reality in which the aggressor is the one who has been wronged, and to reassert a mode of relationality that, to use Jacques Rancière's terms, attempts to silence any whisper of disagreement. This is perhaps what McElroy would describe as a false form of vulnerability, but the issues at hand cannot be addressed through terminological accuracy. Rather, we must ask: How does the claim to being vulnerable work, and for whom? And what is the particular relational dynamic founding the assertion of vulnerability and enabling the subsequent use of that claim?

With these questions in mind, in this chapter I ask after the implications of recent work in feminist philosophy that seeks to reclaim vulnerability in order to provide a new way of reckoning with socially sanctioned violence, and ultimately a new ethical orientation, in a time of perpetual warfare. While addressing specifically gendered, sexualized, and/or racialized violences serves as the impetus for such work, I argue that its appeal to a humanity defined by the ontological condition of vulnerability risks replicating the very understanding of humanity that subtends those particular violences. To explore this issue, I take up a reading of Judith Butler's and Erinn Gilson's work. These authors have devoted serious, sustained attention to developing an ethics and indeed an ethical practice that could help work toward bringing systemic, oppressive violence to an end. I take that project seriously, even as I register a concern about their use of vulnerability as the conceptual foundation for their entry into that project. As Ann V. Murphy argues in a reading of Butler and others, authors working in this area tend to employ a "humanistic ethic" in which vulnerabilities are both "unique" and "generalized"/"anonymous" due to being a definitional feature of the human body.[3] Murphy goes on to argue that "because humanistic ideology has in the past demonstrated its own vulnerability to being corrupted and co-opted, bent in the service of some groups and not others, it is right that the prescriptive sway of the new corporeal humanism be marked by hesitation."[4] Yet I would suggest that a distortion of the meaning of vulnerability and the fact that humanity in its current sociohistorical configuration cannot admit every human being are not the key issues here, but rather (and more seriously) that the appeal to vulnerability elides the strange and ever-shifting qualities of humanity's formation as variously marked categories of people continue to be called into and out of an array of (in)human positionings. Moreover, the understanding of vulnerability largely being promoted—as an ontological condition of exposure that opens one to both intimacy and violence—is resonant with and arguably reiterates the historical constitution of humanity as defined by an internal civilizational/racialized hierarchy. In this scholarly context, rooting an ethics of nonviolence in ontology without a concomitant interrogation of the constitution of that very ontology has the effect of suspending a long line of thinking about imperial and military violence. Along these lines, André Lepecki crucially reminds us of Frantz Fanon's argument that "ontology's putatively transcendental mode of addressing the question of being is but the indispensable political strategy sustaining the colonialist-racist project: a project that reveals how politics and philosophy join forces by discursively framing all modes of appearing and of being present."[5]

In raising these issues, I do not want to dismiss authors like Gilson and Butler, but rather look at how this use of the concept of vulnerability ultimately leads to a critical impasse. In other words, I believe that the project of developing a feminist anti-war ethics needs to follow a different line of inquiry than the concept of vulnerability as ontological condition can provide. Indeed, Gilson and Butler themselves point to other possible modes of doing this work in their use of figurative languages of space, distance, and location in thinking about what vulnerability is and what modes of thinking and feeling it might facilitate. On my reading, the orientation of their arguments toward vulnerability has a hampering effect on what such language can make possible, and in Butler in particular the use of a figural language of distance/proximity seems to reiterate the current alignment of geographical location with ontology that is characteristic of the very geopolitical order that Butler wishes to transform. But there are other thinkers who have worked with similar figurations toward much different ends, and it is to these thinkers that I turn in the second part of this chapter.

Earlier in this book, I argued that humanity has been commonly conceived as defined by the capacity to enact world-ending violence, a capacity that is treated as a necessary resource for the development of a humanitarian ethics. Many feminist scholars have seriously contended with the racial/gender/imperial ordering that gave rise to and sustains this formation of humanity and its archetypal human subject, and taken together, they demonstrate the necessity of doing this work before any questions of ethics or indeed other ways of being human can be considered. In putting humanity and its ontology under pressure, these authors share a necessary twofold critique: first, of efforts to assert humanity's internal coherence; and second, of the imperialist/racist violence that is the necessary outcome of the drive to achieve that illusion of coherence. In forwarding that critique, they have sought to discern the relationship between instances of socially sanctioned violence and violence as constitutive, or in other words, how the infliction of harm and suffering creates the order of meaning and being that defines humanity; and they have developed this notion of constitutive violence in a variety of ways that allow us to see humanity's defining difference-to-itself, which in turn opens up possibilities for its questioning and potential refusal (if not dissolution).

Some, as articulated in Fanon's famous provocation that "every ontology is made unattainable in a colonized and civilized society,"[6] argue that ontology is aligned with whiteness, and that it is the right and capacity to commit violence that defines who is/can be human; thus, potential entry into fully human status has become a point of refusal for some of those who have been conceived as ontology's constitutive outside, for even supposing one could, why would one *want* to claim such status? The insight that humanity can only claim self-defined presence through a series of foundational violences leads these authors to the critical rejection of the effort to establish one's own humanity. For others, being human is a position that cannot be rejected per se; one's relationship to humanity is inherently variable and shifting because of its constitutive difference-to-itself, its intimate and defining relationship to the inhuman. Either way, humanity's difference-to-itself as necessitating a relationship of indistinction with what it supposedly is not—that is, différance—becomes a kind of critical resource for these authors, as it exposes the fact that humanity is not what it is often claimed to be. On this point, I turn our attention back to Denise Ferreira da Silva's critical insight (as discussed in the introduction to this book) about what she names as the two "distinct kinds of human beings . . . the self-determined subject and its outer-determined others,"[7] with the former, the "transparent I," relying on the notion of the latter in order to claim its self-determining status. As a counter to this foundational violence that establishes the subject of humanity, Ferreira da Silva offers a call "to produce a modern contra-ontology, that is, an account of the transparent I that shows how it can emerge—in a relationship, always already contending with its others."[8] Producing a contra-ontology is, I argue, a project undertaken by the second set of authors I engage with in this chapter. This contra-ontological project is, must be, what Chela Sandoval refers to as differential—a type of project that produces engagements with humanity that are necessarily multiplicitous, at times incommensurable, and irreducible to each other. Read alongside each other in this way, these authors imagine and enact modes of relationality that are precisely not premised on the achievement of a universalized expression of humanity. They do not necessarily agree with each other, and indeed it is in holding space for the irresolvability of those disagreements that humanity becomes visible as an exceedingly fraught category. Here I follow Sandoval's call to work against the strictures imposed by the fact that "critical and cultural studies in the U.S. academy, and the theoretical literature on oppositional forms of consciousness, difference, identity, and power, have been developed as divided and racialized, genderized, and sexualized theoretical domains," a situation she refers to as a "dangerous state of theoretical apartheid."[9] Seen as siloed and separate, what Sandoval might call the differentiality of their relationship is erased, and it becomes difficult to see the many possibilities that arise from that differentiality.

In putting these authors' works alongside each other, I read them as engaging a differential contra-ontology of humanity that has the potential for a kind of entry into a feminist anti-war ethics that those analyses reliant on the concept of ontological vulnerability cannot provide. The work of differential contra-ontology is to break open the bonding of identity to social and geographical location that is a hallmark of what Rancière would call the police order, in which whether one's articulation of membership in the community of humanity is understood as such is overdetermined by essentialist modes of rendering human being. These authors describe relationships of proximity, nearness, alongsideness—for example, in the notion of the perihuman, or in the idea that one might be seen as simultaneously inhabiting subhuman, human, and suprahuman positions, or in the necessary intimacy of so-called humans and so-called objects—that are less about sharing or commonality and more about exposing the differentiality that makes the formation of humanity possible. They pursue movements within and between social categories, identities, and positionings that are not so much about a freedom of motion across space but rather about the reconfiguration of space. In other words, differential contra-ontology has the potential to rework the given distribution of the sensible—the aesthetic order in which massive imperial military violence is the organizing telos—and, thus, to form an ethics that does not presume the necessity of consensus or the development of a consciousness of something shared that renders humanity as an undivided whole.

The New Feminist Ethics of Vulnerability

In the introduction to their edited collection on feminist philosophies of vulnerability, Catriona Mackenzie, Wendy Rogers, and Susan Dodds give a detailed account of possible "sources" and "states" of the condition of vulnerability, dwelling on the elaboration of vulnerability's signature characteristics.[10] On their account, the category of vulnerability includes various kinds of suffering under its reach, and indeed the authors seek to locate new ethical possibility in the painstaking cataloging of vulnerability's forms. "An ethics of vulnerability must begin by addressing four questions: What is vulnerability? Why does vulnerability give rise to moral obligations and duties of justice? Who bears primary responsibility for responding to vulnerability? And how are our obligations to the vulnerable best fulfilled?"[11] Here we see vulnerability defined as both a universal state of being, and as a social status characterizing some individuals and groups more than others. Indeed, the authors trace these two invocations of vulnerability across the literature and note the questions scholars have raised about their in/compatibility. While some have expressed concern that the ontological approach "obscures rather than enables the identification of the context-specific needs of particular groups or individuals within populations at risk," others have articulated the "dangers attendant upon labeling particular subgroups or populations as vulnerable, arguing that this can lead to discrimination, stereotyping, and unwarranted and unjust paternalistic responses."[12] Mackenzie, Rogers, and Dodds themselves seek to connect these two understandings of vulnerability in order to articulate a responsibility to the "'more than ordinarily vulnerable,'" by elaborating what they call a taxonomy of vulnerability.[13]

In their emphasis on the concept of vulnerability as a means to understand the origin and existence of suffering and harm, Mackenzie, Rogers, and Dodds exemplify a common approach, one that Erinn Gilson asserts a need to expand upon. Gilson seeks to define vulnerability not primarily as a state of victimization to which some are especially susceptible, but rather as a state of openness that is the basic condition of any kind of relationality. It is the recognition of this actual and universal state of vulnerability that, Gilson posits, has the potential to overturn those social conditions that maintain the façade of a self-defining non-interdependent subject, thus making vulnerability into a resource for social justice action. In order to make this claim, Gilson must contend with the relationship between vulnerability and violence, a concern for which is an animating feature of her work. In *The Ethics of Vulnerability: A Feminist Analysis of Social Life and Practice*, in the context of a close engagement with Butler, Gilson asks "whether vulnerability can be an ethical resource if there is a privileged relationship between vulnerability and violence. If vulnerability is always bound up with violence, as it seems to be in Butler's work, can we conceive of vulnerability apart from violence?"[14] The identification of this problematic founds Gilson's effort to detach vulnerability from a necessary relationship to violence. Elsewhere, Gilson describes her project along these lines in a way that captures the goals she articulates across much of her work, noting that she "seeks to elaborate how and why a denial of vulnerability appears to be a common phenomenon, why it is an ethically and politically dangerous one, and why an awareness of vulnerability is central to undoing not just violence but oppressive social relations in general."[15] She thus proposes "a more fundamental understanding of vulnerability" as "a basic kind of openness to being affected and affecting in both positive and negative ways, which can take diverse forms in different social situations."[16]

Gilson does engage with the ways that the concept of vulnerability has come under critique, specifically for reifying the characterization of certain populations as inherently lacking in agency, as in need of protection that they cannot give themselves, and as naturally inhabiting a lesser position in a hierarchical sociopolitical order.[17] But in her own work she calls for an advance beyond these critiques, pointing out that they can reduce vulnerability to the state of exposure to harm rather than understanding it in the more expansive way she proposes. She characterizes vulnerability as "part of the shared human condition insofar as we are all social and embodied beings, insofar as we are receptive and impressionable in myriad ways,"[18] and her larger argument hinges on this characterization, because she locates oppressive dynamics within the aspiration to be "the prototypical, arrogantly self-sufficient, independent, invulnerable master subject," an aspiration that requires the denial of one's essential vulnerability.[19] Gilson thus asserts that vulnerability is the very "ground for our responsiveness to one another": "It is because we are vulnerable that we need ethics and social justice, but it is also because we are vulnerable—because we can be affected and made to feel sorrow, concern, or empathy—that we feel any compulsion to respond ethically or seek justice."[20] Gilson acknowledges that "we cannot imagine that responsibility simply follows from an avowal of shared vulnerability,"[21] and thus that an ethics born of shared vulnerability is ultimately a practice that must be cultivated with intention.[22] Yet the very process of making the distinction between "ontological vulnerability" and "situational vulnerability"[23] is also key to this ethics, for without doing so "we may be prone to think of it as the reified, fixed property of certain types of individuals."[24]

Gilson posits the failure to make this distinction as a problem of knowledge, one that could be rectified through a more correct discernment of the realities of vulnerability. Awareness, apprehension, recognition, and the absence of these in the form of ignorance become chief concerns for Gilson. She posits the existence of the prevailing account of vulnerability as a symptom of ignorance, which accrues force as a kind of self-perpetuating feedback loop: "ignorance of vulnerability takes shape through an unthinking adherence to a negative conception of it," and this negative conception then enables "maintaining ignorance of the more fundamental sense of vulnerability, ontological vulnerability."[25] Correct and full knowledge of this shared condition of vulnerability is proposed as the necessary foundation for understanding the "social constitution of the perception of vulnerability," which in turn is necessary to cultivating an ethical response to oppression, because "assuming responsibility for vulnerable others, or demanding that other parties take responsibility, requires that one first have perceived and recognized someone's condition as a vulnerable one."[26] Gilson builds upon this claim while engaging Butler's work on the concept of grievability, arguing that accurate perception and understanding of vulnerability is necessary for the kind of social recognition that constitutes an ethical approach to the problem of injustice: "One must, for instance, be able to apprehend someone's life as precarious and the loss of that life as grievable in order to recognize the existence of a right to life. Conversely, the inability to apprehend someone's suffering as undue, grievous, or distressing precludes recognition of that person's humanity."[27]

For me, Gilson's critique of invulnerability as "a central feature of masterful subjectivity because it solidifies a sense of control"[28] sits uneasily next to the argument that it is an ignorance of vulnerability that subtends the desire for an impossible invulnerability. Gilson's call for the alleviation of ignorance in order to open to vulnerability is itself a call for knowledge of something posited as real. But this claim to having a greater proximity to something real also subtends any claim to mastery or invulnerability. Indeed, in the following passage, this conundrum seems to be implicitly acknowledged and then contended with in the form of a distinction between incomplete or "simple" knowledge and full or "deeper" knowledge:

Underlying and supporting such oppressive relations is a denial of responsibility in its most fundamental sense: vulnerability as openness to being affected and affecting in relation to others. In the context of such ignorance, one may make use of knowledge of who is particularly vulnerable, who is susceptible to harm, to exploit that vulnerability; overt forms of oppression entail such exploitation. The knowledge in this instance is a *simple* knowledge that someone is situated so as to be especially vulnerable; it involves no *deeper comprehension* of this vulnerability as a shared condition and rather involves reading such vulnerability as solely negative, exploitable. Thus, oppressive exploitation of vulnerability is an expression of the belief that vulnerability is a negative condition; it is an expression of the desire to continue to avoid, ignore, and repudiate vulnerability by projecting it onto others.[29]

Here, Gilson's account comes up against the limits of what the category of humanity demands. If we follow those thinkers who insist that humanity as both epistemological category and ontology is founded in a racial différance, then to say that vulnerability is a fundamental condition of human existence is to reiterate humanity's foreclosures. Moreover, the call to "refuse to conflate vulnerability in its *most profound and general sense—* openness to being affected and altered—with specifically negative forms of vulnerability, such as susceptibility to harm,"[30] in its alignment of accurate knowledge with openness and affectability, risks reinforcing that formative partitioning of humanity on the basis of a racialized characterization of some as having an understanding of the generalized human condition and others as not. To be human has arguably been defined precisely in this way—that is, to be open and affectable—in the context of a racist set of conditions. According to Hortense Spillers's famous argument, for example, chattel slavery's specific techniques of torture were designed to transform the body into flesh, that is, to make people illegible as differentiated bodies and to create race as a static feature of the very material substance of the no-longer-body: "'slave' is perceived as the essence of *stillness* . . . or of an undynamic human state, fixed in time and space."[31] Affectability takes its form over and against such stillness and unchangeability. Gilson's contention that "it is precisely because we are vulnerable—can be affected and made to feel sorrow, concern, or empathy—that we feel any compulsion to respond ethically"[32] takes on a new set of implications in the context of this genealogy of humanity.

Another way to put this is that the long shadow of violence remains even in the effort to reconceptualize and repurpose the concept of vulnerability away from it. Violence keeps reappearing as an issue to be contended with in Gilson's work, and in the effort to attend to it, it is bracketed off into a mode of relationality that could, the bracketing implies, be done away with. Alyson Cole observes this attempt to "unfetter vulnerability from violence and injury"[33] as a feature of vulnerability scholarship in general, linking it to the tendency to "conceptualize vulnerability in contradistinction to victimization."[34] For Cole, this move risks erasing the fact of victimization, the fact that certain people are targeted for violence, and blaming the victim all over again by turning the focus away from the violent actor, the one who victimizes.[35] To seriously contend with socially sanctioned violence would require that a series of questions about the complex landscape of vulnerability discourse be addressed. Who is positioned so as to be able to *claim their own* vulnerability? What if the mechanism for recognizing oneself as vulnerable is itself violent, for example, because one presses others already recognized as vulnerable into an affective service, as a kind of resource for one's own self-recognition? How do we contend with the common characterization of the inhuman by the commission of what are deemed to be immoral and unjust forms of violence, and the simultaneous reestablishment of humanity through the commission of violence that is deemed to be just? The invocation of vulnerability as ontological condition does not address the differential distribution of either violence or the capacity to represent and speak for a generalized human condition.

Gilson and Butler come into a simultaneous distinction and connection here. Gilson works diligently to distinguish vulnerability from violence, whereas Butler stays with violence in order to consider its complex relationship with ethical responsibility. At the same time, I note a similarity to Gilson in Butler's treatment of vulnerability as an ethical resource, expressed in the assertion that unprecedented suffering and loss in the lives of those who are not usually the target of socially sanctioned violence can radically shift individual and societal orientations toward a deeper appreciation of generalized human vulnerability. This is so particularly in the work that Butler began publishing shortly after 9/11, which contends directly with the war on terror and how it can be resisted, refused, and responded to. In *Precarious Life*, Butler characterizes 9/11 as offering a novel experience of *situational* vulnerability for the imperial aggressor that allows a conscious apprehension of vulnerability as an *ontological* condition, which can then be put to ethical use to countermand retaliatory violence:

"Despite our differences in location and history, my guess is that it is possible to appeal to a 'we,' for all of us have some notion of what it is to have lost somebody. Loss has made a tenuous 'we' of us all."[36] Butler is wary of reinstituting a sovereign subject, and notes that "although I am insisting on referring to a common human vulnerability, one that emerges with life itself, I also insist that we cannot recover the source of this vulnerability; it precedes the formation of 'I.'"[37] But in positing that the targeting of the United States for violence "can be a point of departure for a new understanding if the narcissistic preoccupation of melancholia can be moved into a consideration of the vulnerability of others,"[38] the very possibility of a new ethics is premised on an understanding of violence that is routed through the consciousness of those who are not used to being its target. Indeed, in remarking on the violent sociality born of US militarism, Butler moves from considering the effects of this violence on its targets to a reflection on what it can teach us about a generalized vulnerability: "To the extent that we commit violence, we are acting on another, putting the other at risk, causing the other damage, threatening to expunge the other. In a way, we all live with this particular vulnerability, a vulnerability to the other that is part of bodily life, a vulnerability to a sudden address from elsewhere that we cannot preempt."[39] Butler then gestures toward differential exposures to harm, asking, "is there something to be learned about the geopolitical distribution of corporeal vulnerability from our own brief and devastating exposure to this condition?"[40] Yet even here the main object of concern and the key point of possibility for a new ethical orientation remains "our own brief and devastating exposure," which I take to mean the new and unprecedented experience that 9/11 ostensibly constituted.

In regard to how that new ethical orientation might be cultivated, Butler ends *Precarious Life* with this statement:

> If the humanities has a future as cultural criticism, and cultural criticism has a task at the present moment, it is no doubt to return us to the human where we do not expect to find it, in its frailty and at the limits of its capacity to make sense. We would have to interrogate the emergence and vanishing of the human at the limits of what we can know, what we can hear, what we can see, what we can sense. This might prompt us, affectively, to reinvigorate the intellectual projects of critique, of questioning, of coming to understand the difficulties and demands of cultural translation and dissent, and to create a sense of the public in which oppositional voices are not

feared, degraded or dismissed, but valued for the instigation to a sensate democracy they occasionally perform.[41]

Here I see Butler as arguing for an opening toward political dissent via the recognition of humanity's constitutive difference-to-itself. At the same time, that the recognition of humanity's vulnerability is already a common intellectual/political modality makes it unclear whether a "dislocation from First World privilege" would in fact be the outcome of the privileged subject's new experience of threat and whether such a dislocation would in fact provide "a chance to start to imagine a world in which that violence might be minimized, in which an inevitable interdependency becomes acknowledged as the basis for global political community."[42] The dislocation Butler describes does not emerge from a reconfigured distribution of the sensible, but rather from the individual's greater attunement to a sensibility taken to be pre-given by virtue of its ontological status. And the experience of "First World safety"[43] being interrupted is exactly what has been cited as making the nuclear bomb exceptional in its capacity to jar humanity into a true understanding of its vulnerability and prevent future unjustifiable violence.

In much of their writing on war, those who retain enough privilege to experience its disruption remain the focal point of Butler's examination of the potential for vulnerability to found a new ethics. In both *Frames of War: When Is Life Grievable?* and "Precarious Life, Vulnerability, and the Ethics of Cohabitation," the "we" under consideration, those being addressed, are not only consumers of global media culture, but also those for whom war feels like it is at a distance—that is, those who find themselves being presented with images of violence from afar and wondering what one's responsibility to respond to that violence is.[44] Considering the circulation of a heavily edited set of images from the latest US military incursions, Butler asks what possibilities exist for an engagement with these objects of visual culture to produce the kind of understanding of precariousness that would then lead to "an ethical and political opposition to the losses war entails."[45] For Butler, it is the very circulation of such images that is key to any such possibility: "When those frames that govern the relative and differential recognizability of lives come apart—as part of the very mechanism of their circulation—it becomes possible to apprehend something about what or who is living but has not been generally 'recognized' as a life."[46] Central to Butler's abiding argument about vulnerability is this insistence on the need to value those not yet considered fully human or as worthy of life, by realizing that ethical obligations "emerge"[47] not only in situations of close community but under conditions of distance and difference. Butler cautions in particular against an ethics based only in proximity, for "if I am only bound to those who are close to me, already familiar, then my ethics are invariably parochial, communitarian, and exclusionary."[48] I am concerned about the potential implications of this latter assessment; given the ascription of parochialism to certain groups who are themselves the target of Western imperial violence in so many contexts, it is at the very least challenging to make the kind of assertion that Butler does without evoking this general sensibility. Moreover, Butler goes on to suggest that genocide has its origins in parochialism, as the archetypal example of the refusal to engage in an ethics of nonproximity:

> The possibility of whole populations being annihilated through either genocidal policies or systemic negligence follows *not only* from the fact that there are those who think that they can decide whom they will inhabit the earth with but because such thinking presupposes a disavowal of an irreducible fact of politics: the vulnerability to destruction by others that follows from a condition of precarity in all modes of political and social interdependency. We can make this into a broad existential claim, namely, that everyone is precarious, and this follows from our social existence as bodily beings who depend upon one another for shelter and sustenance and who, therefore, are at risk of statelessness, homelessness, and destitution under unjust and unequal political conditions.[49]

In *Frames of War*, Butler makes a similar claim that the problem with colonialism, US militarism, and other sorts of institutions that want to justify their enactments of violence against particular groups of people is that they make an epistemological error, failing to understand the precariousness of all humans (including those they claim to protect) and indeed their own vulnerability.[50] But claiming oneself to be vulnerable when presented with another's vulnerability has been, as I have tried to show, one primary way in which genocidal logics work. I also take it to be questionable whether a commitment to interdependency is necessarily oppositional to the genocidal. Genocide has never been just about a valuing of one's proximate community over others. As a central mode of Western empire, it has in fact often been about a terrifying *commitment* to humanity writ large, a commitment that has often been expressed as an aspiration toward the eradication of (significant) difference per se such that there is no more space defined by proximity or distance, just an undivided singularity.

The idea that the ontological condition of vulnerability might be turned toward the particular, toward a considered attention to the self or toward the cultivation of a specific community *not* coextensive with humanity, is, in vulnerability scholarship, invoked only in the negative. This risks precluding, and potentially vilifying or even positing as needing to be eradicated, the work of particularly vulnerable individuals and groups to *take care of themselves* in the face of demands to remain targets of violence, to inhabit the kinds of quasi-human status against which full/elevated humans might define themselves, or to participate more fully in serving humanity as a whole. As Cole usefully summarizes it, "the project of vulnerability studies constitutes an effort to address the epistemological ignorance of the privileged, theorizing vulnerability primarily from their point of view. It remains unclear what benefit the acceptance of constitutive vulnerability offers the disadvantaged."[51] Cole's point indicates another problem with the assertion that recognition of the fact of universal vulnerability will lead to a new valuing of people who have been disproportionately targeted for socially sanctioned violence: the problem of value itself. As Lisa Cacho has powerfully argued, there is no "(re)valuing" that is not "already linked to the devaluation of an/other."[52] Because in the context of US politics and law any claim to human rights must be made in the idiom of value, any such claim also ends up being an implicit argument for some other group's lack of a basis for making such a claim themselves; thus, as Cacho points out, what is often represented as different marginalized groups being at odds with each other over issues of inclusion and recognition is in fact a constitutive and inescapable feature of a political and legal system in which access to basic resources is premised on the fundamentally differential order of value.[53] Cacho's argument thus illuminates exactly where vulnerability ethics break down, that is, in the moment where it locates the possibility for a new social justice in the ethical subject's claiming of ownership of her response to the fact of vulnerability. If Butler's subject is the kind of member of a colonial/imperial state who could make the willful choice to turn her grief and loss over becoming a target toward an understanding of shared human precariousness, Cacho's subject is a denizen of a geopolitical locality that *relies on her recognition as excluded* in order to constitute its own self, which means that her grief and loss are not precisely hers to claim as they are already presumed as a structural feature constitutive of democratic governance. For such a subject to assert a place in humanity is not only virtually impossible, but perhaps actively harmful: For those "located in the spaces of social death ... demands for humanity are ultimately disempowering because they can be interpreted only as asking to be given something sacred in return for nothing at all."[54] This highlights the restrictive nature of the idiom of loss: Not only does it presume a subject with something to lose, it also presumes that loss would be the primary experience for the privileged subject experiencing a significant shift in power relations.

In continuing to insist on the necessity of understanding vulnerability as ontological rather than strictly situational, I see Butler as missing the opportunity to engage with the critical aporias opened up by the differential exposure to violence that characterizes the US imperial sociopolitical order and its reign of terror. For example, writing counter to the specific ontological claims that are made in the common characterization of only certain populations as vulnerable, Butler asserts that "if and when any of us were to be fully relieved of our vulnerability, we would have lost the social bond on the basis of which obligations can be grasped as reciprocal. Reciprocity depends upon vulnerability.... So one reason vulnerability cannot be the foundation of who I am, or of any politics I might wish to construct, is that it is the lack of foundation in myself with which I must live, if I am to live at all."[55] In other words, no particular individual—or population—"is" vulnerable; rather, vulnerability is the defining characteristic and generative force of sociality. In *The Force of Nonviolence: An Ethico-Political Bind*, Butler similarly focuses on the necessity of "a critique of individualism as the basis of ethics and politics alike,"[56] via the practice of nonviolence. Violence is a basic feature of relationality, as there is always the chance for "conflict, anger, and aggression,"[57] and as such is a kind of potentiality that, in being responded to, can give rise to an ethics and practice of nonviolence:

> Relationality is not by itself a good thing, a sign of connectedness, an ethical norm to be posited over and against destruction: rather, relationality is a vexed and ambivalent field in which the question of ethical obligation has to be worked out in light of a persistent and constitutive destructive potential. Whatever "doing the right thing" turns out to be, it depends on passing through the division or struggle that conditions that ethical decision to begin with.... Indeed, when the world presents as a force field of violence, the task of nonviolence is to find ways of living and acting in that world such that violence is

checked or ameliorated, or its direction turned, precisely at moments when it seems to saturate that world and offer no way out.[58]

The notion of relationality as fundamentally fraught and as defined by a kind of incalculability[59] is appealing because it refuses to engage the humanitarian logic according to which violence can be categorized as legitimate or illegitimate, can be justified on the basis of a cost-benefit analysis, or can indeed be seen, known, and understood in a complete way. The possibility of violence—as unjustified, irremediable, unredeemable—is always there, and it is by remembering this and yet still returning, again and again, to the practice of an always incomplete nonviolence that any sort of ethics becomes possible. Indeed, Butler asserts that "there is no practice of nonviolence that does not negotiate fundamental ethical and political ambiguities, which means that 'nonviolence' is not an absolute principle, but the name of an ongoing struggle."[60] And yet the abstraction of Butler's formulation takes questions of vulnerability, ethics, and violence out of the particular and indeed parochial contexts of relationality in which they become possible and take on form and meaning in the first place.

Ronak Kapadia's highlighting of one horrific example of the kind of "relational predicament" that is actively produced as a tool of US imperial warfare reminds us of the stakes of such abstraction. In discussing the "double-tap phenomenon," in which a military drone operator hits a target with multiple strikes, Kapadia argues that for people who live in target zones this "forces an ethical predicament when one must decide between one's own life and the lives of others when deciding to aid the wounded and to honor the dead, producing a kind of institutionalization of callousness."[61] This example shows how the very ground of US imperial warfare is a weaponizing of ethics in the attempt to determine "our way of knowing each other and ourselves."[62] And it exceeds and, I would say, deeply troubles the terms of an ethics of nonviolence premised on a refusal to "distinguish between preserving oneself and preserving the other."[63] It also suggests that the ascription of the willingness to kill, or to not take committed action against US imperial violence, to a failure to value all human lives as such is incapable of addressing the brutal ways in which such violence imposes the incapacitation of the ability to care for another as the price of survival. This is the kind of incalculability that exposes the terrible logic of value itself. In the face of these effects of drone warfare, does it still make sense to pose the problem of violence as one to be addressed through efforts to "recast the living as worthy of value"?[64]

Toward a Differential Contra-Ontology

In *Methodology of the Oppressed*, Chela Sandoval takes on the question of how to enact a feminist anti-oppressive shift in consciousness, yet she does so by engaging a different notion of subjectivity, taking as interlocutors a group of differently positioned people and invoking a quite different social and political terrain than does feminist scholarship on vulnerability. Sandoval traces the articulation of what she dubs differential consciousness in the work of a variety of critical theorists, but is particularly interested in its cultivation and enactment by US Third World feminists, a group of thinkers from "varying internally colonized communities" whose work prioritized connections to decolonizing efforts across the globe.[65] Differential consciousness is one of five skills or technologies Sandoval identifies as constituting the methodology of the oppressed—"a set of processes, procedures, and technologies for decolonizing the imagination"[66]—as well as the fifth of five modes of oppositional consciousness that arise from the approach to social movement that is "the theory and method of U.S. third world feminism."[67] The concept of the differential also takes on a third meaning here, as a kind of movement "through meaning," "through consciousness," and "through the social order."[68] Movement and motion are key to Sandoval's theory of how a refusal of prevailing ideology and the practice of a different form of relationality could be enacted in the midst of profound hierarchy. The form of relationality that an anti-racist, anti-colonial feminist in a sense must pursue in such a context (of being positioned on the margins of white-centered feminism's narrative of oppositionality) has been enacted and refined by US Third World feminists through the movement into, out of, and through various different modes of oppositional consciousness.[69] While the first four modes of oppositional consciousness are "politically effective means for transforming dominant power relations," the differential mode is both this and more: The first four "are *kaleidoscoped into an original, eccentric, and queer sight* when the fifth, differential mode is utilized as a theoretical and methodological device for retroactively clarifying and giving new meaning to any other.... Its powers can be thought of as *mobile—not nomadic, but rather cinematographic: a kinetic motion* that maneuvers, poetically transfigures, and orchestrates while demanding alienation, perversion, and reformation in both spectators and practitioners."[70] I am drawn to Sandoval's distinction between an entitlement to nomadically traverse a literal and/or figural terrain, and a kind of movement that offers a kaleidoscopic "sight." The sight that differential consciousness makes possible is characterized by an internally highly differentiated vision, one that breaks up whatever falls within its field of view, transforming it into a new arrangement. Moreover, referencing how the experience of watching a film takes on the illusion of seamlessness and wholeness only through motion—the display of still images in sequence at a particular speed attuned to human visual perception and processing capacities—the concept of differential consciousness attends to the différance that enables consciousness, subjectivity, and meaning-making. This kaleidoscopic vision is, as I take it, the product of a kind of disordering of the given distribution of the sensible. Here, it is not the new experience of a privilege-mitigating loss but rather the alienating and perverting experience of seeing a variety of ideological positions as they relate to each other in a new way—some of which one might have held near and dear to one's heart as they used to be, and yet now appear forever changed—that enacts a reconceptualization and reordering of what might have been previously taken to be reality. Bodies, subjectivities, and epistemologies are rearranged in a way that exposes the aesthetic rules of their previous ordering.

Sandoval's understanding of the conditions under which differential consciousness came to be articulated and enacted emphasizes the margin as an internally diverse and differential space, where the possibility of relationality is rooted not in a generalized human condition but rather in the forms of experience, understanding, and committed action that arise in the context of being targeted for violence: "During the 1970s, U.S. feminists of color identified common grounds on which to make coalitions across their own profound cultural, racial, class, sex, gender, and power differences. The insights gained during this period reinforced a common culture across difference comprised of the skills, values, and ethics generated by a subordinated citizenry compelled to live within similar realms of marginality. This common border culture was reidentified and claimed by a particular cohort of U.S. feminists of color who came to recognize one another as countrywomen—and men—of the same psychic terrain."[71] What is shared here is not an understanding of the ontological status of humanity, but rather a space that is inhabited by force, a space defined by its elsewhereness and in which differences in sociopolitical location remain the necessary basis for the development of oppositional consciousness. In proposing that "this new cartography is best thought of not as a *typology*, but as a *topography* of consciousness in opposition,"[72] Sandoval works against the common suturing of oppositional consciousness to identity on the one hand and universalized human experience on the other:

This *cultural topography* delineates a set of critical points within which individuals and groups seeking to transform dominant and oppressive powers can constitute themselves as resistant and oppositional citizen-subjects. These points are orientations deployed by those subordinated classes who seek subjective forms of resistance other than those determined by the social order itself. These orientations can be thought of as repositories within which subjugated citizens can either occupy or throw off subjectivities in a process that at once enacts and decolonizes their various relations to their real conditions of existence. This kind of kinetic and self-conscious mobility of consciousness was utilized by U.S. third world feminists when they identified oppositional subject positions and enacted them *differentially*.[73]

This differential topography resists the spatialization of time that is the hallmark of colonial epistemology and cosmology.[74] In doing so, it allows for a variety of relationships to time to exist simultaneously (just as an automobile differential allows individual wheels on a vehicle to simultaneously turn at different speeds). The movement that the differential allows is "'between and among' ideological positionings.... The differential represents the variant; its presence emerges out of correlations, intensities, junctures, crises."[75] This approach imagines and enacts a way of contending with socially sanctioned violences that is not predicated upon coming to a shared understanding of human ontology—a shared understanding that, as the notion of a differential topography reveals, would be predicated upon a civilizationist and evolutionary understanding of humanity, and would require an agreement that would itself only be made possible through a series of violences. This is why it is so crucial that "the differential resides in the place where meaning escapes any final anchor point, slipping away to surprise or snuggle inside power's mobile contours—it is part and parcel of the undefinable meaning that constantly escapes every analysis."[76]

In the spirit of Sandoval's differential mode of engagement, I offer a discussion of several lines of inquiry mobilized by authors contending with questions of how, and whether, to relate to humanity. In addition to offering a variety of crucial ways to engage the problem of massive imperial violence at the level of the very configuration of humanity, reading these authors' varying approaches as differentially related to each other can potentially offer another mode of developing a feminist anti-violence ethics. Here I attempt to follow Sandoval's committed analysis of how social positioning profoundly affects one's ways of seeing and knowing, which is also precisely the means by which she seeks to de-essentialize the relationship between identity and consciousness—that is, to thoroughly know the meaning that social categories of identity have for us so that we can effect a reordering of our lives, relationships, communities. As such, the authors I take up here engage in analyses of the racialized/gendered formation of humanity from perspectives and positions that, by definition, cannot be conflated with each other. In other words, reading them together while refusing to resolve them into each other or somehow decide between them can perhaps offer the kind of kaleidoscopic view that is productively alienating in regard to the order of things within which genocide is presumed necessary to the survival of humanity.

One line of inquiry involves what Eunjung Kim calls the "humanness of violence."[77] Kim illuminates how arguments that identify the dehumanization of targeted peoples as the main problem with racist/colonialist/ableist violence retain humanity as their uninterrogated point of reference. Contra the common understanding of such violence as itself inhuman and as arising from the failure to recognize other humans as such, she asserts that it is in fact premised on an initial *recognition* of shared humanity that is then forcibly and actively denied. Rather than being a good process gone wrong (i.e., in which an inherently positive recognition is contorted away from its original purpose), the dynamic of recognition and denial is itself foundational to the enactment of the kind of violence that explicitly targets other humans, such that the recognition of another's humanity becomes profoundly compromised as the basis for any ethics. For Kim, "the blasphemy of thingification, it seems, is not the misrecognition of one entity (humans) for another (things)," but that the thingification of beings originally recognized as human "hinges on a particular way to treat an object."[78] Thus, "viewing perpetrators of violence as non-human animals and victims as objects"[79] simply reconsolidates the normative power of the category of humanity. Kim is particularly interested in the importance of efforts to embrace objecthood—rather than reclaim status within humanity—for an anti-ableist project. As such, she proposes that "positioning violence inside the human . . . compels a movement out of humanness to practice nonviolence, in this way refusing to exercise violence and embracing the vulnerability involved in becoming objects."[80]

Below I will return to a more in-depth consideration of the implications of becoming object, but for now I would like to highlight the assertion Kim is making about violence and its relationship to vulnerability. I find it crucial that Kim describes the possibility for nonviolent practice as a "movement out of humanness," for which one "suspends what are conventionally viewed as uniquely human capacities and values."[81] For Kim, it is this movement that can "open up an anti-ableism, antiviolence queer ethics of proximity that reveals the workings of the boundary of the human," an ethics in which difference is acknowledged as central to the workings of relationality—not by understanding difference per se but by refusing to subsume it to a logic of evaluation according to which the human as the larger/superior category takes on greater importance than the differences that putatively inhere within it.[82] Kim's "movement out of humanness" I see as a refusal of humanity's typical evaluative mandate, a decoupling of humanness from value, or, to use Kim's words, a process of "leaving humanness without qualification":[83] "To suspend humanness is to abandon the appraisal of difference and move toward a nonjudgmental ontology of copresence and proximity."[84] I take Kim's notion of proximity to not assume that closeness automatically yields a mutual understanding of shared interests that in turn interrupts the capacity to perceive the humanity of those made distant by geography and/or identity (i.e., the kind of proximity that on Butler's account would lead to parochialism and exclusion). Rather, Kim's proximity is a name for the simultaneous existence of non-taxonomized forms of being whose relationships with and to each other would not be codified by the evaluating force of recognition.

The critical choice to position violence within the human is not meant to naturalize violence but rather to denaturalize the human—and in doing so, to first expose and then to dismantle the historical, material, and ideological apparatuses that have constituted human ontology as defined by violence. This work of exposure and dismantling is taken up by Patrice Douglass. In an article in which she considers Korryn Gaines's murder by the state, and white-centered feminism's constitutive incapacity to account for the particularity of violence against Black women, Douglass argues that "Blackness is gendered through violence that structures it outside of humanity and defines the perimeters of what it means to *be* for the Human and its discontents."[85] What it means to be human/part of humanity is defined through the enactment of anti-Black violence; to be human is to be violent/anti-Black. Elsewhere, Douglass has elaborated on the implications of this problem for historiographical engagements with chattel slavery. Contrary to common renderings of chattel slavery as inhuman in its expression of violence, Douglass asserts that it was, in fact, very human, the very expression of humanity. Thus, "if humanity is what commits such violence," what are the consequences of articulating redress as involving recognition of one's humanity? If the enactment of such violence is the qualifying factor for entrance into humanity, she asks, what does it mean to say that the person targeted for such violence "is human too"?[86] If this is what it means to be human, then Black humanity is a contradiction that exposes the profound incapacities of the human as the ground for an antioppressive ethics. Pursuing a similar line of inquiry, while arriving at a somewhat different conclusion than Douglass, Zakiyyah Iman Jackson argues that "the recognition of humanity and its suspension act as alibis for each other's terror, such that the pursuit of human recognition or a compact with 'the human' would only plunge one headlong into further terror and domination. Is the black a human being? The answer is hegemonically yes. However, this, in actuality, may be the wrong question as an affirmative offers no assurances. A better question may be: If being recognized as human offers no reprieve from ontologizing dominance and violence, then what might we gain from the rupture of 'the human'?"[87] While Jackson proposes that the human does not establish itself so much through the constitutive exclusion of Blackness but rather through "black(ened) people" being "cast as sub, supra, and human *simultaneously*,"[88] both Douglass and Jackson establish the human as incompatible with nonviolent relationality. Jackson argues that this simultaneity of multiple positionings "puts being in peril because the operations of simultaneously being everything and nothing for an order—human, animal, machine, for instance—constructs black(ened) humanity as the privation and exorbitance of form. Thus the demand placed on black(ened) being is not that of serialized states nor that of the in-between nor partial states but a statelessness,"[89] a plasticity that is instrumentalized in whatever way is needed in order to consolidate humanity as such.[90] Jackson's argument about how the ascribed plasticity of Blackness "puts being in peril" puts a fine point on the differential constitution of the category of humanity, its need to form and reform itself again and again—and, thus, the structured impossibility for all human beings to share the same part in the order of humanity.

Axelle Karera also speaks to these incapacities of the human, posing a foundational challenge to those feminist efforts to properly recognize and assess oppressive violence reviewed in the first part of this chapter: "critical black philosophies . . . question what it means to inhabit a structural position whereby the black philosopher is always already forced to align herself with exclusionary terms in order to register anti-black violence as violence."[91] I read this statement as illuminating the obscured truth around which the anti-violence feminist ethics of vulnerability is logically structured. When she asks the question, "I wonder here what would an ethics based on the radically non-relational look like?,"[92] she is, like Kim, Douglass, and Jackson, suggesting that humanity never has and never could contain the possibility of a variety of humanities conceived nonhierarchically. Because, for Karera, the very form of relationality is premised on the reproduction of white life,[93] the focus on life and "mutual dependency" that characterizes attempts to develop a humanitarian ethics for the Anthropocene "anticipates a post-apocalyptic 'recalibration' of anti-black racist practices."[94] This reinvestment in the value of interdependent vitality both fails to grapple with the origins of prevailing forms of relationality and elides the violences through which those forms have been sustained. In such a context, argues Karera, nonrelationality "becomes a modality of disruption intended to jam discursive syntax, ethical arrangements, and a discourse's desire to secure its coherence by discarding the earth's vulnerable inhabitants."[95] Karera does not explicitly invoke feminist vulnerability scholarship, yet I find that she directly addresses and raises crucial questions about its aesthetic features—namely, its imagining of modal subjects who are either located in geopolitical and identitarian spaces of privilege and whose new experiences of suffering will somehow reorient their affective and ethical capacities, and/or who are able to respond to their own experiences of harm by embracing the ethical possibilities of the shared condition of vulnerability. Her attention to the violent purposes that invocations of "mutual dependency" might serve in arguments that take no account of racialization and racism as fundamental to the establishment of humanity's order suggests the need for a critical questioning of whose experiences of harm and suffering are seen as being able to provide the material foundation for a vulnerability ethics.

Anne Anlin Cheng's deep attention to the complexities and complications of relationality given human life's reliance on that which has been categorized as neither human nor alive—and indeed on the very establishment of such inevitably untenable boundaries—resonates with Karera's question about the nonrelational. Reminding us that any inquiry into ontology must take into account the role of Asiatic femininity and the figure of the "yellow woman" in the composition of the human, Cheng argues that Asiatic femininity has been rendered not as flesh but as ornament,[96] asking, "what happens to our notions of the subject when carnality is cultivated not out of flesh but out of its fusion with inorganic matter? What happens when we accept that style (mediated through yet detached from a racial referent) may be not simply the excess or the opposite of ontology but a precondition for embodiment, an insight that challenges the very foundation of the category of the human? What is at stake here is not just the objectification of people but how that objectification opens up a constitutive estrangement within the articulation of proper personhood and life."[97] Objectification is not about the reduction of persons to flesh and hence things, but rather about the proximity to things and status as thing that in fact makes the human.[98] Indeed, Cheng describes ornamentalism as "a theory about the profound imbrication of things and persons"[99] and offers the reader a series of thoughtful provocations regarding the human's complicated relations to various non-, in-, quasi-, and other-than-human people, beings, and objects. In Cheng's deft hands, the human and the inhuman are revealed to be in a relation of fundamental indistinction, an indistinction wrought not by their fungibility but by their interdependency; she makes it impossible to find any place to alight in trying to articulate a concrete understanding of what the experience of being human is. Ornament—that which is supposedly exterior to the psyche, a mere embellishment of an already existing body, and/or inert object fabricated by a preconstituted subject—turns out to be necessary to establish any semblance of ontology.[100] This is a way to understand the insecurity of the category of the human, resonant with Ferreira da Silva's argument about man as thing, yet that even more deeply explores the ramifications and experience of that insecurity for differently positioned individuals.

The particular relationship of Asiatic femininity to ornament both reveals the reliance of ontology on objectification and raises a specific set of contingencies for the Asiatic woman:

> Simultaneously consecrated and desecrated as an inherently aesthetic object, the yellow woman calls for a theorization of persons and things that considers a human ontology inextricable from synthetic extensions, art, and commodity. Instead of being pure capture or representing fugitive flight from the nominative biological or anatomical raced body, the yellow woman emerges as a "body ornament" whose perihumanity demands that we approach ontology, fleshliness, and aliveness differently. By perihumanity, I mean to identify the peculiar in-and-out position, the peripherality and the proximity of the Asiatic woman to the ideals of the human and the feminine. At once closely linked to ideas of ancient civilizational

values and yet far removed from the core of Western humanist considerations, she circles but is excluded from humanity.[101]

If humanity is not a fixed or sound category in the first place, then Asiatic femininity is neither precisely within nor outside of it.[102] Being human is not a state to be either claimed or disclaimed, or to recognize oneself as always already outside of; rather, its reliance on the object as "a vexing, constitutive potential" makes it a perilous if inescapable imposition for the racialized subject to have to navigate.[103] In focusing on the "making of an aesthetic ontology that is the ornamental personhood of Asiatic femininity,"[104] Cheng offers a crucial way of understanding ontology as having everything to do with the "'aesthetics' at the core of politics"[105]—the distribution of subjects, bodies, and objects in social space, in patterns of relationality that take meaning and value from the preferentialization of certain forms and sensibilities. This exposure of the aesthetic formation of humanity and human persons in general highlights what the rendering of humanity as ontologically vulnerable misses, which is the racialized/ imperial political ordering that figures Asiatic femininity as perihuman.

Cheng's work has important bearing on how we think about the relationship between violence and vulnerability. We might say that her assertion that "commodification and fetishization, the dominant critical paradigms we have for understanding representations of racialized femininity, simply do not ask the harder question of what constitutes being at the interface of ontology and objectness,"[106] invokes a more radical form of vulnerability—the vulnerability of being human *as object*—than that posited by the scholarship discussed earlier in this chapter. This is a quite different mode of engaging with the question of how to understand the forms of relationality wrought by racist violence. In a profound passage, Cheng reckons with such violence by describing human ontology not as defined by the openness to being affected, but rather as the condition shared with all other life of being food, which one becomes precisely by virtue of consuming others:

> Cannibalism might be the condition of, rather than an exception to, civilization. We have to be willing to eat ourselves and others in order to be the privileged humans that we are. . . . Being "nonhuman" and "other" may be *the very mode of our ontology*. Consumption makes otherness our own, but also opens us up to an

unruly sociality where what seems properly ours becomes food for the other. This insight into our fundamental, ontological alienation, which also plays itself out externally over and over again as racial differentiation, does not dilute the impact of racism. On the contrary, it underscores how quotidian, inescapable, voracious, and vulnerable our appetite for the other is.[107]

Here, vulnerability is invoked not so much as a potentiality that grounds the possibility of ethical relation, but rather as alienation, as the difference-to-itself that is the paradoxical possibility of consciousness but also of the very material substance of being; in consuming and being consumed, one comes into being quite literally through making objects and becoming object. The suggestion that alienation is the "very mode of our ontology" has implications for how we understand the functions that racism serves. When racist violence is understood as in part the product of a desire to make the constitutive movements of différance purely external—that is, to project the very conditions of being outside of the self in order to posit, say, whiteness as having a putative essence—it becomes difficult to say that it could be adequately addressed by getting more deeply in touch with one's human nature. I think that here, Cheng is suggesting that racism serves a deep set of functions that cannot be simply rooted out by recognizing one's own susceptibility to suffering, applying willpower to curb one's aggressive impulses, or cultivating an accurate understanding of vulnerability as an object of knowledge.

If things and persons are not so distinct, then it becomes more difficult (perhaps even impossible) to locate a distinctly other-than-human in those things. In other words, forwarding the non- or other-than-human does not necessarily facilitate the decentering or deprivileging of the human. I take it that for Cheng, Jackson, and some others, the decentering/deprivileging of the human is not really possible and is also beside the point—and worse, because of its impossibility, the claim to do so risks reiterating the very racialized and gendered violence that establishes the human as we know it as a meaningful category. Along these lines, Cheng notes that posthumanism, "even as its intention has been to unsettle a tradition of insular humanism and anthropocentrism . . . has forgotten that the crisis between persons and things has its origins in and remains haunted by the material, legal, and imaginative history of persons made into things."[108] It is from the articulation of a responsibility to address this problem that several scholars engage their own inquiry into the human, in part by drawing attention to the perils of two main, interconnected premises of posthumanism: the notion of the dead or no-longer subject, and the failure to account for the foundational role of race in the construction of the human.

As a discourse that engages humanitarian ethics by attempting to decenter the human without deep engagement with the profound violences that brought the hegemonic Western human subject into being, posthumanism reveals what happens when violence is not theorized from the perspective of those who have experienced its deepest and most abiding effects. As scholars like Tiffany Lethabo King and Ferreira da Silva point out, the notion of the dead subject is predicated on a profound obfuscation of the role of actual genocidal death in creating the very conditions for the declaration of the supposed "death" of this (in fact, still-existent) subject. The posthumanist subject appropriates the deaths of others in order to enact a grand denial of responsibility for those deaths. Or, as King puts it, "the erasure of the (white) body-as-subject-as-ontology has been more effective in covering the bloody trail of white/human-self-actualization than it has been at successfully offering a way around and beyond the entrapments of liberal humanism."[109] This simultaneous denial and appropriation/use of genocidally aimed death is, I have argued, also characteristic of bomb ethics. What it feels like to be so positioned—as useful insofar as one's death becomes the material for a theory that is supposedly for everyone, and as responsible for the aggressor's well-being so that your annihilation can be justified when you fail at your given task—is taken up by both King and Ferreira da Silva. It is Ferreira da Silva's point of departure in *Toward a Global Idea of Race*, which she opens by describing the experience of encountering posthumanist articulations of the death of the subject precisely as she was witnessing the actual deaths of actual people. Indeed, the preface begins with the perspective of those people, Black and Brown, who have been positioned within a Western colonial episteme and sociality as dead, as marked and defined by death.[110] At the same time as the actual, systemized deaths of actual people, "the Subject is dead! we have been told. So why is its most effective strategy of power [the analytics of raciality] still with us?"[111] Thus, not only is the declaration of the death of the subject beside the point, from the perspective of the need to address racist violence and the various deaths it requires. It is also that the announcement of the death of the subject, as an object of self-generated fear on the part of the same episteme that called forth that subject, is itself a mechanism of elision of the "various and diverse kinds of human beings . . . that stood differentially before universality when it deployed the powerful weapon, the concept of the racial, which manufactured both man and his 'others' as subjects that gaze on the horizon of their finite existence."[112]

Declaring the death of the subject is an act that, indeed, (re)constitutes the subject. It is through such declarative acts that the subject has any existence in the first place, because the subject is (despite claims to the contrary) not self-constituting, and always reliant upon others to (re)produce an existence that is never its own. In other words, the declaration of the subject's death is best understood as a tactic, one for claiming ownership and control, for reinstituting critique and the development of oppositional consciousness as a propertized relationship. Not only is there still, of course, a subject here, but his secretly desired presence and solidity is projected outward, in yet another reiteration of the profound dereliction of responsibility that defines whiteness as a propertized relation to subjectivity. This way, he gets to enact the critique of himself, thus claiming ownership over his own (putative) undoing. The only possible outcome of this posthumanist move is a radical denial of the constitutive foreclosures that humanism relies upon, a denial that must be enacted again and again, for example, in the form of what King calls the "strange assumption" that Black women scholars are incapable of nonattachment to identity as the basis of subjectivity (strange "given the foreclosure of the possibility of subjecthood to black flesh made female").[113] This strange assumption reinforces that foundational move of racist humanism, the "compulsion to ground Black female flesh in the knowable immanence of a particular body with familiar, anticipated, and already-knowable speech."[114] Moreover, this post/humanist compulsion is then blamed on those who are its very targets, as if they were responsible for post/humanism's racist moves. Here, the posthumanist's continued (unacknowledged) investment in a particular kind of human subject—one who is entitled to everything, to the very limits, ends, outside, and other to the human—is revealed by the material and historical conditions that enable post/humanist thinking itself.

What Ferreira da Silva and King describe as standard posthumanist moves sound very much like what McElroy names "toxic vulnerability," or the notion of vulnerability that is symptomatic of bomb ethics: There is the simultaneous projection onto the aggressor's targets the very qualities that the aggressor wishes to deny in their own self, and the usurpation of the target's state of exposure to violence for the purpose of the aggressor justifying the annihilation of the other to save the self. While the feminist ethics of vulnerability is definitively not invested in the effort of such justification, its account of what violence is and what to do about it shares with bomb ethics a post/humanism that posits violence as a natural feature of being human that can be gotten under control by cultivating the right conception of humanity. As a case in point, in *The Force of Nonviolence*, Butler argues this:

> Even if none of us are freed of the capacity for destruction, or precisely because none of us are freed of that capacity, that ethical and political reflection converges on the task of nonviolence. It is precisely because we can destroy that we are under an obligation to know why we ought not to do it, and to summon those countervailing powers that curb our destructive capacity. Nonviolence becomes an ethical obligation by which we are bound precisely because we are bound to one another; it may well be an obligation against which we rail, in which ambivalent swings of the psyche make themselves known, but the obligation to preserve the social bond can be resolved upon without precisely resolving that ambivalence.[115]

Butler's nonviolence is, to be sure, not to be conflated with the vision of peace that is a central term of bomb ethics. And yet the invocation of destructive capacity as a defining characteristic of humanity and furthermore as precisely what will lead to the realization that it should not be used is foundational to the establishment of humanity as needing to be defended and preserved by those whose advanced civilizational state confers upon them the unique capacity and responsibility to do so. In response to Butler's call to "curb our destructive capacity," I would add a caution regarding who it is that is most commonly imagined as having the ability to do so and the particular forms and experiences of vulnerability that are imagined to be properly conducive to an ethical reorientation characterized by increased attention to both others' and one's own suffering.

This leads me to assert that a feminist ethics of nonviolence would need to seriously contend with the fact that "the crisis between persons and things has its origins in and remains haunted by the material, legal, and imaginative history of persons made into things"[116]—the forgetting of which is, according to Cheng, the critical void over and around which posthumanism constructs itself. Directly taking on this history means, among other things and at the least, critically questioning the specific form of human subjectivity called into being by vulnerability ethics and taking seriously the kinds of intimacy and proximity that cannot be so readily understood as expressions of nonviolent openness to difference. Thus, in the final pages of this chapter, I consider human being as object being from the perspective of what it might look like to root a feminist anti-war ethics in the recognition that the modal subject of vulnerability ethics' aesthetic order—a self- and other-aware agent who has the capacity to cultivate a humanitarian consciousness of the value of the lives of others—has an enabling history and present of making some persons into things. In suggesting that they push back on the expectation to preserve humanity's onto-political order, I do not mean that the authors I invoke here are not interested in questions of ethics, responsibility, or deep relationality. Rather, I suggest that they pursue those questions by centering sensory experiences of intimacy with objects and the condition of objecthood to mobilize humanity's foundational différance.

In her critical review of vulnerability scholarship, Alyson Cole makes the provocative point that the attempt to recuperate vulnerability, "to uncover hidden agency or to endow passivity with expansive agential capacity is arguably not unlike the desire for invulnerability. Both ultimately disavow weakness and inaction as shameful."[117] I take it that Cheng is in part motivated by the need to reconfigure weakness, inaction, and related "shameful" states when she articulates a call to "take seriously the life of a subject who lives as an object,"[118] that is, without attempting to grant agency or status as fully human. Indeed, in proposing that "parsing the transformative magic of ornamentalism will allow us to address those bodies that, even as they are deprived of it, do not seek humanity"—thus "making room for stranger forms of less-than-human agency"—she seeks to move beyond "the impasse between victimization and agency, antiessentialism and authenticity" that feminist anti-racist work can get caught in.[119] The key here, as I take it, is to root out the logic and discourse of value that ultimately lies at the base of these binary terms through which the experience of human existence is so commonly thought. Eunjung Kim speaks directly to this problem of value,[120] which leads her to suggest that "moments of object-becoming yield an opportunity—one that is perhaps counterintuitive yet potentially generative—to fashion an ethics of nonpurposive existence."[121] Such an ethics could, I think, offer a quite different way to approach the problem of violence in regard to human sociality, positing violence as generated not by the fact of being human but rather by the effort to make meaning of being human by distinguishing and valuing it. This is precisely the problem Kim points to when she lists the terms against which feminist subjectivity has often been defined: "unintentionality, speechlessness, unseeing, acquiescence, immobility, inertness, incompetence, asexuality, and disconnection."[122] In naming such qualities and projecting them onto certain populations, indeed reifying those populations through this operation of projection, those discourses and projects invested in humanity's endurance have also relied on a deeply racialized and gendered bifurcation of humanity from objecthood. What both Kim and Cheng offer in response is to insist upon taking these expressions and experiences of objecthood seriously, on their own terms, precisely by not reinjecting them into humanity's order of onto-political value.

In a discussion of the film *Ex Machina*, which ends with the android Ava killing her human maker, trapping and abandoning her (also human) would-be savior, and escaping into human society after being confined to her maker's home for her entire existence up to that point, Cheng asks, "Could this fantasy of living on as a thing, undetected by humans, serve as a fable for the social subject who is an object? Not to assimilate . . . but to exist, somehow, alongside?"[123] I am interested in what Cheng describes as existing alongside humanity. In one way, Ava arguably proves her humanity according to the standards set by the Western imperial epistemological/ontological regime: She exerts her capacity to kill (other) humans in order to ensure her own freedom, and indeed plays out a racist civilizationist narrative in being the first of her kind to do so (the android models who preceded her were made to appear like women of color, while Ava appears white). Yet it is also left unclear whether Ava possesses any sense of responsibility to humanity writ large, and whether she would willingly curb her capacity for destruction due to an understanding of her own potential place within humanity. From this perspective, the film could be said to thematize the hegemonic rendition of humanity's relationship to violence that I have traced in this book: The capacity for destruction is precisely what will allow humanity to survive, but only in the hands of those with a properly advanced understanding of what it means to be human and commitment to humanity as a whole. But in addition to considering the role Ava arguably plays in the filmic narrative as cipher for questions regarding race, gender, and violence, I understand Cheng to be attending to how those who have served as the multiplicity of human/perihuman/inhuman forms upon which humanity has reluctantly relied might themselves choose to relate—or, very possibly, not relate—to the project of maintaining humanity. Existing alongside humanity, the social subject who is an object does not seek the recognition of mutual vulnerability so much as live with and in another kind of relationality that exposes the violence of the social bond.

From the standpoint of those who have been expected to take care of humanity as a whole precisely as they are denied the right to take care of themselves, the *obligation* to preserve the bonds that ensure humanity's social order has arguably been devastating in the most literal of ways, where binding together surpasses the wretched and becomes the very means of annihilation. I think of the expectation that hibakusha understand and narrate their experiences as useful and even necessary to the project of peace; of how the suffering of women like Rukhsana facilitates the cultivation of a humanitarian geopolitical order that they themselves are seen as a threat to; of the utter inability to imagine a place for the uncontacted in the world given their putative incapacity to understand (their own) humanity. A feminist anti-violence/anti-war ethics needs to take the deadly effects of this obligation seriously, to seek out the seemingly unlikely places where this implicit expectation to pay the ultimate price of one's self might lurk, and to refuse the humanitarian logics and processes of evaluation, recuperation, and integration when it comes to those who have been rendered by humanity's aesthetic order as disposable. The disposable signify and materialize what is excessive to humanity or what must be ejected to produce the illusion of its totalizing presence, and indeed the most horrific of violences are committed in the production of this illusion. To reinscribe the disposable within humanity's order, then, would be to eliminate what their presence continues to expose: the inevitable breakdown of humanity's absolutist aspirations. Taking seriously life lived as object means acknowledging the existence of the disposable alongside but not as part of humanity and hence uninscribed within humanity's totalitarian consensus. In attending to the question of "what is possible in a life of precariousness," Cheng offers the insight that "sometimes, disposable lives find themselves through disposable objects.... Freedom for the captured may not be the gift of uncompromised liberty but instead the more modest and demanding task of existing within an entombed shell. It is not only that bodies can leave their residue in the things they produce (an insight that object studies has taught us), but also that objectness reveals the divergent, layered, and sometimes annihilating gestures that can make up personhood."[124] The notion that annihilating gestures can also make up personhood is both a challenge to the genocidal fantasy of total elimination and a reckoning with the reality of violence as so woven into the fabric of social life that it cannot be separated out from it. It also suggests that suffering and the sense of loss it entails is neither measurable nor predictable in its evolution, and that something else can happen when those who have been subjected to its severest forms are not instrumentalized for a greater purpose but simply let be, to live in the midst of it in the best way that they/we can come up with, perhaps somewhere away from those who caused it. Here I am reminded once again of Jinah Kim's thoughts on grief,[125] as the refusal to forget or to get over that provides the possibility of an ethical reorientation not by way of empathy based in the shared condition of vulnerability, but by holding a place for what is not recuperable or recoverable, what is gone and never coming back.

Coda

ZERO LOGICS, ATOMIC SEMIOTICS; OR, AN AESTHETICS OF DEBRIS

> Zero, as a nondegree, silences the claim that there could be anything other than what already is.
>
> –Eric A. Stanley, *Atmospheres of Violence*

First in an article and later in a monograph, Eric A. Stanley explores an abiding concern about how statistics betray queer and trans people and are key to social processes that move to obliterate the actuality of queer and trans existence through extreme violence, perhaps most especially when they are motivated by humanitarian sensibilities.[1] Stanley makes the statement with which I begin this coda, about zero as a nondegree, in the context of a deep critique of the prison as a structuring set of relations in the contemporary United States (and beyond). Referring to the phenomenon of prisons implementing zero-tolerance policies regarding sexual assault, Stanley asserts that because the prison is founded on and reproduces itself through the commission of sexual violence especially against queer and trans individuals, the function of the zero-tolerance policy in regard to the imprisoned is to deny "the experiences they are living as fact."[2] In other words, the peculiar reality fabricated by this prison policy is that the people caged there cannot be, and therefore are not, assaulted. Zero-tolerance policies and hate crimes statistics alike do not just fail to prevent such socially prescribed violences, they work to provide supposed evidence that there is something natural, something given about them. Stanley expresses this argument with the concept of overkill, which is both a legal term and, on Stanley's reading, a way to name the kind of anti-queer/trans violence that goes beyond murder to enact "the ending of trans/queer life itself."[3] As Stanley explains its work as a legal concept, overkill is what authorizes the trans/gay-panic defense: "Here, trans/queer life is a threat that is so unimaginable that one is *forced* to not simply murder but to push the dead backward out of time, out of history, and into that which comes before. Yet this overkill registers as little in the social—the double bind of inhabiting the place of both menace and void."[4] Overkill's definitional failure to register socially, given its centrality to the operation of the very social order itself, cannot be corrected by the gathering of statistics and the attendant codification of violence's forms and meanings. The real issue here is the impossibility of reckoning with loss through its measurement; given that fact, "our task, it seems, is to radically resituate the ways we conceptualize the meaning of violence as fundamental and not antagonistic to our current condition."[5] With this call, I read Stanley as providing another way to see and understand how genocidal humanitarianism has simultaneously founded a general relational order and has profoundly differential impacts for individuals and groups inhabiting identities and onto-political positions that have been marked as nothing.

If "overkill names the technologies necessary for, and the epistemic commitment to, doing away with that which is already gone"[6]—that is, the drive to prove that something that is there is in fact not, for which to simply kill is not enough—it also designates a genocidal fantasy similar to the animating doctrine of US nuclear war policy during the so-called Cold War, a fantasy of the absolute surety of absolute destruction. Joseph Masco explains that "overkill is a theory of nuclear targeting that accounts for imagined technical failures in the system by exponentially multiplying the number of nuclear weapons launched," originally conceived and "designed to enable a simultaneous global nuclear strike on all communist states."[7] An image from an exhibit at the Titan Missile Museum explains that what are "*apparently* excessive numbers of weapons" are actually necessary "to account for the probability of failure among items of equipment as complicated as ICBMs, and ensure that 100% saturation is achieved at the designated targets."[8] In other words, the overkill arsenal has a built-in fail-safe ensuring against the possibility of failing to destroy everything. The ideology of overkill drove the build-up of the US nuclear arsenal to "a peak of over 35,000 nuclear weapons by the end of the 1960s, enough to destroy every major city on the planet many times over," a capability that the United States still retains.[9] Thus, as Masco puts it, "this overkill installs a new kind of biopower, which fuses an obliteration of the other with collective suicide"[10]—that is, it ensures the eradication not only of life but of the history of that life, all trace of it ever having existed.

The kinship between the doctrine of overkill and the concept of zero is found in the interchange between everything and nothing, both forms of totality. "Zero" names both nothing and the potential of that nothing in the hands of those who would authorize themselves to orchestrate life and death: Ground zero identifies destruction as controlled rebirth, while the climate initiative World War Zero offers the goal of reaching nothing (in this case, net zero carbon emissions) as a point of possibility and even sanctuary. As such, zero is the object of desire, seeming to offer control over meaning, over knowledge, over human civilization—and indeed, in the form of nuclear technology, over the very stuff of the universe, atoms themselves—but also the object of dread. For nuclear technology is premised on a form of power that can be unleashed but not contained, a process of dismantling and destruction that by definition cannot be controlled: This is precisely what radioactivity is, the decay of the atom's nucleus that occurs in an element's unstable forms.[11]

The recognition of and attempt to resolve this fundamental problem has profoundly shaped extant approaches to the problem of radioactive waste storage and containment. The impossibility of radioactive waste's containment—which has partly to do with the qualities of radioactive material itself and partly to do with the incapacities that define human existence—has seemed to only further elicit ambitious attempts to prove otherwise.[12] In serving as a consultant on a report submitted to the US Nuclear Regulatory Commission in 1981 that made just such an attempt, semiotician Thomas A. Sebeok was tasked with producing "a reasonably fail-safe means of communicating information" about radioactive waste repositories "such that the system's effectiveness would be maintained for up to 10,000 years,"[13] or in other words, to try to ensure that unsuspecting future humans would not unwittingly create a nuclear disaster. Based on the understanding of communication developed by semiotics and accounting for the inevitability of massive shifts in systems of meaning over that length of time, what Sebeok proposed was an "atomic priesthood," a select group of experts who would be entrusted with the true understanding of radioactive waste's dangers and with maintaining an "artificially created and nurtured ritual-and-legend" so that "the uninitiated will be steered away from the hazardous site for reasons other than the scientific knowledge of the possibility of radiation and its implications; essentially, the reason would be accumulated superstition to shun a certain area permanently."[14] In imagining the continued production of knowledge (and other forms of) hierarchy as key to humanity's future, this proposal fantasizes about the kind of control of meaning that prevailing understandings of nuclear technology have been predicated upon from the beginning, even as Sebeok suggests that due to the operation of entropy, "information tends to decay over time"[15] and that therefore the atomic priesthood should implement a "'relay system' of information transmission . . . to divide the 10,000-year epoch envisaged into manageable segments of . . . reasonably foreseeable periods."[16] The timescales invoked in plans for the storage of radioactive waste are in some way driven by rates of radioactive decay,[17] but perhaps more so by this illusion of control, the absurdity of which is revealed by both Masco's and Valerie Kuletz's discussions of the proposed deep geological repository at Yucca Mountain. While in order to be approved by the federal government the proposal for the Yucca Mountain project had to include a 10,000-year safety plan, the plan really could not be anything other than a fiction; both authors learned from some of those involved in the project themselves that it is reasonable to expect a containment lifetime of only about a hundred to a few hundred years for that facility.[18]

Sebeok's invocation of entropy—the disorder, randomness, and unpredictability that is part of any system—is interesting because it speaks to the fact that radioactive waste achieves what humanity cannot, an endurance and a power to affect the very matter of the universe across a potential span of millions of years. Even the concept of half-life itself expresses the incapacity of humans to control what is supposedly our own invention. Half-life is a calculation of probability, the average time it takes for half of the atoms present in any given quantity of radioactive material to decay; because of random variation, the point in time at which any individual radionuclidic atom will experience decay cannot be known in advance.[19] Half-life is thus a measurement the very form of which is also an expression of its own incapacities as a measurement. Seen in this light, the imagining of nuclear weapons fallout as a potential indelible mark of humanity's presence—as proposed by some Anthropocene writers—is revealed as a particularly strange and tragic way of making exactly that which threatens us with demise into that which will ensure our longevity. Radioactive waste storage planning serves another purpose in addition to its most obvious one: to impose a forgetting of the fact that human-produced radioactivity is already defining the very materiality of existence. Recording and forgetting are in dynamic interplay here, both merely different strategies in the larger project of the attempted control of meaning. This is the legacy of overkill: the fallout that defines our lives, that cannot be contained, that has no spatial or temporal parameters. We are living in the debris of the nuclear project, and some are figured as the waste of that project, that is, the unwanted by-product that gives the lie to the always already failed mission of constructing humanity's ruins. In invoking the "we," I want to be careful to note that this is a differential "we," defined by the internal differences and differentiations that the Western imperial project has both needed and wanted to exterminate. Indeed, precisely because of its aspiration to do so, the possibility of worldwide nuclear annihilation has created neither a common human experience nor a self-same humanity. The figural work of the nuclear waste storage facility is not unlike that of the planned ruins in the genocidal imagining of the future. Like Speer's imagined crumbling amphitheater, the storage facility stands as a testament to humanity's ontological singularity, and yet it is empty of actual living human beings, and it cannot itself be witnessed or known by future humans—a fact clearly understood by Sebeok, as the role of the atomic priesthood was articulated not simply as to keep people away but as to eradicate broader knowledge of the existence of this supposed triumph of human civilization.[20] This attempt to manage decay and indeed impermanence itself, the planned ruins—in the absence of anyone to decipher its meaning—thus becomes debris, a field of unstructured rubble and strewn objects giving no indication of their prior arrangement in a now forever-gone set of relations.

If humanity's ruins define an architecture of idealized consensus, in which onto-political space is structured by an eradication of difference/disagreement so total that it registers simply as reality as-it-is, debris represents a dismantling that is simultaneously a rearrangement of constituent parts that become something else in that rearrangement. In invoking debris, I am specifically thinking of Ocean Vuong's description of his novel *On Earth We're Briefly Gorgeous*, when he noted that he "wanted the book to feel like debris" in order to deflect the kind of reading that would see it as a "guided tour" through Global South pain.[21] I took Vuong, a MacArthur Fellowship winner, to be expressing in that statement a keen awareness of the stature he had achieved and the attendant expectation that he would indeed provide such a guided tour, given his identity and life story as well as the themes covered in his work (the aftermath of the US war in Vietnam, life as a refugee in the midst of layered histories of racism and colonialism, growing up poor and queer in the classist and homophobic society of the US, to name a few). Vuong spoke of knowing that many readers would look for indications of the reality of his life in *On Earth We're Briefly Gorgeous*, and that as a result he saw the book as in part an experiment in "positioning autobiographical lenses around a fictional work," a way to test the current state of the long-lived expectation for writers of color to act as "recorders" of suffering. Thus, instead of a guided tour through planned ruins, debris; instead of offering meaning through the piecing together of what was broken into a new whole, for Vuong in the very writing of the novel "fracture became a technology of self-knowledge." I see in this use of fracture a reinterpretation of technology itself, as well as a refusal of the expectation to embody suffering for others' use—that is, a refusal of the instrumentalization of the suffering of those targeted for horrific death and violence for the purposes of humanity's survival, an instrumentalization that is a key technique and motive of what I have been calling genocidal humanitarianism.

In describing the autobiographical as itself a kind of technology, where autobiography involves the use of "lenses" through which to produce a particular kind of view, Vuong indicts the presumed transparency of the racialized/ethnicized subject that underwrites the aesthetics of ruination and its attendant ethics. The autobiographical lens as a technology of fracture that allows the unfurling of a self-knowledge predicated on such a refusal of instrumentalization and indeed transparency is, it seems to me, at work in Vuong's poem "Notebook Fragments." Written in the form of a list of lines and short sequences with no necessary relationship to each other taken from a journal, a sense of organization and order nonetheless emerges from the repeated invocation of bombs and grenades and their alignment with figures of life (fruit, food, flowers). In the lines "An American soldier fucked a Vietnamese farmgirl. Thus my mother exists. / Thus I exist. Thus no bombs = no family = no me," the repetition of "thus" suggests a logical structure supported by what is in essence a placeholder for meaning rather than a definitive meaning itself: The sequence of "thuses" fails to explain the complexity of the existence of this author of notebook fragments, suggesting the sheer weight of realizing that bombs condition one's existence here and now and the impossibility of ever fully reckoning with what that might mean, but also that the existence of bombs cannot possibly unilaterally determine the existence of the speaker. These are lines that buckle under their own weight, disassemble themselves precisely in their performance of capturing the supposed facts of a supposed reality.

In the terrain of debris, a possibility for another ethics arises, not bomb ethics with its totalizing brightness of transparent meaning but an ethics of anti-transparency and uncontainability, an ethics not caught up in the trappings of humanitarianism. Debris is what one might see looking through Chela Sandoval's kaleidoscope, fragments of what used to appear as a seamless whole, a new view, a recomposition into "an original, eccentric, and queer sight."[22] These fractured and redistributed parts describe the possibility of another ordering. As Jane Bennett reminds us, Rancière's notion of the political is apropos here: "a political act not only disrupts, it disrupts in such a way as to change radically what people can 'see': it repartitions the sensible; it overthrows the regime of the perceptible."[23] Debris is both the figurality of repositioned bodies and subjects who take on new identities and new orientations toward each other precisely in that repositioning, and the materiality of other-than-human presences, entities, and objects that exert what Bennett describes as a kind of vitality or "efficacy" not located within strictly human agency.[24] In considering such efficacies, Bennett suggests that "Rancière's model contains inklings of and opportunities for a more (vital) materialist theory of democracy. Consider, for example, the way it imagines the being of the demos: not as a formed thing or fixed entity, but as an unruly activity or indeterminate wave of energy. The demos is, we read, 'neither the sum of the population nor the disfavored element within,' but an 'excess' irreducible to the particular *bodies* involved."[25]

I see here an opening for bringing together a critique of the impossible control fantasized by the planned ruins of the nuclear waste repository with a consideration of what becomes possible in resistance to and refusal of the consensual political ordering that defines genocidal humanitarianism. Nuclear waste has the habit of exerting its own vital efficacy by breaching and indeed changing the nature of the structures meant to contain it; in this sense, it is a kind of debris, not just representing a reordering of the nature of reality but actively engaging in that reordering, a technology of reordering that moves beyond its purposiveness for humanity. It both represents and is the necessary excessivity of humanity's efforts to define itself in a complete and total way—and thus, articulating a true sense of responsibility to the fact and nature of its existence would of necessity fracture and break open humanity proper. The kind of ethics made possible by the decompositional efficacy of the aesthetics of debris would orient its practice toward a right relationship to waste, to the disposable, to the uncontainable unwanted—all of which are part of life and indeed are especially present characteristics of some lives. As Salar Mameni puts it in their meditation on crude oil and the presence of toxicity in life, "we are composite, contaminated beings mired within multiple bodies, histories, generations, and geographies. Contamination is what makes life possible."[26] I take "contamination" here to reference the entangled, differential relations that vitalize the possibility of any being's presence, relations that call for an ethics of being-with rather than making meaning from, as Mameni suggests in articulating a refusal of the "distanciation from terror" that is common in accounts of warfare and genocidal violence: "instead, I think with Terrans, those bodies and lands that are contaminated, extracted, flooded, and burned."[27] An ethics with this kind of orientation could be a way to take the project of actually contending with the suffering imposed by the colonial war machine with the utmost seriousness; it could offer a more honest engagement with the concept of half-life, as the closest we can get to some kind of necessarily incomplete reckoning with the inevitability of decay and the immeasurability of violence.

Notes

Introduction

1   "I.2. Originally: resembling the Cynic philosophers in having contempt for comfort, wealth, or pleasure, or in a tendency to be scornfully critical of others. Now *esp*.: inclined to believe that people are motivated purely by self-interest." "Cynical (adj.)," *Oxford English Dictionary Online.*

2   Rancière, *The Politics of Aesthetics*, 12–13.

3   This thought was inspired by Ocean Vuong. Answering a question about his novel *On Earth We're Briefly Gorgeous*, he noted that he "wanted the book to feel like debris," to subvert a white gaze that would expect what he described as a "guided tour" through Global South pain. A ruin is tourable—debris is not. Ocean Vuong, virtual book reading and discussion, School of the Art Institute of Chicago, October 6, 2020.

4   As just one example, Michael Barnett characterizes the establishment of the UN in the following way: "The Geneva Conventions were less a breakthrough for humanity than a belated recognition that the brutality of war had exceeded acceptable limits. The Universal Declaration of Human Rights was less a climactic moment in the indefatigable march of human rights than a mournful recognition of humankind's deficit of humanity. These human rights institutions, and many of the edifices constructed after World War II, were testimony not to compassion but rather to the fear of further acts of barbarism" (Barnett, *Empire of*

Humanity, 102–3). While mournful rather than triumphalist, this kind of narrative is typical in generalizing and hence depoliticizing the "barbarism" of the war, and in recentering Western actors and eliding, yet again, the anti-colonialist movements to which those actors responded with such brutality.

5   Falcón, *Power Interrupted*; Rajagopal, *International Law from Below*, 43, 77.
6   Rajagopal, *International Law from Below*, 72.
7   Grewal, *Transnational America*, 121–22.
8   Williams, *The Divided World*, xx.
9   Williams, *The Divided World*, xvi.
10 Williams, *The Divided World*, xxi.
11 Rajagopal, *International Law from Below*, 9–13, 174–86.
12 Rajagopal, *International Law from Below*, 194–95.
13 Asad, "What Do Human Rights Do?," 13.
14 Asad, "What Do Human Rights Do?," pa. 27, 31, 50.
15 Falcón, *Power Interrupted*, 4–5, 8–10, 12–14, 22. See also Laura Hyun Yi Kang's fantastic *Traffic in Asian Women* for a detailed inquiry into the development of the prevailing epistemologies that guide UN-related accounts of gender inequality, particularly in regard to the conceptual categories of sex, violence, and slavery.
16 Grewal, *Transnational America*, 137.
17 Fernandes, "The Boundaries of Terror," 62.
18 Keating, Rasmussen, and Rishi, "The Rationality of Empowerment," 154; Harvey, *The New Imperialism*.
19 See, for example (to name just a few), Ahuja, *Bioinsecurities*; Amar, *The Security Archipelago*; Morgensen, *Spaces Between Us*; Puar, *The Right to Maim*; Puar, *Terrorist Assemblages*; Schuller, *The Biopolitics of Feeling*; Stoler, *Race and the Education of Desire*; Valencia, *Gore Capitalism*; Weheliye, *Habeas Viscus*. I also want to point out that the genealogy of biopower/necropower, so often anchored in the reference to Foucault, is also contestable. Brady Thomas Heiner argues that Foucault's late-career interest in the investigation of power was a product of his engagement with the work of Black Panther Party thinkers—which of course was unacknowledged by Foucault (Heiner, "Foucault and the Black Panthers"). Relatedly, Orlando Patterson offers a different genealogical focal point for some scholars working on biopower/necropower. Patterson's concept of social death, developed within his work on the institution of chattel slavery in the US, has been taken up by scholars investigating the continuing depredations imposed on Black life in con-

temporary institutions coextensive with chattel slavery; it has also been taken up by those interested in working through the co-construction of various racialized groups in relation to each other (Patterson, *Slavery and Social Death*; Cacho, *Social Death*).

20   Mbembe, "Necropolitics," 13–25.
21   Mbembe, "Necropolitics," 20.
22   Mbembe, "Necropolitics," 40 (emphasis in original).
23   Lindqvist, *"Exterminate All the Brutes"*, 3.
24   Lindqvist, *"Exterminate All the Brutes"*, 9.
25   Lindqvist, *"Exterminate All the Brutes,"* 97–107.
26   Lindqvist, *"Exterminate All the Brutes,"* 9; Bouchard, "Humanitarian."
27   Lindqvist, *Terra Nullius*, 126.
28   Wolfe, "Settler Colonialism," 401.
29   Wolfe, "Settler Colonialism," 402.
30   Wolfe, "Settler Colonialism," 402.
31   Wolfe, "Settler Colonialism," 399, 403.
32   Bartov, *Murder in Our Midst*, 32.
33   Wolfe, "Settler Colonialism," 398.
34   Wolfe, "Settler Colonialism," 400.
35   Rancière, *The Politics of Aesthetics*, 13.
36   Rancière and Engelmann, *Politics and Aesthetics*, 66.
37   Rancière, *Disagreement*, 28.
38   Rancière, *Disagreement*, 17.
39   Rancière, *Disagreement*, 8–9, 27.
40   Rancière, *Disagreement*, 123.
41   Rancière, "The Ethical Turn of Aesthetics and Politics," 6.
42   Rancière, "The Ethical Turn of Aesthetics and Politics," 6 (emphasis in original).
43   For Rancière's more extensive argument along these lines, see chapter 6, "Politics in Its Nihilistic Age," in *Disagreement*.
44   Rancière, "The Ethical Turn of Aesthetics and Politics," 2.
45   Rancière, "The Ethical Turn of Aesthetics and Politics," 6–7, 10.
46   Mamdani, *When Victims Become Killers*, 6.
47   Mamdani, *When Victims Become Killers*, 5–10, 14.
48   Mamdani, *When Victims Become Killers*, 43 (emphasis in original).
49   Rodríguez, *Suspended Apocalypse*, 135.

50 Rodríguez, *Suspended Apocalypse*, 138 (emphasis in original).

51 Rodríguez, *Suspended Apocalypse*, 30 (my emphasis).

52 "Humanitarian (n. and adj.)," *Oxford English Dictionary Online*.

53 "Whole (adj., n., and adv.)," *Oxford English Dictionary Online*.

54 Hua, *Trafficking Women's Human Rights*, 17.

55 Wynter, "Unsettling." Wynter distinguishes between Man1 and Man2, as two distinct forms of the "de-supernaturalizing of our modes of being human" (Wynter, "Unsettling," 263–64). She makes this distinction on the basis of a periodization: Man1, in place "from the Renaissance to the eighteenth century," enabled the development of the physical sciences; Man2, in place from the nineteenth century through the present, enabled the development of the biological sciences (Wynter, "Unsettling," 264).

56 Wynter, "Unsettling," 282.

57 Wynter, "Unsettling," 282.

58 Lisa Lowe offers a detailed historical examination of this work in *The Intimacies of Four Continents*.

59 Hartman, *Scenes of Subjection*, 19.

60 Atanasoski, *Humanitarian Violence*, 82.

61 Ticktin, *Casualties of Care*, 2–6.

62 Ticktin, *Casualties of Care*, 80.

63 Ticktin, *Casualties of Care*, 8.

64 Atanasoski, *Humanitarian Violence*, 14.

65 Ticktin, *Casualties of Care*, 61.

66 In regard to the United States' incarceration of refugees from Haiti during the early 1990s, Neel Ahuja describes "two types of state force" used against these people—"militarized exclusion" and "the exercise of a certain type of care" (Ahuja, *Bioinsecurities*, 171).

67 Ahuja, *Bioinsecurities*, 170.

68 Ahuja, *Bioinsecurities*, 170.

69 Ahuja, *Bioinsecurities*, 171.

70 Ahuja, *Bioinsecurities*, 178.

71 For an argument that the ongoing siege of Gaza has come to be enacted through "'humanitarian management,' exercised as the calibration of life-sustaining flows of resources through the physical enclosure, one meant to keep the entire population close to the minimum limit of physical existence" (81), see chapter 3 in Weizman, *The Least of All Possible Evils*.

72 Puar, *The Right to Maim*, 129–35.

73 Butler, *Frames of War*, 42.
74 Ferreira da Silva, *Toward a Global Idea of Race*, xiii.
75 Ferreira da Silva, *Toward a Global Idea of Race*, xxxix.
76 Ferreira da Silva, *Toward a Global Idea of Race*, 44.
77 Ferreira da Silva, *Toward a Global Idea of Race*, 26.
78 Ferreira da Silva, *Toward a Global Idea of Race*, xxiv (emphasis in original).
79 Ferreira da Silva, *Toward a Global Idea of Race*, 162.
80 Rajagopal, *International Law from Below*, 171–72.
81 Browne, Danely, and Rosenow, "Vulnerability and the Politics of Care," 1–7.
82 Schuller, *The Biopolitics of Feeling*, 15 (my emphasis).
83 Schuller, *The Biopolitics of Feeling*, 3–4, 7.
84 Schuller, *The Biopolitics of Feeling*, 4.
85 Schuller, *The Biopolitics of Feeling*, 13.
86 Yoneyama, *Hiroshima Traces*, 113–14.
87 Weizman, *The Least of All Possible Evils*, 8.
88 Weizman, *The Least of All Possible Evils*, 9.
89 Weizman, *The Least of All Possible Evils*, 11–14. For more on the concept of proportionality, see Dower, *Cultures of War*.
90 Virilio, *War and Cinema*, 70 (emphasis in original).
91 Speer, *Inside the Third Reich*, 56.
92 Speer, *Inside the Third Reich*, 56.
93 Speer, *Inside the Third Reich*, 56.
94 See Cartwright, *Screening the Body*; Chow, *The Age of the World Target*; Lippit, *Atomic Light*; Mirzoeff, *The Right to Look*; Rony, *The Third Eye*.
95 "It was in 1861, whilst travelling on a paddle-steamer and watching its wheel, that the future Colonel Gatling hit upon the idea of a cylindrical, crank-driven machine gun. In 1874 the Frenchman Jules Janssen took inspiration from the multi-chambered Colt (patented in 1832) to invent an astronomical revolving unit that could take a series of photographs. On the basis of this idea, Etienne-Jules Marey then perfected his chronophotographic rifle, which allowed the user to aim at and photograph an object moving through space" (Virilio, *War and Cinema*, 15).
96 Kaplan, *Aerial Aftermaths*, 9.
97 Virilio, *War and Cinema*, 4.
98 Kapadia, *Insurgent Aesthetics*, 29.

99 Kapadia, *Insurgent Aesthetics*, 2.
100 Kapadia, *Insurgent Aesthetics*, 69.
101 Rony, *The Third Eye*; Rony, *On Cannibalism*.
102 Trinh, *Woman, Native, Other*, 73 (emphasis in original).
103 Rajagopal, *International Law from Below*, 26.
104 Rajagopal, *International Law from Below*, 108.
105 Rajagopal, *International Law from Below*, 112.
106 Rajagopal, *International Law from Below*, 105 (emphasis in original).
107 Wynter, "Africa, the West and the Analogy of Culture," 25–26.
108 Wynter, "Africa, the West and the Analogy of Culture," 29, 32, 35–37.
109 Wynter, "Africa, the West and the Analogy of Culture," 37.
110 Spillers, "Mama's Baby, Papa's Maybe," 65–69.
111 Mbembe, "Necropolitics," 40.
112 Mbembe, "Necropolitics," 35.
113 Mbembe, "Necropolitics," 35.
114 Asad, *On Suicide Bombing*.
115 Rony, *How Do We Look?*, 187–89.
116 Kim, *Postcolonial Grief*, 12, 19.
117 Kim, *Postcolonial Grief*, 11, 12.
118 Kim, *Postcolonial Grief*, 25.
119 Singh, *Unthinking Mastery*, 223.
120 Dower, *Cultures of War*.
121 Kim, *Postcolonial Grief*, 25.

Chapter 1. Bomb Ethics

Epigraph 1. John W. Dower, *Cultures of War*, 269.

1 "The Clock Shifts."
2 Rabinowitch, "Scientists and World Government," 346.
3 Bromwich, "Doomsday Clock Moves Closer to Midnight."
4 Krauss and Titley, "Thanks to Trump."
5 Chan, "Doomsday Clock Is Set"; Mecklin, ed., "It Is Now Two Minutes to Midnight"; Mecklin, ed., "It Is 100 Seconds to Midnight"; Bulletin Science and Security Board, "Bulletin Science and Security Board Condemns Russian Invasion of Ukraine."
6 Mecklin, ed., "It Is 100 Seconds to Midnight," 3.

7   Mecklin, ed., "It Is 100 Seconds to Midnight," 7–8.
8   Mecklin, ed., "A Time of Unprecedented Danger."
9   Fabian, *Time and the Other*, 31.
10 "Ground zero (n.)," *Oxford English Dictionary Online*. The OED gives a reference to a *New York Times* article from July 1946 as the first appearance of the term. Journalist William L. Laurence writes of the use of Zero as the code name for the location of the Trinity test, in *Dawn over Zero* (4–12). Dower sees the original use of "Zero" as well as the use of "zero areas" to denote destroyed Japanese targets as an expression of the fact that the "language of Apocalypse had already been introduced to war talk" (Dower, *Cultures of War*, 207).
11 Chow, *The Age of the World Target*, 35–36.
12 Yoneyama, *Hiroshima Traces*, 20. See also Bird and Lifschultz, eds., *Hiroshima's Shadow*. The historical documents and scholarly commentaries collected in this volume offer an indispensable historical analysis of both the development of the official narrative of the bomb's use, and challenges to that narrative; see in particular Lifschultz and Bird, "The Legend of Hiroshima"; and Sayle, "Did the Bomb End the War?" See also Takaki, *Hiroshima*.
13 Boyer, *Fallout*, 11–15; Harrison, *Dark Trophies*, 130–53; Takaki, *Hiroshima*, 7–8, 69–100; Tchen and Yeats, eds., *Yellow Peril!*
14 Dower, *War Without Mercy*, 9, 52–56, 142.
15 Dower, *Cultures of War*, 223.
16 Dower, *Cultures of War*, 272.
17 Voyles, *Wastelanding*, 1–15.
18 Voyles, *Wastelanding*, 15.
19 Voyles, *Wastelanding*, 90.
20 "Vulnerable (adj.)," *Oxford English Dictionary Online*.
21 See Voyles, *Wastelanding*, for a book-length history and analysis of US reliance on the Diné people and Diné lands for the existence of its nuclear program. For a discussion of uranium mining in Congo and Australia, see Schwab, *Radioactive Ghosts*, 85–87.
22 Kuletz, *The Tainted Desert*, 6.
23 Lilienthal, *Change, Hope, and the Bomb*, 9.
24 Denooyer and Wolfinger, *The Bomb*.
25 Boyer, *By the Bomb's Early Light*, 5–10, 13–22, 65–70, 193–95.
26 Boyer, *By the Bomb's Early Light*, 14.
27 Einstein and Russell, "The Peril of Universal Death," 485.

28 Rotblat, "A Social Conscience for the Nuclear Age," xvii.

29 Morley, "The Return to Nothingness," 272.

30 Takaki, *Hiroshima*, 64–65.

31 Kelly, ed., *The Manhattan Project*, 291.

32 Laurence, *Dawn over Zero*, 12. Laurence was in a unique position to shape the public discourse around the bomb. A science journalist who was recruited to work with the Manhattan Project, he had a rare level of access to the development of the bomb; he also accompanied the mission that dropped the bomb on Nagasaki as its official reporter, and prepared press releases for the War Department (Laurence, *Dawn over Zero*, xi–xv, 224–43).

33 Nacht, *The Age of Vulnerability*, 8.

34 Gusterson, *People of the Bomb*, 63.

35 Gusterson, *People of the Bomb*, 64–65.

36 Gusterson, *People of the Bomb*, 68.

37 Gusterson, *People of the Bomb*, 69.

38 Voyles, *Wastelanding*, 113.

39 Lippit, *Atomic Light*, 5.

40 Lippit, *Atomic Light*, 86, 93–95. "Seared organic and nonorganic matter left dark stains, opaque artifacts of once vital bodies, on the pavements and other surfaces of this grotesque theater. The 'shadows,' as they were called, are actually photograms, images formed by the direct exposure of objects on photographic surfaces" (Lippit, *Atomic Light*, 94).

41 Frank, excerpt from *Downfall*, 334.

42 Lippit, *Atomic Light*, 95.

43 Lippit, *Atomic Light*, 25. Derrida refers to the fact that "a non-localizable nuclear war has not occurred; it has existence only through what is said of it, only where it is talked about. Some might call it a fable, then, a pure invention" (Derrida, "No Apocalypse, Not Now," 23). For Derrida, this fable of ultimate nuclear catastrophe seems to allow an encounter with "radical precariousness" (27), which I take to be the abyssal foundation of anything claiming presence. Still, I think it has largely been invoked to serve the opposite function, that is, to attempt a preservation of plenitude, in the name of a humanity that is ultimately a differential humanity.

44 Zwigenberg, *Hiroshima*, 19, 14.

45 Zwigenberg, *Hiroshima*, 66–67.

46 Oé, *Hiroshima Notes*, 115–16.

47 Oé, *Hiroshima Notes*, 116.

48 Oé, *Hiroshima Notes*, 118 (my emphasis).

49 Yoneyama, *Hiroshima Traces*, 15. Yoneyama is careful to speak to the particularities of Hiroshima—why it was bombed, the effects of that bombing, and how Hiroshima has since been discursively rendered in reference to the bombing—without assuming a continuity with Nagasaki (Yoneyama, *Hiroshima Traces*, 224–25, n. 23).

50 Yoneyama provides the English translation of hibakusha as "one who was subjected/exposed to the bomb/radiation" (Yoneyama, *Hiroshima Traces*, 35).

51 Yoneyama, *Hiroshima Traces*, 96.

52 Yoneyama, *Hiroshima Traces*, 212–13.

53 Yoneyama, *Hiroshima Traces*, 12.

54 Yoneyama, *Hiroshima Traces*, 72.

55 Zwigenberg, *Hiroshima*, 19.

56 Kennett, *A History of Strategic Bombing*, 177.

57 Franklin, *War Stars*, 117.

58 Kennett, *A History of Strategic Bombing*.

59 Lindqvist, *A History of Bombing*, 45, 109, 115, 123–24, 134–36.

60 Franklin, *War Stars*, 88.

61 Lindqvist's *A History of Bombing* gives an in-depth account of this history. As Caren Kaplan puts it in her discussion of the period between World War I and World War II, "the advocates of airpower in Europe and the United States had argued that it was more moral to plan for massive bombing raids on cities because the scale of violence would force an early surrender, potentially saving large numbers of lives. . . . [W]hile this debate ground on in the West, there was no 'moral or legal taboo' to prevent the bombing of largely civilian populations in colonized or Mandate zones. . . . The 'peacetime' that followed the Armistice in 1918 saw British bombing raids in India, Egypt, Afghanistan, Somaliland, Iraq, and South West Africa while Spain bombed Morocco, France fought anticolonial groups from the air in Syria, and Italy continued its air war in North Africa" (Kaplan, *Aerial Aftermaths*, 175).

62 Voyles, *Wastelanding*, 114.

63 Franklin, *War Stars*, 20–21, 42–45, 51–53.

64 Lindqvist, *A History of Bombing*, 28, 38, 55.

65 Franklin, *War Stars*, 133; Kelly, ed., *The Manhattan Project*, 17, 22. For speculation on the possibility that Robert A. Heinlein's work influenced members of the Manhattan Project, and that President Harry Truman

was impacted by the future war narratives prevalent in American popular culture during his childhood, see Franklin, *War Stars*, 142, 153.

66 Lindqvist, *A History of Bombing*, 171.

67 Franklin, *War Stars*, 43.

68 See Harrison's examination of the racialized practice of human trophy-taking in Western warfare for an argument in this vein (Harrison, *Dark Trophies*, 1–4, 53–57, 60–61, 73–77, 86–92).

69 Rajagopal, *International Law from Below*, 25.

70 On the post–World War II British "emergencies" (anti-colonial wars), see Harrison, *Dark Trophies*, 156–63; Rajagopal, *International Law from Below*, 176–82. In *Cultures of War*, Dower reminds us of the post–World War II campaigns to quickly reestablish Western control over Southeast Asian nations that had been invaded by Japan (377–93), as well as the fact that "[m]ore noncombatants were killed in America's subsequent wars in Korea and Indochina than in the Allied bombing in World War II" (222). And in *Ends of Empire*, Jodi Kim points out that "by the time Saigon fell to North Vietnamese forces on April 30, 1975, America's Vietnam War had escalated to one ton of bombs dropped for every minute Nixon was in office, $150 billion spent between 1954 and 1975, a deployment of 2.7 million servicemen, and the dropping of a total of 10 million tons of bombs" (196).

71 Gusterson, *People of the Bomb*, 23.

72 Gusterson, *People of the Bomb*, 24.

73 Gusterson, *People of the Bomb*, 22, 37.

74 Gusterson, *People of the Bomb*, 28–44.

75 Denooyer and Wolfinger, *The Bomb*.

76 Gusterson, *People of the Bomb*, 26 (my emphasis).

77 Rotblat, "A Social Conscience for the Nuclear Age," xxvii.

78 Davies, *The Birth of the Anthropocene*, 4–5. The most frequently cited inaugural text on the Anthropocene is a short piece by Paul J. Crutzen and Eugene F. Stoermer, "The 'Anthropocene.'" Crutzen and Stoermer cite human expansion across the globe, intensive resource use, and the deviation of certain geological and environmental processes far from norms as the reasons for proposing this new designation for the geological epoch we currently inhabit. See also Crutzen, "Geology of Mankind." Davies cites this latter piece as important despite its brevity because it has been widely read and cited (Davies, *The Birth of the Anthropocene*, 43–44).

79 For a history of the Anthropocene Working Group, a subcommittee of the ICS, and its bid for the ratification of the Anthropocene, see Subcommission on Quaternary Stratigraphy, "Working Group on the

'Anthropocene'"; Zhong, "The Human Age Has a New Symbol." For reporting on the no vote, which was controversial, see Zhong, "Geologists Make It Official."

80 Palsson et al., "Reconceptualizing the 'Anthropos,'" 4.

81 Davis and Todd, "On the Importance of a Date," 763–69; Mameni, *Terracene*, 3–5; Whyte, "Indigenous Climate Change Studies," 159; Yusoff, *A Billion Black Anthropocenes or None*.

82 Todd, "Indigenizing the Anthropocene," 244.

83 Mameni, *Terracene*, 25.

84 Whyte, Talley, and Gibson, "Indigenous Mobility Traditions," 320–21, 328; Todd, "Indigenizing the Anthropocene."

85 Moore suggests "Capitalocene" given that "capitalism was built on excluding most humans from Humanity" (Moore, "The Rise of Cheap Nature," 79). See also Mameni, *Terracene*, 6.

86 Although it is not the main point of her argument, Stacy Alaimo touches on this problem in her examination of posthumanist work which is attuned to the exceptionalism of the category of the human but still frequently fails to seriously engage with the fundamental role of race in humanism (Alaimo, "Your Shell on Acid").

87 Mameni, *Terracene*, 14.

88 Yusoff, *A Billion Black Anthropocenes or None*, 26.

89 Karera, "Blackness and the Pitfalls of Anthropocene Ethics," 38.

90 See for example, Clark, "Geo-Politics and the Disaster of the Anthropocene"; Colebrook, "Not Symbiosis, Not Now"; Crist, "On the Poverty of Our Nomenclature"; Moore, "The Rise of Cheap Nature"; Purdy, *After Nature*; Stoner and Melathopoulos, *Freedom in the Anthropocene*.

91 Davies, *The Birth of the Anthropocene*, 145.

92 For example, see Jan Zalasiewicz's thought experiment in which he imagines a future Earth visited by alien geologists (*The Earth After Us*). Commenting on this idea of how aliens might interpret the Earth's stratigraphic layers from what will be the then-ancient time of humanity, Davies suggests that "[w]hat the aliens would lack is just the *illusion* of a transcendent human essence. It is worth trying to see the world somewhat in the same way as those imaginary aliens, then. Doing so could make a difference to the ecological politics and criticism of our own time" (Davies, *The Birth of the Anthropocene*, 83, emphasis in original). Despite Davies's critique of the notion of "transcendent human essence" that undergirds some such imaginings of the record that humanity might leave of itself, there is still an appeal toward transcendence in the turn toward the perspective of future witnesses of humanity's presence.

93 Roitman, *Anti-Crisis*, 3.
94 Lewis and Maslin, "Defining the Anthropocene," 171.
95 Monastersky, "The Human Age," 146.
96 Monastersky, "The Human Age," 145.
97 Bonneuil and Fressoz, *The Shock of the Anthropocene*, 47.
98 Bonneuil and Fressoz, *The Shock of the Anthropocene*, 58–59 (emphasis in original).
99 Though Lewis and Maslin prefer 1964 over 1952 ("Defining the Anthropocene," 176).
100 Lewis and Maslin, "Defining the Anthropocene," 175. See also Monastersky, "The Human Age," 146.
101 Lewis and Maslin, "Defining the Anthropocene," 175.
102 Waters et al., "Can Nuclear Weapons Fallout Mark the Beginning of the Anthropocene Epoch?," 55. See also Waters et al., "The Anthropocene Is Functionally and Stratigraphically Distinct from the Holocene."
103 Yusoff, *A Billion Black Anthropocenes or None*, 31–32. I also want to note Davis and Todd's divergent argument in regard to this date; they argue for setting the start of the Anthropocene at 1610 precisely because it would be a way of defining the ecological devastations of the Anthropocene as predicated upon Western racism and colonialism, and hence of "call[ing] for the consideration of Indigenous philosophies and processes of Indigenous self-governance as a necessary political corrective, alongside the self-determination of other communities and societies violently impacted by the white supremacist, colonial, and capitalist logics instantiated in the origins of the Anthropocene" (Davis and Todd, "On the Importance of a Date," 763). I respect this argument and hope that my own will be read not as foreclosing on theirs but as emerging from a specific orientation to the critique of major trends in the discourse on the Anthropocene and, thus, existing alongside their argument.
104 Palsson et al., "Reconceptualizing the 'Anthropos,'" 4.
105 Scranton, *Learning to Die in the Anthropocene*, 13.
106 Scranton, *Learning to Die in the Anthropocene*, 24 (my emphasis).
107 Scranton, *Learning to Die in the Anthropocene*, 24.
108 Chakrabarty, "The Climate of History," 198.
109 Chakrabarty, "Postcolonial Studies," 14.
110 Chakrabarty, "The Climate of History," 220–21.
111 Chakrabarty, "The Climate of History," 221–22.
112 Chakrabarty, "The Climate of History," 222.
113 Chakrabarty, "Postcolonial Studies," 14.

114 Chakrabarty, "Postcolonial Studies," 15.
115 Clark, *Ecocriticism on the Edge*, 14, 31.
116 Clark, *Ecocriticism on the Edge*, 160.
117 Clark, *Ecocriticism on the Edge*, 14 (emphasis in original).
118 Clark, *Ecocriticism on the Edge*, 145.
119 Ghosh, *The Great Derangement*, 63.
120 Ghosh, *The Great Derangement*, 8–11.
121 Ghosh, *The Great Derangement*, 87.
122 Ghosh, *The Great Derangement*, 92, 110–11, 141.
123 Karera, "Blackness and the Pitfalls of Anthropocene Ethics," 38.
124 Karera, "Blackness and the Pitfalls of Anthropocene Ethics," 39.
125 Scranton, *Learning to Die in the Anthropocene*, 92.
126 Scranton, *Learning to Die in the Anthropocene*, 100.
127 Scranton, *Learning to Die in the Anthropocene*, 25.
128 Davies, *The Birth of the Anthropocene*, 85.
129 Morton, "Ecology Without the Present," 232.
130 Morton, "Ecology Without the Present," 233.
131 Yusoff, *A Billion Black Anthropocenes or None*, 44.
132 Yusoff, *A Billion Black Anthropocenes or None*, 44. See also Subcommission on Quaternary Stratigraphy, "Working Group on the 'Anthropocene.'"
133 Zhong, "The Human Age Has a New Symbol."
134 Lowe, *The Intimacies of Four Continents*, 18, 21; Yusoff, *A Billion Black Anthropocenes or None*, 1–11.
135 Hauser, "U.S. Nuclear Weapons Tests Come to YouTube."
136 Lawrence Livermore National Laboratory, "Physicist Declassifies Rescued Nuclear Test Films."
137 "Operation Dominic—Arkansas 102037"; "Operation Dominic—Housatonic 120256."
138 "Operation Dominic—Bighorn 110764."
139 "Operation Nougat—Danny Boy 81495."
140 Dower, *Cultures of War*, 272.
141 See Gusterson, *People of the Bomb*; Kosek, "Nuclear Natures"; Kuletz, *The Tainted Desert*; Masco, *The Future of Fallout*; Schwab, *Radioactive Ghosts*; Voyles, *Wastelanding*.
142 "Sensible (adj., n., and adv.)," *Oxford English Dictionary Online*.
143 Kosek, "Nuclear Natures," 258–59.

Chapter 2. Postcolonial Histories of the Bomb

Epigraph 1: Souleymane Cissé, "Souleymane Cissé's Light on Africa," interview by Manthia Diawara, 15.

An earlier version of chapter 2 in a different form appeared as "The Limits of the Anthropocene: Anticolonial Humanity in Kidlat Tahimik's *Mababangong Bangungot* and Souleymane Cissé's *Yeelen*," *Interventions: International Journal of Postcolonial Studies* 24, no. 7 (2022): 1161–76.

1. Chakrabarty, "Postcolonial Studies and the Challenge of Climate Change," 14–15.
2. Chakrabarty, "Postcolonial Studies and the Challenge of Climate Change," 9
3. Chakrabarty, "Postcolonial Studies and the Challenge of Climate Change," 9.
4. Roitman, *Anti-Crisis*, 87.
5. Though E. San Juan Jr. suggests the translation "Fragrant Asphyxiations" (San Juan, "Kidlat Tahimik," 172).
6. Murphy and Williams, *Postcolonial African Cinema*, 110.
7. For just one example, see Austen, "Beyond 'History.'"
8. See MacRae, "*Yeelen*," 57–59; Stefanson, "Violence in Souleymane Cissé's Films," 197. Cissé himself states that "what is transmitted is an identity of an ethnic group that existed before the penetration of Islam" (Cissé, "Souleymane Cissé," interview by Ukadike, 23).
9. Barlet, *African Cinemas*, 8.
10. Tahimik, "Cups-of-Gas Filmmaking."
11. Campos, "Kidlat Tahimik and the Determination of a Native Filmmaker," 50.
12. See, for example, Metz, "Technology and National Identity"; Russell, *Experimental Ethnography*.
13. James, "'*Yeelen*,' Based on Myths from Mali." For readings in this vein, see, for example, Kariithi, "Misreading Culture and Tradition"; MacRae, "*Yeelen*"; Merolla, "Filming African Creation Myths."
14. Dovey, *Curating Africa in the Age of Film Festivals*, 53.
15. Dovey, *Curating Africa in the Age of Film Festivals*, 54.
16. Fabian, *Time and the Other*.
17. Roitman, *Anti-Crisis*, 28.
18. Rony, *How Do We Look?*, 14–15.
19. Kim, *Ends of Empire*, 197.

20 San Juan, *After Postcolonialism*, 68.

21 San Juan, *After Postcolonialism*, 3.

22 Pavsek, *The Utopia of Film*, 95. Tahimik's abiding interest in this concept is evident in his recent film *Balikbayan #1: Memories of Overdevelopment Redux VI*.

23 Scott-Heron, "Whitey on the Moon," 21.

24 Austen, "Beyond 'History,'" 37.

25 It was in a class taught by Charlie Sugnet in the early 2000s that I first saw *Yeelen*. Charlie made the connection to *Star Wars* and Hollywood's use of this part of Africa for producing a scenography of alien places, and suggested that the catastrophe at the end of the film was a gesture toward nuclear apocalypse. A few other writers discuss *Yeelen* in relation to science fiction, though mostly in passing. See Austen, "Beyond 'History'"; MacRae, "*Yeelen*."

26 O'Driscoll, "Explosive Challenge," 43–44.

27 Pravalie, "Nuclear Weapons Tests and Environmental Consequences," 738.

28 O'Driscoll, "Explosive Challenge."

29 Pfaff, "Souleymane Cissé (1940–), Mali," 52.

30 Dovey, *Curating Africa in the Age of Film Festivals*, 36.

31 Cirincione, Wolfsthal, and Rajkumar, *Deadly Arsenals*, 190.

32 Schmitt, "A Shadowy War's Newest Front"; Schmitt, Walsh, and Peltier, "Coup in Niger Upends U.S. Terrorism Fight."

33 Schmitt, "A Shadowy War's Newest Front."

34 Insofar as this film also levels a critique against nationalism, particularly as violently expressed by the US-backed Marcos government against its own people, Kidlat's refusal to be a subject of humanity can be read as a simultaneous refusal to be a subject of the nation. Noting how dangerous it would have been for Tahimik to engage in a direct critique of the Marcos government, several authors read the film's critique of US imperialism as an allegorical critique of Marcos. For such arguments, see Jameson, "'Art Naïf' and the Admixture of Worlds," 191–92; Metz, "Technology and National Identity," 127, 138. While acknowledging the conditions of political necessity these authors rightly point to, I am interested in what happens when the film's critiques of Marcos and of US empire are seen not as allegorically related but rather as mutually constitutive. I like Harrod Suarez's suggestion of "the possibility that metonymy best describes the relationship between the US and the Philippines, such that the latter is not separated but a part of the very staging of US nationalism and imperialism" (Suarez, "Among the Sensuous," 67).

35   Tahimik, interview by Nash, 75.

36   Jameson, "'Art Naïf' and the Admixture of Worlds," 186–91. For pieces that weigh in on Jameson's reading, see Dixon and Zonn, "Confronting the Geopolitical Aesthetic"; San Juan, "Kidlat Tahimik"; Tolentino, *National/Transnational*.

37   San Juan, "Kidlat Tahimik," 183. For a similar reading, see Russell, *Experimental Ethnography*, 299.

38   Zimmerman, "Benevolent Assassination," 6.

39   Zimmerman, "Benevolent Assassination," 6–7.

40   Zimmerman, "Benevolent Assassination," 8.

41   I use "Third World" here following Tahimik's own articulation of the relationship between his subject position and his artistic work; I discuss this further below.

42   Pavsek, *The Utopia of Film*, 252, n. 37 (my emphasis).

43   Tahimik, "Cups-of-Gas Filmmaking," 83. It should be noted that the spelling of the second appearance of "fillmaking" in the title is purposeful; in the essay, Tahimik notes that it originated as a typographical "error" that he then chose to keep.

44   Neufeld, *Von Braun*, 5–6; Biddle, *Dark Side of the Moon*, x–xi.

45   Neufeld, *Von Braun*, 5, 96, 142–45, 159–66, 176–79; Biddle, *Dark Side of the Moon*, xii, 115–17.

46   Neufeld, *Von Braun*, 221–22, 260, 266–67.

47   Biddle, *Dark Side of the Moon*, 149.

48   Biddle, *Dark Side of the Moon*, x.

49   Biddle, *Dark Side of the Moon*, 38, 114, 134–36, 141.

50   Pavsek, *The Utopia of Film*, 128.

51   Dower, *War Without Mercy*, 154. This theory, glossed by the phrase "ontogeny recapitulates phylogeny," was widely influential and had impact lasting far beyond its scientific application. David Eng notes the broad influence of this theory in his discussion of the racist implications of Freud's thinking about the relationship between individual psychological traits and the features of advanced human society (Eng, *Racial Castration*, 7).

52   Pavsek notes, in regard to Tahimik's notion of overdevelopment, that "it becomes at once obligation and, as every one of Tahimik's major films demonstrates, a nearly compulsory object of desire" (Pavsek, *The Utopia of Film*, 139).

53   See San Juan for discussion of the particularities of how Filipino men were/are so figured (San Juan, *After Postcolonialism*, 101–3, 124–25).

54   Eng, *Racial Castration*, 6.

55 Eng, *Racial Castration*, 11.

56 I was able to find two books with this title. See Haggerty, *Man's Conquest of Space*; Shelton, *Man's Conquest of Space*. Haggerty's is a children's book, while Shelton invokes man as a singular subject, for example, by employing singular verb tense to describe "man's" thoughts and actions.

57 It was reading Suarez that initially drew my attention to the first mispronunciation of the word as "monkey" (Suarez, "Among the Sensuous," 80).

58 Suarez, "Among the Sensuous," 80.

59 Dylan Rodríguez adds to this discussion the important point that the characterization of Filipino people as monkeys also served a specifically political purpose in its connection to the "U.S. colonial project's foundational diagnosis of 'Filipinos as infantile, immature subjects, unready yet for self-government of body or polity'" (Rodríguez, *Suspended Apocalypse*, 151).

60 Shelton, *Man's Conquest of Space*, 78–82.

61 Suarez reads *Mababangong Bangungot* as presenting a straightforward valorization of men's role in revolutionary postcoloniality: "Judging by the visual diegesis that authorizes meaning, one must accept the gendered rescue of the working classes and the colonized, both feminized, across the globe. A surreal, masculinized resistance provides the opposition to the realism of ethnography, capitalism, and colonialism: a battle staged in both plot and narrative" (Suarez, "Among the Sensuous," 68). My own reading differs from Suarez's in this regard.

62 Dixon and Zonn, "Confronting the Geopolitical Aesthetic," 111.

63 Pavsek, *The Utopia of Film*, 110.

64 Rony, *The Third Eye*; Rony, *How Do We Look?*

65 Pavsek, *The Utopia of Film*, 139–40.

66 Bourdeau, "Auguste Comte."

67 Bourdeau, "Auguste Comte."

68 Frederic Jameson notes the "hideous concrete supermarkets, not without a certain resemblance to atomic power-stations," though I think he is referring to the super chimneys (Jameson, "'Art Naïf' and the Admixture of Worlds," 190).

69 Cissé, "Souleymane Cissé," interview by Ukadike, 22.

70 Ukadike notes that Cissé is himself Muslim, like 90 percent of Malians (Ukadike, "*Yeelen* (1987), Souleymane Cissé," 769). And Kariithi cites Cissé as stating, "'I am Soninké, but I express myself in Bambara'" (Kariithi, "Misreading Culture and Tradition," 177).

71 Murphy and Williams, *Postcolonial African Cinema*, 126.

72 Pfaff, "Souleymane Cissé (1940–), Mali."
73 Tcheuyap, *Postnationalist African Cinemas*, 151.
74 Tcheuyap, *Postnationalist African Cinemas*, 151 (emphasis in original).
75 Dovey, *Curating Africa in the Age of Film Festivals*, 52. Thackway also notes the role *Yeelen* has played in this controversy (Thackway, *Africa Shoots Back*, 20, 40, 70–71).
76 Osinubi, "Cognition's Warp," 257.
77 Tcheuyap, *Postnationalist African Cinemas*, 175.
78 Wynter, "Africa, the West and the Analogy of Culture," 35 (emphasis in original).
79 Murphy and Williams, *Postcolonial African Cinema*, 114–16.
80 Barlet, *African Cinemas*, 212.
81 Osinubi, "Cognition's Warp," 258.
82 Cissé, cited in Barlet, *African Cinemas*, 90. Barlet cites the source of this statement as being the press pack for *Yeelen*.
83 Cissé, "Souleymane Cissé's Light on Africa," 15.
84 Washington, "'The Sea Never Dies,'" 236.
85 Austen, "Beyond 'History,'" 37.
86 Austen, "Beyond 'History,'" 38.
87 Cissé, "Souleymane Cissé's Light on Africa," interview by Diawara, 14.
88 Stefanson, "Violence in Souleymane Cissé's Films," 199.
89 Stefanson, "Violence in Souleymane Cissé's Films," 199.
90 Stefanson, "Violence in Souleymane Cissé's Films," 199.
91 MacRae, "*Yeelen*," 64.
92 Hoffman, "*Yeelen*," 100.
93 Cissé, "Souleymane Cissé," interview by Ukadike, 23.
94 Austen, "Beyond 'History,'" 36.

Chapter 3. Converting Absences into Signs

Epigraph 1: Atanasoski, *Humanitarian Violence*, 127.

A much earlier version of chapter 3 appeared in a different form as "Daring to Look: Women Without 'Faces' and Humanitarian Resentment," *Feminist Formations* 29, no. 3 (2017): 110–31.

1 Feminist Majority Foundation, "Feminist and Human Rights Groups to Biden and Harris"; Gupta and Donner, "'Lost Between Borders'"; Nader and Ferris-Rotman, "Freedom at Stake."

2 NWSA Executive Committee, "Solidarity with Afghan Women and Feminists."
3 Samar, "If the U.S. Doesn't Learn from the Past."
4 Atanasoski, *Humanitarian Violence*, 15.
5 Atanasoski, *Humanitarian Violence*, 74.
6 Khalili, *Time in the Shadows*, 211.
7 Khalili, *Time in the Shadows*, 211.
8 Khalili, *Time in the Shadows*, 198.
9 Khalili, *Time in the Shadows*, 212.
10 Kapadia, *Insurgent Aesthetics*, 2. Kapadia refers to Af-Pak as the "region that sutures Afghanistan to Pakistan" (2). For an extensive history of the colonialism in this part of the world, the emergence of Af-Pak as a zone of competing national, imperial, and military interests, and the part it has come to play in the US war on terror, see Fitzgerald and Gould, *Crossing Zero*. In short, Af-Pak is not simply a geographical designation but a geopolitical one.
11 Mohammadzai's first name is spelled differently by different sources, sometimes as "Aisha." I chose "Aesha" for consistency and because it appears to be used more often; however, it is not clear which spelling she herself might prefer.
12 See Chowdhury, *Transnationalism Reversed*; Hesford, *Spectacular Rhetorics*; Kozol, *Distant Wars Visible*.
13 In his address to a joint session of Congress on September 20, 2001, President George W. Bush declared that "the United States respects the people of Afghanistan—after all, we are currently its largest source of humanitarian aid," and that "this is the world's fight. This is civilization's fight. This is the fight of all who believe in progress and pluralism, tolerance and freedom" (Bush, "Address to a Joint Session of Congress"). This framing would hold steady during the years of the Barack Obama presidency, and while with the US Defense Strategic Guidance of January 2012 the US military "indicated a shift from population-centric counterinsurgency to a counterterrorism policy of special operations and drone warfare" (Khalili, *Time in the Shadows*, 247), the enmeshment of special operations and drone strikes with humanitarian logics is evident in their common characterization as cleaner, more modern and precise methods of achieving military aims while minimizing collateral losses. See Khalili and Kapadia for additional discussions of this, including consideration of the so-called revolution in military affairs and the debates over the relative merits of and proper relationship between "emotionally intelligent" and "more rational, bureaucratized, and technologically savvy" warfare (Khalili, *Time in the Shadows*, 45)—both of which have been

conceived through and justified by humanitarian logics (Kapadia, *Insurgent Aesthetics*, 49–51, 60–62; Khalili, *Time in the Shadows*, 45–48). Furthermore, as Olwan details, the Obama administration explicitly articulated a commitment to addressing "gender-based violence" as a means to authorize US national security endeavors (Olwan, *Gender Violence*, 95–104).

14 For incisive critiques of Western/imperial feminist investment in US militarism as a project of Muslim women's putative liberation, see, for example, Fernandes, "The Boundaries of Terror"; Grewal, *Saving the Security State*; Russo, "The Feminist Majority Foundation's Campaign." This is a well-established and rich line of critique which I will not rehearse in detail here. I note that the inquiry I undertake in this chapter is built on the foundation established by such scholars, and would not be possible without them.

15 Butler, *Precarious Life*, 142.

16 Hesford, *Spectacular Rhetorics*, 7 (emphasis in original).

17 Hesford, *Spectacular Rhetorics*, 1–2.

18 Razack, "Stealing the Pain of Others," 387 (emphasis in original).

19 Griggers, *Becoming-Woman*, 12–14.

20 Griggers, *Becoming-Woman*, 5.

21 Griggers, *Becoming-Woman*, 4 (emphasis in original).

22 See Saba Mahmood's *Politics of Piety*, a classic, groundbreaking study, for an analysis of how Western feminist understandings of politics are deeply informed by secular liberalist notions of agency.

23 Puar, *Terrorist Assemblages*, 98. This largely remains the case. A crucial exception is Tara McKelvey's *Monstering*. McKelvey includes accounts of children and women who were tortured, raped, and/or died at the hands of the US military, at Abu Ghraib and beyond. McKelvey also confirms that government documents specifically regarding violence against women detainees are often redacted and have in some cases been withheld (see especially chapter 16, "State Secrets," 194–208).

24 Kapadia, *Insurgent Aesthetics*, 190.

25 Kapadia, *Insurgent Aesthetics*, 189.

26 Kapadia *Insurgent Aesthetics*, 108.

27 Several authors have engaged in crucial, extensive analyses of such practices. Sarah Haley examines "the necessity of violence against black women's bodies in the maintenance of white supremacy as an ideological, economic, and political order" (Haley, *No Mercy Here*, 7) in the post-slavery southern US, persuasively arguing that "Assault and destruction of the body in specific contexts (riots, scaffolds, penal camps)

were fundamental tools in the construction of white civil society, white human value, and white personhood more broadly" (9). For accounts of the targeting of Muslim women of color for various forms of public violence by members of civil society as well as the state in the wake of 9/11, see Chaumtoli Huq's "The War on Terror on Muslim Women and Girls" and Louise A. Cainkar's *Homeland Insecurity*.

28 Elora Halim Chowdhury examines the work of Bangladeshi survivors of acid violence on their own behalf, many of whom suffered facial injuries, and in doing so engages a crucial analysis of rehabilitative mandates (especially those given by humanitarian groups) to recover and hence rejoin society as economically productive citizens (Chowdhury, *Transnationalism Reversed*).

29 Asad, *On Suicide Bombing*, 24.

30 Weizman, *The Least of All Possible Evils*, 10.

31 Weizman, *The Least of All Possible Evils*, 11.

32 Asad, *On Suicide Bombing*, 20.

33 Asad, *On Suicide Bombing*, 30.

34 Asad, *On Suicide Bombing*, 31.

35 Asad, *On Suicide Bombing*, 30–32. Kapadia adds to our understanding of how the idea of the terrorist psyche plays into military operations beyond torture: "Since at least 2004, the CIA and the US Air Force have discharged an illegal 'targeted killing' program in Pakistan and Afghanistan, where individuals on the borderlands of violence who are deemed to be 'enemies of the state' are assassinated without charge or trial. The executive branch has claimed the unchecked authority to classify citizens and others on what it obliquely terms a 'disposition matrix,' a secret capture/kill database of alleged terrorists and enemy combatants designed by the Obama administration and 'based on secret determinations, based on secret evidence, that individuals meet a secret definition of the enemy'" (Kapadia, *Insurgent Aesthetics*, 65).

36 Asad, *On Suicide Bombing*, 32–34; Puar, *Terrorist Assemblages*, 81–88.

37 For in-depth arguments along these lines, see Asad, *Formations of the Secular*; Koshy, "From Cold War to Trade War"; Rajagopal, *International Law from Below*; Weizman, *The Least of All Possible Evils*; Williams, *The Divided World*.

38 Mameni, "Dermopolitics"; Puar, *Terrorist Assemblages*; Puar and Rai, "Monster, Terrorist, Fag"; Rana, *Terrifying Muslims*; Weheliye, *Habeas Viscus*.

39 See Weheliye, *Habeas Viscus*, especially 53–56, 71–73.

40 Mameni, "Dermopolitics," 98.

41   Rana, *Terrifying Muslims*, 66.
42   Grewal, *Transnational America*, 157.
43   Grewal, *Transnational America*, 137, 154–57.
44   Grewal, *Transnational America*, 156.
45   Herr, "Women's Rights as Human Rights," 123.
46   Herr, "Women's Rights as Human Rights," 128.
47   Kang, *Traffic in Asian Women*, 133 (emphasis in original).
48   Kang, *Traffic in Asian Women*, 139.
49   Olwan, *Gender Violence*, 92–95.
50   Jaleel, *The Work of Rape*, 16.
51   Jaleel, *The Work of Rape*, 51.
52   Jaleel, *The Work of Rape*, 58.
53   Olwan, *Gender Violence*, 11.
54   Olwan, *Gender Violence*, 10–23, 92–94, 114–16.
55   Along these lines, Olwan points out the common assertion that "honor-related violence differs from other forms of violence against women (including intimate partner violence) because its victims are part of patriarchal cultures that see women as the property of men, where men and kin are encouraged to regulate the sexualities and social behaviors of women" (Olwan, *Gender Violence*, 21).
56   Olwan, *Gender Violence*, 115.
57   Atanasoski, *Humanitarian Violence*, 175.
58   Atanasoski, *Humanitarian Violence*, 168.
59   Atanasoski, *Humanitarian Violence*, 178.
60   Amar, *The Security Archipelago*, 204–5.
61   Atanasoski, *Humanitarian Violence*, 170.
62   Jaleel, *The Work of Rape*, 50.
63   Atanasoski, *Humanitarian Violence*, 6.
64   This stance was clearly expressed in President George W. Bush's claim to be saving Muslims from themselves: "The terrorists are traitors to their own faith, trying, in effect, to hijack Islam itself. The enemy of America is not our many Muslim friends; it is not our many Arab friends. Our enemy is a radical network of terrorists, and every government that supports them" (Bush, "Address to a Joint Session of Congress").
65   In making this assertion, I am inspired by Julietta Hua's detailed, incisive analysis of how laws and discourse about sex trafficking deploy human rights frameworks to constitute women as "good" victims *and*

targets of punishment, in ways that reproduce and reinforce the racist project of US empire (Hua, *Trafficking Women's Human Rights*).

66 See Jones, "Our Afghan Demons"; Nordland, "Portrait of Pain Ignites a Debate."
67 Klein, "The Forest and the Trees."
68 Jones, "Our Afghan Demons," 6.
69 Lemmon, "An Unspeakable Crime." This is the first reference to Mohammadzai in English-language media that I was able to locate.
70 Baker, "Afghan Women and the Return of the Taliban," 24.
71 Goldbaum, "Afghan Economy Nears Collapse." I would like to draw attention to a brief news article that appeared earlier that month, published by the Feminist Majority Foundation, which reports that some Afghan families were being forced to sell their young daughters in order to have enough money to eat. The article ascribes this phenomenon to Afghan culture ("child marriage") and the Taliban's rule by misogyny, never mentioning the role of the US or other entities with the power to make globally impactful economic decisions ("Starving Afghan Families Forced to Sell Their Daughters for Food").
72 Ravitz, "Saving Aesha."
73 Maira, *The 9/11 Generation*, 197.
74 Maira, *The 9/11 Generation*, 195.
75 Maira, *The 9/11 Generation*, 203.
76 Ravitz, "Saving Aesha."
77 Khalili describes detention in counterinsurgency as, among other things, a form of attempted "social engineering" (Khalili, *Time in the Shadows*, 170).
78 Nguyen, *The Gift of Freedom*, 53.
79 Nguyen, *The Gift of Freedom*, 54.
80 Nguyen, *The Gift of Freedom*, 74.
81 Nguyen, *The Gift of Freedom*, 60.
82 Badkhen, "PTSDland," 35.
83 Badkhen, "PTSDland," 34.
84 Atanasoski, *Humanitarian Violence*, 14.
85 Hesford, *Spectacular Rhetorics*, 69–70.
86 Badkhen, "PTSDland," 36.
87 Ravitz, "Saving Aesha."
88 Ravitz, "Saving Aesha."
89 "Patients of Courage: Bibi Aisha."

90   Maira, *The 9/11 Generation*, 163.

91   Jolie, "Sharmeen Obaid-Chinoy."

92   Robbins, "The Lifesaver."

93   Sterling et al., "Viewer's Guide," 5.

94   Sterling et al., "Viewer's Guide," 20.

95   Sterling et al., "Viewer's Guide," 7.

96   In contrast, I note Elora Halim Chowdhury's importantly complex account of the causes of acid violence, because she attends to the complicated entanglements of diverse social and economic phenomena that come to bear in a postcolonial nation (in the case of her study, Bangladesh) that must still contend with the desires of Western and Global North financial and political interests and whose government is far from free of these power dynamics (Chowdhury, *Transnationalism Reversed*, 23–26).

97   Toor, "Imperialist Feminism Redux," 150 (emphasis in original).

98   Bina D'Costa coins this term to refer to non-state actors like the Taliban so as to refuse the easy designations of "terrorist" and "militant," and hence calls into question the common distinctions between supposedly legitimate and non-legitimate political actors, showcasing their many entanglements (D'Costa, "Gender Justice and (In)Security in Pakistan and Afghanistan").

99   D'Costa, "Gender Justice and (In)Security in Pakistan and Afghanistan," 415.

100 As with other such objects of knowledge, "honor killing" has a complicated politics. I do not engage a consideration of that politics here, but I do note that I do not take it, or the phenomenon it names, either at face value or for granted. For commentary on the politics of this particular naming, see Olwan, *Gender Violence*; Olwan, "Pinkwashing the 'Honor Crime'"; Razack, *Casting Out*.

101 For a crucial analysis of how humanitarian programs meant to allow women (especially though not exclusively in the Global South) to participate in the global economy reproduce and sometimes strengthen larger economic and political inequalities along the lines of the gender binary, see Keating, Rasmussen, and Rishi, "The Rationality of Empowerment." Inderpal Grewal also gives a fantastic, in-depth overview of how the rise of the framework of "women's rights as human rights" has been intricately connected to the project of development (see especially chapter 3, "'Women's Rights as Human Rights'" in Grewal, *Transnational America*). It should also be noted that Rukhsana has alleged that Obaid-Chinoy promised to provide her with money and a new home, but did not fulfill that promise (Anis, "Sharmeen Obaid Did Not Ful-

fill Promise"). Whether or not the allegation is true, this story raises important questions about the failure of certain feminist analyses of violence to address the fundamental problem of an oppressive and extractivist global economic system.

102 Spivak, "Can the Subaltern Speak?," 285.
103 Spivak, "Can the Subaltern Speak?," 274–75, 279–80, 286, 292.
104 Brudholm, *Resentment's Virtue*, 2.
105 Nguyen, *The Gift of Freedom*, 129 (emphasis in original).
106 Since then, the law has been revised to only allow a pardon in the case of the accused being convicted and sentenced to capital punishment, in which case the convict is still mandated to serve a lifetime prison sentence (Masood, "Pakistan Toughens Laws").
107 That Obaid-Chinoy has sought to use the film to promote legal change is suggested by a news story about it, in which Obaid-Chinoy is quoted as stating, "'the biggest thing (challenge) is making women aware of their rights. Forced marriage is a crime in Pakistan. We're hoping that our awareness campaign will play a role in the change'"; the author reports that "the filmmaker told *Eastern Eye* the country had been galvanised into thinking about honour killings after she won an Academy Award for a documentary which shone a global spotlight on the issue" (Kumar, "'Women Want Control of Lives'"). A piece in the *New York Times* reporting on Obaid-Chinoy's Academy Award win also suggests a direct connection between *A Girl in the River* and growing support for legislative change in Pakistan at the time, with then Prime Minister Nawaz Sharif reported to have seen the film and have been in the process of considering legislative efforts as a result (Imtiaz, "Oscar Win Shines Light on Pakistan Efforts").
108 In a 2018 profile of Obaid-Chinoy, the continuing effects of the film on Saba's life are noted: "Saba later told reporters that her family were deeply 'disturbed' by *A Girl in the River*, and perceived it as another blow to their honor. Last year, Saba left the country with her husband and children" (Okeowo, "Daughter of Pakistan," 26).
109 Mazzei, "Noor Salman Acquitted."
110 I refer here to the notion of US sexual exceptionalism developed by Jasbir Puar in *Terrorist Assemblages*.
111 Epstein and Gruelle, "Should an Abused Wife Be Charged in Her Husband's Crime?" To be absolutely clear, I am not questioning the phenomenon of coercive control as described here. Indeed, it is all too apparent to me that psychological abuse works by leveraging relational bonds so as to dismantle the target's basic trust in her sense of reality. In that sense, the abuse dynamic makes the notion of free choice moot.

At the same time, this seems to me to open up serious questions about the general use of the allied concepts of free choice, intent, and state of mind within jurisprudence, given their deep embeddedness within prevailing notions of gendered and racialized subjectivity.

Chapter 4. Documentation as Eradication

Epigraph 1: Macharia, "On Being Area-Studied," 188.

A very early version of chapter 4 appeared in a different form as "Communities of Ruin: Humanitarian Violence and the Amazon's Uncontacted Tribes," *Culture, Theory and Critique* 58, no. 1 (2017): 62–76.

1. Langewiesche, "The War for the Rainforest."
2. Langewiesche, "The War for the Rainforest."
3. "Awá: Earth's Most Threatened Tribe."
4. Muggah, "A Violent Tragedy Foretold in the Amazon." For more on the Amazon as potentially nearing ecosystem collapse, see Amigo, "When Will the Amazon Hit a Tipping Point?"; Boulton, Lenton, and Boers, "Pronounced Loss of Amazon Rainforest Resilience."
5. Brum, "Was a British Journalist the Latest Victim?"
6. Nicas and Moriyama, "Inside the Amazon Journey."
7. World War Zero is the name of John Kerry's climate initiative, which seeks to achieve net zero carbon emissions by the year 2050. World War Zero's website, perhaps predictably, features the heavy use of militarized language. As just one example, one can sign up for email updates by clicking the "Enlist" link at the top of the page, and the home page features the number of "enlistees" updated in real time ("World War Zero").
8. Nicas and Moriyama, "Inside the Amazon Journey."
9. Mirzoeff, *The Right to Look*, 19.
10. For a discussion of US-based industry's figural and material investment in the Amazon, and the phenomenon of what the author refers to as military corporatism, see Grandin, "Empire's Ruins."
11. Gómez-Barris, *The Extractive Zone*, 67.
12. Gómez-Barris, *The Extractive Zone*, 10.
13. Amar, *The Security Archipelago*, 15.
14. Macharia, "On Being Area-Studied."
15. Macharia, "On Being Area-Studied," 188.
16. Audra Simpson makes this argument about recognition and refusal in "The Ruse of Consent."

17 Ginsburg, "Native Intelligence"; Shohat and Stam, *Unthinking Eurocentrism*.
18 Rony, *The Third Eye*, 8–21.
19 One example is the controversy generated by Patrick Tierney's book *Darkness in El Dorado*. The accusations Tierney makes in the book regarding several individuals known for their work with Amazonian peoples prompted a formal investigation by the American Anthropological Association. For a detailed account of the controversy and ensuing investigation, see Borofsky, *Yanomami*. I note this example not in order to weigh in on the controversy but to draw attention to the cultural capital it generated for the participants in the debate—making it, on some level, more about the debate than the peoples whose treatment was being argued about.
20 Lindqvist, *A History of Bombing*; Lindqvist, *Terra Nullius*.
21 Lindqvist, *"Exterminate All the Brutes,"* 97–107.
22 For example, see Grann, *The Lost City of Z*; Preston, "The El Dorado Machine."
23 Cleary, "Towards an Environmental History of the Amazon"; Geddes, "Ancient Amazon Civilisation Laid Bare"; Heckenberger et al., "Amazonia 1492"; Pärssinen, Schaan, and Ranzi, "Pre-Columbian Geometric Earthworks"; Stokstad, "'Pristine' Forest Teemed with People."
24 Balée, *Cultural Forests of the Amazon*, 6.
25 Balée, *Cultural Forests of the Amazon*, 5–6, 53–55.
26 Parks, "Drones, Vertical Mediation, and the Targeted Class," 231.
27 Parks, "Drones, Vertical Mediation, and the Targeted Class," 230–31.
28 Mirzoeff, *The Right to Look*, 2.
29 Mirzoeff, *The Right to Look*, 7.
30 An exception is Heckenberger et al. Two of the coauthors are identified as members of the Kuikuro people of the Upper Xingu region of the Brazilian Amazon. The piece references "indigenous knowledge systems," which have identified areas that coincide with the sites of "mapped archeological features" (Heckenberger et al., "Amazonia 1492," 1711–12), although the emphasis in this article is on the process of mapping using satellite imagery. Alternatively, William Balée offers a very different understanding of the history of the Amazon forest's shaping by humans, one that is more careful to center Amazonian peoples' knowledge and practices (Balée, *Cultural Forests of the Amazon*).
31 Pearce, *Deep Jungle*, 170.
32 Pearce, *Deep Jungle*, 171.
33 "Jungle (n.)," *Oxford English Dictionary Online*.

34   Wallace, *The Unconquered*, 160.
35   Wallace, *The Unconquered*, 161–62.
36   "Uncontacted Forest."
37   "Uncontacted Tribe, Mato Grosso, Brazil 2013."
38   "The Last of His Tribe."
39   Watson, "This Man Is the Last of His Tribe."
40   Watson, "This Man Is the Last of His Tribe."
41   Wallace, "Why Revealing Uncontacted Tribes May Help Save Them."
42   Wallace, "Why Revealing Uncontacted Tribes May Help Save Them."
43   Neves and Machado, "Nationalising Indigenous Peoples," 165.
44   For an important discussion of FUNAI's history, see Warren, *Racial Revolutions*, especially 103–13.
45   Neves and Machado, "Nationalising Indigenous Peoples," 167.
46   Neves and Machado, "Nationalising Indigenous Peoples," 173.
47   Turner, "Representation, Politics, and Cultural Imagination," 79–80.
48   For one discussion of the place of "objects" in various cosmologies of Amazonian peoples, see Santos-Granero, "Introduction."
49   De la Cadena, "Indigenous Cosmopolitics in the Andes," 337–38.
50   De la Cadena, "Indigenous Cosmopolitics in the Andes," 350.
51   Terborgh, "Out of Contact," 50.
52   Terborgh, "Out of Contact," 51.
53   Terborgh, "Out of Contact," 51.
54   Wallace, *The Unconquered*, 259.
55   Wallace, *The Unconquered*, 259–60.
56   Wallace, *The Unconquered*, 409.
57   Terborgh, "Out of Contact," 50 (my emphasis).
58   Balée, *Cultural Forests of the Amazon*, 54.
59   Wallace, *The Unconquered*, 269.
60   Wallace, *The Unconquered*, 391.
61   Wallace, *The Unconquered*, 298–301.
62   Wallace, *The Unconquered*, 299–300.
63   Wallace, *The Unconquered*, 300.
64   Wallace, *The Unconquered*, 29.
65   Ginsburg, "Native Intelligence," 237.
66   Ginsburg, "Screen Memories," 40.
67   "Human Planet," BBC One.

68 Sweney, "BBC Admits."
69 "Human Planet," BBC One.
70 Watson, "This Man Is the Last of His Tribe."
71 Wallace, "Exclusive: Stunning New Photos."
72 "Awá: Earth's Most Threatened Tribe."
73 "Awá: Earth's Most Threatened Tribe."
74 "Awá: Earth's Most Threatened Tribe."
75 McClintock, *Imperial Leather*, 21–22; Nash, *The Black Body in Ecstasy*, 29, 36.
76 As brilliantly argued by Donna Haraway in "Teddy Bear Patriarchy."
77 Amar, *The Security Archipelago*, 17.
78 Amar, *The Security Archipelago*, 64.
79 Amar, *The Security Archipelago*, 184.
80 Amar notes that while tropicalism has been well analyzed as a feature of Western/Global North colonialist ideology, "much less work has been done on the role that orientalism and tropicalism have played when appropriated by nationalist, state-building, modernizing, and counterhegemonic projects in the postcolonial world" (Amar, *The Security Archipelago*, 59). He explains that the Brazilian embrace of tropicalist modernism has been predicated on "miscegenation as the solution to the 'problems' of essentialized racial difference.... Domestically, this usually played out as a narrative in which black needed white in order to conceive modernity; but displaced into the geopolitical realm, the formula became a narrative of the white Brazilian needing the brown or black Moor. Thus, erotic contact between the races and the resulting progeny—the 'mixed-race' Moor (on the global scale) or the mulatta (on the national scale)—served as central metaphors for a new kind of modernity that was more powerful than exclusionary and hierarchical projects" (Amar, *The Security Archipelago*, 62).
81 Nicas and Andreoni, "Brazil Found the Last Survivors of an Amazon Tribe."
82 Herr, "Women's Rights as Human Rights."
83 Herr, "Women's Rights as Human Rights," 133–36.
84 Melamed, *Represent and Destroy*, 192.
85 Alfred, "Sovereignty," 38.
86 Melamed, *Represent and Destroy*, 183–84.
87 Piore, "Guardians of the Tiger People," 51.
88 Wallace, *The Unconquered*, 108–9.

89   Wallace, *The Unconquered*, 343.
90   Wallace, *The Unconquered*, 224.
91   Wallace, *The Unconquered*, 188.
92   Wallace, *The Unconquered*, 256.
93   Wallace, *The Unconquered*, 257.
94   Wallace, "Exclusive: Stunning New Photos." It is Meirelles who is being quoted here.

Chapter 5. A Differential Humanity

Epigraph 1: Butler, *The Force of Nonviolence*, 146.

1   These thoughts were very much informed by ongoing conversations with Diane Detournay and Daniel Rhodes.
2   McElroy, "This Isn't Your Old Toxic Masculinity."
3   Murphy, "Corporeal Vulnerability and the New Humanism," 578.
4   Murphy, "Corporeal Vulnerability and the New Humanism," 589.
5   Lepecki, *Exhausting Dance*, 89.
6   Fanon, *Black Skin, White Masks*, 109.
7   Ferreira da Silva, *Toward a Global Idea of Race*, xiii.
8   Ferreira da Silva, *Toward a Global Idea of Race*, 16.
9   Sandoval, *Methodology of the Oppressed*, 70. While the connections and divisions Sandoval limns have shifted since the time of *Methodology*'s writing, the problem she names remains with us even as it takes on new forms.
10   Mackenzie, Rogers, and Dodds, "Introduction."
11   Mackenzie, Rogers, and Dodds, "Introduction," 3–4.
12   Mackenzie, Rogers, and Dodds, "Introduction," 6.
13   Mackenzie, Rogers, and Dodds, "Introduction," 7.
14   Gilson, *The Ethics of Vulnerability*, 63.
15   Gilson, "Vulnerability, Ignorance, and Oppression," 308.
16   Gilson, "Vulnerability, Ignorance, and Oppression," 310.
17   Gilson, *The Ethics of Vulnerability*, 32–39.
18   Gilson, "Vulnerability, Ignorance, and Oppression," 311.
19   Gilson, "Vulnerability, Ignorance, and Oppression," 312.
20   Gilson, "Vulnerability and Victimization," 72.
21   Gilson, *The Ethics of Vulnerability*, 59.
22   Gilson, *The Ethics of Vulnerability*, 2.

23 Gilson, *The Ethics of Vulnerability*, 37.
24 Gilson, *The Ethics of Vulnerability*, 38.
25 Gilson, *The Ethics of Vulnerability*, 75.
26 Gilson, *The Ethics of Vulnerability*, 31.
27 Gilson, *The Ethics of Vulnerability*, 43.
28 Gilson, "Vulnerability, Ignorance, and Oppression," 312.
29 Gilson, "Vulnerability, Ignorance, and Oppression," 323 (my emphasis).
30 Gilson, "Vulnerability, Ignorance, and Oppression," 324 (my emphasis).
31 Spillers, "Mama's Baby, Papa's Maybe," 78 (my emphasis).
32 Gilson, *The Ethics of Vulnerability*, 11.
33 Cole, "All of Us Are Vulnerable," 261.
34 Cole, "All of Us Are Vulnerable," 269.
35 Cole, "All of Us Are Vulnerable," 267–71.
36 Butler, *Precarious Life*, 20.
37 Butler, *Precarious Life*, 31.
38 Butler, *Precarious Life*, 30.
39 Butler, *Precarious Life*, 29.
40 Butler, *Precarious Life*, 29.
41 Butler, *Precarious Life*, 151.
42 Butler, *Precarious Life*, xii–xiii.
43 Butler, *Precarious Life*, 30.
44 Butler, *Frames of War*; Butler, "Precarious Life, Vulnerability, and the Ethics of Cohabitation."
45 Butler, *Frames of War*, 13.
46 Butler, *Frames of War*, 12.
47 Butler, "Precarious Life, Vulnerability, and the Ethics of Cohabitation," 134.
48 Butler, "Precarious Life, Vulnerability, and the Ethics of Cohabitation," 138.
49 Butler, "Precarious Life, Vulnerability, and the Ethics of Cohabitation," 148 (emphasis in original).
50 Butler, *Frames of War*, xxv–xxvi, xxx, 43.
51 Cole, "All of Us Are Vulnerable," 274.
52 Cacho, *Social Death*, 17.
53 Cacho, *Social Death*, 14–17.
54 Cacho, *Social Death*, 7.
55 Butler, "Bodies that Still Matter," 36.
56 Butler, *The Force of Nonviolence*, 9.

57 Butler, *The Force of Nonviolence*, 10.
58 Butler, *The Force of Nonviolence*, 10.
59 Butler, "Bodies that Still Matter," 37.
60 Butler, *The Force of Nonviolence*, 23.
61 Kapadia, *Insurgent Aesthetics*, 64.
62 Kapadia, *Insurgent Aesthetics*, 64.
63 Butler, *The Force of Nonviolence*, 87.
64 Butler, *The Force of Nonviolence*, 24.
65 Sandoval, *Methodology of the Oppressed*, 42.
66 Sandoval, *Methodology of the Oppressed*, 69.
67 Sandoval, *Methodology of the Oppressed*, 6.
68 Sandoval, *Methodology of the Oppressed*, 6, 104, 112.
69 Sandoval, *Methodology of the Oppressed*, 43–47, 51–54.
70 Sandoval, *Methodology of the Oppressed*, 44 (my emphasis).
71 Sandoval, *Methodology of the Oppressed*, 53.
72 Sandoval, *Methodology of the Oppressed*, 54 (emphasis in original).
73 Sandoval, *Methodology of the Oppressed*, 54 (emphasis in original).
74 Hoad, "Arrested Development or the Queerness of Savages." I very much appreciate Hoad's analysis of what he calls the spatialization of time in this article.
75 Sandoval, *Methodology of the Oppressed*, 58.
76 Sandoval, *Methodology of the Oppressed*, 180.
77 Kim, "Unbecoming Human," 297.
78 Kim, "Unbecoming Human," 297.
79 Kim, "Unbecoming Human," 297.
80 Kim, "Unbecoming Human," 297.
81 Kim, "Unbecoming Human," 295.
82 Kim, "Unbecoming Human," 296.
83 Kim, "Unbecoming Human," 298.
84 Kim, "Unbecoming Human," 305.
85 Douglass, "Black Feminist Theory for the Dead and Dying," 115 (emphasis in original).
86 Douglass, "Sexualized Black Subjection."
87 Jackson, *Becoming Human*, 20.
88 Jackson, *Becoming Human*, 35 (emphasis in original).
89 Jackson, *Becoming Human*, 35.

90   Jackson, *Becoming Human*, 48.
91   Karera, "Blackness and the Pitfalls of Anthropocene Ethics," 45.
92   Karera, "Blackness and the Pitfalls of Anthropocene Ethics," 47–48.
93   Karera, "Blackness and the Pitfalls of Anthropocene Ethics," 43–49.
94   Karera, "Blackness and the Pitfalls of Anthropocene Ethics," 34.
95   Karera, "Blackness and the Pitfalls of Anthropocene Ethics," 52.
96   Cheng, "Ornamentalism: A Feminist Theory for the Yellow Woman," 428.
97   Cheng, "Ornamentalism: A Feminist Theory for the Yellow Woman," 436.
98   Cheng, *Ornamentalism*. Here, Cheng is directly engaging with Black feminist theorists who, in conversation with Spillers, have worked with the concept of flesh. Rather than posing flesh and ornament in opposition, Cheng is clear to describe "Africanist and Asiatic femininities" as inhabiting a nondiscrete relationship with each other, suggesting that both are constituted in part through "technologies of ornamentalism" (7) and that ornamentalism is "potentially an operative component in what Spillers famously called the vestibular economy of black female flesh, helping us to see that there is in fact no 'zero degree of conceptualization'" (153).
99   Cheng, *Ornamentalism*, 152.
100 Cheng, *Ornamentalism*, 25–27, 42–43.
101 Cheng, *Ornamentalism*, 2.
102 Cheng, "Ornamentalism: A Feminist Theory for the Yellow Woman," 441.
103 Cheng, "Ornamentalism: A Feminist Theory for the Yellow Woman," 442.
104 Cheng, *Ornamentalism*, 91.
105 Rancière, *Politics of Aesthetics*, 13.
106 Cheng, *Ornamentalism*, 22.
107 Cheng, *Ornamentalism*, 124–25 (emphasis in original).
108 Cheng, *Ornamentalism*, 106.
109 King, "Humans Involved," 178.
110 Ferreira da Silva, *Toward a Global Idea of Race*, xi–xii.
111 Ferreira da Silva, *Toward a Global Idea of Race*, xxxvii.
112 Ferreira da Silva, *Toward a Global Idea of Race*, xviii.
113 King, "Post-Identitarian and Post-Intersectional Anxiety," 131.
114 King, "Post-Identitarian and Post-Intersectional Anxiety," 131.
115 Butler, *The Force of Nonviolence*, 148.
116 Cheng, *Ornamentalism*, 106.
117 Cole, "All of Us Are Vulnerable," 271.

118 Cheng, *Ornamentalism*, 92.
119 Cheng, *Ornamentalism*, 19.
120 Kim, "Unbecoming Human," 315.
121 Kim, "Unbecoming Human," 298.
122 Kim, "Unbecoming Human," 302.
123 Cheng, *Ornamentalism*, 150.
124 Cheng, *Ornamentalism*, 105.
125 Kim, *Postcolonial Grief*.

Coda

Epigraph 1: Stanley, *Atmospheres of Violence*, 105.

1 Stanley, *Atmospheres of Violence*; Stanley, "Near Life, Queer Death."
2 Stanley, *Atmospheres of Violence*, 105.
3 Stanley, *Atmospheres of Violence*, 33.
4 Stanley, *Atmospheres of Violence*, 33 (emphasis in original).
5 Stanley, *Atmospheres of Violence*, 31.
6 Stanley, *Atmospheres of Violence*, 33.
7 Masco, *The Future of Fallout*, 131.
8 Masco, *The Future of Fallout*, 134 (my emphasis).
9 Masco, *The Future of Fallout*, 250.
10 Masco, *The Future of Fallout*, 194.
11 "Radioactive Decay," US Environmental Protection Agency.
12 Valerie Kuletz gives an excellent, incredibly in-depth account of the impossibility of containment in *The Tainted Desert*.
13 Sebeok, "Pandora's Box," 449.
14 Sebeok, "Pandora's Box," 460.
15 Sebeok, "Pandora's Box," 463.
16 Sebeok, "Pandora's Box," 464.
17 Sebeok notes that the 10,000-year time frame "is clearly an arbitrary limit" given variable rates of decay depending on the element (Sebeok, "Pandora's Box," 449).
18 Kuletz, *The Tainted Desert*, 275; Masco, *The Future of Fallout*, 95–99.
19 "Radioactive Decay," Wikipedia.
20 For another example of long-term nuclear waste storage being conceived as a kind of planned ruins, see the US Department of Energy's fact sheet detailing proposed architectural designs for communicating

the dangers of the Waste Isolation Pilot Plant, the United States' subterranean nuclear waste storage facility, far into the future. Proposals include creating a landscape of huge stone and/or concrete blocks, spikes, and thorns covering the land over the facility (US Department of Energy, "Site Markers").

21   Ocean Vuong, virtual book reading and discussion, School of the Art Institute of Chicago, October 6, 2020.
22   Sandoval, *Methodology of the Oppressed*, 44.
23   Bennett, *Vibrant Matter*, 106–7.
24   Bennett, *Vibrant Matter*, 20–23.
25   Bennett, *Vibrant Matter*, 106 (emphasis in original).
26   Mameni, *Terracene*, 169.
27   Mameni, *Terracene*, 56.

Bibliography

Agamben, Giorgio. *Homo Sacer: Sovereign Power and Bare Life*. Translated by Daniel Heller-Roazen. Stanford University Press, 1998.

Ahuja, Neel. *Bioinsecurities: Disease Interventions, Empire, and the Government of Species*. Duke University Press, 2016.

Alaimo, Stacy. "Your Shell on Acid: Material Immersion, Anthropocene Dissolves." In *Anthropocene Feminism*, edited by Richard Grusin, 89–120. University of Minnesota Press, 2017.

Alfred, Taiaiake. "Sovereignty." In *Sovereignty Matters: Locations of Contestation and Possibility in Indigenous Struggles for Self-Determination*, edited by Joanne Barker, 33–50. University of Nebraska Press, 2005.

Amar, Paul. *The Security Archipelago: Human-Security States, Sexuality Politics, and the End of Neoliberalism*. Duke University Press, 2013.

Amigo, Ignacio. "When Will the Amazon Hit a Tipping Point?" *Nature* 578, nos. 505–7 (February 25, 2020). https://www.nature.com/articles/d41586-020-00508-4.

Anis, Ema. "Sharmeen Obaid Did Not Fulfill Promise of Rs3m, Plastic Surgery: Acid Victim." *Express Tribune*, June 28, 2012. https://tribune.com.pk/story/400532/obaid-chinoy-did-not-fulfil-promise-of-rs3m-plastic-surgery-acid-victim.

Asad, Talal. *Formations of the Secular: Christianity, Islam, Modernity*. Stanford University Press, 2003.

Asad, Talal. *On Suicide Bombing*. Columbia University Press, 2007.

Asad, Talal. "What Do Human Rights Do? An Anthropological Enquiry." *Theory and Event* 4, no. 4 (2000). https://www.muse.jhu.edu/article/32601.

Atanasoski, Neda. *Humanitarian Violence: The U.S. Deployment of Diversity.* University of Minnesota Press, 2013.

Austen, Ralph A. "Beyond 'History': Two Films of the Deep Mande Past." In *Black and White in Colour: African History on Screen*, edited by Vivian Bickford-Smith and Richard Mendelsohn, 28–40. Double Storey Books, 2007.

"Awá: Earth's Most Threatened Tribe." Survival International. Accessed June 13, 2024. http://www.survivalinternational.org/awa.

Badkhen, Anna. "PTSDland." *Foreign Policy* 195 (2012): 34–36.

Baker, Aryn. "Afghan Women and the Return of the Taliban." *Time* 176, no. 6 (August 9, 2010): 20–28.

Balée, William. *Cultural Forests of the Amazon: A Historical Ecology of People and Their Landscapes.* University of Alabama Press, 2013.

Barlet, Olivier. *African Cinemas: Decolonizing the Gaze.* Translated by Chris Turner. Zed, 2000.

Barnett, Michael. *Empire of Humanity: A History of Humanitarianism.* Cornell University Press, 2011.

Bartov, Omer. *Murder in Our Midst: The Holocaust, Industrial Killing, and Representation.* Oxford University Press, 1996.

Bennett, Jane. *Vibrant Matter: A Political Ecology of Things.* Duke University Press, 2010.

Berger, John. "Twelve Theses on the Economy of the Dead." In *Hold Everything Dear: Dispatches on Survival and Resistance.* Pantheon, 2007.

Biddle, Wayne. *Dark Side of the Moon: Wernher von Braun, the Third Reich, and the Space Race.* W. W. Norton, 2009.

Bird, Kai, and Lawrence Lifschultz, eds. *Hiroshima's Shadow: Writings on the Denial of History and the Smithsonian Controversy.* Pamphleteer's Press, 1998.

Bonneuil, Christophe, and Jean-Baptiste Fressoz. *The Shock of the Anthropocene: The Earth, History, and Us.* Translated by David Fernbach. Verso, 2015.

Borofsky, Robert. *Yanomami: The Fierce Controversy and What We Can Learn from It.* University of California Press, 2005.

Bouchard, Danielle. "Communities of Ruin: Humanitarian Violence and the Amazon's Uncontacted Tribes." *Culture, Theory and Critique* 58, no. 1 (2017): 62–76.

Bouchard, Danielle. "Daring to Look: Women Without 'Faces' and Humanitarian Resentment." *Feminist Formations* 29, no. 3 (2017): 110–31.

Bouchard, Danielle. "Humanitarian." In *Rethinking Women's and Gender Studies II*, edited by Catherine Orr and Anne Braithwaite, 257–66. Routledge, 2024.

Bouchard, Danielle. "The Limits of the Anthropocene: Anticolonial Humanity in Kidlat Tahimik's *Mababangong Bangungot* and Souleymane Cissé's *Yeelen.*" *Interventions: International Journal of Postcolonial Studies* 24, no. 7 (2022): 1161–76.

Boulton, Chris A., Timothy M. Lenton, and Niklas Boers. "Pronounced Loss of Amazon Rainforest Resilience Since the Early 2000s." *Nature Climate Change* 12, no. 3 (March 2022): 271–78. https://www.nature.com/articles/s41558-022-01287-8.

Bourdeau, Michel. "Auguste Comte." Translated by Mark van Atten, Béatrice Fink, and Mary Pickering. *Stanford Encyclopedia of Philosophy*, 2015 ed., edited by Edward N. Zalta. Accessed June 27, 2017. https://plato.stanford.edu/entries/comte/.

Boyer, Paul. *By the Bomb's Early Light: American Thought and Culture at the Dawn of the Atomic Age*. University of North Carolina Press, 1994 (1985).

Boyer, Paul. *Fallout: A Historian Reflects on America's Half-Century Encounter with Nuclear Weapons*. Ohio State University Press, 1998.

Bromwich, Jonah Engel. "Doomsday Clock Moves Closer to Midnight, Signaling Concern Among Scientists." *New York Times*, January 26, 2017.

Browne, Victoria, Jason Danely, and Doerthe Rosenow. "Vulnerability and the Politics of Care: Transdisciplinary Dialogues." In *Vulnerability and the Politics of Care: Transdisciplinary Dialogues*, edited by Victoria Browne, Jason Danely, and Doerthe Rosenow, 1–29. Oxford University Press for the British Academy, 2021.

Brudholm, Thomas. *Resentment's Virtue: Jean Améry and the Refusal to Forgive*. Temple University Press, 2008.

Brum, Eliane. "Was a British Journalist the Latest Victim of Bolsonaro's War on the Amazon?" *New York Times*, June 11, 2022.

Bulletin Science and Security Board. "Bulletin Science and Security Board Condemns Russian Invasion of Ukraine; Doomsday Clock Stays at 100 Seconds to Midnight." *Bulletin of the Atomic Scientists*, March 7, 2022. https://thebulletin.org/2022/03/bulletin-science-and-security-board-condemns-russian-invasion-of-ukraine-doomsday-clock-stays-at-100-seconds-to-midnight/?utm_source=ClockPage&utm_medium=Web&utm_campaign=DoomsdayClockMarchStatement.

Bush, George W. "Address to a Joint Session of Congress and the American People." *White House*, September 20, 2001. https://georgewbush-whitehouse.archives.gov/news/releases/2001/09/20010920-8.html.

Butler, Judith. "Bodies that Still Matter." In *Vulnerability and the Politics of Care: Transdisciplinary Dialogues*, edited by Victoria Browne, Jason Danely, and Doerthe Rosenow, 33–42. Oxford University Press for the British Academy, 2021.

Butler, Judith. *The Force of Nonviolence: An Ethico-Political Bind*. Verso, 2021.

Butler, Judith. *Frames of War: When Is Life Grievable?* Verso, 2010.

Butler, Judith. *Precarious Life: The Powers of Mourning and Violence*. Verso, 2004.

Butler, Judith. "Precarious Life, Vulnerability, and the Ethics of Cohabitation." *Journal of Speculative Philosophy* 26, no. 2 (2012): 134–51.

Byrd, Jodi. *The Transit of Empire: Indigenous Critiques of Colonialism*. University of Minnesota Press, 2011.

Cacho, Lisa Marie. *Social Death: Racialized Rightlessness and the Criminalization of the Unprotected*. New York University Press, 2012.

Cainkar, Louise A. *Homeland Insecurity: The Arab American and Muslim American Experience After 9/11*. Russell Sage Foundation, 2009.

Campos, Patrick F. "Kidlat Tahimik and the Determination of a Native Filmmaker." *Kritika Kultura* 25 (2015): 46–81.

Cartwright, Lisa. *Screening the Body: Tracing Medicine's Visual Culture*. University of Minnesota Press, 1995.

Cervoni, Albert. "A Historic Confrontation in 1965 Between Jean Rouch and Ousmane Sembène: 'You Look at Us as if We Were Insects.'" Translated by Muna El Fituri. In *Ousmane Sembène: Interviews*, edited by Annett Busch and Max Annas, 3–6. University of Mississippi Press, 2008.

Chakrabarty, Dipesh. "The Climate of History: Four Theses." *Critical Inquiry* 35, no. 2 (2009): 197–222.

Chakrabarty, Dipesh. "Postcolonial Studies and the Challenge of Climate Change." *New Literary History* 43, no. 1 (2012): 1–18.

Chan, Sewell. "Doomsday Clock Is Set at 2 Minutes to Midnight, Closest Since 1950s." *New York Times*, January 25, 2018.

Cheng, Anne Anlin. *Ornamentalism*. Oxford University Press, 2019.

Cheng, Anne Anlin. "Ornamentalism: A Feminist Theory for the Yellow Woman." *Critical Inquiry* 44 (2018): 415–46.

Chow, Rey. *The Age of the World Target: Self-Referentiality in War, Theory, and Comparative Work*. Duke University Press, 2006.

Chowdhury, Elora Halim. *Transnationalism Reversed: Women Organizing Against Gendered Violence in Bangladesh*. State University of New York Press, 2011.

Cirincione, Joseph, Jon B. Wolfsthal, and Miriam Rajkumar. *Deadly Arsenals: Nuclear, Biological, and Chemical Threats*, 2nd ed. Carnegie Endowment for International Peace, 2005.

Cissé, Souleymane. "Souleymane Cissé." Interview by N. Frank Ukadike. Translated by Kathryn Lauten. In *Questioning African Cinema: Conversations with Filmmakers*, by N. Frank Ukadike, 19–28. University of Minnesota Press, 2002.

Cissé, Souleymane. "Souleymane Cissé's Light on Africa." Interview by Manthia Diawara. *Black Film Review* 4 (1988): 12–16.

Cissé, Souleymane, dir. *Yeelen*. Kino International, 2002 (1987).

Clark, Nigel. "Geo-Politics and the Disaster of the Anthropocene." *Sociological Review* 62, no. 1 (2014): 19–37.

Clark, Timothy. *Ecocriticism on the Edge: The Anthropocene as a Threshold Concept*. Bloomsbury Academic, 2015.

Cleary, David. "Towards an Environmental History of the Amazon: From Prehistory to the Nineteenth Century." *Latin American Research Review* 36, no. 2 (2001): 65–96.

"The Clock Shifts." *Bulletin of the Atomic Scientists.* n.d. Accessed December 17, 2021. https://thebulletin.org/doomsday-clock/timeline/.

Cole, Alyson. "All of Us Are Vulnerable, but Some Are More Vulnerable Than Others: The Political Ambiguity of Vulnerability Studies, an Ambivalent Critique." *Critical Horizons: A Journal of Philosophy and Social Theory* 17, no. 2 (May 2016): 260–77.

Colebrook, Claire. "Not Symbiosis, Not Now: Why Anthropogenic Change Is Not Really Human." *Oxford Literary Review* 34, no. 2 (2012): 185–209.

Crist, Eileen. "On the Poverty of Our Nomenclature." *Environmental Humanities* 3, no. 1 (2013): 129–47.

Crutzen, Paul J. "Geology of Mankind." *Nature* 415 (January 3, 2002): 23.

Crutzen, Paul J., and Eugene F. Stoermer. "The 'Anthropocene.'" *Global Change Newsletter* 41 (May 2000): 17–18.

"Cynical (adj.)." *Oxford English Dictionary Online.* Oxford University Press, March 2024. https://doi.org/10.1093/OED/7812544209.

Davies, Jeremy. *The Birth of the Anthropocene.* University of California Press, 2016.

Davis, Heather, and Zoe Todd. "On the Importance of a Date, or Decolonizing the Anthropocene." ACME: *An International Journal for Critical Geographies* 16, no. 4 (2017): 761–80.

D'Costa, Bina. "Gender Justice and (In)Security in Pakistan and Afghanistan." *Postcolonial Studies* 19, no. 4 (2016): 409–26.

de la Cadena, Marisol. "Indigenous Cosmopolitics in the Andes: Conceptual Reflections beyond 'Politics.'" *Cultural Anthropology* 25, no. 2 (2010): 334–70.

Denooyer, Rushmoore, and Krik Wilfinger, dirs. and prods. *The Bomb.* Public Broadcasting Service, 2015.

Derrida, Jacques. "No Apocalypse, Not Now (Full Speed Ahead, Seven Missiles, Seven Missives)." Translated by Catherine Porter and Philip Lewis. *Diacritics* 14, no. 2 (1984): 20–31.

Dixon, Deborah, and Leo Zonn. "Confronting the Geopolitical Aesthetic: Fredric Jameson, 'The Perfumed Nightmare,' and the Perilous Place of Third Cinema." In *Cinema and Popular Geo-Politics,* edited by Marcus Power and Andrew Crampton, 95–120. Routledge, 2007.

Douglass, Patrice. "Black Feminist Theory for the Dead and Dying." *Theory and Event* 21, no. 1 (January 2018): 106–23.

Douglass, Patrice. "Sexualized Black Subjection: Reproducing the Social Body." Talk given at the University of North Carolina–Greensboro, February 26, 2020.

Dovey, Lindiwe. *Curating Africa in the Age of Film Festivals.* Palgrave Macmillan, 2015.

Dower, John W. *Cultures of War: Pearl Harbor/Hiroshima/9-11/Iraq.* W. W. Norton/New Press, 2010.

Dower, John W. *War Without Mercy: Race and Power in the Pacific War.* Pantheon Books, 1986.

Einstein, Albert, and Bertrand Russell. "The Peril of Universal Death." In *Hiroshima's Shadow: Writings on the Denial of History and the Smithsonian Controversy*, edited by Kai Bird and Lawrence Lifschultz, 485–87. Pamphleteer's Press, 1998.

Eng, David. *Racial Castration: Managing Masculinity in Asian America*. Duke University Press, 2001.

Epstein, Deborah, and Kit Gruelle. "Should an Abused Wife Be Charged in Her Husband's Crime?" *New York Times*, March 12, 2018.

Fabian, Johannes. *Time and the Other: How Anthropology Makes Its Object*. Columbia University Press, 2002 (1983).

Falcón, Sylvanna M. *Power Interrupted: Antiracist and Feminist Activism Inside the United Nations*. University of Washington Press, 2016.

Fanon, Frantz. *Black Skin, White Masks*. Translated by Charles Lam Markmann. Grove Press, 1967.

Feminist Majority Foundation. "Feminist and Human Rights Groups to Biden and Harris: Do Not Recognize Taliban Regime and Honor U.S. Commitments to Aid Afghan Women and Girls." August 18, 2021. https://feminist.org/news/press/feminist-and-human-rights-groups-to-biden-and-harris-do-not-recognize-taliban-regime-and-honor-u-s-commitments-to-aid-afghan-women-and-girls/.

Fernandes, Leela. "The Boundaries of Terror: Feminism, Human Rights, and the Politics of Global Crisis." In *Just Advocacy? Women's Human Rights, Transnational Feminisms, and the Politics of Representation*, edited by Wendy Hesford and Wendy Kozol, 56–74. Rutgers University Press, 2005.

Ferreira da Silva, Denise. *Toward a Global Idea of Race*. University of Minnesota Press, 2007.

Fitzgerald, Paul, and Elizabeth Gould. *Crossing Zero: The AfPak War at the Turning Point of American Empire*. City Lights Books, 2011.

Frank, Richard B. Excerpt from *Downfall: The End of the Imperial Japanese Empire*. In *The Manhattan Project: The Birth of the Atomic Bomb in the Words of Its Creators, Eyewitnesses, and Historians*, edited by Cynthia C. Kelly, 334. Black Dog and Leventhal, 2007.

Franklin, H. Bruce. *War Stars: The Superweapon and the American Imagination*. Oxford University Press, 1988.

Garland, Alex, dir. *Ex Machina*. A24, 2014.

Geddes, Linda. "Ancient Amazon Civilisation Laid Bare by Felled Forest." *New Scientist* 204, no. 2738 (December 12, 2009): 11.

Ghosh, Amitav. *The Great Derangement: Climate Change and the Unthinkable*. University of Chicago Press, 2016.

Gilson, Erinn C. *The Ethics of Vulnerability: A Feminist Analysis of Social Life and Practice*. Routledge, 2014.

Gilson, Erinn. "Vulnerability, Ignorance, and Oppression." *Hypatia: A Journal of Feminist Philosophy* 26, no. 2 (2011): 308–32.

Gilson, Erinn Cunniff. "Vulnerability and Victimization: Rethinking Key Concepts in Feminist Discourses on Sexual Violence." *Signs: Journal of Women in Culture and Society* 42, no. 1 (2016): 71–98.

Ginsburg, Faye. "Native Intelligence: A Short History of Debates on Indigenous Media and Ethnographic Film." In *Made to Be Seen: Perspectives on the History of Visual Anthropology*, edited by Marcus Banks and Jay Ruby, 233–55. University of Chicago Press, 2011.

Ginsburg, Faye. "Screen Memories: Resignifying the Traditional in Indigenous Media." In *Media Worlds: Anthropology on New Terrain*, edited by Faye D. Ginsburg, Lila Abu-Lughod, and Brian Larkin, 39–57. University of California Press, 2002.

Goldbaum, Christina. "Afghan Economy Nears Collapse as Pressure Builds to Ease U.S. Sanctions." *New York Times*, November 27, 2021.

Gómez-Barris, Macarena. *The Extractive Zone: Social Ecologies and Decolonial Perspectives*. Duke University Press, 2017.

Grandin, Greg. "Empire's Ruins: Detroit to the Amazon." In *Imperial Debris: On Ruins and Ruination*, edited by Ann Laura Stoler, 115–28. Duke University Press, 2013.

Grann, David. *The Lost City of Z: A Tale of Deadly Obsession in the Amazon*. Doubleday, 2005.

Grewal, Inderpal. *Saving the Security State: Exceptional Citizens in Twenty-First Century America*. Duke University Press, 2017.

Grewal, Inderpal. *Transnational America: Feminisms, Diasporas, Neoliberalisms*. Duke University Press, 2005.

Griggers, Camilla. *Becoming-Woman*. University of Minnesota Press, 1997.

"Ground zero (n.)." *Oxford English Dictionary Online*. Oxford University Press, July 2023. https://doi.org/10.1093/OED/9127509120.

Gupta, Alisha Haridasani, and Francesca Donner. "'Lost Between Borders': Afghan Women on the Lives They Left Behind." *New York Times*, September 14, 2021.

Gusterson, Hugh. *People of the Bomb: Portraits of America's Nuclear Complex*. University of Minnesota Press, 2004.

Haggerty, James J. *Man's Conquest of Space*. Scholastic Book Services, 1966.

Haley, Sarah. *No Mercy Here: Gender, Punishment, and the Making of Jim Crow Modernity*. University of North Carolina Press, 2016.

Haraway, Donna. "Teddy Bear Patriarchy: Taxidermy in the Garden of Eden, New York City, 1908–1936." In *Primate Visions: Gender, Race, and Nature in the World of Modern Science*, 26–58. Routledge, 1989.

Harrison, Simon. *Dark Trophies: Hunting and the Enemy Body in Modern War*. Berghahn Books, 2012.

Hartman, Saidiya. *Scenes of Subjection: Terror, Slavery, and Self-Making in Nineteenth-Century America*. Oxford University Press, 1997.

Harvey, David. *The New Imperialism*. Oxford University Press, 2003.

Hauser, Christine. "U.S. Nuclear Weapons Tests Come to YouTube." *New York Times*, March 17, 2017.

Heckenberger, Michael J., Afukaka Kuikuro, Urissapá Tabata Kuikuro, J. Christian Russell, Morgan Schmidt, Carlos Fausto, and Bruna Franchetto. "Amazonia 1492: Pristine Forest or Cultural Parkland?" *Science* 301, no. 5640 (September 19, 2003): 1710–14.

Heiner, Brady Thomas. "Foucault and the Black Panthers." *City* 11, no. 3 (2007): 313–56.

Herr, Ranjoo Seodu. "Women's Rights as Human Rights and Cultural Imperialism." *Feminist Formations* 31, no. 3 (2019): 118–42.

Hesford, Wendy. *Spectacular Rhetorics: Human Rights Visions, Recognitions, Feminisms*. Duke University Press, 2011.

Hoad, Neville. "Arrested Development or the Queerness of Savages: Resisting Evolutionary Narratives of Difference." *Postcolonial Studies* 3, no. 2 (2000): 133–58.

Hoffman, Rachel. "*Yeelen*." *African Arts* 22, no. 2 (February 1989): 100–101.

Hua, Julietta. *Trafficking Women's Human Rights*. University of Minnesota Press, 2011.

Human Planet. BBC Home Entertainment, 2011.

"Human Planet." BBC One. Accessed July 1, 2022. https://www.bbc.co.uk/programmes/boollpvp.

"Humanitarian (n. and adj.)." *Oxford English Dictionary Online*. Oxford University Press, September 2023. https://doi.org/10.1093/OED/8300114784.

Huq, Chaumtoli. "The War on Terror on Muslim Women and Girls: Forging Transformative Solidarities." *Scholar and Feminist Online* 15, no. 3 (2019). https://sfonline.barnard.edu/unraveling-criminalizing-webs-building-police-free-futures/the-war-on-terror-on-muslim-women-and-girls-forging-transformative-solidarities/.

Imtiaz, Saba. "Oscar Win Shines Light on Pakistan Efforts to Stop 'Honor Killings.'" *New York Times*, March 2, 2016.

Jackson, Zakiyyah Iman. *Becoming Human: Matter and Meaning in an Anti-Black World*. New York University Press, 2020.

Jaleel, Rana M. *The Work of Rape*. Duke University Press, 2021.

James, Caryn. "'*Yeelen*,' Based on Myths from Mali." *New York Times*, October 8, 1987, C37.

Jameson, Fredric. "'Art Naïf' and the Admixture of Worlds." In *The Geopolitical Aesthetic: Cinema and Space in the World System*, 186–213. Indiana University Press, 1992.

Jolie, Angelina. "Sharmeen Obaid-Chinoy." *Time* 179, no. 17 (April 30, 2012): 95.

Jones, Ann. "Our Afghan Demons." *Nation*, August 30, 2010, 4–6.

Junge, Daniel, and Sharmeen Obaid-Chinoy, dirs. *Saving Face*. Home Box Office, 2011.

"Jungle (n.)." *Oxford English Dictionary Online*. Oxford University Press, July 2023. https://doi.org/10.1093/OED/9672950235.

Kang, Laura Hyun Yi. *Traffic in Asian Women*. Duke University Press, 2020.

Kapadia, Ronak. *Insurgent Aesthetics: Security and the Queer Life of the Forever War*. Duke University Press, 2019.

Kaplan, Caren. *Aerial Aftermaths: Wartime from Above*. Duke University Press, 2018.

Karera, Axelle. "Blackness and the Pitfalls of Anthropocene Ethics." *Critical Philosophy of Race* 7, no. 1 (2019): 32–56.

Kariithi, Nixon K. "Misreading Culture and Tradition: Western Critical Appreciation of African Films." In *L'Afrique et le Centenaire du Cinéma/Africa and the Centenary of Cinema*, edited by Panafrican Federation of Filmmakers (FEPACI), 166–87. Présence Africaine, 1995.

Keating, Christine, Claire Rasmussen, and Pooja Rishi. "The Rationality of Empowerment: Microcredit, Accumulation by Dispossession, and the Gendered Economy." *Signs: Journal of Women in Culture and Society* 36, no. 1 (2010): 153–76.

Kelly, Cynthia C., ed. *The Manhattan Project: The Birth of the Atomic Bomb in the Words of Its Creators, Eyewitnesses, and Historians*. Black Dog and Leventhal, 2007.

Kennett, Lee. *A History of Strategic Bombing*. Charles Scribner's Sons, 1982.

Khalili, Laleh. *Time in the Shadows: Confinement in Counterinsurgencies*. Stanford University Press, 2012.

Kim, Eunjung. "Unbecoming Human: An Ethics of Objects." *GLQ: A Journal of Lesbian and Gay Studies* 21, nos. 2–3 (2015): 295–320.

Kim, Jinah. *Postcolonial Grief: The Afterlives of the Pacific Wars in the Americas*. Duke University Press, 2019.

Kim, Jodi. *Ends of Empire: Asian American Critique and the Cold War*. University of Minnesota Press, 2010.

King, Tiffany Lethabo. "Humans Involved: Lurking in the Lines of Posthumanist Flight." *Critical Ethnic Studies* 3, no. 1 (2017): 162–85.

King, Tiffany Lethabo. "Post-Identitarian and Post-Intersectional Anxiety in the Neoliberal Corporate University." *Feminist Formations* 27, no. 3 (2015): 114–38.

Klein, Joe. "The Forest and the Trees." *Time* 176, no. 6 (August 9, 2010): 19.

Kosek, Jake. "Nuclear Natures: In the Shadows of the City on the Hill." In *Understories: The Political Life of Forests in Northern New Mexico*, 228–75. Duke University Press, 2006.

Koshy, Susan. "From Cold War to Trade War: Neocolonialism and Human Rights." *Social Text* 17, no. 1 (1999): 1–32.

Kozol, Wendy. *Distant Wars Visible: The Ambivalence of Witnessing*. University of Minnesota Press, 2014.

Krauss, Lawrence M., and David Titley. "Thanks to Trump, the Doomsday Clock Advances Toward Midnight." *New York Times*, January 26, 2017.

Kuletz, Valerie. *The Tainted Desert: Environmental Ruin in the American West*. Routledge, 1998.

Kumar, Reena. "'Women Want Control of Lives': Director Debates Honour Killings in Pakistan After Baloch Murder." *EasternEye*, July 29, 2016, 2.

Langewiesche, William. "The War for the Rainforest." *New York Times Magazine*, March 16, 2022, updated April 18, 2022.

"The Last of His Tribe." *YouTube*, July 6, 2007. Accessed July 3, 2022. https://www.youtube.com/watch?v=ffh9QT8I6fQ.

Laurence, William L. *Dawn over Zero: The Story of the Atomic Bomb*, 2nd ed. Alfred A. Knopf, 1947.

Lawrence Livermore National Laboratory. "Physicist Declassifies Rescued Nuclear Test Films." March 14, 2017. https://www.llnl.gov/news/physicist-declassifies-rescued-nuclear-test-films.

Lemmon, Gayle Tzemach. "An Unspeakable Crime." *Daily Beast*, December 27, 2009. http://www.thedailybeast.com/articles/2009/12/28/afghanistans-unspeakable-crime.html.

Lepecki, André. *Exhausting Dance: Performance and the Politics of Movement*. Routledge, 2006.

Lewis, Simon L., and Mark A. Maslin. "Defining the Anthropocene." *Nature* 519 (March 12, 2015): 171–80.

Lifschultz, Lawrence, and Kai Bird. "The Legend of Hiroshima." In *Hiroshima's Shadow: Writings on the Denial of History and the Smithsonian Controversy*, edited by Kai Bird and Lawrence Lifschultz, xxxi–lxxvii. Pamphleteer's Press, 1998.

Lilienthal, David E. *Change, Hope, and the Bomb*. Princeton University Press, 1963.

Lindqvist, Sven. *"Exterminate All the Brutes": One Man's Odyssey into the Heart of Darkness and the Origins of European Genocide*. Translated by Joan Tate. New Press, 1992.

Lindqvist, Sven. *A History of Bombing*. Translated by Linda Haverty Rugg. New Press, 2001.

Lindqvist, Sven. *Terra Nullius: A Journey Through No One's Land*. Translated by Sarah Death. Granta, 2012 (2007).

Lippit, Akira Mizuta. *Atomic Light (Shadow Optics)*. University of Minnesota Press, 2005.

Lowe, Lisa. *The Intimacies of Four Continents*. Duke University Press, 2015.

Macharia, Keguro. "On Being Area-Studied: A Litany of Complaint." *GLQ: A Journal of Lesbian and Gay Studies* 22, no. 2 (April 2016): 183–89.

Mackenzie, Catriona, Wendy Rogers, and Susan Dodds. "Introduction: What Is Vulnerability and Why Does It Matter for Moral Theory?" In *Vulnerability:*

New Essays in Ethics and Feminist Philosophy, edited by Catriona Mackenzie, Wendy Rogers, and Susan Dodds, 1–29. Oxford University Press, 2014.

MacRae, Suzanne H. "*Yeelen*: A Political Fable of the *Komo* Blacksmith/Sorcerers." *Research in African Literatures* 26, no. 3 (1995): 57–66.

Mahmood, Saba. *Politics of Piety: The Islamic Revival and the Feminist Subject*. Princeton University Press, 2005.

Maira, Sunaina Marr. *The 9/11 Generation: Youth, Rights, and Solidarity in the War on Terror*. New York University Press, 2016.

Mamdani, Mahmood. *When Victims Become Killers: Colonialism, Nativism, and the Genocide in Rwanda*. Princeton University Press, 2020 (2001).

Mameni, Salar. *Terracene: A Crude Aesthetics*. Duke University Press, 2023.

Mameni, Sara. "Dermopolitics and the Erotics of the Muslim Body in Pain." *Women and Performance: A Journal of Feminist Theory* 27, no. 1 (2017): 96–103.

Masco, Joseph. *The Future of Fallout, and Other Episodes in Radioactive World-Making*. Duke University Press, 2021.

Masood, Salman. "Pakistan Toughens Laws on Rape and 'Honor Killings' of Women." *New York Times*, October 6, 2016.

Mazzei, Patricia. "Noor Salman Acquitted in Pulse Nightclub Shooting." *New York Times*, March 30, 2018.

Mbembe, Achille. "Necropolitics." Translated by Libby Meintjes. *Public Culture* 15, no. 1 (2003): 11–40.

McClintock, Ann. *Imperial Leather: Race, Gender and Sexuality in the Colonial Contest*. Routledge, 1995.

McElroy, Alex. "This Isn't Your Old Toxic Masculinity. It Has Taken an Insidious New Form." *New York Times*, January 13, 2022.

McKelvey, Tara. *Monstering: Inside America's Policy of Secret Interrogations and Torture in the War on Terror*. Carroll and Graf, 2007.

Mecklin, John, ed. "It Is Now Two Minutes to Midnight: 2018 Doomsday Clock Statement." *Bulletin of the Atomic Scientists*, January 25, 2018. https://thebulletin.org/doomsday-clock/2018-doomsday-clock-statement/.

Mecklin, John, ed. "It Is 100 Seconds to Midnight." *Bulletin of the Atomic Scientists*, January 23, 2020. https://thebulletin.org/wp-content/uploads/2020/01/2020-Doomsday-Clock-statement.pdf.

Mecklin, John, ed. "A Time of Unprecedented Danger: It Is 90 Seconds to Midnight: 2023 Doomsday Clock Statement." *Bulletin of the Atomic Scientists*, January 24, 2023. https://thebulletin.org/doomsday-clock/2023-doomsday-clock-statement/.

Melamed, Jodi. *Represent and Destroy: Rationalizing Violence in the New Racial Capitalism*. University of Minnesota Press, 2011.

Merolla, Daniela. "Filming African Creation Myths." *Religion and the Arts* 13 (2009): 521–33.

Metz, Anneke. "Technology and National Identity in Kidlat Tahimik's 'Perfumed Nightmare.'" *ARIEL: A Review of International English Literature* 28, no. 3 (July 1997): 119–42.

Mirzoeff, Nicholas. *The Right to Look: A Counterhistory of Visuality*. Duke University Press, 2011.

Monastersky, Richard. "The Human Age." *Nature* 519 (March 12, 2015): 144–47.

Moore, Jason W. "The Rise of Cheap Nature." In *Anthropocene or Capitalocene? Nature, History, and the Crisis of Capitalism*, edited by Jason W. Moore, 78–115. PM Press, 2016.

Morgensen, Scott Lauria. *Spaces Between Us: Queer Settler Colonialism and Indigenous Decolonization*. University of Minnesota Press, 2011.

Morley, Felix. "The Return to Nothingness." In *Hiroshima's Shadow: Writings on the Denial of History and the Smithsonian Controversy*, edited by Kai Bird and Lawrence Lifschultz, 272–74. Pamphleteer's Press, 1998.

Morton, Timothy. "Ecology Without the Present." *Oxford Literary Review* 34, no. 2 (2012): 229–38.

Muggah, Robert. "A Violent Tragedy Foretold in the Amazon." *National Public Radio*, June 17, 2022. https://www.npr.org/2022/06/17/1105852069/opinion-dom-phillips-bruno-pereira-brazil-amazon-environmental-crime.

Murphy, Ann V. "Corporeal Vulnerability and the New Humanism." *Hypatia: A Journal of Feminist Philosophy* 26, no. 3 (2011): 575–90.

Murphy, David, and Patrick Williams. *Postcolonial African Cinema: Ten Directors*. Manchester University Press, 2007.

Nacht, Michael. *The Age of Vulnerability: Threats to the Nuclear Stalemate*. Brookings Institution, 1985.

Nader, Zahra, and Amie Ferris-Rotman. "Freedom at Stake: What Afghan Women Stand to Lose Under the Taliban." *Time*, September 13–20, 2021, 24–27.

Nash, Jennifer. *The Black Body in Ecstasy: Reading Race, Reading Pornography*. Duke University Press, 2014.

Neufeld, Michael J. *Von Braun: Dreamer of Space, Engineer of War*. Alfred A. Knopf, 2007.

Neves, Maria Beatriz Correa, and Marco Antonio Calil Machado. "Nationalising Indigenous Peoples, Legalising Indigenous Lands: A (Post)Colonial Critique of the Land Demarcation Process in Brazil by the Analysis of the Guarani-Mbyá Case." *Postcolonial Studies* 20, no. 2 (2017): 163–75.

Nganang, Alain P. "Of Cameras, Trains, and Roads: French Colonial Conquest and Cinematographic Practice." *Black Renaissance/Renaissance Noire* 5, no. 1 (2003): 15–25.

Nguyen, Mimi Thi. *The Gift of Freedom: War, Debt, and Other Refugee Passages*. Duke University Press, 2012.

Nicas, Jack, and Manuela Andreoni. "Brazil Found the Last Survivors of an Amazon Tribe. Now What?" *New York Times*, August 19, 2023.

Nicas, Jack, and Victor Moriyama. "Inside the Amazon Journey That Left a Journalist and an Activist Dead." *New York Times*, July 11, 2022.

Nolan, Christopher, dir. *Oppenheimer*. Universal Pictures, 2023.

Nordland, Rod. "Portrait of Pain Ignites a Debate over the Afghan War." *New York Times*, August 5, 2010.

NWSA Executive Committee. "Solidarity with Afghan Women and Feminists." *National Women's Studies Association*, August 2021. https://mailchi.mp/nwsa/nwsa-statement-of-solidarity-with-afghan-women-and-feminists.

Obaid-Chinoy, Sharmeen, dir. *A Girl in the River: The Price of Forgiveness*. Home Box Office, 2016 (2015).

O'Driscoll, Mervyn. "Explosive Challenge: Diplomatic Triangles, the United Nations, and the Problem of French Nuclear Testing, 1959–1960." *Journal of Cold War Studies* 11, no. 1 (2009): 28–56.

Oé, Kenzaburo. *Hiroshima Notes*. Translated by David L. Swain and Toshi Yonezawa. Marion Boyars, 1981 (1965).

Okeowo, Alexis. "Daughter of Pakistan." *New Yorker*, April 9, 2018, 22–28.

Olwan, Dana M. *Gender Violence and the Transnational Politics of the Honor Crime*. Ohio State University Press, 2021.

Olwan, Dana M. "Pinkwashing the 'Honor Crime': Murdered Muslim Women and the Politics of Posthumous Solidarities." *Signs: Journal of Women in Culture and Society* 44, no. 4 (2019): 905–30.

"Operation Dominic—Arkansas 102037." Lawrence Livermore National Laboratory. *YouTube*, March 20, 2018. https://www.youtube.com/watch?v=UsY1bTKbSYY.

"Operation Dominic—Bighorn 110764." Lawrence Livermore National Laboratory. *YouTube*, July 2, 2018. https://www.youtube.com/watch?v=Hj8j6RpAQco.

"Operation Dominic—Housatonic 120256." Lawrence Livermore National Laboratory. *YouTube*, March 20, 2018. https://www.youtube.com/watch?v=IZZ_IsyE_iE.

"Operation Nougat—Danny Boy 81495." Lawrence Livermore National Laboratory. *YouTube*, July 3, 2018. https://www.youtube.com/watch?v=UXbpIIBqjNU.

Osinubi, Taiwo Adetunji. "Cognition's Warp: African Films on Near-Future Risk." *African Identities* 7, no. 2 (May 2009): 255–74.

Palsson, Gisli, Bronislaw Szerszynski, Sverker Sörlin, et al. "Reconceptualizing the 'Anthropos' in the Anthropocene: Integrating the Social Sciences and Humanities in Global Environmental Change Research." *Environmental Science and Policy* 28 (2013): 3–13.

Parks, Lisa. "Drones, Vertical Mediation, and the Targeted Class." *Feminist Studies* 42, no. 1 (2016): 227–35.

Pärsinnen, Martti, Denise Schaan, and Alceu Ranzi. "Pre-Columbian Geometric Earthworks in the Upper Purús: A Complex Society in Western Amazonia." *Antiquity* 83, no. 322 (December 2009): 1084–95.

"Patients of Courage: Bibi Aisha." American Society of Plastic Surgeons. *YouTube*, November 4, 2014. https://www.youtube.com/watch?v=oRAokVK_R2w.

Patterson, Orlando. *Slavery and Social Death: A Comparative Study*. Harvard University Press, 1982.

Pavsek, Christopher. *The Utopia of Film: Cinema and Its Futures in Godard, Kluge, and Tahimik*. Columbia University Press, 2013.

Pearce, Fred. *Deep Jungle*. Eden Project, 2005.

Pfaff, Françoise. "Souleymane Cissé (1940–), Mali." In *Twenty-Five Black African Filmmakers: A Critical Study, with Filmography and Biobibliography*, 51–67. Greenwood Press, 1988.

Piore, Adam. "Guardians of the Tiger People." *Scientific American* 320, no. 2 (February 2019): 46–55.

Pravalie, Remus. "Nuclear Weapons Tests and Environmental Consequences: A Global Perspective." *Ambio: A Journal of the Human Environment* 43, no. 6 (2014): 729–44.

Preston, Douglas. "The El Dorado Machine." *New Yorker*, May 6, 2013, 34–40.

Puar, Jasbir. *The Right to Maim: Debility, Capacity, Disability*. Duke University Press, 2017.

Puar, Jasbir. *Terrorist Assemblages: Homonationalism in Queer Times*. Duke University Press, 2007.

Puar, Jasbir K., and Amit S. Rai. "Monster, Terrorist, Fag: The War on Terrorism and the Production of Docile Patriots." *Social Text* 20, no. 3 (2002): 117–48.

Purdy, Jedediah. *After Nature: A Politics for the Anthropocene*. Harvard University Press, 2015.

Rabinowitch, Eugene. "Scientists and World Government." *Bulletin of the Atomic Scientists* 3, no. 12 (December 1947): 345–46.

"Radioactive Decay." United States Environmental Protection Agency. Accessed July 22, 2022. https://www.epa.gov/radiation/radioactive-decay.

"Radioactive Decay." Wikipedia. Accessed July 23, 2022. https://en.wikipedia.org/wiki/Radioactive_decay#Mathematics.

Rajagopal, Balakrishnan. *International Law from Below: Development, Social Movements and Third World Resistance*. Cambridge University Press, 2003.

Rana, Junaid. *Terrifying Muslims: Race and Labor in the South Asian Diaspora*. Duke University Press, 2011.

Rancière, Jacques. *Disagreement: Politics and Philosophy*. Translated by Julie Rose. University of Minnesota Press, 1999.

Rancière, Jacques. "The Ethical Turn of Aesthetics and Politics." Translated by Jean-Philippe Deranty. *Critical Horizons: A Journal of Philosophy and Social Theory* 7, no. 1 (2006): 1–20.

Rancière, Jacques. *The Politics of Aesthetics*. Translated by Gabriel Rockhill. Continuum, 2006.

Rancière, Jacques, and Peter Engelmann. *Politics and Aesthetics*. Translated by Wieland Hoban. Polity, 2019.

Ravitz, Jessica. "Saving Aesha." CNN, May 21, 2012. http://www.cnn.com/interactive/2012/05/world/saving.aesha/.
Razack, Sherene H. *Casting Out: The Eviction of Muslims from Western Law and Politics*. University of Toronto Press, 2008.
Razack, Sherene H. "Stealing the Pain of Others: Reflections on Canadian Humanitarian Responses." *Review of Education, Pedagogy, and Cultural Studies* 29 (2007): 375–94.
Reddy, Chandan. *Freedom with Violence: Race, Sexuality, and the US State*. Duke University Press, 2011.
Robbins, Sarah J. "The Lifesaver: Sharmeen Obaid-Chinoy." *Glamour* 110, no. 12 (December 2012): 227.
Rodríguez, Dylan. *Suspended Apocalypse: White Supremacy, Genocide, and the Filipino Condition*. University of Minnesota Press, 2010.
Roitman, Janet. *Anti-Crisis*. Duke University Press, 2014.
Rony, Fatimah Tobing. *How Do We Look? Resisting Visual Biopolitics*. Duke University Press, 2022.
Rony, Fatimah Tobing, dir. *On Cannibalism*. Women Make Movies, 2010.
Rony, Fatimah Tobing. *The Third Eye: Race, Cinema, and Ethnographic Spectacle*. Duke University Press, 1996.
Rotblat, Joseph. "A Social Conscience for the Nuclear Age." In *Hiroshima's Shadow: Writings on the Denial of History and the Smithsonian Controversy*, edited by Kai Bird and Lawrence Lifschultz, xvi–xxviii. Pamphleteer's Press, 1998.
"Ruin (n.)." *Oxford English Dictionary Online*. Oxford University Press, March 2024. https://doi.org/10.1093/OED/4285531933.
Russell, Catherine. *Experimental Ethnography: The Work of Film in the Age of Video*. Duke University Press, 1999.
Russo, Ann. "The Feminist Majority Foundation's Campaign to Stop Gender Apartheid: The Intersections of Feminism and Imperialism in the United States." *International Feminist Journal of Politics* 8, no. 4 (December 2006): 557–80.
Samar, Sima. "If the U.S. Doesn't Learn from the Past, Afghan Women and Girls Will Pay the Price." *Ms.*, August 12, 2021. https://msmagazine.com/2021/08/12/afghanistan-taliban-violence-women-children-minorities/.
Sandoval, Chela. *Methodology of the Oppressed*. University of Minnesota Press, 2000.
San Juan, E., Jr. *After Postcolonialism: Remapping Philippines-United States Confrontations*. Rowman and Littlefield, 2000.
San Juan, E., Jr. "Kidlat Tahimik: Cinema of the 'Naïve' Subaltern in the Shadow of Global Capitalism." *Communal/Plural* 6, no. 2 (1998): 171–85.
Santos-Granero, Fernando. "Introduction: Amerindian Constructional Views of the World." In *The Occult Life of Things: Native Amazonian Theories of Materiality and Personhood*, edited by Fernando Santos-Granero, 1–29. University of Arizona Press, 2009.

Sayle, Murray. "Did the Bomb End the War?" In *Hiroshima's Shadow: Writings on the Denial of History and the Smithsonian Controversy*, edited by Kai Bird and Lawrence Lifschultz, 22–50. Pamphleteer's Press, 1998.

Schmitt, Eric. "A Shadowy War's Newest Front: A Drone Base Rising from Saharan Dust." *New York Times*, April 22, 2018. https://www.nytimes.com/2018/04/22/us/politics/drone-base-niger.html.

Schmitt, Eric, Declan Walsh, and Elian Peltier. "Coup in Niger Upends U.S. Terrorism Fight and Could Open a Door for Russia." *New York Times*, August 16, 2023.

Schuller, Kyla. *The Biopolitics of Feeling: Race, Sex, and Science in the Nineteenth Century*. Duke University Press, 2018.

Schwab, Gabriele. *Radioactive Ghosts*. University of Minnesota Press, 2020.

Scott-Heron, Gil. "Whitey on the Moon." In *Now and Then . . . : The Poems of Gil Scott-Heron*, 21. Payback Press, 2000.

Scranton, Roy. *Learning to Die in the Anthropocene: Reflections on the End of a Civilization*. City Lights Books, 2015.

Sebeok, Thomas A. "Pandora's Box: How and Why to Communicate 10,000 Years into the Future." In *On Signs*, edited by Marshall Blonsky, 448–66. Johns Hopkins University Press, 1985.

"Sensible (adj., n., and adv.)." *Oxford English Dictionary Online*. Oxford University Press, March 2024. https://doi.org/10.1093/OED/8057348185.

Shelton, William Roy. *Man's Conquest of Space*. National Geographic Society, 1968.

Shohat, Ella, and Robert Stam. *Unthinking Eurocentrism: Multiculturalism and the Media*, 2nd ed. Routledge, 2014.

Simpson, Audra. "The Ruse of Consent and the Anatomy of 'Refusal': Cases from Indigenous North America and Australia." *Postcolonial Studies* 20, no. 1 (2017): 18–33.

Singh, Julietta. *Unthinking Mastery: Dehumanism and Decolonial Entanglements*. Duke University Press, 2018.

Sissako, Abderrahmane, dir. *Bamako*. New Yorker Films, 2006.

Speer, Albert. *Inside the Third Reich: Memoirs by Albert Speer*. Translated by Richard Winston and Clara Winston. Macmillan, 1970.

Spillers, Hortense. "Mama's Baby, Papa's Maybe: An American Grammar Book." *Diacritics* 17, no. 2 (1987): 65–81.

Spivak, Gayatri. "Can the Subaltern Speak?" In *Marxism and the Interpretation of Culture*, edited by Cary Nelson and Lawrence Grossberg, 271–313. University of Illinois Press, 1988.

Stanley, Eric A. *Atmospheres of Violence: Structuring Antagonism and the Trans/Queer Ungovernable*. Duke University Press, 2021.

Stanley, Eric. "Near Life, Queer Death: Overkill and Ontological Capture." *Social Text* 29, no. 2 (2011): 1–19.

"Starving Afghan Families Forced to Sell Their Daughters for Food." *Feminist Majority Foundation*, November 5, 2021. https://feminist.org/news/starving-afghan-families-sell-their-daughters-for-food/.

Stefanson, Blandine. "Violence in Souleymane Cissé's Films." *Journal of African Cinemas* 1, no. 2 (2009): 189–205.

Sterling, Fran, et al. "Viewer's Guide." *Saving Face*, directed by Daniel Junge and Sharmeen Obaid-Chinoy. Home Box Office, 2011.

Stokstad, Eric. "'Pristine' Forest Teemed with People." *Science* 301, no. 5640 (September 19, 2003): 1645–46.

Stoler, Ann Laura. *Race and the Education of Desire: Foucault's 'History of Sexuality' and the Colonial Order of Things*. Duke University Press, 1995.

Stoner, Alexander M., and Andony Melathopoulos. *Freedom in the Anthropocene: Twentieth-Century Helplessness in the Face of Climate Change*. Palgrave Macmillan, 2015.

Suarez, Harrod. "Among the Sensuous: Listening to Film, Listening to the Philippines." *Communication and Critical/Cultural Studies* 8, no. 1 (March 2011): 67–84.

Subcommission on Quaternary Stratigraphy. "Working Group on the 'Anthropocene.'" Accessed February 17, 2020. http://quaternary.stratigraphy.org/working-groups/anthropocene/.

Sweney, Mark. "BBC Admits Treehouse Scene from Human Planet Series Was Faked." *The Guardian*, April 4, 2018.

Tahimik, Kidlat, dir. *Balikbayan #1: Memories of Overdevelopment Redux VI*. dafilms.com, 2017.

Tahimik, Kidlat. "Cups-of-Gas Filmmaking vs. Full Tank-cum-Credit Card Fillmaking." *Discourse: Journal for Theoretical Studies in Media and Culture* 11, no. 2 (1989): 80–86.

Tahimik, Kidlat. Interview by Aily Nash. In *Speaking Directly: Oral Histories of the Moving Image*, edited by Federico Windhausen, 74–88. San Francisco Cinematheque, 2013.

Tahimik, Kidlat, dir. *Mababangong Bangungot*. Flower Films, 2006 (1977).

Takaki, Ronald. *Hiroshima: Why America Dropped the Bomb*. Little, Brown, 1995.

Tchen, John Kuo Wei, and Dylan Yeats, eds. *Yellow Peril! An Archive of Anti-Asian Fear*. Verso, 2014.

Tcheuyap, Alexie. *Postnationalist African Cinemas*. Manchester University Press, 2011.

Terborgh, John. "Out of Contact." Review of *The Unconquered: In Search of the Amazon's Last Uncontacted Tribes*, by Scott Wallace. *New York Review of Books* 59, no. 6 (April 5, 2012): 48–51.

Thackway, Melissa. *Africa Shoots Back: Alternative Perspectives in Sub-Saharan Francophone African Film*. Indiana University Press, 2003.

Ticktin, Miriam. *Casualties of Care: Immigration and the Politics of Humanitarianism in France*. University of California Press, 2011.

Tierney, Patrick. *Darkness in El Dorado: How Scientists and Journalists Devastated the Amazon*. W. W. Norton, 2000.

Todd, Zoe. "Indigenizing the Anthropocene." In *Art in the Anthropocene: Encounters Among Aesthetics, Politics, Environments and Epistemologies*, edited by Heather Davis and Etienne Turpin, 241–54. Open Humanities Press, 2015.

Tolentino, Rolando B. *National/Transnational: Subject Formation, Media, and Cultural Politics in and on the Philippines*. Ateneo de Manila University Press, 2001.

Toor, Saadia. "Imperialist Feminism Redux." *Dialectical Anthropology* 36, nos. 3–4 (December 2012): 147–60.

Trinh T. Minh-ha. *Woman, Native, Other: Writing Postcoloniality and Feminism*. Indiana University Press, 1989.

Turner, Terence. "Representation, Politics, and Cultural Imagination in Indigenous Video: General Points and Kayapo Examples." In *Media Worlds: Anthropology on New Terrain*, edited by Faye D. Ginsburg, Lila Abu-Lughod, and Brian Larkin Berkeley, 75–89. University of California Press, 2002.

Ukadike, N. Frank. "*Yeelen* (1987), Souleymane Cissé." In *Film Analysis: A Norton Reader*, edited by Jeffrey Geiger and R. L. Rutsky, 756–75. W. W. Norton, 2005.

"Uncontacted Forest." Survival International. Accessed June 14, 2024. https://www.survivalinternational.org/awa.

"Uncontacted Tribe, Mato Grosso, Brazil 2013." *YouTube*, August 20, 2013. Accessed July 18, 2022. https://www.youtube.com/watch?v=OUVqF4kLJKA.

US Department of Energy. "Site Markers." Accessed May 31, 2024. https://wipp.energy.gov/pdfs/site_markers.pdf.

Valencia, Sayak. *Gore Capitalism*. Translated by John Pluecker. Semiotext(e), 2018.

Virilio, Paul. *War and Cinema: The Logistics of Perception*. Translated by Patrick Camiller. Verso, 1989.

Voyles, Traci Brynne. *Wastelanding: Legacies of Uranium Mining in Navajo Country*. University of Minnesota Press, 2015.

"Vulnerable (adj.)." *Oxford English Dictionary Online*. Oxford University Press, March 2024. https://doi.org/10.1093/OED/1136519195.

Vuong, Ocean. "Notebook Fragments." In *Night Sky with Exit Wounds*, 68–72. Copper Canyon Press, 2016.

Vuong, Ocean. *On Earth We're Briefly Gorgeous*. Penguin, 2019.

Vuong, Ocean. Virtual Reading and Discussion, School of the Art Institute of Chicago, October 6, 2020.

Wallace, Scott. "Exclusive: Stunning New Photos of Isolated Tribes Yield Surprises." *National Geographic*, December 21, 2016. https://www.nationalgeographic.com/culture/article/uncontacted-tribe-amazon-brazil-photos.

Wallace, Scott. *The Unconquered: In Search of the Amazon's Last Uncontacted Tribes*. Crown, 2011.

Wallace, Scott. "Why Revealing Uncontacted Tribes May Help Save Them." *National Geographic*, November 21, 2018. https://www.nationalgeographic.com/culture/article/brazil-uncontacted-tribe-indigenous-people-amazon-video.

Walzer, Michael. *Arguing About War*. Yale University Press, 2004.

Warren, Jonathan W. *Racial Revolutions: Antiracism and Indian Resurgence in Brazil*. Duke University Press, 2001.

Washington, Teresa N. "'The Sea Never Dies': Yemoja: The Infinitely Flowing Mother Force of Africana Literature and Cinema." In *Yemoja: Gender, Sexuality, and Creativity in the Latina/o and Afro-Atlantic Diasporas*, edited by Solimar Otero and Toyin Falola, 215–66. State University of New York Press, 2013.

Waters, Colin N., James P. M. Syvitski, Anthony Barnosky, et al. "Can Nuclear Weapons Fallout Mark the Beginning of the Anthropocene Epoch?" *Bulletin of the Atomic Scientists* 71, no. 3 (2015): 46–57.

Waters, Colin N., Jan Zalasiewicz, Colin Summerhayes, et al. "The Anthropocene Is Functionally and Stratigraphically Distinct from the Holocene." *Science* 351, no. 6269 (2016): 137–47.

Watson, Fiona. "This Man Is the Last of His Tribe. Let Him Live in Peace." *Survival International*, July 2018. Accessed June 14, 2024. https://www.survivalinternational.org/articles/3599-Last%20of%20his%20tribe%20new%20footage%202018.

Weheliye, Alexander G. *Habeas Viscus: Racializing Assemblages, Biopolitics, and Black Feminist Theories of the Human*. Duke University Press, 2014.

Weizman, Eyal. *The Least of All Possible Evils: Humanitarian Violence from Arendt to Gaza*. Verso, 2011.

"Whole (adj., n., and adv.)." *Oxford English Dictionary Online*. Oxford University Press, March 2024. https://doi.org/10.1093/OED/3310946030.

Whyte, Kyle. "Indigenous Climate Change Studies: Indigenizing Futures, Decolonizing the Anthropocene." *English Language Notes* 55, nos. 1–2 (2017): 153–62.

Whyte, Kyle, Jared L. Talley, and Julia D. Gibson. "Indigenous Mobility Traditions, Colonialism, and the Anthropocene." *Mobilities* 14, no. 3 (2019): 319–35.

Williams, Randall. *The Divided World: Human Rights and Its Violence*. University of Minnesota Press, 2010.

Wolfe, Patrick. "Settler Colonialism and the Elimination of the Native." *Journal of Genocide Research* 8, no. 4 (2006): 387–409.

"World War Zero." Accessed July 14, 2022. https://worldwarzero.com/.

Wynter, Sylvia. "Africa, the West and the Analogy of Culture: The Cinematic Text After Man." In *Symbolic Narratives/African Cinema: Audiences, Theory and the Moving Image*, edited by June Givanni, 25–76. British Film Institute, 2000.

Wynter, Sylvia. "Unsettling the Coloniality of Being/Power/Truth/Freedom: Towards the Human, After Man, Its Overrepresentation—an Argument." CR: The New Centennial Review 3, no. 3 (2003): 257–337.

Yoneyama, Lisa. *Hiroshima Traces: Time, Space, and the Dialectics of Memory.* University of California Press, 1999.

Yusoff, Kathryn. *A Billion Black Anthropocenes or None.* University of Minnesota Press, 2018.

Zalasiewicz, Jan. *The Earth After Us: What Legacy Will Humans Leave in the Rocks?* Oxford University Press, 2008.

Zhong, Raymond. "Geologists Make It Official: We're Not in an 'Anthropocene' Epoch." *New York Times*, March 20, 2024.

Zhong, Raymond. "The Human Age Has a New Symbol. It's a Record of Bomb Tests and Fossil Fuels." *New York Times*, July 11, 2023.

Zimmerman, Patricia R. "Benevolent Assassination: An Interview with Filipino Filmmaker Kidlat Tahimik." *Afterimage* 20 (1992): 6–10.

Zwigenberg, Ran. *Hiroshima: The Origins of Global Memory Culture.* Cambridge University Press, 2014.

Index

Page locators in italics indicate figures

abjection, 42, 56, 85, 121
absences, converted into signs, 120, 146
academy, theoretical divides in, 189
acid attacks on women, 38, 114, 127, 136–42, 247n28
Acid Control and Acid Crime Prevention Act (Pakistan), 137, 138, 140, 142
aesthetics, 3, 5–6; bombing as aesthetic event, 46, 72–73, *73*; "breast" as aesthetic object, 176; at core of politics, 209. *See also* ruination, aesthetics of
affect/affectability, 24–26, 67, 119; and uncontacted peoples, 152, 154; and vulnerability, 192–93
Afghanistan, 245–46n13; Af-Pak region, 113–14, 137, 245n10; Female Engagement Teams, 113; as "PTSDland," 126, 131–32; US withdrawal from, 111–13, 129; as "war-wrecked," 131
Afghanistan Independent Human Rights Commission, 111–12

"Afghan Women and the Return of the Taliban" (Baker), 128–29
Africa: decolonization in, 84–85; as destined to disappear, 2–3; reconfiguration of, 85, 100–101
Agamben, Giorgio, 121
agency, 6; agency/non-agency binary, 71; collective, 66–67; of "earth-beings," 166; inaction as "shameful," 214; of Indigenous peoples erased, 171–72; liberal secular standards for, 143; of uncontacted peoples, 173, 180–81
The Age of Vulnerability: Threats to the Nuclear Stalemate (Nacht), 51
Ahuja, Neel, 22
Alfred, Taiaiake, 179
Algeria, French nuclear testing in, 84
Amar, Paul, 125, 154, 177
Amazon rainforest, 38, 252n10; Awá people, 151, 160–61, 175; battlefield trope of, 39, 150; created by pre-contact ecological management, 38, 157; criminality associated

Amazon rainforest (continued) with, 150, 151, 155; ecosystem collapse, 39, 151; as "ground zero," 157, 182; humanity's future linked to imagination of, 149–50, 153, 155, 157; imagined as ruins of disappeared civilization, 39, 156–65; "lost cities" tourism, 157; securitization of, 39, 150, 154–55, 176–78. *See also* Brazil; uncontacted peoples

American Society of Plastic Surgeons (ASPS), 133

Anthropocene, 60–71; alternative names for, 61, 237n85; anti-black racist practices recalibrated by, 207; anti-colonial and anti-racist thought as in past, 78–79; atmospheric carbon dioxide level and systematic murder, 64; as authorized narrative of the Earth, 63; and bomb ethics, 36–37, 69–71; critiques of, 60–61; "derangement" in discourse of, 62, 67–68; effect on human beings elided by discourse of, 61, 70; genocidal conceptualization of humanity in discourse of, 45–46, 69; geologic timescale, 60, 63–64, 69–70, 238n103; initial holocaust visited on Americas in 1610, 64, 238n103; knowledge transmission as disrupted by, 45–46, 60, 62, 67; nuclear weapons as originary marker of, 45, 48, 221; preoccupation with humanity as a whole, 45, 59; as redemptive, 67–69; refusal of discourse on, 80; stratigraphic markers for, 60, 63–64, 70–71; survival, discourse of, 36–37, 67, 84; uncontacted people as figures in, 153; universalism of, 60, 66–67, 110. *See also* climate crisis/environmental protection

"The 'Anthropocene'" (Crutzen and Stoermer), 236n78

Anthropocene Working Group, 70–71

anti-ableist project, 204–5, 214–15

anti-colonial/anti-imperial movements, 46, 56, 86; critique as form of overcoming, 35–36; decolonization, 33, 35, 66, 84–85; human rights as technology for managing, 10–11, 24–25; nuclear deterrence to prevent north-south confrontation, 58–59

anti-violence/anti-war ethics, feminist, 9, 30, 39–40, 187, 189, 203–7, 214, 216

apartheid, theoretical, 189

"Architectural Megalomania" (Speer), 28–29

architecture, ruins as purpose of, 28–29

Arguing About War (Walzer), 119

Arsala, Mati, 133–34

"'Art Naïf' and the Admixture of Worlds" (Jameson), 86, 243n68

Asad, Talal, 11, 34, 118, 119, 124, 129

Asiatic femininity, as ornament, 207–10

Atanasoski, Neda, 21, 111, 112–13, 124

Auschwitz, 56

Austen, Ralph, 84, 104

authenticity, 81, 164, 214; and BBC productions, 172–73; cultural, 173, 175; repurposing of, 100–101; "voice-consciousness," 143

autobiographical lens, 223

Badkhen, Anna, 131–33
Baker, Aryn, 128–29
Balée, William, 157, 169
Balian, 79
Bamako (Sissako), 2–5
Barnett, Michael, 227–28n4
Bartov, Omer, 14–15
Bennett, Jane, 224
Berlin, destruction of, 28
Biddle, Wayne, 89
Biden, Joe, 129
bin Laden, Osama, 133, 137
"biological precarity," 23
biopolitics/necropolitics, 3, 5, 7, 2–13, 156, 228n19
Blackness, gendered through violence, 205–6

blame of victim, 115, 117, 125, 131–32, 138, 186, 212; function of, 147–48
bomb ethics, 36–37, 69–71, 83; death appropriated by, 48–49, 52, 59, 74, 211–13; lives mobilized for, 44–45, 47, 55, 75. *See also* nuclear weapons technology; peace
The Bomb (documentary), 47–48, 49, 52
Bonneuil, Christophe, 63
Boyer, Paul, 48–49
Brazil, 149–50; instrumentalization of Indigenous territory, 164; tropicalism, 177, 255n80; US support for coups and death squads, 153. *See also* Amazon rainforest; uncontacted peoples
"breast," as aesthetic object, 176
Bretton Woods institutions, 33
Brudholm, Thomas, 143–44
Brum, Eliane, 151
Bulletin of the Atomic Scientists, 41
Bush, George W., 245n13, 248n64
Butler, Judith, 23, 114–15, 183, 186, 187, 191; Works: *The Force of Nonviolence: An Ethico-Political Bind*, 199–200, 213; *Frames of War: When Is Life Grievable?*, 196–98; *Precarious Life*, 194–96; "Precarious Life, Vulnerability, and the Ethics of Cohabitation," 196

Cacho, Lisa, 198
cannibalism, literal and figurative, 33, 155–56, 209–10
"Can the Subaltern Speak?" (Spivak), 143
capitalism, 237n85; abject predation on women, 12; and Anthropocene, 65–66; carbon-based, 65, 153; mass-produced objects, 166–67; racial, 33, 46, 84, 153
Capitalocene, 61, 237n85
care, 230n66; disciplines of, 22–23; incapacitation of ability to, 200; regime of, 21, 35
Castile, Philando, 35
celebrity ambassadors, 135–36, 152

Centers for Disease Control and Prevention, 132
Chakrabarty, Dipesh, 66–67, 77–78, 81
Cheng, Anne Anlin, 207–10, 213–16, 259n98
Chow, Rey, 43
Chowdhury, Elora Halim, 247n28, 250n96
Cissé, Souleymane, 37, 76–77, 79, 99, 240n8; explicit politics as danger to, 101–2; filmmaking studies, 85; in knowledge possession, 102–3. *See also Yeelen* (Cissé)
civilians: atomic bomb used on, 27, 56; legal killing of, 119; population-centric counterinsurgency tactics, 113–14; "strategic bombing" of, 56, 57, 235n61
"civilization," 6; Amazon rainforest imagined as site of ruins, 156; Anthropocene discourse of, 62; "learning to die," 65; nuclear threat to, 49–50; psychoanalytic view, 92, 242n51; vision privileged, 31–32
civilizationism, 8, 37, 80, 82, 123, 203, 215; in *Mababangong Bangungot*, 86, 90, 96–97, 110; US Cold War, 86
Clark, Timothy, 67
climate crisis/environmental protection, 9, 13, 37–38, 42, 61; narratives of as alibis for extractivism, 153–54. *See also* Anthropocene
coevalness, denial of, 42, 82
Cold War, 51, 86; overkill arsenals, 219–20; US imperialism during, 75–76
Cold War/post–Cold War era, 5, 10; geopolitical reorganization, 7, 30, 51–52, 56, 136
Cole, Alyson, 194, 198, 214
colonialism and conquest, 5, 21, 45–46, 82; conquest geography, 64; "culture of experimentation," 52–53; eradicatory drive of, 2, 6–7; human rights as reiteration of, 11; nuclear, 37, 83–85; recognition as

INDEX   285

colonialism and conquest (continued) mechanism of, 155; settler colonialism. 14, 21, 44, 155, 164; and uncontacted peoples, 153, 155. *See also* imperialism
commitment to humanity, 150, 155, 197–98, 215
Committee on the Elimination of Discrimination Against Women (UN), 12
Compton, Arthur, 50
Comte, Auguste, 96
concentration camps: Guantánamo, 22–23; "Muselmann" figure in, 121; Nazi, 89, 97, 121
consciousness, 80; cultural topography of, 202–4; delinked from identity, 204; differential and oppositional, 201–4; "voice-consciousness," 143. *See also* humanitarian consciousness
consensus, 16–18, 81, 190, 216, 222
consumption of the other, 32, 100, 115, 175–76
contamination, 224–25
contra-ontology, 188–90, 201–4
cosmologies, 61, 70, 82, 203; of "the end," 29–30; and uncontacted peoples, 165, 167, 176; voiding of, 34
counterinsurgency: as gender-based violence, 124; meaning-making functions of, 132–33; population-centric, 113–14; "social engineering," 113, 131, 249n77; women of color as targets for, 38, 117, 124, 146. *See also* military violence
Crawford Lake (Ontario, Canada), 71
crisis, 45, 62, 78; between persons and things, 210, 213
critical fabulation, 82
Crutzen, Paul J., 236n78
"Cups of Gas Filmmaking vs. Full Tank-cum-Credit Card Fillmaking" (Tahimik), 88, 242n43
cynicism, 2–5, 12, 227n1

Davies, Jeremy, 62, 69, 237n92
Davis, Heather, 238n103
D'Costa, Bina, 137, 250n98
death: appropriated by bomb ethics, 48–49, 52, 59, 74, 211–13; dead subject distinguished from, 211; death-oriented practices of looking, 3–4; failure to register/non-events, 46, 65; and humanity as a whole, 46, 57; humanity defined by capacity to master, 13–14; "learning to die," 64–65, 69; "living dead" metaphor, 13, 141–42; management and ownership of, 5; progress's reliance on, 89–91, 96; social, 199, 211, 228–29n19; and uncontacted peoples, 156, 162, 171. *See also* genocidalism
"death ratio," 28
"death-worlds," 13, 34
debris, 1, 222–24, 227n3; as dismantling, 9, 40, 222
decolonization, 33, 66, 84–85, 201; "postcolonial grief" at deferral of, 35–36
Deep Jungle (Pearce), 158–59
de la Cadena, Marisol, 166, 168
Deleuze, Gilles, 116
demos, 224
depoliticization, 16, 21–22, 29, 228n4
"derangement," 62, 67–68
"Dermopolitics," 121
Derrida, Jacques, 24, 53, 234n43
destruction/devastation: climate crisis narratives as alibi for, 153; of colonialism and conquest, 2, 6–7, 13; of disagreement, 29; eradication intertwined with documentation, 156, 160, 171; eradication of difference, 64–65, 198; "missing destructiveness," 157; torture as access to, 120. *See also* extermination; ruination, aesthetics of
development: debt-based financing, 12; extractivism linked with, 3, 33–34, 83; as "ideology of governance," 33; "overdevelopment," 8–854, 242n52; post-World War II project of, 30; subjects of as

accomplices in own "pauperization," 4; "underdeveloped," the, 33–34, 78, 85
Diawara, Manthia, 77
différance, 24, 188, 193, 202, 210, 214
difference: differential consciousness, 201–4; differential humanity, 6, 8, 39–40; eradication of, 64–65, 198; feminist approaches to, 195–98, 201–5, 210; as temporal distancing, 42, 82; transcendence of in Anthropocene discourse, 66–67
Diné people, 44, 233n21
disagreement, 7, 16, 29, 67, 186, 189, 222
disappearance: aestheticization of, 3; of bombing victims, 52–54; double, 52, 54; genocidal instrumentalization of, 25; of "indifferent native," 155; institutionalized, 84; invisibilization, 134; by state denials, 117; and uncontacted peoples, 151, 154–55, 157, 159, 163, 173, 178, 181–82; without remainder, fear of, 181–82
disease threats, military response to, 22–23
disposability, 40, 216, 224
dispossession, 12, 179–80
Dixon, Deborah, 94
documentation: atrocities redacted, 115, 246n23; eradication intertwined with, 156, 160, 171; impossibility of reckoning with loss through, 219; of Mohammadzai's activities, 129–30; queer and trans people betrayed by, 218–19; recording and forgetting, 221–22; and securitization, 155, 173–82; of uncontacted peoples, 154–58, 160–65, 171; victims reincarnated as bodies of data, 52–53; of violated female body, 121–23; of vulnerability, 30. *See also* surveillance
Dodds, Susan, 190
"domestic violence," feminist concept of, 123

Doomsday Clock, 41–43, 46
Douglass, Patrice, 205–6
Dovey, Lindiwe, 81
Dower, John, 36, 41, 75, 236n70
drone footage of uncontacted people, 162
drone warfare, 31–32; "double-tap" method, 32, 200; "targeted class" of people, 157–58; US Air Force base in Niger, 85

"earth-beings," 166
Egypt, 154
Einstein, Albert, 49
Eng, David, 92, 242n51
entropy, 221
"The Ethical Turn of Aesthetics and Politics" (Rancière), 17
The Ethics of Vulnerability: A Feminist Analysis of Social Life and Practice (Gilson), 191–94
ethnography, 172, 174; desire for total knowledge, 32–33; entrenchment of, 80–81; knowledge production, modes of, 30; visual technologies of, 32, 158, 162
evolutionary theory, 26, 33, 50–51; extinction in context of, 13–14, 156; positivism, 96; prediction of particular racial groups' extinction, 156, 158–59; recapitulationist, 90–91
Ex Machina (film), 215
extermination: to ensure survival of humanity, 6, 113, 156; genocidal project of, 6, 156; humanism's reliance on, 13; humanity imagined through, 6, 9; knowledge production linked with, 30. *See also* destruction/devastation
extinction, 15, 39, 80, 96–97, 180; Anthropocenic, 62–63; in context of evolutionary theory, 13–14, 156; environmental devastation narrativized, 30; as inevitable for humanity, 156. *See also* humanity's end

extractivism: development linked with, 3, 33–34, 83; elided by Anthropocene discourse, 61; environmental protection entangled with, 153–54; on Indigenous lands, 44, 153–54, 169; wastelanding, 44, 85, 159–60
extrajudicial killing, 4, 237n35

Fabian, Johannes, 42, 82
faciality, 115–18, 138, 143
Falcón, Sylvanna M., 10, 12
Fanon, Frantz, 35, 187
Female Engagement Teams, 113
feminism: anti-violence/anti-war ethics, 9, 30, 39–40, 187, 189, 203–7, 214, 216; Black theorists, 259n98; difference, approaches to, 195–98, 201–5, 210; "domestic violence," concept of, 123; ethics of vulnerability, 190–200, 207; oblique threat to support white-ascendant form of, 135; suffering as key feature in scholarship, 114–15; third world, 201–4; and UN initiatives, 12, 121; US feminism of color, 202; violence against women as focus of, 122–23; vulnerability scholarship, 39, 194–98, 207; and war on terror, 12, 137; Western understandings of politics, 246nn14, 23
Feminist Majority Foundation, 249n71
Fernandes, Leela, 12
Ferreira da Silva, Denise, 24, 188, 211–12
Figueiredo, Wellington, 170–71
filmmaking: African, 85, 100; looking, practices of, 3–4; racism of reviews, 80–81; realist mode, 81–83. *See also* media; specific films
flesh, concept of, 193, 259n98
The Force of Nonviolence: An Ethico-Political Bind (Butler), 199–200, 213
forests, human relationships with, 158
forgiveness: required of victims, 143–45, 217; and weak legal system, 145–46

Foucault, Michel, 13, 228n19
"fourth eye," 34–36, 95
fracture, 40, 223
Frames of War: When Is Life Grievable? (Butler), 196–98
France, 21, 84, 85
Frank, Richard B., 53
Franklin, H. Bruce, 56
Fressoz, Jean-Baptiste, 63
Freud, Sigmund, 92

Gaines, Korryn, 205
Geneva Conventions, 227n4
genocidal humanitarianism, 28, 36, 153, 183, 219; defined by consensual political ordering, 224; distribution of the sensible, 40, 62, 223. *See also* ruination, aesthetics of
genocidalism: in Anthropocene, 45–46, 69; as defining characteristic of aesthetics of ruination, 15–16; of Europe in and around World Wars I and I, 14; and formation of "humanity," 7–8, 12–13, 15; humanitarianism intertwined with, 5, 125; and human rights, 10–19; intensive labor of, 18, 30; positioned as racial/gender enlightenment, 125; realism implicated in, 81; as self-negating project, 36; as specific form humanity "should" take, 8; as spectacle, 44; survival linked with, 6–7, 25, 29, 204. *See also* death; extermination
geologic timescale, 60, 63–64, 69–70
geopolitical reorganization, 7, 30, 51–52, 56, 136
Ghosh, Amitav, 68
Gilson, Erinn, 186, 187, 190–94
A Girl in the River: The Price of Forgiveness (Obaid-Chinoy), 137–38, 144–45
Global South, 11–12, 25, 179, 222; characterization of women in, 122; extraction from under guise of development, 81; securitization in, 154, 177
Gómez-Barris, Macarena, 154

governance: development as ideology of, 33; humanitarianism as central to imperial modes of, 5, 7, 10; human-security, 154–55, 177
governmentality, 11, 13, 90. *See also* biopolitics/necropolitics
Grewal, Inderpal, 11, 122, 250n101
grief, 133, 198, 217; postcolonial, 35–36
grievability, 186, 192, 196
Griggers, Camilla, 115
"ground zero": Amazon as, 157, 182; nuclear, 43, 157, 233n10; World War Zero, 220
Guantánamo, as HIV concentration camp, 22–23
Guattari, Félix, 116
guilt, 119
Gusterson, Hugh, 58–59

Haitian refugees, HIV positive, 22, 230n66
Haley, Sarah, 246–47n27
Hartman, Saidiya, 21
healing: as colonizing idea, 35, 40; killing as prerequisite to, 133; victim's responsibility for, 138, 198
Heart of Darkness (Conrad), 21
Herr, Ranjoo Seodu, 122
Herzog, Werner, 80–81
Hesford, Wendy, 115, 132
hibakusha (bomb survivor), 27, 54–55, 215, 235n50
hierarchical differentiation: grouphoods, 6, 15; of human rights principles, 11–12; "proper" social roles for different subjects, 3, 135–36, 166–69; and sensibility, 16; and vulnerability discourse, 187. *See also* onto-political order
Hill, Kim R., 180
Hiroshima, atomic bombing of, 234n49; Atomic Bomb Dome peace memorial, 55; as part of plan to destroy Japan, 56–57; possibility for world peace signified by, 27, 54
Hiroshima and Nagasaki, atomic bombing of, 27, 43, 47–48, 54–55; and containment ideology, 55–56; as expected event, 56; omitted from nuclear bomb footage, 73–74
Hitler, Adolf, 28–29
holocaust: atomic, 47, 48, 64; Holocaust as implied founding event of genocide, 14; initial visited on Americas, 64, 238n103
Holocene, 62
Homo oeconomicus, 33, 101
Hua, Julietta, 20, 248–49n65
humanitarian consciousness, 10, 23, 115; and Anthropocene discourse, 45–47, 69; and bomb ethics, 43, 47–48, 51, 57; torture and wounding as resources for, 120, 129–30, 137; uncontacted peoples as resources for, 29–30, 162, 164, 169–71, 178, 180; and vulnerability discourse, 184. *See also* consciousness; humanitarian subject
humanitarian discourses, 6–10, 18, 29, 44; genocidal aspirations in, 7, 9; ordering of reality, 9–10; resistance managed by, 23–24
humanitarianism: cannibalizing mode of, 155–56; as central to neocolonial governance and militarism, 10; genocidalism intertwined with, 5, 125; in historical context, 7; militarized, 112–13, 126; and nuclear weapons discourse, 36, 39, 43, 46–47, 50–51; reconciliation processes, 143–44; suffering, reliance on, 8, 19, 26, 38; "transnational regime of care," 21; as Western discourse, 5–6
humanitarian subject, 32, 40; conditioned through gazing upon torture, 120; necessity of violence to the production of, 38, 117–25, 144, 146; racialization of, 26; uncontacted peoples required for development of, 162, 164, 169–71, 178, 180, 182. *See also* humanitarian consciousness; subject

humanity: agency/non-agency binary, 71; Asian women rendered as ornamental, 207–10; defined by the capacity to master death, 13–14; enactment of violence as entry into, 206–7; Eurocentric, white-ascendant conceptualizations of, 5, 21, 25, 156; exclusions from, 15, 23–24, 42–43, 178–79, 186–87, 196–99, 208–9; existing alongside, 215; genocidal formation of, 7–8, 12–13, 15; "genres" of, 75; illusion of internal coherence, 8, 9, 23–24, 29, 188; Indigenous peoples not admitted to, 170, 179; as irredeemable category, 68; "movement out of humanness," 205, 210; non-self-sameness of, 23–24, 69–70, 78, 82, 188, 195–96; parochial views of, 20, 25, 197; perihumanity, 189, 208–9; refusal to claim, 188, 203–6, 210; self-determined subject and outer-determined others, 23–24, 188; vulnerability used to describe, 8–9, 186–87. *See also* onto-political order

humanity as a whole, 5, 8–9, 19–25; assimilation into, 166–67; commitment to, 150, 155, 197–98, 215; eradication of difference, 64–65, 198; as focus of Anthropocene discourse, 45, 59; large-scale death not threat to, 57; not capable of self-awareness, 66; types of lives under threat from nuclear bomb, 46–47

humanity's end: Amazon rainforest linked to, 149–50; cosmology of, 29–30; destruction linked with imaginings of, 6–7, 28–29; social technologies for naming and managing, 42–43. *See also* Anthropocene; extinction; nuclear weapons technology

"humanity's ruins," 18, 29, 32, 222

Human Planet "Jungles" episode (BBC), 149, 152, 172

human rights: as biopolitically/necropolitically motivated, 12–13; duties associated with for victims, 138; and genocidal humanity, 10–19; hierarchical differentiation involved in, 11–12; institutionalization of, 10; as "regime of truth," 11; as spectacle, 115; women's rights as, 122, 147, 250n101. *See also* international juridical apparatus; law

hyperobjects, 70–71

"idealistic annihilation," 36, 43–44

imperialism: and Anthropocene discourse, 68; colonizers' self-critique as part of, 21; fantasies of superweapon that brings peace, 57–58; humanitarianism and militarism linked, 112–13; liberation projects as militarized strategy, 114–15, 135; Muslim-majority nations subject to, 37–38; US, during Cold War, 75–76; US, in Philippines, 17, 83, 87, 241n34, 243n59; women, focus on, 12, 113–14. *See also* anti-colonial/anti-imperial movements; colonialism and conquest; onto-political order

Indigenous peoples: agency of erased through representations, 171–72; already-contacted Amazonian peoples, 167; in the Andes, 166; Awá people, 151, 160–61, 175; dependency narrative of, 169; Diné people, 44, 233n21; as evacuated of interiority, 169; extinction predicted for, 156, 158–59; extractivism on lands of, 44, 153–54, 169; as foil for humanitarian subject's own musings, 169–70; humanity denied to, 170, 179; grouphood of eliminated, 15; "indifferent native," 155; media projects of, 156, 172, 173; permanent war against, 154; portrayed as lacking understanding, 167–68; racist accounts of assimilation programs, 166–67; sovereignty as inappropriate political objective for, 179; UN role in colonizing and displacing, 179; US targeting of, 83; wastelanding on lands of, 44, 85, 159–60; women racialized, 175–76. *See also* uncontacted peoples

inhumanity: figures of, 2, 39, 59, 160, 166; of "improper" responses to images, 135–36; as justification for humanitarian warfare, 21–22, 120, 127–28; of violence, 204

interdependency, 196–97, 207–8

Interim Committee, Science Panel of, 50

International Commission on Stratigraphy, 60, 71

International Criminal Tribunal for the Former Yugoslavia, 124–25

International Geologic Time Scale, 60

international governance regimes, 10–11, 24, 124; international financial institutions, 2–3, 83; neoliberal multiculturalism, 179–80. *See also* geopolitical reorganization; United Nations

international juridical apparatus, 112, 122–25, 177; "necro-economy" of, 27; rejected by anti-colonial movements, 46; shadow side of, 58; and spectacle, 115; war crimes adjudicated by, 123–25. *See also* human rights; law

Iraq, 64–65, 125, 132

Islam: atavism attributed to, 116, 136–37; honor-related violence attributed to, 124; as justification for US violence, 125; "Muslim" as ambiguous identifier, 120–21; Western knowledge claims about, 116. *See also* women, Muslim

Israel, 23, 183–84

Jackson, Zakiyyah Iman, 206, 210
Jaleel, Rana, 123
Jamal, Asad, 145
Jameson, Fredric, 86, 243n68
January 6, 2021 events, 185

Japan, 236n70; colonizing violence in history of, 55; US destruction and occupation of, 115. *See also* Hiroshima, atomic bombing of; Hiroshima and Nagasaki, atomic bombing of

Jawad, Mohammad, 138–39, 140
Jolie, Angelina, 135–36
Jones, Ann, 126
Junge, Daniel, 114
"jungle," as term, 159–60

kaleidoscopic "sight," 201–2, 204, 224
Kang, Laura Hyun Yi, 122–23
Kapadia, Ronak, 31–32, 116–17, 200, 245n10
Kaplan, Caren, 31, 235n61
Karera, Axelle, 61, 68, 206–7
Keating, Christine, 12
Kennett, Lee, 56
Kerry, John, 252n7
Khalili, Laleh, 113
Kim, Eunjung, 204–5, 214–15
Kim, Jinah, 35, 36, 40, 216
Kim, Jodi, 83, 236n70
King, Tiffany Lethabo, 211, 212
Klein, Joe, 126

knowledge: crisis as object of, 78; Muslim women as objects of, 126; possession of as impossible, 101, 102–3, 108; "simple" versus "deeper," 192–93; terrorist as object of, 118, 124; as totality, 77, 78, 103; and vulnerability, 192–93. *See also* understanding

knowledge production, 7–8; Anthropocene as disruptive of, 45–46, 60, 62, 67; authenticity as concern, 172–73; and bombing, 27, 48, 53; documentary and ethnographic modes of, 30; and entropy, 221; mental health and trauma, instrumentalization of, 130–33; militarized, 8, 63; and war on terror, 118, 146. *See also* meaning-making

Kosek, Jake, 74
Krauss, Lawrence M., 42
Kuletz, Valerie, 221

Latham, Kerry P., 134
Latour, Bruno, 67
Laurence, William L., 50–51, 234n32
law: alternatives not considered, 141; demands of on victims, 138, 143, 144; hierarchical ordering of bodies by, 3; jurisprudence against acid violence, 136–38, 140, 141–42. *See also* human rights; international juridical apparatus
Lawrence Livermore National Laboratory (LLNL), 3, 71–73
Learning To Die in the Anthropocene: Reflections on the End of a Civilization (Scranton), 64–65, 69
Lemmon, Gayle Tzemach, 127–28
Lepecki, André, 187
"lesser evil" principle, 27–28, 119, 162
Lewis, Jeff, 127
Lewis, Simon L., 63–64
liberation, humanitarian subject's view of, 20–21, 149–50, 169–70
liberation projects, 33; as imperial/military strategy, 114–15, 135; surveillance tactics characterized as, 150; Western concepts of, 115, 141, 246n14
Lilienthal, David E., 47, 52
Lindqvist, Sven, 13–14, 156
Lippit, Akira Mizuta, 53, 234n40
"living dead," 13, 141–42
Los Alamos, 74–75
loss, idiom of, 199

Mababangong Bangungot (Tahimik), 75–76, 85–99, 99; alternatives to Anthropocene discourse in, 37; "benevolent assassination" "mistake," 87–88; at Berlin Film Festival, 87; bridge trope in, 86, 89–90, 94, 96; circumcision scene as third eye/fourth eye act, 95; conditions of cheapened labor in, 83–84; ethnographic and culturalist readings of, 80–81; formal and intellectual complexities of, 79; institutions critiqued in, 84; Kidlat as caricature of a caricature, 87–88, 91–92; Kidlat character read as naïve, 86–87; locality in, 81; "low-tech" qualities, 79; masculinity in, 243n61; mispronunciations in, 88, 93; monkeys, references to, 93, 243n57; non-diegetic shots in, 96; as *The Perfumed Nightmare*, 75, 79; progress rejected in, 90–91, 96–98, 110; space race in, 83, 85–86, 88–89, 92–93, 96–97; surrealism, switch to, 98; Tagalog voice-over narration, 90; transformation of consciousness enacted by, 80; white carabao image in, 91, 94–95. *See also* Tahimik, Kidlat
Machado, Marco Antonio Calil, 164
Macharia, Keguro, 149, 155
Mackenzie, Catriona, 190
Maira, Sunaina Marr, 130
Mali, 79–80, 84–85
Mamdani, Mahmood, 17–18, 224–25
Mameni, Salar, 60–61, 121
Man, 20, 230n55; as *Homo oeconomicus*, 33, 101
Manhattan Project, 41, 50, 73, 234n32
Mars Project (von Braun), 89
Masco, Joseph, 219–20, 221
masculinity, white-ascendant, 91–92
Maslin, Mark A., 63–64
Mateen, Omar, 146–47
Mbembe, Achille, 13–14, 34
McElroy, Alex, 184–86, 212
McKelvey, Tara, 246n23
meaning-making, 168, 202; and nuclear weapons technology, 27, 36–37, 48, 52; objects of as absent from, 154; pathologization of victims', 129–30, 132–33; torture as official suspicion about, 121; women's images and stories as objects of, 114. *See also* knowledge; knowledge production
media: citizen viewing of nuclear test footage, 52, 71–74, 73; consumer of as humanitarian actor, 152, 196; disappearance of war casualties from, 52; Indigenous agency erased in representations, 171–72;

Indigenous projects, 146, 172, 173; role in targeting of Muslim women by counterterrorism tactics, 38. *See also* filmmaking
Meirelles, José Carlos, 149, 174
Melamed, Jodi, 179
memory, 35, 54–55, 82; of *Homo oeconomicus*, 33, 101; vulnerability of, 69
mental health and trauma, instrumentalization of, 130–33
Methodology of the Oppressed (Sandoval), 201
militarism: disease threats, military response to, 22–23; humanitarianism linked with, 112–13; and knowledge production, 63; liberation projects as imperial/military strategy, 114–15, 135; provision of aid to injured women as tactic, 113. *See also* visual knowledge systems, militarized
military violence: ability to distinguish right from wrong as justification for, 119–20; "lesser evil" justification, 27–28, 119, 162; suffering used to legitimize, 22–23, 34, 183; US denials of, 116–17; US incursion into Muslim-majority nations, 37–38; women as targets of occupying forces and aggressors, 116, 125, 128. *See also* counterinsurgency; warfare; war on terror
Mirzoeff, Nicholas, 152, 158
mispronunciation, politics of, 88, 93, 242n43
modernity: genocide as core feature of, 14; as hellish, 75–76; nuclear weapons technology as origin of, 45, 48; tropicalism, 255n80; world-system, 64
Mohammadzai, Aesha, 38, 114, 126, 133, 245n11; face of as key link to continuing necessity of the war on terror, 129; facial reconstruction, 133–34; as "Nadia," 127; *Time* magazine cover and article, 38, 114, 126–28; and Women for Afghan Women, 127, 129–30
Morley, Felix, 50
Morton, Timothy, 70
Muggah, Robert, 151
Murphy, Ann V., 186

Nacht, Michael, 51
Nation, 126
National Geographic, 173–74
National Indian Foundation of Brazil (Fundação Nacional do Indio; FUNAI), 149, 150, 160–64; no-contact policy, 154, 170–71
Nazi Germany, 28, 89, 97, 121
neoliberal multiculturalism, 179–80
Neves, Maria Beatriz Correa, 164
New York Times, 150, 151, 184–85
Nguyen, Mimi Thi, 131, 144
Non-Aligned Movement, 84
nonhuman beings, 39, 175–76; as hyperobjects, 70–71. *See also* objects
Non-Proliferation Treaty (1970), 58
nonviolence, 187, 199–200, 204–6, 211
North Africa, nuclear contamination in, 84
"Notebook Fragments" (Vuong), 223
nuclear colonialism, 37, 83–85
"nuclear orientalism," 58
nuclear weapons technology: atomic bombing justified for purposes of peace, 27, 36, 43, 51, 54, 58–59, 73, 213; atomic bomb used on civilians, 27, 54–56, 215, 235n50; Bikini Atoll test, 52; bomb ethics, 36–37, 40, 44–47, 69–71, 83, 211–13; bombing as aesthetic event, 46, 72–73, 73; containment, ideological strategy of, 55–56; deterrence discourse, 51, 58–59, 71–76; Diné lands used for, 44, 233n21; Doomsday Clock, 41–43, 46; early novels about, 57–58, 235–36n65; extermination as reason for development and use, 43; global nuclear regime, 58–59; grandiose rhetoric, 46–47; "ground zero," 43, 157, 233n10; hibakusha (bomb

nuclear weapons (continued)
survivor), 27, 54–55, 215, 235n50; Hiroshima and Nagasaki, atomic bombing of, 27, 43, 47–48, 54, 73–74; holocaust, atomic, 47–48; humanitarian discourse of, 36, 39, 43, 46–47, 50–51; "idealistic annihilation," 36, 43–44; Manhattan Project, 41, 50, 73, 234n32; meaning-making about, 27, 36–37, 48, 52; as origin of modern era, 45, 48; and racialization, 36, 55–56, 58; radioactive waste repositories, 220–22, 224, 260–61n20, 260n17; test subjects exposed to radioactive material, 52–53, 74; Third World challenges to, 84; Trinity test, 43–44, 48, 50, 71, 233n10; and vulnerability trope, 26–27, 44–46, 51, 60; witnessing by others than victims, 44, 52. *See also* Hiroshima, atomic bombing of; Hiroshima and Nagasaki, atomic bombing of

Obaid-Chinoy, Sharmeen, 114, 135–38, 144–46, 250n101, 251n108; aligned with law, 136; awards won by, 38, 114, 136–37, 251n107. *See also A Girl in the River: The Price of Forgiveness* (Obaid-Chinoy); *Saving Face* (Obaid-Chinoy)
Obama administration, 245–46n13, 247n35
object, 189; becoming, 204, 213–17; "breast" as, 176; dependency narrative as alibi for predation, 169; "earth-beings" seen as, 166; hyperobjects, 70–71; human/object divide, 166; history of people made into things, 210, 213; Indigenous people assumed to lack proper relationship to, 166–69; ornamentalism, 207–10; posthumanist approach to, 210–11; relationship to seen as dependency, 33–34, 167–68; subject as, 214–15; "things" of mass capitalist production, 166–67; Western preoccupation with, 165–73. *See also* nonhuman beings
Oé, Kenzaburo, 54
Olwan, Dana, 123–24, 246n13, 248n55
On Cannibalism (Rony), 32
On Earth We're Briefly Gorgeous (Vuong), 222–23, 227n3
ontology: as aesthetics at core of politics, 209; contra-ontology, 188–90, 201–4; and ethics of nonviolence, 187; geographical location aligned with, 188; Muslim, 121; "ontological" and "situational" vulnerability, 192, 194–95, 199; and perihumanity, 189, 208–9; racialization of, 174, 193; and realist mode, 81; of victim, 144; whitened, 26, 188
onto-political order, 3, 13, 30, 214–15; absence and presence, reliance on, 155; geopolitical reorganization, 7, 30, 51–52, 56, 136; grouphoods, 6, 15; "humanity's ruins" as, 18; Indigenous people excluded from, 166–67; international governance regimes, 10–11, 24, 124, 179; visual experience in, 48. *See also* colonialism and conquest; hierarchical differentiation; imperialism
Oppenheimer (film), 48, 72–73
Oppenheimer, J. Robert, 50, 73
oppositional consciousness, 201–4
ornamentalism, 207–10, 259n98
Osinubi, Taiwo Adetunji, 100, 102
"overdevelopment," 84–85, 170, 242n52
overkill, 219–20

Pakistan, 113–14, 126, 135–43; Acid Control and Acid Crime Prevention Act, 137, 138, 140, 142; Af-Pak region, 113–14, 137, 245n10; ASLSIS, 137; legal system, 145–46
Palestine, 23; Gaza, siege of, 183, 230n71; genocide said to be good for Gazans, 183; vulnerability of as justification for violence against, 184

Pan-African Movement, 84
Parks, Lisa, 157–58
parochialism, 20, 25, 197, 205
pathologization: of resentment, 143–44; of victims, 129–30, 132–33; of violence, 131, 144
Patterson, Orlando, 228–29n19
Pavsek, Christopher, 87–88, 95, 242n52
peace: atomic bomb mobilized for purposes of, 27, 36, 43, 51, 54, 58–59, 73, 213; "atoms for peace" program, 58; fantasies of superweapon to bring about, 57–58. See also bomb ethics; nuclear weapons technology
Pearce, Fred, 158–59
"people," 15, 17
Pereira, Bruno, 151, 152
perihumanity, 189, 208–9
"The Peril of Universal Death" (Einstein and Russell), 49
Philippines, 18; "benevolent assimilation" policy, 87; Marcos regime, 90, 241n34; Miss Universe 1974 pageant, 91; "refeudalization" of, 83–84; US imperialism in, 17, 83, 87, 241n34, 243n59; wars, 93–94
Phillips, Dom, 151
police, 16, 35, 189
Possuelo, Sydney, 160–61, 169, 171, 180–81
post-9/11 politics, 12, 17, 118–19. See also war on terror
postcolonial, the, 77–78, 81–82; myth and epic, turn to, 100–101
postcolonial cultural studies, 9, 30–31
"postcolonial grief," 35–36
"Postcolonial Studies and the Challenge of Climate Change" (Chakrabarty), 77–78
postcolonies, management of, 37, 83
posthumanism, 210–13
"post-panoptic visuality," 152
poverty, 5; Africa as enslaved to production of, 101; in dominant discourse about Indigenous peoples, 167–68; symbolics of, 30, 33

Precarious Life (Butler), 194–96
"Precarious Life, Vulnerability, and the Ethics of Cohabitation" (Butler), 196
precarity: "biological," 23; of humanity, 46, 53, 69, 75, 114; and vulnerability, 192, 196–98
primitive, characterization of, 26, 50–51, 81, 159, 169, 171
prison, and zero-tolerance policies, 218–19
progress: devastation wrought by, 96; as nightmare, 75–76; predations of, 79; rejection of, 90–91, 96–98, 110; reliance on death, 89–91, 96; as temporality of genocide, 81
proportionality, legal precept of, 28, 119
"Protecting the Nation from Foreign Terrorist Entry into the United States" (Executive Order 13769), 124
proximity, queer ethics of, 205, 213
psychoanalysis, 92, 242n51
"PTSDland" (Badkhen), 131–33
Puar, Jasbir, 23, 116
Pulse nightclub shooting (2016), 146–47

queer and trans people, 218–19

racialization, 9, 204; of Asian femininity, 207–10; of contemporary threats, 30; flattening of geopolitics by, 55; human/nonhuman animal categorical divide, 175–76; of "Muslim," 120–21; "nuclear orientalism," 58; and nuclear weapons technology, 36, 55–56, 58; and objecthood, 215; and securitization, 176–77; sexual dynamics of, 92, 209–10
racism: assimilation programs, 166–67; of film reviews, 80–81; targets of expected to relinquish resentment, 38; of US military involvement in Pacific, 43; violence of internal coherence, 8–9, 188

radioactive waste, 220–22, 224, 260–61n20, 260n17
Rajagopal, Balakrishnan, 10–11, 33, 58
Rana, Junaid, 121
Rancière, Jacques, 6, 16–17, 186, 189, 224
Rankin, John, 21
Rasmussen, Claire, 12
Ravitz, Jessica, 129–30, 132
Razack, Sherene, 115
realism, 81–83, 102, 243n61; alternative versions of, 99–101
reality, 78; colonialist logics of, 17–18; humanitarian subject's attachment to fantasy of, 169–70
recapitulationist theory, 90–91
recognition: denial of, 204; humanitarian need for, 155, 181
reconciliation processes, 143–44
recuperation, refusal of, 217
refugees: Afghan girl figure, 115; Haitian, 22, 230n66; as objects of biomedical study, 131
relationality, 15, 35, 148; and affect/affectability, 24–26; as feature of violence, 185–86, 199–200, 207; and injured women, 117; and "movement out of humanness," 205; new modes of, 39; nonrelationality as modality of disruption, 207; oppositional consciousness, 201–4; and uncontacted peoples, 163, 166
remainder, 18–19, 69–70, 154, 170, 181–82
resentment, 38, 119, 143–48; instrumentalized toward juridical progress, 145–46; pathologization of, 143–44
resistance: anti-ableist project, 204–5, 214–15; in bomb survivors' testimonies, 55; defiance of the modes of sensibility, 75; managed by humanitarian discourses, 23–24, 37. *See also* anti-colonial/anti-imperial movements; anti-violence/anti-war ethics, feminist; social justice projects

responsibility, and vulnerability, 191–93, 196–98, 215
responsibility to protect, doctrine of, 21–22, 112
retaliation, vulnerability linked with, 185–86, 194–95
Rishi, Pooja, 12
Rodríguez, Dylan, 18
Rogers, Wendy, 190
Roitman, Janet, 62, 78, 82–83
Rony, Fatimah Tobing, 32–33, 34–35, 82, 95
Rotblat, Joseph, 49–50
ruination, aesthetics of: atomic bomb's role in, 27, 46; and conquest geography, 64; drone base as embodiment of, 85; genocidalism as defining feature of, 15–16; realism as key technique of, 81; and vulnerability, 25–36. *See also* aesthetics; genocidal humanitarianism
ruins: Amazon rainforest conceptualized as, 39, 156–65; "humanity's ruins," 18, 29, 32, 222; planned, 25–36, 40, 97, 108, 157, 222–24, 260–61n20; as purpose of architecture, 28; radioactive waste repositories as, 220–22, 224, 260–61n20, 260n17; "ruin," defined, 1–2, 18; "ruin value," theory of, 29
Russell, Bertrand, 49
Rwandan genocide, 17–18

Saar, Ibrahima, 105
Salman, Noor, 146–47
Samar, Sima, 111–12
Sandoval, Chela, 189, 201–4, 224
San Juan, E., Jr., 83, 86
"Saving Aesha" (CNN), 129–30
Saving Face (Obaid-Chinoy), 38, 114, 135–43; as alibi for extractivism, 141; filmmakers positioned as unimplicated in violence, 142–43; "improper" responses to images as inhuman, 135–36
Schuller, Kyla, 26

science fiction, 76, 100, 241n25
Scranton, Roy, 64–66, 69
Sebeok, Thomas A., 220–22, 260n17
securitization, 39, 150; controlled boundary of the human, 177–78; against disease threats, 22–23; and documentation, 155, 173–82; and gender norms, 177; human-security governance, 154–55, 177; "human-security products," 154, 155; and racialization, 176–77. *See also* war on terror
sensibility, 16, 87, 166, 196–97; and contra-ontology, 189–90, 201; humanitarian, 17, 38, 179; moral, 119; nuclear, 74–75; and vulnerability, 184, 196
sensory perception, 6, 26, 83, 164, 214
sentimentalism, 26
September 11, 2001, 132, 194–95, 245n13
settler colonialism, 14, 21, 44, 155, 164
"Settler Colonialism and the Elimination of the Native" (Wolfe), 14
Sissako, Abderrahmane, 2–3
slavery, chattel, 101, 228–29n19; as expression of humanity, 206–7; torture central to, 34, 193
social death, 199, 211, 228–29n19
"social engineering," 113, 131, 249n77
social justice projects: anti-oppressive, 184–85; and discourse of vulnerability, 25, 184–85; effect of humanitarian logics on, 8; invocations of suffering in approaches, 23. *See also* anti-colonial/anti-imperialist projects; resistance
South Africa, 143–44
sovereignty, 82, 98, 195; achieved through destruction, 101; as inappropriate political objective for Indigenous peoples, 179; onto-political asserted through devastation, 13; over the consumed, 33; unequal, 125
Soviet Union, 51, 84, 85

space race, 83, 85–86, 88–89, 92–93, 96–97
spectacle, 34, 44, 115
Speer, Albert, 28–29, 222
Spillers, Hortense, 34, 193, 259n98
Spivak, Gayatri Chakravorty, 143
Spriggs, Gregory D., 71–72
Stanley, Eric A., 218–19
Star Wars, 76, 84
statistics, betrayal by, 218
Stefanson, Blandine, 105
Stoermer, Eugene F., 236n78
Stuckert, Ricardo, 173–74
style, as precondition for embodiment, 207–8
Suarez, Harrod, 93, 241n34, 243n61
subject: death of, 211–12; limited conditions of legibility for Third World, 87; Muslim, fraught vulnerability of, 120; as object, 214–15; panhuman eschatology of, 54; "transparent I," 24, 188; whitened, 26. *See also* humanitarian subject; object
suffering: appropriation of, 46, 48–49, 52, 59, 115; attunement of subject to, 26; and feminist ethical critique, 114–15; hierarchical delineations of, 19; humanitarianism and militarism linked in alleviation of, 112–13; "human suffering," concept of, 8–9, 15, 19–25; racist proposals for alleviating, 166–67; refusal to embody, 223; reliance of humanitarianism on, 8, 19, 26, 38; required to produce universalist human subject, 20–21; as setup, 23; used to legitimize militarized responses, 22–23, 34, 183; writers of color expected to record, 223. *See also* torture and wounding; vulnerability
Sundiata Epic (Mali), 84
surveillance, 32, 85, 116–17; as intimacy, 134; normalization of, 130; "post-panoptic visuality," 52; of uncontacted peoples, 150. *See also* documentation; vision

survival: Anthropocene discourse of, 36–37, 60, 62–67, 84; genocidalism linked with imaginings of, 6–7, 25, 29, 204; hibakusha (bomb survivor), 27, 54–55, 215, 235n50; holding on to grief as, 36, 217; incapacitation of the ability to care for another, 200; uncontacted peoples linked with, 150–53, 162, 164, 170
Survival International, 151, 152, 161–62, 173
Szilard, Leo, 57–58

Tahimik, Kidlat, 37, 75–76, 79, 170; "Cups of Gas Filmmaking vs. Full Tank-cum-Credit Card Fillmaking," 88; MBA earned by, 86; name change, 86–87. See also *Mababangong Bangungot*
Taliban: abuses of women, 111–12; low-level, 128–29; Pakistani agreement with, 137
Tcheuyap, Alexie, 100
teleological narratives: antiteleological temporality, 82; of Doomsday Clock, 42; impossibility of, 110; of uncontacted peoples, 174
temporality, 81–82, 88, 110; colonial spatialization of, 203; difference as temporal distancing, 42, 82; "near-future," 100; nonlinear, 83, 105–7
Terborgh, John, 166–68
terrorism: acid violence classified as, 136; "Islamic," 118–19; Terracene designation, 61. See also war on terror
"terrorist": deceptive nature attributed to, 120; injury of as sign of, 120; as object of knowledge, 118, 124; terrorist psyche, concept of, 34, 118, 120, 124, 247n35, 248n64. See also torture
"third eye," 32, 35, 95
Third World: challenges to nuclear weapons proliferation, 84; as "inept," 179–80; nuclear deprivation of, 58–59; uses of term, 88

Ticktin, Miriam, 21
Time magazine: cover and article on Mohammadzai, 38, 114, 126–28; "The World's 100 Most Influential People: 2012," 135
Titan Missile Museum, 219
Titley, David, 42
Todd, Zoe, 60, 61, 238n103
Toor, Saadia, 137
topography, cultural, 202–3
torture: absences converted into signs by, 120; central to slavery, 34; as hermeneutic, 118; and humanitarian necessity of violence, 118–25; injured bodies as sign of necessity of, 120; and inner truth of devastation, 120; as main technique of war on terror, 34; meaning-making functions of, 132–33. See also suffering; terrorism; wounding, visible
totality/totalization, 8; consensus as, 16–18, 81, 190, 216, 222; of Doomsday Clock, 42; of ethnographic project, 32–33; of "humanity as a whole," 20; knowledge as, 77, 78, 103; and visual technologies, 31
Toward a Global Idea of Race (Ferreira da Silva), 211–12
trans/gay-panic defense, 219
transparency, 24, 53, 81, 116–17, 223–24; "transparent I," 24, 188
Traoré, Moussa, 85
trauma, production and study of, 132–33
Trinh T. Minh-ha, 32–33
tropicalism, 177, 255n80
Trump, Donald, 41–42, 124
Truth and Reconciliation Commission (South Africa), 143–44

Ukraine, invasion of, 42
The Unconquered: In Search of the Amazon's Last Uncontacted Tribes (Wallace), 152, 160–63, 166–71, 180–82
uncontacted peoples: as absent presences, 150, 154, 160–62; aerial

restructurings of, 158; agency of, 173, 180–81; consent not given for contact, 152, 161–62, 167, 173–74; "contact" defined, 165; as "contemporary peoples," 173, 174; and death, 156, 162, 171; as descendants or escapees from genocide, 150; and disappearance, 151, 154–55, 157, 159, 163, 173, 178, 181–82; documentation of, 154–58, 160–65, 171; effect of colonial and imperial dynamics on, 153; figurality in discourses of climate crisis and global capitalism, 38–39; freedom attributed to, 149–50, 169–70; as "human-security products," 154, 155; naming of after weapons, 171–72; as Neolithic, 173–74; no-contact policy, 154, 170–71, 180; nuclear metaphors for contact with Europeans, 158–59; objects, Western preoccupation with, 165–73; as objects of philosophical use, 39; Piripkura people, 177–78; portrayal of as degraded, almost-dead, or already vanished, 38; portrayed as lacking understanding, 39, 150, 153, 154–55, 157–59, 179–81, 215; proliferation of portrayals of, 152–53; as remnants of disappeared peoples, 154; required for development of humanitarian subject, 29–30, 162, 164, 169–71, 178, 180, 182; survival of humanity linked to, 150–53, 162, 164, 170; usefulness of to survival discourse, 153–54; women racialized, 174–76. *See also* Amazon rainforest; Indigenous peoples

"underdeveloped," the, 33–34, 78, 85

understanding: crisis in, 45; Indigenous peoples portrayed as lacking, 167–68; uncontacted peoples portrayed as lacking, 39, 150, 153, 154–55, 157–59, 179–81, 215; victims portrayed as lacking, 20–21, 29, 34, 118, 131–33, 143, 215. *See also* knowledge; knowledge production

United Nations, 227–28n4; Bretton Woods institutions, 33; Commission on the Status of Women, 12; and continued projects of destruction, 58; documents and treaties, 115; feminist thought and activism enmeshed with, 12, 121; gender inequality, structures for, 12, 118; neocolonial order upheld by, 10–11; role in colonizing and displacing Indigenous peoples, 179

United Nations Development Fund for Women, 122–23

United Nations Security Council, 125

United States: Afghan Americans invisibilized, 134; Afghanistan, interests in, 112–14; appropriation of nuclear terror by, 49; citizen viewing of nuclear test footage, 52; coups and death squads supported by, 153; credibility, loss of, 112; denials of military practices, 116–17; exceptionalist discourse of, 132, 135; Guantánamo used as HIV concentration camp by, 22–23; humanitarian responsibilities abandoned by, 112; January 6, 2021 events, 185; imperialism in Philippines, 17, 83, 87, 241n34, 243n59; military incursion into Muslim-majority nations, 37–38; nuclear arsenal, 219–20; refugees created by, 131; Soviet Union, relations with, 51; surveillance and intelligence practices, 116–17; value, idiom of, 198. *See also* Afghanistan

Universal Declaration of Human Rights (1948), 11, 227n4

universalism, 11; Africa positioned at center of, 102–3; of Anthropocene discourse, 60, 66–67, 110; critiques of, 19–20; hierarchies within, 20–21; shared sense of catastrophe, 66–67; suffering required to produce, 20–21; of vulnerability, 190; white ascendancy in notion of, 91

"An Unspeakable Crime" (Lemmon), 127–28
US Air Force, 85
US Division of Public Health Services studies, 52–53
US Nuclear Regulatory Commission, 220

V-2 rocket, 89
value, idiom of, 198
victims: appropriation of suffering and terror away from, 48–49, 52, 59, 115; blame imputed to, 115, 117, 125, 131–32, 138, 146–47, 186, 212; censorship of, 53–54; depoliticization of, 21–22; deserving, 115; double disappearance of, 52, 54; forgiveness required of, 143–45, 217; and nuclear technology, 44; portrayed as lacking understanding, 20–21, 29, 34, 118, 131–33, 143, 215; psychological abuse of, 117, 251–52n111; reincarnated as bodies of data, 52–53; responsibility for own healing, 138, 198; witnessing required of, 53–54, 215. *See also* women, injured; women, Muslim
Vietnam, 83, 112–13, 131, 236n70
violence: Blackness gendered through, 205–6; and *différance*, 24, 210; as form of intimacy, 134; "gender violence" as object, 118; "humanness" of, 204; human rights as means of managing, 11; of internal coherence, 8–9, 188; just and unjust hermeneutic, 118, 119; justified by vulnerability, 184; just warfare/violence ideology, 119, 120; necessary to production of humanitarian subject, 38, 117–25, 144, 146; non-intentionality claim, 119; pathologization of, 131; pedagogy of, 165–73; relationality as feature of, 185–86, 199–200, 207; right to as benevolent responsibility, 21–22; trauma used to theorize, 132; and vulnerable subject, 183–90, 191, 194. *See also* wounding, visible
Virilio, Paul, 28, 31, 158
visuality: death-oriented practices of looking, 3–4; kaleidoscopic "sight," 201–2, 204, 224; photographic technology, 31, 231n95; "post-panoptic," 152; privileged in Western imperial epistemes, 30–31; return look, 156; seeing as destructive, 32; as visualization of history, 158; X-ray photography technology, 53. *See also* surveillance; witnessing
visual knowledge systems, militarized: bombs as cameras, 53, 234n40; and descriptions of nuclear bombing, 27, 48; development of technology, 31, 231n95; seeing as capacity for destruction, 30. *See also* spectacle; surveillance
visual media: addressees of, 48; archive of nuclear tests, 71–74, 73; sanitized footage, 73–74
visual technologies: ethnographic, 32, 152, 157–58, 173–74, 182; of ethnography, 32, 158, 162
"voice-consciousness," 143
von Braun, Wernher, 85–86, 88–89, 92–93, 97
Voyles, Traci Brynne, 44, 52–53
vulnerability: and aesthetics of ruination, 25–36; aggressor's appropriation of, 185, 194; and anti-oppressive projects, 184–85; as basic to all humans, 184, 186, 190–91, 195; claims to, 194; and differentiality, 189, 195; distance/proximity discourse, 187, 196–97; documentation of, 30; of Earth, 64; feminist ethics of, 190–200; feminist scholarship, 39, 194–98, 207; forms of, 190; as generative force of sociality, 199; of human as object, 209; "humanistic ethic" of, 186; instrumentalized to justify violence, 184; and knowl-

edge, 192–93; of memory, 69; of Muslim subject, 120; and nuclear weapons discourse, 26–27, 44–46, 51, 60; "ontological" and "situational," 192, 194–95, 199; as openness, 190–93, 209; *Oxford English Dictionary* entry, 44; petulant/toxic, 185, 212; and precarity, 192, 196–98; racialization of, 26; and responsibility, 191–93, 196–98, 215; retaliation linked with, 185–86, 194–95; social justice–oriented discourse of, 25, 184; true and false forms of, 185–86; unexpected in First World, 195–96, 199; universality of, 190; used to describe humanity, 8–9; variety of roles, 25–26; victimization distinguished from, 190, 194; violence and the vulnerable subject, 183–90, 191, 194. *See also* suffering

Vuong, Ocean, 40, 222–23, 227n3

Wallace, Scott, 152, 160–63, 166–71, 180–82
Walzer, Michael, 119
war crimes, 123–25
war ethics, 8, 25
warfare: across natural life support systems, 151; asymmetric, 58, 123–25, 146, 157, 183–84; civilians targeted, 27–28, 56; conventional bombing campaigns, 56; global, grand narrative of, 151–52; humanitarian warfare mediascape, 134; human rights relationship to, 7; just warfare/violence ideology, 119, 120; responsibility to intervene, 21–22; "strategic bombing," 56, 57, 235n61; total, 28, 56; undivided political community as purpose of, 17. *See also* military violence
war on terror, 64; and Anthropocene discourse, 61; and feminist human rights approach, 12, 137; framed as humanitarian effort, 114; "gender-based violence" as justification for, 246n13, 248n64; gendered racial project at the heart of, 137; knowledge project of, 118, 146; Mohammadzai's face as link to continuation of, 129; "Muslim" as racial category in, 121; and neo-imperial aspirations, 85; torture as main technique of, 34; women as targets of occupying forces, 116. *See also* military violence; securitization; terrorism
wastelanding, 44, 85, 159–60
Waters, Colin, 64
Watson, Fiona, 162, 163, 173, 174
weaponry, development of, 31, 231n95. *See also* nuclear weapons technology
Weheliye, Alexander, 121
Weizman, Eyal, 27, 119
Wells, H. G., 57–58
"West, the," 5–6
Whyte, Kyle, 61
Williams, Randall, 11
witnessing, 237n92; authentication by, 127; bombing redeemed by, 55; call to, 71–73; genocidal destruction needed for, 73; by other than victims, 44, 52; required of victims, 53–54, 215; and survival of humanity, 149–50; survivor-witness as response to loss of faith, 56. *See also* vision
Wolfe, Patrick, 14–15
women, 250n101; as both to-be-saved and to-be-punished, 146, 248–49n65; category stabilized by gendered human rights abuses, 122; implied blameworthiness of, 115, 117, 125, 138; non-white targeted to maintain white supremacy, 246–47n27; psychological abuse of, 117, 251–52n111; as targets of occupying forces and military aggressors, 116, 125, 128; women's rights as human rights, 122, 147, 250n101

women, injured: acid attacks on, 38, 114, 127, 136–42, 247n28; as blameworthy, 118, 125, 147; faces of as imperial focus, 114; and faciality, 115–18, 138, 143; facial reconstructive surgery portrayed as humanitarian intervention for, 117–18, 133–34, 138–39; honor-related violence against, 123–24, 137, 144–45, 248n55, 250n100, 251n107; humanitarian creation of conditions for punishment, 141; provision of aid to as military tactic, 113; as symbol of American charity and compassion, 115; Western knowledge claims about, 116. *See also* Islam; victim, figure of; wounding, visible

women, Muslim: Bosnian racialized as white, 124–25; codification of, 121–22; faciality required of, 141; as objects of knowledge, 126; targeted by counterinsurgency and counterterrorism tactics, 38, 117, 124, 146; as unreliable figures, 146–47. *See also* Islam

Women, Peace, and Security (UN Resolution 1325), 125

Women for Afghan Women, 127, 129–30

The World Set Free (Wells), 57–58

World War II, 10, 50; continuation of genocidal killing justified by, 57; "strategic bombing," 56, 57, 235n61

World War Zero, 152, 220, 252n7

wounding, visible, 30; of Muslim women, 37–38; of nuclear bombing victims, 44; pedagogical and a hermeneutic function of, 34, 129; as sign of "terrorist," 120; test subjects exposed to radioactive material, 52–53. *See also* women, injured

Wynter, Sylvia, 20, 25, 33, 75, 101, 230n55

Yeelen (Cissé), 76, 79–84, 99–110; alternatives to Anthropocene discourse in, 37; as double refusal, 101; ending of, 107–8; epistemic breaks in, 104; ethical and political engagements, 79; ethnographic and culturalist readings of, 80–81; historical moment of, 80; history repurposed in, 99–101; knowledge possession as impossible, 101, 102–3, 108; Komo practitioners in, 100, 103–4; locality in, 81; Mande culture in, 84, 99–100, 104; non-diegetic shots in, 105–6; nonlinear temporalities in, 105; nuclear catastrophe referenced in, 101, 103, 106–7, *107*; plot structure, 104–5; realism altered in, 99–100; science fiction mode in, 76, 100, 102, 241n25; spatial relations in, 102, 105–7; temporalities in, 100, 104–5, 107. *See also* Cissé, Souleymane

Yoneyama, Lisa, 27, 43, 54–55

Yucca Mountain radioactive waste depository, 221

Yusoff, Kathryn, 61, 64, 70–71

Zahan, Dominique, 104

zero-tolerance policies, 218–19

Zonn, Leo, 94

Zwigenberg, Ran, 54, 56

www.ingramcontent.com/pod-product-compliance
Lightning Source LLC
Chambersburg PA
CBHW021850230426
43671CB00006B/330